Global Responses to T

The terrible attacks on September 11 and more recent atrocities in Russia, Indonesia, Kenya and Saudi Arabia have demonstrated that terrorism is a global threat to stability, democracy and prosperity. This text examines how the world has reacted to, and been affected by, September 11, the ensuing war in Afghanistan and President George W. Bush's declaration of a 'war on terror' as the 'first war of the twenty-first century.'

The contributors trace the reactions of individual governments and public opinion across North America, Europe, the Middle East, Africa and Asia to terrorism, the war in Afghanistan and Iraq. The discussion of individual countries is placed in context through an examination of wider issues such as the future of al-Qaeda, the growing refugee problem, the effect on the world economy and a significant revisiting of our approaches to understanding international relations.

There are now many books available on terrorism but few can boast the quality and range of the contributions to this volume, which locate the war on terror in a truly global intellectual context. It is essential reading for all students of international relations and terrorism as well as the general reader wishing to understand this complex subject.

Contributors: Paul Wilkinson, Rohan Gunaratna, Robert Singh, Andrew Dorman, Richard McAllister, Adrian Hyde-Price, Philip A. Daniels, Roland Dannreuther, Raymond Hinnebusch, Gwenn Okruhlik, David Newman, David Kenda Adaka Kikaya, James Putzel, Samina Yasmeen, Raju G. C. Thomas, Rex Li, Sally N. Cummings, Joanne Wright, Joanne van Selm, Brigitte Granville, Christopher Coker and Barry Buzan.

Mary Buckley is currently an independent scholar living in London having previously enjoyed research affiliations at Michigan, Kiev, Moscow, and Azerbaijan universities, and teaching posts at Edinburgh and London universities. Her books include *Women and Ideology in the Soviet Union* (1989), *Redefining Russian Society and Polity* (1993), *Post-Soviet Women: From the Baltic to Central Asia* (edited, 1997) and *Kosovo: Perceptions of War and its Aftermath* (co-edited, 2002).

Rick Fawn is a Senior Lecturer in International Relations at the University of St. Andrews. Among his books are *International Society after the Cold War: Anarchy and Order Reconsidered* (co-edited, 1996), *The Czech Republic: A Nation of Velvet* (2000) and *Ideology and National Identity in Post-Communist Foreign Policies* (edited, 2003).

Global Responses to Terrorism

9/11, Afghanistan and beyond

**Edited by Mary Buckley and
Rick Fawn**

Routledge
Taylor & Francis Group

LONDON AND NEW YORK

First published 2003
by Routledge
11 New Fetter Lane, London EC4P 4EE

Simultaneously published in the USA and Canada
by Routledge
29 West 35th Street, New York, NY 10001

Routledge is an imprint of the Taylor & Francis Group

Typeset in Baskerville by RefineCatch Limited, Bungay, Suffolk
Printed and bound in Great Britain by The Cromwell Press, Trowbridge,
Wiltshire

British Library Cataloguing in Publication Data
A catalogue record for this book is available from the British Library

Library of Congress Cataloging in Publication Data
Global responses to terrorism: 9/11, the war in Afghanistan and beyond/
   edited by Mary Buckley and Rick Fawn.
      p.   cm.
   Includes bibliographical references and index.
   1. Terrorism – Prevention.   2. International relations.   I. Buckley, Mary
   (Mary E. A.)   II. Fawn, Rick.
   HV6431.G56   2003
   303.6′25 – dc21   2003003799

ISBN 0–415–31429–1 (hbk)
ISBN 0–415–31430–5 (pbk)

This volume is dedicated to the
memory of Professor John Erickson
who would have joined us in this project if he could have
with provocative reflections on geopolitics

Contents

Contributors

EDITORS

Mary Buckley taught for seventeen years at the University of Edinburgh and was Professor of Politics at Royal Holloway, University of London, from September 2000 to December 2002. Her books include *Women and Ideology in the Soviet Union* (Harvester/Wheatsheaf, 1989); *Redefining Russian Society and Polity* (Westview, 1993); *Post-Soviet Women: From the Baltic to Central Asia* (editor, CUP, 1997); and *Kosovo: Perceptions of War and its Aftermath* (as co-editor, Continuum, 2002). Recent articles have appeared in the *Journal of Communist Studies and Transition Politics, Social History* and *European Security.*

Rick Fawn is Senior Lecturer in International Relations at the University of St Andrews, Scotland. He has published several books, including works on international relations and foreign policy such as *Ideology and National Identity in Post-Communist Foreign Policies* (editor, Frank Cass, 2003); *International Society after the Cold War: Anarchy and Order Reconsidered* (as co-editor, Macmillan, 1996); and articles in journals such as *Democratization, European Security, Europe-Asia Studies* and *Geopolitics.*

CONTRIBUTORS

Barry Buzan is Professor of International Relations at the London School of Economics and a Project Director at the Copenhagen Peace Research Institute (COPRI). Among his recent books are *Security: A New Framework for Analysis* (Lynne Rienner, 1998, with Ole Wæver and Jaap de Wilde); *Anticipating the Future* (Simon & Schuster, 1998, with Gerald Segal); *The Arms Dynamic in World Politics* (Lynne Rienner, 1998, with Eric Herring); *International Systems in World History: Remaking the Study of International Relations* (Oxford, 2000, with Richard Little); and *Regions and Powers: A Guide to the Global Security Order* (Cambridge, 2003, with Ole Wæver).

Christopher Coker is Professor of International Relations at the London School of Economics, where he has been since 1982. He is the author of several books including *War and the Illiberal Conscience* (Westview, 1998); *The Twilight of the West* (Westview, 1997); *War and the Twentieth Century* (Brassey's, 1994); *Britain's Defence Policy in the 1990s: An Intelligent Person's Guide to the Defence Debate* (Brassey's, 1992); *A Nation in Retreat* (Brassey's, 1991); and *Humane Warfare* (Routledge, 2001). His latest books are *Waging War without Warriors: The Evolution from Pre human to Post human Warfare* (Lynne Rienner, 2002) and *Globalisation and Insecurity in the Twenty-first Century* (International Institute for Strategic Studies Adelphi Paper 345, 2002).

Sally N. Cummings is a Lecturer in Politics at the University of Edinburgh. She is the author of *The Dynamics of Centre-Periphery Relations in Kazakhstan* (Brookings Institution and Royal Institute of International Affairs, 2000), editor of *Oil, Transition and Security in Central Asia* (Routledge, 2003), *Power and Change in Central Asia* (Routledge, 2001) and co-editor of *Kosovo: Perceptions of War and its Aftermath* (Continuum, 2002).

Philip A. Daniels is Senior Lecturer in Politics at the University of Newcastle. He has written articles and book chapters on Italian and West European politics, including 'The 1999 Elections to the European Parliament', in M. Gilbert and G. Pasquino (eds.), *Italian Politics: The Faltering Transition* (Berghahn, 1999); 'Italy: Rupture and Regeneration?', in D. Broughton and M. Donovan (eds.), *Changing Party Systems in Western Europe* (Continuum, 2000); and 'Italy', in J. Lodge (ed.), *The 1999 Elections to the European Parliament* (Palgrave, 2001).

Roland Dannreuther is Senior Lecturer in Politics at the University of Edinburgh. He has also been the Director of the New Issues in Security Course at the Geneva Centre for Security Policy (2000–1) and Research Associate at the International Institute for Strategic Studies (IISS) (1991–4). His publications include *The Gulf Conflict: A Strategic and Political Analysis* (IISS Adelphi Paper 264, 1991–2); *Creating New States in Central Asia* (IISS Adelphi Paper 288, 1994); *The Soviet Union and the PLO* (Macmillan, 1998); (ed. with K. Hutchings) *Cosmopolitan Citizenship* (Macmillan, 1999); and (co-authored with Philip Andrews-Speed and X. Liao) *The Strategic Implications of China's Energy Needs* (IISS, 2002).

Andrew Dorman is a Lecturer in Defence Studies in the Defence Studies Department, King's College London based at the Joint Services Command and Staff College. He was previously a Lecturer at the University of Birmingham and a Senior Lecturer at the Royal Naval College Greenwich. He has published widely and his books include: *Defence under Thatcher, 1979–89* (Palgrave, 2002); *Britain and the Changing Face of Military Power* (as co-editor, Palgrave, 2002); *Britain and Defence 1945–2000: A Policy Re-evaluation* (as co-editor, Longman, 2001); *The Changing Face of Maritime Power* (co-author, Palgrave, 1999); *European Security: An Introduction to Security Issues in post-Cold War Europe* (Dartmouth, 1995); and *Military Intervention: from Gunboat Diplomacy to Humanitarian Intervention* (as co-editor, Dartmouth, 1995).

Brigitte Granville is Head of the International Economics Programme at the Royal Institute for International Affairs. She has written widely on inflation, exchange rate and sovereign debt resolution in transition economies. Recent publications include: 'The Problem of Monetary Stabilisation', in B. Granville and P. Oppenheimer (eds), *Russia's Post-Communist Economy* (Oxford, 2001). Among her other works are *Essays on the World Economy and its Financial System* and *Sovereign Debt: Origins, Management, and Restructuring* (with Vinod Aggarval, published by RIIA distributed by Brookings, forthcoming). Dr. Granville is presently working on an edited volume on sovereign debt.

Rohan Gunaratna is Research Fellow at the Centre for the Study of Terrorism and Political Violence, University of St Andrews. He also served as the Principal Investigator of the UN University Terrorism Prevention Branch and as Co-Director of the UN Project on Managing Contemporary Insurgencies. He has spent fifteen years working on terrorism at the operational and policy levels, for the last eight of which he has researched on al-Qaeda in Central and South Asia. He is author of six books on armed conflict and wrote the background paper on Asia-Pacific terrorism for the G8 Okinawa Summit. He is also a consultant to several governments and corporations on terrorism. Immediately after 9/11, the US Congress invited him to testify on the al-Qaeda organization before its Committee on National Security.

Raymond Hinnebusch is Professor of International Relations and Middle East Politics at the University of St Andrews. His books include *Egyptian Politics under Sadat* (Lynne Rienner, 1988); *Peasant Bureaucracy in Ba'thist Syria: The Political Economy of Rural Development* (Westview, 1989); *Authoritarian Power and State Formation in Ba'thist Syria: Army, Party and the Peasant* (Westview, 1990); *Syria and Iran: Middle Powers in a Penetrated Regional System* (as co-author, Routledge, 1997); *Syria: Revolution from Above* (Routledge, 2001); *The Foreign Policies of Middle East States* (as co-editor, Lynne Rienner, 2001); and *The International Politics of the Middle East* (Manchester, 2003).

Adrian Hyde-Price is Professor of Politics at the University of Leicester. His books include *European Security Beyond the Cold War* (Sage, 1991); *The International Politics of East Central Europe* (Manchester, 1996); *Germany and European Order* (Manchester, 2000); *Europe's New Security Challenges* (as co-editor, Lynne Rienner, 2000); and *Security and Identity in Europe* (as co-editor, Palgrave, 2000).

David Kenda Adaka Kikaya received a BA from the University of Nairobi and an MA and PhD from the University of Bradford. He worked at UN Headquarters in New York before returning to Kenya as Foreign News Editor with the Nation Group of Newspapers. Thereafter he held several appointments in the Kenyan government, including in the Office of the President and in the Ministry of Foreign Affairs and International Cooperation, and served as First Secretary at the Kenyan High Commission in London for eight years and as Director of the Asian and Australasian and the Europe and Commonwealth Divisions of the Foreign Ministry. Since January 2001 he has served as Kenya's Ambassador to the United Nations Human Settlement Programme (UN-HABITAT).

Rex Li is Senior Lecturer in International Relations at Liverpool John Moores University and an Associate Editor of *Security Dialogue*. He has published widely on Asia-Pacific security issues and China's foreign relations. His recent articles have appeared in *The Journal of Strategic Studies, The World Today, World Defence Systems, Pacifica Review, Journal of Contemporary China* and elsewhere.

Richard McAllister is Senior Lecturer in Politics at the University of Edinburgh. He is author of *From EC to EU* (Routledge, 1997) and of contributions to journals such as *Common Market Law Review* and *The Journal of Common Market Studies* and to many volumes on French politics, the European Union and on France's reactions to the Kosovan conflict.

David Newman is Professor of Political Geography and Chairperson of the Department of Politics and Government at Ben Gurion University in Israel. He is also editor of the international journal *Geopolitics* and writes a weekly political commentary column in the *Jerusalem Post*. His research and publications have focused on territorial dimensions of the Israel–Palestine conflict, and the changing nature of state territory, boundaries and geopolitics in a globalizing world. He has published extensively on these topics in both geographical and political science literature.

Gwenn Okruhlik is a Visiting Scholar at the University of Texas at Austin and a Fulbright Scholar currently conducting research in Saudi Arabia on identity and citizenship. Her publications include chapters in *Islam and Politics: A Social Movement Theory Approach* (Indiana University Press, forthcoming); *Iran, Iraq and the Gulf* (St. Martin's Press, 2001); and *The Global Color Line: Racial and Ethnic Inequality and Struggle From a Global Perspective* (JAI Press, 1999). Her articles have appeared in such journals as *Comparative Politics, Current History, International Journal, Middle East Journal*, and *Middle East Report*. Her online essay on 'Understanding Political Dissent in Saudi Arabia' (October 2001 at www.merip.org) has been widely disseminated.

James Putzel is Director, Development Research Centre and Crisis States Programme, London School of Economics. His recent publications include: 'The Asian Crisis: Developmental States and Crony Capitalists', in Pietro Massina (ed.), *Rethinking Development in East Asia: From the Miracle Mythology to the Economic Crisis* (RoutledgeCurzon, 2002); 'Social Capital and the Imagined Community: Democracy and Nationalism in the Philippines', in Michael Liefer (ed.), *Asian Nationalism* (Routledge, 2000); and 'The Survival of an Imperfect Democracy in the Philippines', *Democratization*, Vol. 6, No. 1 (Spring 1999).

Joanne van Selm is Senior Policy Analyst at the Migration Policy Institute, a Washington DC-based think tank devoted to the study of international migration, where she focuses on issues of refugee protection, most particularly in

Europe, and questions of migration management. Since 1998 she has also been affiliated as an Associate Professor to the University of Amsterdam's Department of Political Science and the Institute for Migration and Ethnic Studies. Her publications include *Kosovo's Refugees in the European Union* (as editor, Continuum, 2000) and *Refugee Protection in Europe: Lessons of the Yugoslav Crisis* (Martinus Nijhoff, 1998). She has also published widely on global migration, European integration in asylum and migration affairs, Dutch politics and international refugee policies.

Robert Singh is Senior Lecturer in Politics at Birkbeck College, University of London. His research interests include domestic US politics, public policy and American foreign policy. His books include *The Farrakhan Phenomenon: Race, Reaction and the Paranoid Style in American Politics* (Georgetown, 1997); *The Congressional Black Caucus: Racial Politics in the US Congress* (Sage, 1997); *Contemporary American Politics and Society* (Sage, 2002); and *American Government and Politics* (Sage, 2002).

Raju G. C. Thomas is the Allis Chalmers Distinguished Professor of International Affairs at Marquette University in Milwaukee, Wisconsin. He has published more than a dozen books and edited/co-edited books, including: *Indian Security Policy* (Princeton University Press, 1986); *South Asian Security in the 1990s* (IISS-London/Oxford University Press, 1993); *Democracy Security and Development in India* (St. Martin's Press/Macmillan, 1996); *Perspectives on Kashmir* (Westview Press, 1992); *The South Slav Conflict: Religion, Nationalism and War* (Garland/Taylor & Francis, 1996); *The Nuclear Non-Proliferation Regime* (Macmillan/St. Martin's Press, 1998); *Nuclear India in the 21st Century* (Palgrave-Macmillan, 2002), and *Yugoslavia Unraveled: Sovereignty, Self-Determination, Intervention* (Lexington Books, 2003). He is currently completing *India's Search for Security*, and co-editing with Stanley Wolpert a 4-volume Encyclopedia of India for Macmillan-Gale.

Paul Wilkinson is Professor of International Relations and Chairman of the Advisory Board of the Centre for the Study of Terrorism and Political Violence (CSTPV) at the University of St Andrews. His publications include *Political Terrorism* (Macmillan, 1974); *Terrorism and the Liberal State* (Macmillan, 1977/1986); *The New Fascists* (Pan, 1981/1983); *Contemporary Research on Terrorism* (as co-editor, Aberdeen, 1987); *Aviation Terrorism and Security* (as co-editor, Frank Cass, 1999) and *Terrorism versus Democracy: The Liberal State Response* (Frank Cass, 2001). He is co-editor of the academic journal *Terrorism and Political Violence*, and is currently director of a research project funded by the ESRC on the domestic management of terrorist attacks in the UK.

Joanne Wright is Director of European Studies and Jean Monnet Professor at Royal Holloway, University of London where she is also currently Dean of the Faculty of History and Social Science. She is co-author with K. Bryett of *Policing and Conflict in Northern Ireland* (St Martin's, 2001) and of *Terrorist Propaganda: The Red Army Faction and the Provisional IRA, 1968–86* (Macmillan, 1991), and has contributed recent articles to *European Security* and *Contemporary British History*. She is on the editorial board of *Terrorism and Political Violence*.

Samina Yasmeen is a Senior Lecturer in International Politics at the University of Western Australia (UWA), Perth. Her publications include: 'Is Pakistan's Nuclear Bomb an Islamic Bomb?', *Asian Studies Review*, 2001; 'South Asia after the Nuclear Tests: Prospects for Arms Control', *Pacifica Review*, October 1999; 'Pakistan's Nuclear Tests: Domestic Debate and International Determinants', *Australian Journal of International Affairs*, April 1999; 'The Case for a South Asian Nuclear Weapon Free Zone', in Ramesh Thakur (ed.), *Nuclear Weapons-Free Zones* (Palgrave, 1998); and 'Sino-Pakistan Relations and the Middle East', *China Report* (New Delhi), January 1999.

Acknowledgments

We are most grateful to Craig Fowlie and Zoë Botterill at Routledge for their enthusiasm for this project and ready help, making the editorial process a pleasant one. Thanks are also due to Liz Dawn for her efficient copy-editing, to Michael Solomons for preparing the index, and to Nicole Krull for overseeing the production process. Linda Kunzli at Royal Holloway, University of London, also deserves thanks for her willing assistance. Miss Moira Courtman of the Map Room at the University of London main library provided invaluable advice on maps.

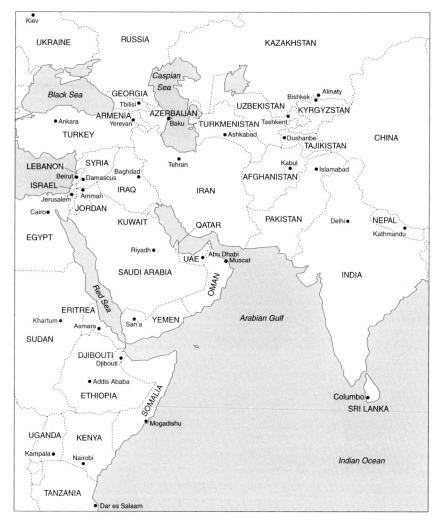

Map 1 Overview of Middle East, East Africa, southern Russia, Central Asia, Afghanistan, Pakistan and India

Map 2 Afghanistan

Introduction

World reactions to September 11 and the 'war on terror'

Mary Buckley

After the events of September 11 2001, a stunned US President George W. Bush declared that 'night fell on a different world.'[1] There was indeed horror around much of the globe that a new and insidious precedent had been set for terror against states, making everyone vulnerable.

Quite how that different world was perceived, however, like the world before it, varied across and within states, notwithstanding similarities in interpretation. For some it was just the old world continued. What vulnerability meant to leaders and to citizens also showed variation ranging from US fears of further attacks, to Russian concerns about remaining marginalized on the world stage, to African anxieties about the reduced priority in the developed world to tackling AIDS or financing projects in less developed nations. By contrast, the vulnerabilities of Afghan refugees revolved around the daily basics of the human condition – obtaining food, shelter and security.

The main aims of this book, like those of *Kosovo: Perceptions of War and its Aftermath*, are: first, to discuss the reactions of leaders, political parties and public opinion in different states of the world to the events of September 11, to war in Afghanistan and to threatened war against what US leaders have branded 'rogue states' in order to assess similarities and differences; and second, to explore broader issues of terrorism, war, peace, alliances, international organization, world economy, the plight of refugees and international relations theory.[2]

The states selected for discussion include those central to the action in the war against terrorism but in different parts of the world and in different ways, namely the USA, Britain, France, Pakistan, Russia, the Central Asian states and Canada. Inclusion of Germany and Italy also highlights contrasts in linkages between domestic and foreign policy in two member states of the European Union (EU) and North Atlantic Treaty Organization (NATO). Both are committed to the war against terrorism, but Silvio Berlusconi's right-wing coalition government – Italy's most Euro-skeptic in the postwar period – exhibited inertia and confusion over Italy's role and public opinion was reluctant to commit troops, while Germany, after swiftly endorsing action against terrorism and redefining its own security policy, spearheaded a call for European multilateralism in the face of US unilateralism.

The situation in the Middle East is more complicated since it is the locus of the accused and the accusers. States here supported a condemnation of terrorism to differing degrees and for varying reasons. We focus on Iran, Iraq, Syria, Saudi Arabia, Israel and the Israel–Palestine peace process. On the periphery of key decision-making but none the less seriously affected by international developments, albeit in very different ways and with various regional consequences, are states in Southeast Asia and Africa and also China and India.

States of different types are thus included, drawing attention to: the relevance of categories which include 'superpower' even 'mega-power,' 'former superpower,' 'less developed nation,' 'middle ground power' and 'aspiring global actor'; the formulation of foreign policy; and leaders' expectations of leaders' reactions in other states. Geopolitics is crucial to our discussion since recent developments in Pakistan and Central Asia – such as US aid to Pakistan and the provision of bases for US troops in three states of Central Asia – would not have occurred without proximity to the war in Afghanistan. Geopolitical dynamics have huge consequences for relations within regions and between those regions and the USA. Situated far away from the main theatre of war, leaders in other states, such as some in Africa, fear further neglect from the advanced industrial world.

The presence of Muslim populations within states also illustrates complex variations in reactions to September 11 linked to the history of a given state, size of its Muslim population, constellation and nature of religious beliefs, type of government, presence of terrorist groups and region. Comparison across France, Indonesia, Pakistan, Iran, Iraq and Israel nicely confirms the importance of multivariate explanations to account for attitudes among different groups, including Muslims, within a state.

ORGANIZATION: FROM SEPTEMBER 11 TO AFGHANISTAN

Rick Fawn (Chapter 1) sets the context for discussion by tracing the chronology of key events and outcomes after September 11 up to the close of 2002. Paul Wilkinson (Chapter 2) then provides an analytic setting by sketching the use and misuse of the concept of terrorism. He provides a typology of terrorists and poses questions concerning effectiveness, motivation and significance. He also draws attention to the consequences for terrorism studies of the destruction of the World Trade Center. Against this backdrop, Rohan Gunaratna (Chapter 3) gives a detailed account of the history of al-Qaeda, explains its global structures, networks and operations and concludes that it can only be defeated by a multinational, multidimensional and multi-agency response.

A close examination of US foreign policy by Robert Singh (Chapter 4) suggests that 9/11 (as it is popularly referred to in the USA) accelerated trends, policies and approaches that were already well established, rather than marking a transformation. According to Singh, it reconfirmed Bush's approach that military strength was vital to assuring national security of a hegemonic power – to some a 'hyper-power' or 'mega-power' – 'with neither peer nor precedent.'

Britain was the only state, as Andrew Dorman (Chapter 5) discusses, that provided military forces to the USA on the first day of action. Initially Tony Blair was seen as Bush's 'friend' offering political, moral and military backing. War in Afghanistan, however, inflamed the debate in Britain about Islam and citizenship and carried on from Kosovo questions about the creation of Europe's own rapid reaction force. Later on strains emerged between Blair and Bush over the Middle East and the newly established International Court of Human Rights.

It was Britain rather than Canada that emerged as the USA's most loyal ally in the war against terrorism, despite the fact that Canada shares the world's longest undefended border with its superpower neighbor and notwithstanding the largest volume of bilateral trading in the world. Rick Fawn (Chapter 6) stresses the importance of Canada's self-perceived status as a non-militaristic international humanitarian assistant, explores the strains of reliance on the USA, and discusses the significance of Canada's commitment to multiculturalism and open immigration – commitments which critics can now dub facilitators of terrorism. For these reasons, Fawn categorizes Canada as distinct for being a 'reluctant moral middle power.'

In France, as in Britain and Canada, there was immediate sympathy after 9/11 for the USA but, as Richard McAllister (Chapter 7) notes, evident concern after Bush's reference to an 'axis of evil' and possible action against Iraq. McAllister examines the gradually increasing French role in military action in Afghanistan, despite tensions in the 'bicephalous executive' and attempts by president and prime minister to use the situation to their respective electoral advantages. He also explores reactions among France's Muslim population which is the largest in Europe.

The shock at 9/11 in Germany was fueled by knowledge that terrorists had worked in Hamburg. Adrian Hyde-Price (Chapter 8) discusses how the Bundestag showed 'unconditional solidarity' to the USA with the exception of the Party of Democratic Socialism. Foreign Minister Joschka Fischer, leader of the Green Party, played a central diplomatic role in consolidating the international alliance against terrorism. Germany also funded an important UN-sponsored conference held in November 2001 in Bonn on the creation of a post-Taliban interim regime. Above all, argues Hyde-Price, war in Afghanistan made a huge impact on the redefinition of Germany's military contribution to security, as had Kosovo before it. Whether or not to support war against Iraq was also an important issue for Germany, seriously affecting the September 2002 parliamentary elections, and resulting in bolstered support for Schröder and Fischer and their stance against US unilateralism and for multilateralism.

Italy stands out within the European Union, as Philip A. Daniels (Chapter 9) notes, for having a leader whose legitimacy was questioned in international newspapers due to outstanding corruption charges against him and also to the inclusion of the postfascist National Alliance in his coalition government. Berlusconi hoped that September 11 would help to increase his credibility. Among the consequences, however, were strained relations with both EU states and the USA. Daniels argues that the Italian government gave mixed messages on the role Italy would play in the war on terrorism and generally mishandled the crisis. Berlusconi was also reported to have made the gaffe that Western civilization was 'superior' to Islamic. His lack of diplomacy contrasted hugely with the constructive role played by Germany's Fischer. In fact, the Italian Greens argued against a military response, as did Catholic pacifist groups and the Pope who advocated a dialogue in search for peace.

Whereas Europe was in shock at 9/11, the Middle East was under an immediate world spotlight. Roland Dannreuther (Chapter 10) examines reactions in Iran and Iraq, noting that these states had histories of anti-Americanism and were potential suspects for the attacks. Dannreuther explains why the USA has labeled Iran, Iraq and North Korea as an 'axis of evil,' and challenges the automatic coupling of Iran and Iraq due to important differences between them. Iran defines itself as a radical Islamist state while Iraq is committed to secular Arab nationalism. They each have different compositions, political systems and regimes. Iranian leaders supported an Afghanistan without the Taliban, but Saddam Hussein did not take this stand. Dannreuther also traces reactions in Iraq to UN Resolution 1441 and to world pressures on Saddam to disarm.

By contrast, Syrian leaders, as Raymond Hinnebusch (Chapter 11) outlines, were willing to cooperate with the international coalition against terrorism, but with qualifications. This, however, was complicated by a growing rapprochement with Iraq, an irritant to the Bush leadership, and also by Syria's dissatisfaction with Israel's continued occupation of the Golan Heights. Syria attempted to balance openings with Europe and Iraq against US interventionism in the Middle East. Saudi Arabia, home of Osama bin Laden, gave support to the US coalition against terrorism and cut ties with the Taliban. Gwenn Okruhlik (Chapter 12) explores the self-searching within the country that spawned the prime terrorist and the painful conflicting pressures from domestic sources and from the USA. As in most of the Arab world, there was conviction that US foreign policy in their region was seriously flawed.

There was, however, predictable dissent in Israel. David Newman (Chapter 13) notes how Israel, much to its leaders' surprise, was omitted by the Bush administration from its coalition against terrorism in preference to having Arab states on board. Prime Minister Sharon had expected to be a key ally of the USA in its battle and also to see Palestinian organizations, such as Hamas and Jihad, on the hit-list, but they were not. The Israeli government was quick to argue that US policy towards Israel was not the cause of 9/11. Unswerving Israeli backing for the war on terror and an increase in Palestinian suicide bombings in Israel ultimately resulted in a strengthening of US–Israeli relations.

Harsh criticism of US foreign policy was common in the developing world where it was dubbed 'the root cause' of the problem that triggered terrorism. Views varied on the African continent but as David Kenda Adaka Kikaya (Chapter 14) argues, there was deep-seated concern that 9/11 meant that donor countries would marginalize Africa even more as funds were channeled into the fight against terrorism. Leaders in most states favored concerted UN involvement rather than a unilateral US approach. In May 2003 President Bush's AIDS bill was passed in the US Congress, finally granting $15 billion in aid to Africa.

Anxieties about US foreign policy were evident in Southeast Asia too. James Putzel (Chapter 15) discusses how Malaysian leaders opposed strikes against Afghanistan, Thailand was wary of offering unconditional support fearing that use of its military bases would be requested and Singapore was slow to endorse US action. The situation in Indonesia was more complex due to its large Islamic population. Although the president expressed solidarity with the USA in an attempt to reverse the US ban on assistance to the Indonesian armed forces because of domestic criticism from opposition Islamic organizations, Indonesia's administration called for UN authority over any military action.

By contrast, Putzel explains in more detail why President Macapagal-Arroyo of the Philippines was a more ardent supporter of the US action than Britain's Tony Blair. He traces the decline and poverty of Muslims in the Philippines, examines different politically active Muslim organizations and Macapagal-Arroyo's strategies to 'wipe out terrorism.' Partnership with the USA against terrorism was hoped to bolster the Philippines longstanding war with its own Islamic separatists. Putzel also explores the significance of subsequent bombings in Bali and Sulawesi in October 2002, then new attacks in the Philippines, and holds that legitimacy for draconian security measures in their aftermath could backfire by empowering repressive military forces and thereby weakening chances for democratic consolidation.

Samina Yasmeen (Chapter 16) shows how, like the Philippines, Pakistan experienced serious domestic cross-pressures. But bordering Afghanistan, Pakistan unexpectedly found itself at center-stage in a global attack on terrorism and received US financial assistance. To its benefit, sanctions were lifted against its nuclear program and against its military takeover, to the envy of some African leaders, as noted by Kikaya. According to Yasmeen, General Musharraf adopted a liberal approach to domestic and foreign policy whilst Islamists viewed the situation in terms of a clash of civilizations. Musharraf has a keen interest in the reconstruction of Afghanistan, but is attempting not to offend Iran over this.

India has a history of non-alignment. Like Russia and China, India had been against NATO intervention in Kosovo, and like Russia was quick to offer support to the US coalition against terrorism. As Raju G.C. Thomas (Chapter 17) explains, India's bases were passed over by US leaders in favor of facilities in Pakistan, closer to Afghanistan. Growing tensions between India and Pakistan complicated the question in this region of what constituted a war on terrorism. From the Indian side came the argument that it was waging war against terrorists in Kashmir. The response from Pakistan was that India was meting out state terrorism. Thomas holds that 'the Pakistan factor' has stymied any great Indo–US strategic cooperation, just as it did during the Cold War.

Leaders of states in the developing world shared the goal of wanting something back from the USA if they showed support for the 'war against terrorism.' Rex Li (Chapter 18) discusses the significance of China as a rising power with global aspirations. Like the Prime Minister of Malaysia, President Jiang Zemin supported a US policy to hunt down terrorists – but opposed war against Afghanistan. Chinese leaders' hopes of concessions from the USA on Taiwan and of a reversal of sanctions imposed after the massacre in Tiananmen Square in 1989 were, however, dashed. Li explores the views of Chinese security experts and examines the consequences of 9/11 for regional relationships.

The Russian Federation (Chapter 19) is distinct here for being the only former superpower, which had seen its empire in Eastern Europe collapse, its state implode and its economy, polity and society suffer endemic organized crime, instability and poverty. President Vladimir Putin skillfully took advantage of 9/11 to join the coalition against terrorism to bring Russia more centrally back to the stage of world politics after its disagreements with the West over Kosovo and after the election of President George W. Bush who had downgraded Russia in Washington's eyes, in contrast to his predecessor Bill Clinton.

Among the benefits for Russia are agreements on arms reductions and recognition from the USA of market economy status. Communists and nationalists at home, however, remain critical with China of US plans for a missile defense system and of the USA's reneging of the 1972 Anti-Ballistic Missile (ABM) Treaty. They deplored NATO expansion, US troops in Central Asia, US advisors in Georgia, Putin's pulling out of bases in Cuba and Vietnam and Congress's unwillingness to overturn the Jackson–Vanik amendment. Putin's critics accused him of contributing to the geopolitical weakening of Russia. After the siege of a Moscow theatre from 23–26 October 2002, fresh critics lambasted Putin for imitating Bush's rhetoric of fighting world terror and for confusing the struggle for Chechen independence with actions of al-Qaeda.

The states of Central Asia were formerly republics in the USSR, but were 'led' rather than 'leading,' and generally opposed to independence from Moscow in contrast to other republics such as Lithuania, Latvia, Estonia and Georgia whose nationalists had demanded 'sovereignty.' Sally N. Cummings (Chapter 20) points out that the US war on terrorism gave Kazakhstan, Kyrgyzstan, Tajikistan, Turkmenistan and Uzbekistan enhanced strategic importance. Leaders in all five offered intelligence to the USA and air transport, and Kyrgyzstan, Tajikistan and Uzbekistan were used as bases by Western forces as front-line states. Cummings explains why support for the USA was a risk for the region and what leaders wanted to extract from the USA for their backing. She also considers the significance of internal dissent and notes the deteriorating relations among these five states and special concern that Uzbek leaders will intensify their aggressive policies.

Discussion of the role of international organizations after 9/11 is both topical and controversial. Joanne Wright (Chapter 21) focuses on reactions in the UN Security Council and General Assembly, noting the resolutions and arguments that came out of them. She maintains that the UN's lack of a prominent public role in the war against Afghanistan is due to the fact that it was clear that the USA was going to respond on its own. Member states, however, are keen for the UN to adopt a long-term strategy. Wright argues that NATO's reaction to 9/11 was symbolic with a minimal military contribution. The EU was also a limited actor, highlighting the inadequacies of the Common Foreign and Security Policy. If anything, 9/11 may prompt more integration within the EU.

This book would be incomplete if it scrutinized reactions within states and international organizations alone. It goes on to consider the consequences for refugees in Afghanistan, the impact on the world economy and, more broadly, what constitutes war. It is also timely to ask whether international relations theory itself needs an overhaul.

For refugees, whether it is war, terrorism or 'expressive violence' as later defined by Christopher Coker, is irrelevant. Displacement, lack of shelter and food are what matter. Joanne van Selm (Chapter 22) argues that the public imagination in the West was not fired to think of Afghan refugees as people in need of large-scale protection, as had been the case for Kosovo's refugees, but rather as those needing food, blankets and tents.[3] Limited media access to Afghanistan was one key reason behind this. The resulting lack of spellbinding media images contributed. The Taliban's destruction of Buddha statues hit the headlines, not desperate refugees. Van Selm examines where the refugees are in Pakistan and Afghanistan and the role of the UNHCR.

Whereas refugees suffered, the global economy, according to Brigitte Granville (Chapter 23), did not. Although markets initially showed panic and stock prices plummeted, rapid economic policy responses prevented fears being realized. Granville makes a sound case that the international economic order needs to adopt effective strategies to reduce global poverty since this is what poses a threat to international security.

In a wide-ranging discussion, Coker (Chapter 24) questions whether 9/11 really does mean 'year zero' and argues that it reintroduced Americans to a different way of warfare similar to that of Japanese Kamikaze pilots. He muses on nihilism, anarchism, expressive violence as affirmation of a way of life, Conrad and the existential dimension of war. The issue for Coker is the dialectical relationship of twenty-first century warfare between the modern and postmodern worlds.

International relations theory, however, according to Barry Buzan (Chapter 25), does not need rethinking. He outlines the four main theoretical approaches: neorealist, globalist, regionalist and constructivist and suggests that, in the light of 9/11, they all still capture important aspects of the complex world system. Thus, in Buzan's view, major changes are not needed in debates about these theories or to agendas in international relations.

In the concluding chapter (26) the editors consider the significance of September 11 and its aftermath for the pressing issues of civil rights abuses in the pursuit of terrorism and the nature of foreign policies in a unipolar world. Buckley and Fawn argue that liberal democracies are prone to perpetuating civil wrongs in certain historical contexts, thereby compromising the democratic tradition. War, crisis and perceived state necessity can result in the internment of certain target groups, the suspension of habeas corpus and employment restrictions. The danger in the means/end argument of justifying present 'bad' practices as 'regrettable but necessary' for the future 'good' is that they may become institutionalized and take on a permanence. The editors also concentrate here on the making of foreign and security policies with the threat of global terrorism in mind and on the political dimensions of obtaining consensus, especially when the interpretation of religion is a complicating factor. They argue that bringing domestic and international levels together effectively demands both tolerant societies and considerable international agreement.

FROM AFGHANISTAN TO IRAQ

The US war against terrorism continues after Afghanistan. Increasingly keen to wage war against Iraq and to topple Saddam Hussein, Bush was held back by world pressure in September and October 2002 against acting unilaterally and ignoring the UN. Tony Blair played a deft role in this. The USA's National Security Strategy, however, confidently declared the US right to wage preemptive war against states which posed immediate risk to national security and against any country deemed a 'potential risk.'[4] This confirmed for many throughout the world that it was unchecked US unilateralism that was a dangerous world threat.

In November 2002, republican gains in mid-term elections in the USA, as Singh's chapter notes, were a boost to Bush's leadership. His constant push for a fresh UN resolution on Iraq finally brought dividends. Even Syria, France, Russia and China came on board, although how they interpreted its significance varied. Bush wanted war whereas Putin commented that war might now be averted. Dannreuther's chapter discusses how the Iraqi regime had, through intensive regional and international diplomacy, attempted to undermine US objectives. But with erstwhile close friends in Moscow and Beijing now turning cool, Saddam finally became conciliatory towards the UN and agreed for weapons inspectors to enter Iraq.

The story of Iraq's treatment by the world is the next stage in the US war on terror, falling outside the scope of this volume. The following chapters, however, discuss the significance of the course of events in the year after September 11, including terrorist incidents in 2002 in Daghestan, Kuwait, offshore Yemen, Bali, Moscow and Mombasa and in 2003 in Riyadh. By November, increased 'chatter' warned security services of imminent 'spectacular attacks' from al-Qaeda, with rumors flying of Heathrow airport and the London underground being favored targets.[5] On 28 November, however, the Paradise Hotel in Mombasa was blown up and there was an attempt to shoot down an Israeli charter jet departing from Mombasa. Terror had returned to Kenya. Then in January 2003, traces of the deadly poison, ricin, were found in a flat in Wood Green in London, and four men were the first to be charged under the 1996 Chemical Weapons Act as well as under section 57 of the Terrorism Act for 'possession of articles of value to a terrorist.'[6] Debates were refueled about the unpreparedness of states for chemical and biological terrorist attacks.

While ricin was hitting the headlines, a military build-up was taking place in the Gulf in preparation for possible war with Iraq. Bush's most steadfast ally in Britain was enduring more vociferous opposition to war from within his own

Labour Party, prompting further debate about stability and tensions in the US–British relationship. In his State of the Union address in January, Bush argued passionately for war, claiming that he possessed evidence of a link between Saddam Hussein and al-Qaeda. 'Old Europe,' as US Defense Secretary Donald Rumsfeld undiplomatically dubbed France and Germany, remained critical, hesitant or neutral. Alongside Bush, Blair continued to back firm action, although prevailed yet again in persuading Bush not to act unilaterally since this would harm the transatlantic relationship. Blair also pressed Bush to give weapons inspectors in Iraq more time to complete their work, as backed by leaders in Russia and in many other states. But Bush's message remained blunt: 'Saddam Hussein is not disarming. He is a danger to the world.'[7] Thus Bush advocated a preemptive war. World leaders, however, were now divided in their views with Britain, Spain and Bulgaria at the opposite end of the spectrum from France, Germany, Syria and Pakistan. Amid this, North Korea announced that it would withdraw from the nuclear Non-Proliferation Treaty.[8] Worldwide, leaders protested. Intelligence from satellites suggested that North Korea subsequently moved 8,000 nuclear fuel rods out of storage, appearing to move towards producing atomic weapons.

War on Iraq was formally declared on 18 March without the support of the UN Security Council.[9] Frantic diplomatic efforts on the part of the USA and Britain to secure a second UN resolution eventually stalled due to Jacques Chirac's insistence that France would veto it. Attempts had been made to persuade the 'undecided' on the Security Council, namely Mexico, Pakistan, Angola, Cameroon, Guinea and China, to back one.[10] The opponents of war on the Council were still France, Germany, Russia and Syria with Spain and Bulgaria supporting the British/American stand. Under the intense pressure of opposition within the population and within his party, Blair stood shoulder to shoulder with Bush arguing that he believed this course to be 'right.' Bush told his nation that 'we will accept no outcome but victory.'[11]

The UN secretary general, Kofi Annan, regretted that it was a 'sad day for the United Nations and the international community.'[12] The leaders of France, Russia and Germany reiterated their critical stand, with Russia's Foreign Minister Igor Ivanov stressing that the USA and Britain were violating the UN Charter and had no authorization for war or for the overthrow of a leader of a sovereign state.[13] Earlier they had protested that there were no grounds for stopping the work of the weapons' inspectors.[14] On 20 March President Putin condemned the war as 'a big political mistake' and worldwide from Sydney to Moscow and San Francisco, demonstrators took to the streets in protest.[15] Bush's war on terror had indeed shifted from Afghanistan to the Middle East with many questioning the proclaimed link between Saddam Hussein and al-Qaeda. In his televised broadcast on 20 March, a very gaunt Blair told the nation that tyrannical leaders with weapons of mass destruction had to be tackled to prevent those weapons from falling into the hands of terrorists who threatened democracy, prosperity and a way of life worth preserving.[16] By contrast, Bush seemed upbeat, calm and ready for action, not under the same degree of strain as Blair. Both Bush and Blair emphasized 'total' commitment to the reconstruction of Iraq and to persistent efforts to secure a stable Israel and viable Palestine.

The chapters which follow explore in some detail the chain of events across the world from September 11, 2001 which built up into 'phase two' of the war against Iraq. The issues raised here concerning the reconstruction of war-torn states, the plight of refugees, the meaning of citizenship, the role of the UN and the significance of war are relevant to both Afghanistan and Iraq and also to any future military operations.

NOTES

1 Quoted in *The Economist*, 27 Oct.–2 Nov. 2001, p. 22.
2 Mary Buckley and Sally N. Cummings (eds), *Kosovo: Perceptions of War and its Aftermath* (London and New York: Continuum, 2001).
3 See Joanne van Selm, 'Perceptions of Kosovo's Refugees', in ibid., pp. 251–65.
4 See   http://www.thepanamanews.com/pn/v_08/issue_18/news_01.html;   http://www.onlinejournal.com/Commentary/Thomas100302/thomas100302.html
5 *The Guardian*, 12 Nov. 2002, p. 1; *The Observer*, 17 Nov. 2002, p. 1.
6 *The Independent on Sunday*, 12 Jan. 2003, p. 2.
7 *The Guardian*, 1 Feb. 2003, p. 1.
8 *The Independent on Sunday*, 12 Jan. 2003, p. 2.
9 *The Guardian*, 19 March 2003, p. 1.
10 *The Independent*, 6 March 2003, p. 5.
11 Radio Free Europe, Radio Liberty (RFERL), *Newsline*, Vol. 7, No. 53, Part III, 20 March 2003, p. 1.
12 *The Independent*, 20 March 2003, p. 6.
13 Ibid.
14 RFE/RL, *Newsline*, Vol. 7, No. 50, Part 1, 17 March 2003, p. 1.
15 Ibid., Vol. 7, No. 51, Part 1, 18 March 2003, p. 1; *Rossiiskaia gazeta*, 21 March 2003, p. 1.
16 *10 O'clock News*, BBC 1, 22.00 hours, 20 March 2003.

1 From ground zero to the war in Afghanistan

Rick Fawn

The attacks of September 11 may almost have been predictable. While the name al-Qaeda was not used publicly by its members before 9/11, its adherents had bombed the World Trade Center eight years before, in an attack that, if fully successful, would have killed an estimated 200,000.[1] The group had planned to bomb multiple aircraft over the Pacific in Project *Bojinka* and to crash a jet into an American government building. The same group succeeded in the simultaneous bombing of US embassies in Dar-es-Salaam and Nairobi in 1998. A related group hijacked an Air France airbus from Algeria in December 1994 with the intention of crashing it into Paris. The operative group, the type of target, and the means had all been in evidence before.

Before 9/11 Osama bin Laden was also identified as the leading terrorist threat to the USA – the CIA revealed after the 9/11 attacks that it had offered a bounty three years earlier for bin Laden dead or alive. This should perhaps not be surprising as bin Laden's 1998 declaration of war on the USA could have been taken seriously in light of tangible attacks rather than rhetoric. Bill Clinton admitted in late September 2001 that as President 'we did everything' to apprehend him: 'I authorized the arrest and, if necessary, the killing of Osama bin Laden, and we actually made contact with a group in Afghanistan to do it.'[2] Not apprehending bin Laden was, Clinton said, the greatest regret of his presidency. Preparations by US intelligence agencies before 9/11 for mass terrorism against mainland America were among the fastest expanding federal programs and also unprecedented among countries.[3]

US intelligence reports in summer 2001 are now known to have warned of attacks against the American mainland. The specific operatives behind the attacks took exploratory or preparatory measures that caused suspicion, but tragically not enough for a rights-based, liberal society to conduct a full-scale investigation or arrest.[4] Zacarias Moussaoui, believed to have been the twentieth hijacker, was arrested a month before 9/11, but his computer was not searched because the FBI could not secure a warrant.

By mid-2002, allegations – some perhaps politically motivated, others probably neutral – abounded about how much intelligence services and even the White House knew about some sort of terrorist attack on the USA. In May 2002 Democrat Senator and Senate Majority Leader Tom Daschle charged that the Bush administration had warnings in August 2001 of a major attack by al-Qaeda that included a hijacking. Two weeks later CIA Director George Tenet was 'in denial' about the CIA's receipt of information on two 9/11 hijackers connected to al-Qaeda two years before the attacks, but accounts by September 2002 suggested that in July 2001 leading US officials already expected a 'spectacular attack' by bin Laden within weeks.[5]

This chapter traces the major events made in response to the September attacks. Its focus is on: coalition building – both diplomatic and military; the decision to wage both war and undertake peacekeeping in Afghanistan; and the measures taken to stabilize that war-ravaged country.

FROM GROUND ZERO TO AFGHANISTAN

By mid-morning on 9/11 the world knew that the impact from two 767s had collapsed the two 110-story towers of the World Trade Center, ignited neighboring buildings, and also completely destroying adjacent several buildings. This devastated area of Manhattan promptly gained the mournful nickname of 'ground zero,' a term previously used by Pentagon staff for the center of their building as a euphemism for the Cold War nuclear strike that never came. But this hub of American military coordination was also in disarray, a third aircraft having slammed into a side of the Pentagon. Buildings throughout the capital, including key government facilities like the White House and Congress, were evacuated amid fears of additional attacks. Speculation grew over the intended target of a fourth hijacked plane – most likely a political target like the White House or Camp David or possibly an east coast nuclear power plant; but this plane was heroically downed by its passengers over Pennsylvania, foiling further malevolence.

Through the attacks, bin Laden achieved more than he expected. In a videotape released in November 2001 bin Laden explained that he had hoped that three or four floors of each tower would burn and that the towers' steel structure would melt from the heat of the detonating fuel, causing only the floors above to collapse. Even he, in self-professed, if diabolic 'optimism,' appeared not to expect each tower to disintegrate completely.

While US forces were caught unaware and were arrayed against a seemingly invisible enemy, retaliatory planning began immediately. Unlike right after the 1995 Oklahoma bombing, in which blame turned quickly to foreign Muslim terrorists rather than home-grown American fundamentalists, forthright statements of culpability were few on the day.

In circumstances of uncertainty and expectations of additional attacks, President Bush was hurried to the safety of a nuclear-bomb-proof bunker briefly while the US government sought not only to operate but also to respond. Bush warned on 9/11 that retaliation was imminent. Planning began that morning for a war in Afghanistan. Bilateral and multilateral diplomacy were used for almost a month before they were complemented by military measures.

On 12 September the essence of the American response was already outlined. Bush labeled the attacks as 'acts of war' and declared that no distinction would be made between those who conducted them and those who shelter the perpetrators. His slogan 'Either you are with us or with the terrorists' defined allegiances. International support was immediately forthcoming from traditional American allies. Unprecedented in its half-century existence, NATO invoked Article 5, offering immediate assistance from all members to the USA, although the Bush administration would pursue its war effort outside NATO structures. The UN Security Council also passed Resolution 1368 that day, which recognized 'the inherent right of individual or collective self-defence' of Article 51 of the UN Charter and which also declared the body's 'readiness to take the necessary steps to respond to the terrorist attacks of September 11 2001 and to combat all forms of terrorism, in accordance with the Charter of the UN.'

A day later US Secretary of State Colin Powell pronounced bin Laden the chief suspect. Bush reiterated this on 15 September when he also declared the USA to be at war. Vice-President Dick Cheney followed with warnings of a protracted war. But before applying military might, US authorities approached the Taliban for the release of bin Laden and top associates. The Taliban asked the USA for its proof and offered to try bin Laden in its own courts.

The nature of the attack was assessed on numerous fronts. The New York Stock Exchange was closed for four days; when it reopened on 17 September it suffered its largest single-day loss. The airline industry was perhaps the first economic-sector casualty. Swissair was the first of many Western airlines to declare bankruptcy, citing September 11 as a cause, while others blamed the event for thousands of redundancies, some of which may have occurred regardless. Lost American output in the first week after the attack was estimated at US$40 billion; Chairman of the Federal Reserve Alan Greenspan said the US economy had 'ground to a halt.'[6] The International Monetary Fund (IMF) warned on 26 September of the first global recession in a decade. While the economic impact may have been overstated, the costs of providing additional security have diverted public funds in the USA and elsewhere. Expectations of recession pushed down the price of oil; and Gulf states, as well as Russia, assisted the industrial West by pledging nevertheless to increase petroleum production. And the world remained jittery – New York's Dow Jones Industrial Average lost 163 points when the crash of a light plane into Milan's Pirelli tower was initially feared as terrorism; with prompt news of an accident or the pilot's suicide, the Dow Jones regained 110 points by early afternoon. But this was a mild indication of the effects which further terrorism would have on markets. Initial economic fears were so grave, and the deviousness of the attacks so unprecedented, that al-Qaeda was believed to have placed 'put options' on US airlines before the attacks, allowing it to sell the shares at the pre-attack price but to pay only the depressed post-attack prices. If true, al-Qaeda would have netted billions for its own use and inflicted further insolence to the US economy. While the economic damage could thus have been greater, the saying remained 'Never have so few cost so many so much.'

The emerging American response combined diplomacy with assurances of righting the wrongs of 9/11. At a joint session of Congress on 20 September Bush pledged justice would be done, and demanded that the Taliban surrender al-Qaeda leaders and all terrorists to US authorities, close permanently terrorist camps and allow American verification. The importance of Britain was evident, with Blair attending a White House dinner beforehand (despite being late due to new airport security) and then seated prominently in Congress for Bush's speech in which the President said his country 'had no truer friend than Great Britain.'[7]

Despite being bolstered by the support of Britain and other Western countries, any US-led military operations in landlocked Afghanistan hinged on the support of Pakistan. The Pakistani government, particularly its Inter-Services Intelligence (ISI) agency had nurtured the Taliban, had vested interests in its continued domination of Afghanistan, and was one of only three states to recognize the Taliban as the official regime. Sacrificing bin Laden for the continuation of the Taliban thus seemed a major Pakistani strategic interest. But on 18 September, and again on 28 September, Pakistani representatives were unable to convince the Taliban to surrender bin Laden, and the Taliban signaled the expectation of an attack by closing its air space and putting its defences on alert. However, in a possible bow to American pressure, a Council of 1,000 clerics agreed to turn over bin Laden to the USA and asked him to leave Afghanistan. The Taliban took the extraordinary measure of overturning that, and downgrading it to a 'suggestion.' The Taliban's ambassador to Pakistan, Mullah Abdul Salam Zaeef, rejected Bush's demand of the same day for extradiction of bin Laden as 'an insult of Islam' and proclaimed 'We will never surrender to evil and might.' What diplomatic standing the Taliban had was beginning to erode: while still recognizing the regime, Pakistani diplomats were withdrawn from Kabul. The United Arab Emirates ended its recognition on 22 September; Saudi Arabia followed three days later, declaring that the Taliban harbored, armed and encouraged terrorists.

Apart from the Taliban's increased isolation, the Bush administration now engaged in changing Pakistani policy towards Afghanistan. American sanctions imposed on Pakistan for its 1998 nuclear testing were lifted (as were the corresponding ones on India). On 7 October Musharraf removed Lieutenant-General Mahmood Ahmed as head of the ISI, and other military figures believed to be supportive of the Taliban were 'sidelined.'

In the USA, Bush issued an Executive Order on 24 September to disrupt terrorist finances, with several accounts believed connected to bin Laden or al-Qaeda frozen immediately. His administration made clear that the 'war on terrorism' would have phases, the first of which would be against Afghanistan, a policy underlined by the continuing assembly of American military power in the country's vicinity. Russian President Putin not only said he would increase Russian military supplies to anti-Taliban forces but also would provide intelligence to the USA. Moscow acquiesced as American aircraft arrived in Uzbekistan within days of 9/11 and personnel began arriving in other former Soviet Central Asian republics by early October.[8] Recognizing the need for international, multi-ethnic and multi-faith support, the US government altered the name of its preparation from 'Operation Infinite Justice' to 'Operation Enduring Freedom.' The UN

Security Council passed an American-drafted resolution on 28 September imposing extensive requirements on member states to counteract terrorism on their territory.[9]

On 30 September, the Taliban admitted that bin Laden was at an undisclosed location in Afghanistan 'for his safety and security.' The Taliban's ambassador to Pakistan, Mullah Abdul Salam Zaeef, announced that bin Laden was 'under the control of the Islamic Emirate of Afghanistan,' although he added that only those responsible for his security knew his whereabouts, and that 'He's in a place which cannot be located by anyone.'[10] In these circumstances, Pakistani President Musharraf announced on 1 October that his government had done everything possible to achieve a diplomatic solution and that war was not inevitable. At the same time, hundreds of Pakistanis were reported crossing into Afghanistan to prepare for jihad against the United States.[11]

The start of October suggested that strategic shifts might occur within Afghanistan. The Northern Alliance declared that it had made an agreement with exiled Afghan King Zahir Shah to overthrow the Taliban. But the fate of Afghanistan did not hang only on internal machinations. On 6 October Bush told the Taliban its time was short and rejected its suggestion of considering the release of Western aid workers held on charges of proselytizing Christianity as an implied compromise on surrendering bin Laden. What diplomacy had existed between the USA and the Taliban was finished.

START OF WAR IN AFGHANISTAN

On 7 October US attacks began, with British participation, using cruise missiles and aircraft. After repeating demands that bin Laden be surrendered, Bush announced on television that 'None of these demands were met. And now the Taliban will pay the price.' The President said the decision was made 'only after the greatest care and a lot of prayer' and 'We did not ask for this mission, but we will fulfill it.' In terms of the emerging fight Bush concluded that 'The battle is now joined on many fronts' and warned 'We will not falter. And we will not fail.'[12]

The first strikes by tomahawk missiles and about forty aircraft hit targets in Kabul including a presidential palace, a media center and anti-aircraft weapons, and Kandahar's airport, but mostly outlying areas where terrorist training camps were suspected. Bin Laden was believed to have survived. In a videotape released on 7 October, bin Laden took credit for the 9/11 attacks, thereby changing his organization's previous practice of not claiming responsibility for its terrorism. He also called on Muslims to engage in a jihad against the USA and its supporters.

The first indication that the strikes would not necessarily be precise was the accidental bombing of a UN facility that killed four mine-clearance personnel. With augmented Anglo–American bombing underway, the strength of the international coalition was questioned when Blair, on a Middle Eastern diplomatic tour, was refused reception by Saudi officials.

Blair's Middle Eastern visits may have been in Bush's stead for fear of hostile popular receptions and diplomatic rebuffs. Israel's adoption of American rhetoric of fighting a war on terrorism to justify its forceful measures against continuing Palestinian protests and suicide attacks, further inflamed wider Arab opinion. But even if the USA risked not having support for its Afghanistan campaign across the Middle East, Bush was undeterred. On 10 October Bush declared the elimination of global terrorism as 'our calling' and proclaimed 'Now is the time to draw the line in the sand against the evil ones.' The American war took on a more tangible form when, on the same day, the FBI published the names and photographs of its twenty-two 'most wanted' terrorists.

Despite this apparent offensive, major alerts of imminent terrorist attack against the USA were declared, first by the FBI on 11 October, with several others following, including Attorney-General John Ashcroft's of 29 October. When such attacks did not occur, US officials said it was impossible to know whether extra vigilance might have prevented renewed attacks. Tom Ridge, freshly installed to the new post of Director of Homeland Security, said the anthrax attacks and 9/11 were likely connected. With four apparently unrelated people dead from anthrax, speculation over its origins turned to Iraq; but tests of the substance indicated that it was an American strain, and suspicions eventually turned to a US government laboratory outside Washington. Even though Bush would come to declare the anthrax outbreak as 'a second wave of terrorist attacks upon our country,'[13] a year later, blame remained undetermined.

Returning to Asia, although many Muslims throughout the region protested the American actions, and a widespread strike was attempted in Pakistan to undermine the government's support for the US war, the Pakistani government moved to full backing of the USA following Powell's mid-October visit when Musharraf was known bluntly to have requested debt relief. Apart from the lifting of the 1998 sanctions, speculation suggested that Pakistan would receive considerable financial benefits from the USA for changing its policy. By 10 November Bush had publicly pledged over US$1 billion aid to Pakistan.

The war entered a further stage when, on 20 October, the Pentagon acknowledged the first deployment of some 200 ground troops, which were operating near the Taliban's spiritual center of Kandahar in southern Afghanistan. The first American personnel were killed when a helicopter crashed in Pakistan; the American military rejected the Taliban's claim of downing it. The next day American attacks refocused on Taliban positions near the northern city Mazar-e Sharif, where the Northern Alliance had made some advances. Rumsfeld indicated that the Northern Alliance could also advance towards Kabul as US air targeting of the Taliban had improved because of intelligence supplied by American special forces on the ground.

On 27 October thousands of Pakistani fighters gathered to fight a jihad against the USA. The transnational composition of the Taliban/al-Qaeda forces was further revealed when five of their members killed by an American attack on Kabul turned out to be British citizens. In Pakistan a day later, six masked attackers, thought to be Islamic supporters of al-Qaeda, shot dead fifteen

Christian worshipers and a policeman at St. Dominic's Church in Bahawalpur, central Pakistan.

By the end of October US troops were known to be operating in support of the Northern Alliance in northern Afghanistan, while early November saw intensified US bombings, including the use of B-52s to assist a major Northern Alliance advance. Al-Jazeera broadcast another declaration by bin Laden in which he called on Pakistanis to oppose their government and support the Taliban against the USA. The American war effort seemed to be succeeding as Rumsfeld declared on 4 November that while it still retained local power, the Taliban no longer functioned as a government. The next day the US military said it was exploring the use of airbases in post-Soviet Central Asia for its bombing missions, while more Northern Alliance forces amassed north of Kabul.

The construction of a multinational force continued. In a remarkable development, considering its constitutional limitations on the geographical deployment of its soldiers and the Green Party's ideological opposition to military operations, the German government agreed on 6 November to an American request for almost 4,000 German soldiers. A day later the Italian parliament accepted a similar request, assigning 2,700 troops, and on 8 November Jordan's King Abdullah gave verbal backing to the war. Musharraf, however, stated that the war needed to be short and that bombing should cease during the approaching Muslim holy month of Ramadan, which the USA did not do, but it increased humanitarian air drops. Musharraf's government also requested that the Taliban withdraw its diplomats from Karachi, although the final Taliban representation would only be asked to leave Pakistan on 22 November. In broader diplomacy, the UN's special envoy indicated plans for a provisional Afghan government that would contain various representations from the population, including potentially parts of the Taliban, and that would be assisted by an international peacekeeping force.

Despite some successes for the USA in international diplomacy, the war looked less successful than desired in late October and early November. As the bombing continued, Chairman of the US Joint Chiefs of Staff Richard Myers said that targets included air defence and command and control facilities, early warning radar, airfields and other infrastructure. But even Rumsfeld conceded that key targets were few. As B-52s were introduced into the campaign at the end of October to pound Taliban positions, the Taliban Foreign Minister mockingly proposed that Bush and Blair duel with Mullah Mohammed Omar using Kalashnikovs.

At the beginning of November reports declared the bombing was 'way behind schedule,' that coming snow would complicate the war and give the Taliban advantage, and that people were beginning to starve in some provinces.[14] The *New York Times* wrote that the Bush administration had 'underestimated the Taliban's resistance' and that Afghanistan was 'an especially difficult battlefield.'[15]

In a major military breakthrough in Afghanistan the Northern Alliance captured Mazar-i-Sharif on 9 November; two days later it claimed half the country, and approached Kabul. On 13 November Northern Alliance troops entered the capital. Military historian John Keegan suggested the fall of the north and Kabul was 'one of the most remarkable reversals of military fortune since Kitchener's victory at Omdurman in the Sudan in 1898.'[16] This may have been a remarkable military achievement, but its timing was unanticipated. Indeed, Bush had requested the Northern Alliance not to enter Kabul until a provisional government was established, and the UN's representative for Afghanistan, former Algerian Foreign Minister Lakhdar Brahimi, rushed to assemble Afghan leaders for discussions.

In the USA fears surged concerning a new terrorist attack following the crash in Brooklyn on 12 November of American Airlines flight 587. Among the dead were two WTC employees who had survived 9/11. The crash was deemed accidental only after national security alerts were imposed and international financial markets plummeted. The spectre of domestic attack did not diminish, however, as by mid-November the US Department of Justice had accumulated 5,000 names of people living in the USA to be questioned about 9/11.[17]

In Kabul, joy at the end of Taliban rule was evident, with music being played publicly for the first time since the Taliban consolidated its power by seizing Kabul in 1996, men's beards being trimmed or shaven off and women able to bare their faces; but victory was not bloodless, with the International Red Cross reporting that hundreds were killed in the earlier taking of Mazar-i-Sharif.

With the north largely secured, save for the area around Konduz in the northeast, near the Tajik border, Western attention turned to other parts of Afghanistan. Taliban control was eroding elsewhere as Jalalabad fell and the Taliban faced revolt in Kandahar. On 15 November an advance group of 100 British Royal Marines was deployed at Bagram airbase. Arriving without prior knowledge of the Northern Alliance, it was nearly fired on. Thereafter British Foreign Secretary Jack Straw told his Northern Alliance counterpart Abdullah Abdullah that he would personally inform the Northern Alliance of future British arrivals. These unannounced British personnel became the first conventional forces, after the small number of American, to be used in Afghanistan. French forces were meanwhile being prepared for deployment to Mazar-i-Sharif to assist with the distribution of humanitarian aid.

US forces also claimed that bombings of Kandahar and Kabul in mid-November had killed enemy leaders, including Muhammed Atef, a leading al-Qaeda military commander, and one of those named on the American 'most wanted' list. US troops were also blocking south-running roads to capture others. As auspicious as these measures may have appeared, Mullah Omar broadcast on the BBC's Pashtun service his intended aim of the 'destruction of America.'[18] If anti-American sentiment could be stoked by such rhetoric, it did not deter the arrival of soldiers from other countries.

With the military dynamic clearly shifting in favor of anti-Taliban forces by the middle of November, postwar jockeying for power began. Former Afghan President Burhanudi Rabbani, forced from office by the Taliban, returned to Kabul. The Northern Alliance consented to send delegates to a UN-sponsored conference in Bonn to discuss the postwar government with other Afghan groups. A large Russian delegation also arrived in Kabul.

Having yet to sight bin Laden, the US military made radio announcements of rewards of up to US$25 million for information on his location or that of his senior associates. Military officials later admitted that many Afghans would not appreciate this value and that offers, such as a flock of sheep, might have been more relevant. Military efforts now concentrated on southern Afghanistan, where the Taliban continued to hold Kandahar, and on the Taliban's last northern bastion of Konduz. There, a peaceful end to the siege was obstructed by the presence of foreign fighters, including Arabs, Pakistanis and Chechens, who were thought to want to fight to the end rather than surrender. Konduz fell on 26 November after intensive fighting over several days during which a Northern Alliance attack was supported by American air attacks. Simultaneously in southern Afghanistan, US air power focused on caves and tunnels around Kandahar.

The brutality of the war was brought home to the West with the uprising of Taliban prisoners held in the Qala-i-Janghi fortress outside Mazar-i-Sharif, in which CIA agent Johnny 'Mike' Spann was killed. The Northern Alliance retook the facility only after three days and repeated bombings of it by US aircraft. The deaths of hundreds of enemy forces prompted international human rights groups to demand investigations and raised questions of the observance of rules of war and of general human rights by the Northern Alliance. If such questions could be avoided because Taliban/al-Qaeda forces were considered non-Western, then the discovery of American John Walker Lindh among them suggested otherwise.

The first conventional US forces – some hundreds of Marines – were deployed on 25 November outside Kandahar, and then took over an airfield. This measure prompted Bush to prepare Americans for the possibility of combat deaths. One US military official described the rules of engagement as 'unrestricted hunting license'; Special Forces were being used, and hundreds of enemy forces were reported killed without any US casualties.[19]

While fighting continued in Afghanistan, the UN conference to determine Afghanistan's postwar order began in Bonn on 27 November. While UN officials were optimistic about the outcome, several obstacles unsurprisingly arose. Among them were that former Afghan President Rabbani first refused to attend the conference in person, staying in his 'presidential palace' in Kabul, and then objected to a large international peacekeeping deployment. The lesser-known Pashtun Hamid Karzai was able to address the conference by a video link and called for unity among the assembled representatives. Rabbani's personal representative at the conference conveyed that Rabbani was under strong international pressure to change his stand, a situation intensified when Russian diplomats, previous supporters of Rabbani, made clear to other members of the faction Moscow's expectation of their conformity to the desired international outcome. Rabbani may even have been facing an insurrection among his ranks, and in these circumstances, modified his position.

By 2 December a draft agreement was circulated which indicated that former King Zahir Shah, who had already returned to Kabul with a triumphant parade, also would not stand as an interim president, and thereafter Rabbani publicly consented to other candidates to head the provisional government. On 5 December the peace agreement was signed. Karzai, fresh from fighting with US forces against the Taliban in the south, where he was also injured by a mistargeted 2,000-pound American bomb, was named President of the interim body. But just after its signing the agreement seemed weakened when ethnic Uzbek Abdul Rashid Dostum objected to what he called the underrepresentation of his people.

A new dimension in the war emerged as the US Defence Department started on 30 November to formulate the procedures to bring Afghan prisoners before military tribunals. Ashcroft stated that not only would human rights be maintained but also that practices applied to non-American detainees would be in keeping with the American Constitution. These declarations laid the groundwork for one of the most contentious measures by the US government in the war: the establishment of the Camp X-Ray detention center at the American military base at Guantanamo Bay, Cuba. Eventually hundreds of foreign nationals captured in Afghanistan were held there, restrained in small chain-link cages and without an agreed legal status conferring protection to them.

In Afghanistan, by 6 December Kandahar seemed set to fall, with Taliban forces in the city agreeing to surrender to Karzai's new government. But the Taliban then promptly reversed its commitment, while Mullah Omar apparently disappeared. US forces intensified ground and air operations to close suspected Taliban escape routes.

At the end of the first week of December, Kandahar collapsed into anarchy as Afghan factions fought against each other. US Marines engaged in their first combat on the ground on 7 December in southern Afghanistan as they fought enemy forces while following information from Afghan warlords that bin Laden and Mullah Mohammed Omar were cornered in caves along the Pakistani border. US bombers pounded the area. Rumsfeld confessed 'I see, literally, dozens and dozens and dozens of pieces of intelligence every day . . . and they don't agree.' As to confirmation of bin Laden in the Tora Bora caves, Rumsfeld said 'One can't know with precision until the chase around the yard is over.' Even though talk was at this point of the Taliban having been defeated, Rumsfeld again signaled caution: 'It would be premature to suggest that once Kandahar surrenders that, therefore, we kind of relax and say "well, that takes care of that," because it doesn't.'[20]

AFTER KANDAHAR

Rumsfeld was right. The fall of Kandahar signaled the formal end of Taliban rule, but the fight against its members and al-Qaeda and the search for their chief leaders remained. The story of international presence in Afghanistan after the fall of Kandahar is one of three parts: the continuing American-led war; the implementation of an international stabilization force; and efforts to build political and social stability in this war-torn country. The latter issues are revisited in the book's conclusion.

Fears of terrorism outside Afghanistan did not subside with the fall of

Kandahar. Most notably, British-born Richard Reid attempted on 22 December to ignite a 'shoe bomb' on American Airlines flight 63 from Paris to Miami. Through the purchase of a computer by American journalists in Kabul, Reid's previous travel across Europe, the Middle East and Asia, were matched to those of an al-Qaeda operative's nickname. Meanwhile, enemy resistance was much greater than expected, particularly in early December around Kandahar and Spin Boldak, along the Pakistani border. By January 2002, the Pentagon acknowledged 'non-trivial pockets' of resistance; some foreign reports said these included a renegade Taliban/al-Qaeda army of 5,000 soldiers with 450 pieces of armor.[21] US Joint Chiefs of Staff Chairman General Richard Myers said that even if military sweeps did not capture al-Qaeda leaders they collected important intelligence. Efforts to apprehend enemy figures resulted in Musharraf consenting on 8 January 2002 to US soldiers operating in Pakistan to pursue al-Qaeda. Chief of Staff Myers said, however, that US forces would not act unilaterally inside Pakistan.

The American-led fighting was no longer conducted as consistently as before, becoming several different types of operations, with specific objectives. The Pentagon invited allied forces to participate in these difficult operations. Thus, 1,700 Royal Marines were deployed to aid Americans. Previously, British forces were involved in missions such as securing Bagram airbase or contributing in a non-combat role to the international peacekeeping force. Likewise, Canadian troops, with a history of peacekeeping, were deployed in combat missions for the first time since the Korean War. The largest such anti-terrorist maneuver in Afghanistan, Operation Anaconda, ended on 18 March, although many enemy forces were believed to have escaped to Pakistan.

The British began combat operations with US and allied Afghan forces on 16 April 2002 in Operation Ptarmigan, named for the northern bird known for camouflage. Operation Snipe, a two-week operation in the first half of May, was declared a success for having eliminated infrastructure and a 'vast arsenal of weapons' and for depriving the opposition of strategic assets that could be used later. While no enemies were killed or captured, British commander Brigadier Roger Lane said 'We have delivered a significant blow to the ability of al-Qaeda to plan, mount and sustain terrorist operations in Afghanistan and beyond.'[22] Even the size of the arsenal seized was later disputed. Operation Condor began on 16 May 2002 with over 1,000 US and foreign personnel and a similar number of Afghans attacking cave complexes along the Pakistani border. This maneuver demonstrated the need to deploy ground forces rather than to rely solely on US air power and indigenous ground troops. Throughout, however, British forces never engaged enemy forces directly. Operation Ptarmigan unfortunately seemed a euphemism not for the international forces but for the enemy.

With such an atypical conflict, the tactics on both sides necessarily diversified. Remnant Taliban and al-Qaeda forces apparently distributed leaflets in early April 2002 offering up to US$50,000 for a captured Westerner and US$100,000 for a dead one. US commanders admitted that this tactic, similar to an American one, had won over Afghan fighters. And while the US paid its Afghan fighters

US$200 per month, vastly more than they could otherwise earn, the practice fuelled inter-Afghan rivalries.[23]

American initiatives continued outside Afghanistan. Yet another new geographic and strategic dimension to the war was added with American use of military bases in Central Asia as coalition aircraft flew military missions from the former Soviet republic of Kyrgyzstan from early March. The Manas base at Bishkek airport would house about 3,000 troops, approximately two-thirds of whom were American who arrived in April. The others were drawn from some dozen additional states.

Even with the sustained international support for the war, and unprecedented American diplomatic and military presence in central and south Asia, many military mistakes and accidents inevitably occurred. In a training exercise near Kandahar an American reservist pilot bombed Canadian troops, killing four and wounding eight. US gunships mistakenly fired on Afghan wedding celebrations in eastern Afghanistan in May – killing as many as a dozen civilians – when they came to support Australian forces under enemy fire.[24] The Afghan government concluded that US bombings had killed forty-six civilians, including twenty-five in the wedding.

Some of these unintended casualties were perhaps an indication of the difficulties of waging the war against an elusive enemy. American and allied Afghan forces encountered heavy resistance in early March 2002 at Shar-i-kot in eastern Afghanistan, where al-Qaeda was believed to be recruiting more local support. On 4 March eight Americans were killed, and forty wounded, in the highest single incident of American combat fatalities. Most were killed when an American Chinook helicopter was shot down, the first time a US aircraft was so destroyed. This suggested that substantial resistance was being mounted in the east of Afghanistan, in what US Central Command described as a 'fight to the death' and in which at least 500 enemy forces were believed killed. At the same time, the Pakistani government announced that it would assign additional troops to its 1,500-mile border with Afghanistan, having already deployed some 60,000.

The continued fighting, its unconventional format and the allied casualties (unlike in Kosovo) may have led US Commander Tommy Franks mistakenly to say: 'First let me say that our thoughts and prayers go to the families and the friends of the service members who have lost their lives in our ongoing operations in *Vietnam*.'[25]

Searches throughout 2002 of suspected al-Qaeda operational centers in Afghanistan by foreign troops gave indications of the movement's broader terrorist intentions. Among them were videotapes instructing on the use of various weapons, including anti-aircraft, and showing what appeared to be tests of crude chemical weapons on dogs, suggesting that al-Qaeda was developing weapons of mass destruction. The ongoing and expanding nature of the 'war on terrorism' was underscored by Bush's 29 January State of the Union Address in which he labeled Iraq, Iran and North Korea 'an axis of evil.'

Terrorist attacks believed related to al-Qaeda nevertheless continued. Apart from lethal attacks on Christians and on French engineers in Pakistan, the French oiltanker *Limburg* was damaged off Yemen on 6 October 2002 after being rammed by an explosive-laden dingy in an operation similar to that against *USS Cole*. American Marines stationed in Kuwait were repeatedly shot at in early October 2002, while one was killed and another wounded on 8 October. The extent of al-Qaeda's activities may not be known, but large inter-religious attacks have also occurred. In predominantly Christian Zamboanga, Philippines, for example, 5 people were killed and some 150 injured from the bombing of a shopping center on 17 October. A Christmas Eve bombing in the Philippines that killed 13 and injured 12 was specifically blamed on 'Islamic militants.'[26]

On 12 November 2002 al-Jazeera's broadcast of an undated audiotape of bin Laden, which US authorities generally accepted as genuine, gave credence to those and other attacks as being part of coordinated operations by al-Qaeda. Instead of being dead, bin Laden condemned Bush as a 'modern-day Pharaoh' and Cheney and Powell as 'Hulega of the Mongols.' He threatened Westerners with 'You will be killed as you bomb. And expect more that will further distress you.' He also commended several of the recent attacks on Western targets, including the tourist-frequented Sari Club bombing in Bali that killed over 200 on 12 October, the three-day Moscow hostage siege and the fatal shooting of an American USAID staffer in Amman, Jordan later that month. Bin Laden's tape also specifically threatened attacks against Australia, Britain, Canada, France, Germany and Italy.

These apparent global dangers make the outcome of Afghanistan more vital. Its future is likely to be punctuated by further enemy resistance and violence. Karzai and key ministers have faced assassination attempts, and Afghan Aviation Minister Abdul Rahman was killed. 'Kamikaze camels,' the ubiquitous beasts strapped with explosives, have been sent wandering towards facilities of the interim government and foreign forces. Even so, a strong recognition, and a smaller tangible commitment, existed among Western governments to secure Afghanistan and begin its wholesale reconstruction. This goal cannot be neglected because as terrorism continues to be a key policy issue, Afghanistan's future will stand in judgment as part of the wider, more permanent goals of the 'war on terrorism.'

NOTES

1 Mark Juergensmeyer, *Terror in the Mind of God: The Global Rise of Religious Violence* (Berkeley, CA: University of California Press, 2000), p. 62; and James Dwyer, David Kocieniewski, Deirdre Murphy and Peg Tyre, *Two Seconds under the World: Terror comes to America – The Conspiracy behind the World Trade Center Bombing* (New York: Crown, 1994).

2 Details of the CIA plan were first published in the *New York Times*, 30 Sept. 2001. An investigation by British-based *Financial Times* found the Clinton administration declined offers of intelligence sharing from Sudan two months before the 1998 East Africa embassy bombings that would have included 300 pages of detailed information on al-Qaeda. Mark Huband, 'US Rejected Sudanese Files on Al-Qaeda', *Financial Times*, 30 Nov. 2001.

3 Richard A. Falkenrath, 'Problems of Preparedness: U.S. Readiness for a Domestic Terrorist Attack', *International Security*, Vol. 25, No. 4 (Spring 2001), pp. 147–8.
4 A leading example was the application by Mohammed Atta, a key instigator of the attacks, to a Florida bank for a loan to finance flying lessons and to buy a cropduster. Despite having a blackeye, threatening the loan officer, and talking of attacking Washington, he provoked no suspicion; he was denied the loan because he did not meet criteria for foreign nationals. *The Times*, 8 June 2002.
5 *Financial Times*, 4 June 2002, p. 6; and 20 Sept. 2002, p. 20.
6 Larry Elliot and Heather Stewart, 'The Cost of War?', *The Guardian*, 22 Sept. 2001.
7 'A Nation Challenged: President Bush's Address on Terrorism Before a Joint Meeting of Congress', *New York Times*, 21 Sept. 2001.
8 John Hooper and Kevin O'Flynn, 'Russia Exploits the War Dividend', *The Guardian*, 26 Sept. 2001, p. 6.
9 Among other features, Resolution 1373 (2001), stipulated that 'all States shall: . . . (c) Deny safe haven to those who finance, plan, support, or commit terrorist acts, or provide safe havens; (d) Prevent those who finance, plan, facilitate or commit terrorist acts from using their respective territories for those purposes against other States or their citizens.'
10 Cited in John F. Burns, 'Taliban Say They Hold Bin Laden, for His Safety, But Who Knows Where?', *New York Times*, 1 Oct. 2001.
11 *The Guardian*, 2 Oct. 2001.
12 Bush's speech was widely reported. The official website is: http://www.whitehouse.gov/news/releases/2001/10/20011007-8.htm/
13 'Bush Says U.S. Will Solve Anthrax Crimes', Radio Address by the President to the Nation, The Oval Office, Radio Transcript, Office of the Press Secretary 3 Nov. 2001.
14 [No author] 'Winter is Coming and the Taliban are Strong as Ever. What Now for the War on Terror?', *The Guardian*, 3 Nov. 2001, p. 6.
15 *New York Times*, 8 Nov. 2001.
16 *Daily Telegraph*, 14 Nov. 2001.
17 Reuters, 14 Nov. 2001.
18 Transcript posted at http://www.news.bbc.co.uk/hi/english/world/south_asia
19 *Washington Times*, 23 Nov. 2001.
20 Quoted in *The Scotsman*, 7 and 8 Dec. 2001.
21 *The Times*, 25 Jan. 2002.
22 Quoted in *Financial Times*, 14 May 2002.
23 Catherine Philip, 'Taleban Offers Reward for Westerners', *The Times*, 6 April 2002.
24 *The Times*, 18 May 2002.
25 Cited in Charles Glover and Richard Wolffe, 'Friends and Foes', *Financial Times*, 6 March 2002, p. 18; emphasis added.
26 'Philippines Bomb Kills 13, Wounds 12', *New York Times*, 24 Dec. 2002.

2 Implications of the attacks of 9/11 for the future of terrorism

Paul Wilkinson

One predictable yet little remarked consequence of the outrages committed in America on 9/11 has been an upsurge of academic interest in the study of terrorism. The number of US institutes and research centres and 'think thanks' which have now added this subject to their research agendas or, in some cases, have been newly established to specialize in this field has mushroomed. In Britain and other European countries the increase in interest has been more modest: some universities are now beginning to recruit specialists in terrorism studies to teach the subject as part of the curriculum of political science or international relations. Yet throughout European academia there is still a deep-seated reluctance, if not outright refusal, to recognize that studying terror as a weapon, whether by sub-state groups or regimes, is a legitimate and necessary scholarly activity.

Most of the standard British introductory texts on politics and international relations make no reference to the concept of terrorism, or if they do it is only to dismiss it on the grounds that it is simply a pejorative term for guerrilla warfare and freedom fighting.[1] Equally remarkable is the neglect of the use of terror by regimes and their security forces. The omission of a reference to these phenomena in the introductory texts is all the more startling in view of the fact that throughout history regimes have been responsible for campaigns of mass terror, of a lethality and destructiveness far greater in scale than those waged by sub-state groups.

After 9/11 it became impossible, even for the most sheltered ivory-towered academic, to deny the reality of terrorism. The hijacked airliners were deliberately flown into the World Trade Center and Pentagon, killing an estimated 3,000 civilians. The attack was carried out by people recruited into the al-Qaeda terrorist network, in pursuit of the explicit aim of al-Qaeda's leader, Osama bin Laden, to terrorize Americans. The post-modernist's pretence that terrorism is simply a subjective mental construct invented by security experts is exposed as a foolish illusion. As those who live in countries such as Algeria, Colombia, Israel, Sri Lanka and parts of India will testify, 'terrorism' is a reality, a scourge which can bring terrible suffering to their communities. I would argue that just as criminologists clearly have a duty to study murder and other serious crimes, so scholars of political science and international relations have a legitimate role in studying the use of terror by sub-state groups and states and responses to these phenomena, by states and societies and the international community.

It is important to note that there is a growing international community of scholars researching terrorism. It is clearly a multidisciplinary field involving not only political scientists and historians, but also sociologists, psychologists, lawyers, and some scientists and technologists with particular interests in chemical, biological, radiological and nuclear weapons or in matters such as techniques of forensic investigation. The range and variety of their work is reflected in the leading journals specializing in terrorism studies,[2] and in a number of valuable bibliographies[3] of the subject.

Those who wish to make a serious contribution to terrorism studies will need to familiarize themselves with the substantial social scientific and historical literature. As will be made clear in this chapter, terrorism takes many forms, and some of the more dangerous and well-resourced terrorist groups and state sponsors of terrorism have been in the business for over a quarter of a century. There are many excellent studies of the specific groups and regimes involved, comparative studies, and specialists' works on different aspects of terrorism, including terrorist ideologies and beliefs, leadership, strategy, tactics, weaponry, propaganda, and links with political parties and organized crime. There is also a rich literature on responses to terrorism, including case studies and analyses of political, diplomatic, law enforcement, legislative, judicial, military, media, and international aspects of response.[4] Of course there are many serious gaps and weaknesses in the specialist literature. This is hardly surprising in view of the relatively small national cadres of researchers expert in this field in most countries around the world, and the extremely limited financial resources allocated for independent academic research in this field prior to 9/11. Obviously there is a considerable amount of in-house research, particularly with counter-terrorism, carried out by the research sections of government ministries and security agencies. However, most of the data and research findings of these studies are classified and tend to be rather narrowly focused on issues of particular immediate relevance to the department concerned. They are not aimed at filling some of the gaps in the terrorism literature, for example: underlying causes; emergence of and evolution of terrorist campaigns; the relationship between leaders and followers; or the dynamics of relations between the 'directors' of terrorist organizations and the political fronts, parties and overseas support networks which they develop and, in some cases, depend upon. The major weaknesses in fundamental research into terrorism can only be remedied if there is far more generous funding and coordination of academic research efforts round the world, and much greater effort to ensure closer formal and informal research cooperation between institutes within countries and across national borders. An interesting and encouraging precedent worth noting is the development of arms control and counter-proliferation studies in the 1960s and 1970s.[5]

In this chapter I review the implications of 9/11 for terrorism internationally. It is a complex subject. Here I restrict myself to brief re-examination of the concept of terrorism, to presentation of a typology of contemporary terrorism, and to a fresh look at the effectiveness of terrorism as a political weapon. I also discuss the significance of 9/11, the key features of al-Qaeda as the archetype of the 'new terrorism,' and the threat it now poses, as well as the continuing threat from 'traditional' terrorism.

TERRORISM: THE CONCEPT

The concept of terrorism is often totally misused, such as when it is employed as a synonym for political violence in general or when it is used as a pejorative term for any insurgency campaign of which we disapprove. It is also frequently used loosely and inconsistently. In this respect it shares the same problem of other key strategic concepts, such as 'revolution,' 'imperialism' and 'democracy'. None of these concepts lends itself to universally agreed one-sentence definition yet all of them are indispensable for political discourse, and there is a sufficiently widely shared acceptance of the core meaning of such concepts for them to play a central role in international political and social scientific debate.

Alex Schmid and Albert Jongman have produced impressive evidence of the extent to which a minimum consensus definition of terrorism has become accepted among the international community of social scientists who study conflict.[6] Equally significant is the development of a whole body of international resolutions, conventions and agreements dealing with aspects of prevention, suppression and punishment of acts of terrorism,[7] in which there is near universal acceptance of the terminology used to describe the form of behavior to be condemned or prohibited. Contemporary international academic, diplomatic, and juridical debates no longer become bogged down in days of definitional debate. The major disputes that arise concern culpability for specific attacks or for sponsoring or directing them, and over the kind of international measures that should be taken in response.

Terrorism is neither a political philosophy nor a movement, nor is it a synonym for political violence in general. It is a special means or method of conflict which has been employed by a wide variety of factions and regimes. It is premeditated and systematic, and aims to create a climate of extreme fear or terror. The modern word *terror* and *terrorism* are derived from the Latin verb *terrere*, to cause to tremble, and *deterre*, to frighten from. *Terrorism* and *terrorist* did not come into use until the period of the French Revolution in the 1790s. The term was used by Edmund Burke in his polemic against the French Revolution, and came to be used to denote those revolutionaries who sought to use terror systematically either to further their views or to govern, whether in France or elsewhere.

A key feature of terrorism is that it is directed at a wider audience or target than the immediate victims. It is one of the earliest forms of psychological warfare. The ancient Chinese strategist, Sun Tzu, conveyed the essence of the method when he wrote, 'kill one, frighten ten thousand.' An inevitable corollary is that terrorism entails attacks on random and symbolic targets, including civilians, in order to create a climate of extreme fear among a wider group. Terrorists often claim to be carefully selective and discriminating in their choice of targets, but to the communities that experience the terrorist campaign the attacks are bound to seem arbitrary and indiscriminate. In order to create the widespread sense of fear he seeks, the terrorist deliberately uses the weapons of surprise and disproportionate violence in order to create a sense of outrage and insecurity. As Raymond Aron observes: 'an action of violence is labeled "terrorist" when its psychological effects are out of all proportion to its purely physical result. . . . The lack of discrimination helps to spread fear, for if no one in particular is a target than no one can be safe.'[8] It is this characteristic which differentiates terrorism from tyrannicide and individual political assassination.

As Hannah Arendt has observed, the belief that one could change a whole political system by assassinating the major figure has clearly been rendered obsolete by the transition from the age of absolutist rulers to an age of governmental bureaucracy.[9] In all but a handful of regimes today real power is wielded by the bureaucratic elite of anonymous or faceless officials. Arendt provides a powerful explanation for the fact that the age of bureaucracy has coincided with burgeoning of political terrorism. Terrorism has become for its perpetrators, supporters and sponsors, the most attractive low-cost, low-risk, but potentially high-yield method of attacking a regime or a rival faction. The bomb plot against Hitler, had it succeed, would have been an act of tyrannicide not terrorism. Who could deny that Hitler was the linchpin of the Nazi system? Is it possible to find an analogous case today where the removal of an all-powerful dictator would dramatically change the system? Some have argued that Saddam Hussein is one such case, but by May 2003 it is too early to tell whether the toppling of Saddam will lead to democracy in Iraq.

The concept of terrorism used in the contemporary academic literature is essentially political. What about the use of terrorism in the name of religious causes? Or of the pursuit of criminal gains? It is true that militant religious fundamentalists have often throughout history waged holy terror as part of a holy war, and there is much concern about the rise of contemporary fanatical Islamic fundamentalist groups such as Hizbollah, Hamas and al-Gama'a Al-Islamiyya and al-Qaeda. The major reason why moderate Muslim leaders and secular movements see these particular fundamentalist groups as such a threat is precisely because their revolutionary Islamic agenda aims not merely at the purifying of religious practice but at the overthrow of existing governments and their replacement by fundamentalist theocracies. Hence these movements are inherently religious *and* political. The worrying trend whereby powerful criminal gangs, such as the Italian Mafia[10] and the Latin American narco-barons,[11] have adopted some of the tactics and weapons of terrorist groups, does pose grave problems for the relevant law-enforcement authorities. But it does not detract from the value of the core concept of political terrorism. In reality the overwhelming majority of perpetrators of contemporary terrorism use the weapon to influence political behavior.

TYPOLOGY

It is important to note the above defining criteria of political terrorism are broad enough to encompass states' use of terror as well as that performed by groups. Typologically it is useful to distinguish *state* from *factional* terror. Normally, in the literature, a state's use of terror is referred to as terror, while sub-state terror is referred to as terrorism. This distinction is employed throughout this chapter. Historically, states have conducted terror on a far more massive and lethal scale than groups. They have employed terror as a weapon of tyranny and repression and as an instrument of war. Another important distinction can be made between *international* and *domestic* terrorism: the former is terrorist violence involving the citizens of more than one country, while the latter is confined within the border of one country, sometimes within a particular locality in the country. This distinction is useful for analytical and statistical purposes. However, in reality, it is hard to find an example of any significant terrorist campaign that remains purely domestic: any serious terrorist campaign actively seeks political support, weapons, financial assistance and safe haven beyond its own borders.

Once we move beyond these very broad categories it is useful to employ a basic typology of contemporary perpetrators of terrorism based on their underlying cause or political motivation.

Nationalist terrorists

These are groups seeking political self-determination. They may wage their struggle entirely in the territory they seek to liberate, or they may be active both in their area and abroad. In some cases they may be forced by police or military action or by threat of capture, imprisonment or execution to operate entirely from their place of exile. Nationalist groups tend to be more capable of sustaining protracted campaigns and mobilizing substantial support than ideological groups. Even those nationalist groups that can only claim the support of a minority of their ethnic constituency (for example the IRA (Irish Republican Army) and ETA (Basque Homeland and Liberty)) can gain political resonance because of their deep roots in the national culture for which they claim to be the authentic voice. There is no sign that groups of this kind are disappearing from the terrorist scene.

Ideological terrorists

These terrorists seek to change the entire political social and economic system either to an extreme left or extreme right model. In the 1970s and 1980s studies of ideological terrorism focused on the extreme left, because of the preoccupation with groups such as the Red Army Faction in Germany and the Red Brigades in Italy. Yet, as Walter Laqueur observes in his magisterial general history of terrorism,[12] the dominant ideological orientation of European terrorism between the world wars was fascist. And it is neo-Nazi and neo-fascist groups that are behind so much of the racist and anti-immigrant violence in present-day Germany and other European countries. The Red Army groups so active during the 1970s and 1980s have now largely faded away, the victims of their own internal splits, determined law enforcement by their respective police and judicial authorities, and changing political attitudes amongst young people in the post-Cold War era. However, in Latin America and parts of Asia and Africa extreme left organizations using terrorism remain a significant challenge to governments.

Religio-political terrorists

The most frequently cited examples of this type of terrorism are groups such as Hizbollah and Hamas. Bin Laden's al-Qaeda network is clearly religio-political. At its core his agenda is political though it is dressed up in language of Islamic holy war.[13] But it is important to bear in mind that militant fundamentalist factions of major religions other than Islam have also frequently spawned their own violent extremist groups. Striking examples can be found among Sikhs, Hindus and Jews, and there is a well-documented link between certain Christian fundamentalist groups and extreme right-wing terrorism in North and Central America.[14]

Single-issue terrorist groups

These groups are obsessed with their desire to change a specific policy or practice within the target society, rather than with the aim of political revolution. Examples included the violent animal rights and anti-abortion groups.

State-sponsored and state-supported terrorists

States use this type of terrorism both as a tool for domestic and foreign policy. For example when the Iranian regime sent hit-squads to murder leading dissidents and exiled political leaders they did so for domestic reasons, to intimidate and eradicate opposition to the regime. However, when North Korea sent its agents to mount a bomb attack on the South Korean government delegation on its visit to Rangoon, the communist regime was engaged in an act of covert warfare against its perceived 'enemy' the government in the South, designed at furthering its foreign policy aim of undermining the Republic of South Korea. State sponsors may use their own directly recruited and controlled terror squads or choose to act through client groups and proxies. They almost invariably go to some lengths to disguise their involvement, in order to sustain plausible denial. The ending of the Cold War and the overthrow of the East European communist one-party regimes and the former Soviet Union certainly removed the Warsaw Pact's substantial network of sponsorship and support for a whole variety of terrorist groups. But this does not mean that state sponsorship has ceased to be a factor in the international scene. Countries such as Iraq, Iran and Syria have been heavily involved.[15] Others, such as Libya appear to have been attempting to distance themselves from past major involvement in state-sponsored terrorism. The post-Cold War environment has made such sponsorship potentially far more costly because of the likelihood of strong US sanctions being imposed.

EFFECTIVENESS AND MOTIVATION

How effective has terrorism been as a weapon for attaining political objectives since 1945? History shows that terrorism has been more effective as an auxiliary weapon in revolutionary and national liberation struggles. Most of the key modern theorists and leaders of revolutionary insurgency, such as Mao Tse-tung and Che Guevara, have recognized the dangers of depending on terrorism and have come down against giving it a major role in the struggle for revolution. The few cases where terrorism played a major part in bringing about sweeping political change arose in a limited number of colonial independence struggles against foreign rule. Included in this group would be the circumstances surrounding the end of the Palestinian Mandate after the terrorist campaign of the Irgun (National Military Organization) and Stern (Fighters for the Freedom of Israel) and the British decision to withdraw from the Suez Canal zone base together with the campaigns which led the British to withdraw from Cyprus and Aden, and the French to withdraw from Algeria. In all these cases special conditions existed which made terrorism a more potent weapon: (i) due to humanitarian and judicial restraints the occupying power was unwilling to carry through draconian measures to wipe out the terrorist organizations; (ii) in each case there were intercommunal power struggles within the colony which rendered peaceful diplomatic settlement and withdrawal difficult if not nigh impossible; (iii) the terrorists who succeeded in these conditions (as in Aden up until 1968) enjoyed massive if not solid support from their own ethnic groups, and this created an almost impenetrable barrier for the intelligence branches on which the government security forces depended for success, and a vast reservoir of active and tacit collaboration and support for their terrorist operatives. Even taking into account the influence of terrorism as an auxiliary tactic in revolutionary and independence struggles and in the rise of fascism between the First and Second World Wars, the overall track record of terrorism in attaining major political objectives is abysmal.

But if this historical assessment is correct we are left with the thorny problem of explaining why, at the beginning of the new millennium, political terrorism remains such a popular weapon among a wide range of groups around the world. There are at least four hypotheses that may help to provide an answer to this question. They are by no means mutually exclusive: (i) some terrorists may be poor students of history and may continue to believe that they can repeat the success of groups such as EOKA (National Organization of Cypriot Fighters in Cyprus) and the FLN (National Liberation Front) in Algeria, not realizing that their own situations are not truly colonial in this sense, and therefore not comparable; (ii) some may fully recognize the severe limitations of terrorism as a means of attaining strategic goals, but may see sufficient tangible short-term rewards from terrorism, such as huge publicity, the gaining of ransoms, securing the release of fellow terrorists from jail, to make it worthwhile to use it as an auxiliary weapon; (iii) some may be motivated by the *expressive* value of the activity rather than the *instrumental/operational* value, and may wish to continue the campaign primarily because it is a relatively quick and easy way to express their hatred of their opponents and of the justice of their cause; and (iv) some may be addicted to the business of terrorist operations and material gain from extortion and racketeering and may be unable to kick the habit. Politically motivated terrorism is generally justified by its perpetrators on one or more of the following grounds: (i) any means are justified to realize an alleged transcendental end (in Weber's terms,[16] 'value rational grounds'; (ii) closely linked to number (i) is the claim that extreme violence is intrinsically beneficial, regenerative, cathartic and an enabling deed regardless of the other consequences; (iii) terrorism can be shown to have 'worked' in the past, and is held to be either the 'sole remaining' or 'best available' method to achieving success (in Weber's terms, 'instrumental rational' grounds); (iv) the morality of the just vengeance 'an eye for an eye, a tooth for a tooth'; and (v) the theory of the 'lesser evil' which assumes that greater evils will befall us or our nation if we do not adopt terror against our enemies.

THE SIGNIFICANCE OF SEPTEMBER 11

Prior to 9/11 the conventional wisdom was that the use of terrorism was endemic in low-intensity conflict around the world but that it rarely, if ever, posed a strategic threat to the security of a major power or the international community. Some specialists in the study of terrorism did point out examples of the use of weapons of terror having a strategic impact on international politics, for example in hastening the withdrawal of colonial powers from countries such as Cyprus and Algeria or derailing the peace process between the Israelis and Palestinians.[17] Others warned of the dangers of terrorists obtaining and using a weapon of mass destruction, but these warnings were largely ignored.[18]

9/11 changed these conventional attitudes towards terrorism dramatically and irrevocably. These attacks had enormous strategic consequences for both the USA and the international community. At the time of writing we are still too close to these tragic events to make a proper assessment of their wider impact and long-term implications. It is possible, however, to identify some of the most significant consequences: the scale of the loss of life caused in the World Trade Center attacks, unprecedented in the history of sub-state terrorism, led the US President, government, and the vast majority of US citizens to view them as an act of war rather than as crimes of terrorism; President Bush decided to respond by declaring a global war on terrorism, not only against the perpetrators of 9/11 but also against other terrorist groups described as having 'global reach.' This obviously had huge implications for US foreign and security policy.

When President Bush took office he and his advisors created the impression that the new administration would be placing its main emphasis on domestic issues, reducing foreign entanglements, and avoiding new ones. This 'Fortress

America' approach has been completely reversed since 9/11. The US administration has embarked on a policy of global activism and military intervention unparalleled since the early days of the Cold War, and extending to a new doctrine of preemptive military attack which Bush seems determined to implement in order to secure 'regime change' in Iraq.

President Bush, with the support of Prime Minister Blair, and other close allies, has enthusiastically, and with a remarkable degree of success, sought to create an international coalition against terrorism. A remarkable feature of this coalition is that it includes two major powers traditionally deeply opposed to US global activism, Russia and China. It is clear that the leaders of Moscow and Beijing view the activities of al-Qaeda as a grave threat to their own national security. President Putin's demonstrated willingness to provide substantial assistance to the USA in the struggle against al-Qaeda, including permission to overfly and use bases in Russia's sphere of influence, has led to much closer US–Russian relations.

Perhaps the most remarkable changes in the strategic environment caused by the 9/11 attacks were the swift toppling of the Taliban regime in Afghanistan, which had provided al-Qaeda with such a valuable safe haven and base, and the decision by General Musharraf, the leader of Pakistan, to reverse his country's policy of support for the Taliban, a policy which had helped the latter to seize control of most of Afghanistan. Moreover, against most predictions, the interim government in Afghanistan, set in place through the aegis of the UN, appears to have survived and is beginning the painful process of rebuilding Afghanistan's shattered economy.

WHAT IS 'NEW' ABOUT THE AL-QAEDA TERRORISM? AND WHY DOES IT STILL POSE A SERIOUS THREAT?

It would be foolish to try to assess the impact of the September 11 attacks without taking into account the responses of the USA, other major states, and the wider world. Yet it would also be wanting to ignore the ways in which al-Qaeda, the perpetrators, have changed the nature and severity of the terrorism threat itself.

Al-Qaeda, 'the Base,' a global terrorist network largely created by bin Laden, can justifiably be characterized as the archetype of the 'New Terrorism.'[19] Unlike the more traditional types of terrorist groups it is transnational in its fullest sense: it has a universalistic ideology aimed not only at forcing the USA to withdraw its forces from the Arabian peninsula and to stop supporting Israel, but also at toppling the governments of Arab and other Muslim states it accuses of collaborating with the USA and its allies, and its ultimate aim is to establish a pan-Islamic Caliphate. It is not dependent on any single regime or government for its survival and financial resources. It has a presence in at least fifty countries. Its activists are drawn from a wide range of Muslim countries, and some originate from the Muslim diaspora within Western societies.

Second, in addition to its central leadership and coordinating committees on military, legal, media, and other matters, al-Qaeda has a worldwide network of operational and preparative cells and affiliated organizations capable of being activated at any time and carrying out terrorist attacks on their own initiative. It is because of this, despite the major setback of losing its safe haven in Afghanistan, that the global network is still capable of continuing the terrorist campaign. This has been clearly demonstrated by a series of terrorist attacks, including a number that have been thwarted by the authorities. The use of overseas support networks and international terrorist attacks are of course nothing new in the history of terrorism. What is new about the al-Qaeda network is the scale of its diffusion around the world, and, as demonstrated in the September 11 attacks, the meticulous long-term planning and terrorist tradecraft the network has been able to deploy.[20]

Last, but not least, there are major differences between the more traditional terrorist groups and al-Qaeda regarding the *nature and scale of the violence* the latter employs. Through its suicide airliner attacks on the World Trade Center, al-Qaeda has been responsible for the most lethal acts of terrorism by a sub-state group in history. It is no accident that bin Laden's network should have been the first sub-state group to have carried out mass destruction terrorism. Bin Laden has called upon his followers and 'dutiful' Muslims everywhere to kill as many Americans as possible. Brian Jenkins, one of the pioneers of modern terrorism studies, once stated 'terrorists want a lot of people watching, not a lot of people dead.'[21] Sadly, for groups such as al-Qaeda and its affiliates this no longer holds. Hence, while such deadly terrorist cells, aimed and equipped at causing carnage on a massive scale, are still at large, the threat to the USA, the UK, Israel and other designated 'enemies' of the bin Laden network remains an ever-present reality. Moreover, it is important to note that al-Qaeda has carried out, planned or attempted terrorist attacks in a wide range of countries, including Singapore, Pakistan, India, Tunisia, Morocco, Jordan, Italy, France, Kenya, Tanzania, Yemen and Saudi Arabia. It is also very clear that a terrorist group like al-Qaeda which sets out to kill as many civilians as possible, would have no compunction about using chemical, biological, radiological or nuclear (CBRN) weapons if they manage to weaponize the appropriate materials. Hence, the threat of CBRN terrorism has been brought a step closer by September 11 attacks.

IS 'TRADITIONAL' TERRORISM IN DECLINE? DOES IT CONTINUE TO POSE A SERIOUS THREAT?

It should be fairly obvious from the preceding discussion that al-Qaeda and its affiliates constitute a particularly intractable and dangerous challenge to governments and the international community. Indeed, the author shares the widely held view of specialists in terrorism studies that bin Laden's network poses the most serious threat to innocent life in the history of terrorist groups. But what of the 'traditional' groups? Are they being eclipsed by the new terrorism and forced to retire from the scene? Sadly, there is no real evidence of this. The roots of the ethnic, ideological and religious conflicts which spawn such terrorism show no signs of withering away, and in the eyes of practitioners and sympathizers terrorism appears an attractive low-cost, low-risk and potentially high-yield weapon which they are unwilling to forgo.

One positive development is that at least in a few of the cases the terrorism appears potentially corrigible, because a combination of political initiatives, diplomacy and peace processes can sometimes even resolve highly intractable conflicts. For example against all predictions the Northern Ireland peace process, though extremely fragile, is still surviving and terrorist killings in the Province have been dramatically reduced.[22] Another remarkable example where a peace initiative has made a breakthrough is the Norwegian-inspired initiative in Sri Lanka, which has led to a ceasefire between the Tamil Tigers and the government security forces and to peace talks, following a conflict which has cost over 64,000 lives.

Unfortunately there are many deep-rooted conflicts which seem stubbornly incorrigible, for example between the Israelis and the Palestinians and the Indians and Pakistanis. In these situations terrorism not only helps polarize the conflict; in both these cases terrorist attacks could all too swiftly escalate into full-scale wider inter-state war with a significant risk that weapons of mass destruction could be used by the belligerents.

CONCLUSIONS

Certain conclusions follow from this brief analysis: first, both 'new' and 'traditional' terrorism pose a significant strategic threat to nation states and to international peace and security generally; second, because there are many different kinds of terrorism with a potentially international reach in the contemporary world it is a dangerous illusion to believe that they can all be eradicated by 'the war on terrorism' or by some simple military or political solution; and third, in view of the risks of terrorism triggering wider wars or escalating to the level where weapons of mass destruction are employed, it is vitally important to develop far more effective and widely supported conflict resolution and peace-building initiatives as well as methods of more effectively preventing and combating terrorist violence.

Conflict resolution methods alone will not eradicate the terrorist violence of incorrigible groups fueled on hatred and revenge. But by significantly reducing the underlying causes of deep-seated conflicts, giving politics and diplomacy a chance to succeed, they can save thousands of lives.

NOTES

1 See for example, Peter Willetts, 'Transnational Actors and International Organizations in Global Politics', in John Baylis and Steve Smith (eds.) *The Globalisation of World Politics* (Oxford: Oxford University Press, 2001), pp. 356–8; and Michael Smith, Richard Little

and Michael Shackleton, *Perspectives on World Politics* (Milton Keynes: Open University Press, 1981).

2 See, *Terrorism and Political Violence*, published quarterly by Frank Cass since 1989 and *Studies in Conflict and Terrorism*, published bimonthly by Taylor & Francis Ltd.

3 For example, Amos Lakos, *International Terrorism: A Bibliography* (Boulder, CO: Westview Press, 1986); Edward F. Mickolus, *Terrorism 1988–91: A Chronology and Selectively Annotated Bibliography* (Westport, CT: Greenwood Press, 1988); and Alex P. Schmid and Albert J. Jongman *et al.*, *Political Terrorism: A New Guide to Actors, Authors, Concepts, Data Bases, Theories and Literature* (Amsterdam: North Holland Publishing Co., 1988).

4 For a review of some of this literature see Schmid and Jongman *et al.*, *Political Terrorism*.

5 Classic contributions include: Bernard Brodie (ed.) *The Absolute Weapon: Atomic Power and World Order* (New York: Harcourt Brace & Co., 1946); Thomas C. Schelling, *The Strategy of Conflict* (Cambridge, MA: Harvard University Press, 1960); and the annual publications of the International Institute for Strategic Studies, London, *Strategic Survey* and *The Military Balance*.

6 Schmid and Jongman *et al.*, *Political Terrorism* pp. 1–32.

7 For a useful collection of these measures, see Robert Friedlander (ed.) *Terrorism: Documents of International and Local Control* (Dobbs Ferry: Oceana Publications Inc., 1970–84).

8 Raymond Aron, *Press and War* (London: Weidenfeld & Nicolson, 1966), p. 170.

9 Hannah Arendt, 'On Violence', in her *Crises of the Republic* (London: Penguin Books, 1973), p. 141ff.

10 Alison Jamieson, *The Modern Mafia* (Conflict Studies, No. 224, Research Institute of the Study of Conflict and Terrorism, London, 1989).

11 Richard Clutterbuck, *Terrorism and Guerrilla Warfare* (London: Routledge, 1990), pp. 89–114.

12 Walter Laqueur, *Terrorism* (London: Weidenfeld & Nicolson, 1977).

13 Rohan Gunaratna, *Inside al-Qaeda* (London: CSTPV-Hurst Series on Political Violence, 2002), Chapter 2.

14 See Jeffrey Kaplan, 'Right-Wing Violence in North America', in Tore Bjorgo (ed.) *Terror from the Extreme Right* (London: Frank Cass, 1995).

15 See *Patterns of Global Terrorism 2001*, Washington, DC: US Department of State, 2002, pp. 63–8 for a discussion of recent and current evidence of state sponsorship.

16 See E. Shields and H. A. Finch (trans. and ed.) *Max Weber on the Methodology of the Social Sciences* (Glencoe, IL: Free Press, 1949).

17 See for example Walter Laqueur, *The Age of Terrorism* (Boston: Little, Brown, 1987); Paul Wilkinson, *Terrorism and the Liberal State*, second edition (Basingstoke: Macmillan Press, 1986); and the latter's *Terrorism Versus Democracy: The Liberal State Response* (London: Frank Cass, 2000).

18 See, for example, Paul Wilkinson, *Terrorism and the Liberal State*, Chapter 13, 'Potential Threats'.

19 For an excellent analysis of the 'New Terrorism', see Walter Laqueur, *The New Terrorism* (London: Phoenix Press, 2001).

20 See Gunaratna, *Inside al-Qaeda*, for a discussion of these features and also his Chapter 3 in this volume.

21 Brian M. Jenkins, *International Terrorism: The Other World War* (Santa Monica: RAND, 1985), p. 22.

22 For a discussion of politics and peace processes as possible pathways out of terrorism, see Wilkinson, *Terrorism versus Democracy*, pp. 78–93.

3 Al-Qaeda

Organization and operations

Rohan Gunaratna

The anti-Soviet multinational Afghan campaign of 1979–1989, fought by Arabs and Asian Muslims and using Pakistan as a launching pad, produced a new generation of fighters – the Mujahidin or the warriors of God. They were driven by a politico-religious ideology of jihad or holy war, articulated by Dr. Abdullah Azzam, a Palestinian Jordanian. In Peshawar, Pakistan, Azzam founded both Maktab al-Khidimat Il Mujahidin al-Arab (MAK: the Afghan Service Bureau) in 1984 and al-Qaeda al-Sulbha (The Solid Base) in 1988.[1]

With over fifty offices in some forty countries worldwide, MAK recruited Muslim youth, arranged for their passage, trained them and inducted them into the battlefield. Azzam's deputy and successor was Osama bin Laden, a Mujahid from the richest non-royal Saudi family. After the Soviet withdrawal in February 1989, MAK evolved into al-Qaeda and the Mujahidin. After bin Laden took over the organization in December 1989, members of al-Qaeda gravitated towards several other conflict zones where the Muslims were suffering or perceived to be suffering. They included Kashmir, Mindanao in the Philippines, Tajikistan, Chechnia, Dagestan, Azerbaijan, Algeria, Somalia and Bosnia. In parallel, al-Qaeda launched a campaign to oust the corrupt Muslim rulers and replace their regimes by establishing pious rulers and Islamic states.

In preparation to wage his global campaign, bin Laden established links with two dozen Islamist terrorist groups and political parties including the Abu Sayaaf Group in the Philippines; Moro Islamic Liberation Front; Islamic Movement of Uzbekistan; Eastern Turkistan Islamic Party; Armed Islamic Group of Algeria; al-Ansar Mujahidin in Chechnia; and Kumpulan Mujahidin Malaysia. As the West was perceived as assisting the opponents of these groups, the trajectory of their guerrilla and terrorist campaigns turned towards the Muslim regimes and Western countries, especially the USA.

Today the challenge before the international community is not only to neutralize al-Qaeda but also its associated groups. Even if bin Laden is killed, the legacy he has established by creating a powerful international alliance of terrorist groups will continue to pose a threat to international security. For instance, the integration of the two Egyptian groups – al-Islamiya al-Gama al-Masri (Islamic Group of Egypt) and al-Islamiya al-Jihad (Egyptian Islamic Jihad) has been pivotal to the success of al-Qaeda. By 1998, bin Laden absorbed and completely integrated the two full-fledged organizations into the al-Qaeda structure. Their leaders were co-opted as leaders of al-Qaeda and the umbrella – al-Jabhah al-Islamiyyah al-'Alamiyyah Li-Qital al-Yahud Wal-Salibiyyin (World Islamic Front for the Jihad Against the Jews and the Crusaders).

To fight the terrorist alliance, an intergovernmental coalition was essential. September 11 provided the reason to develop such a coalition. Within six months of the USA forming an anti-terrorist coalition, the al-Qaeda core and leadership as well as its support and operational infrastructure have suffered gravely.

STRUCTURE AND EVOLUTION

As a multidimensional group, al-Qaeda advances its aims and objectives through a network of cells, associated terrorist and guerrilla groups and affiliated political, religious, social and welfare organizations. In addition to its own cells generating support or executing terrorist operations, al-Qaeda provides a platform for associate groups to come together, share expertise, transfer resources, discuss strategy and even conduct joint operations. While al-Qaeda cells mostly operate in the West (including in Australia and New Zealand), the associate groups mostly operate in the South. Affiliated groups are scattered worldwide, operating in Muslim territorial, migrant and diaspora communities. Al-Qaeda members are better motivated, trained and disciplined than associate members and have a wider reach than localized associate members. While al-Qaeda cells take strategic targets, associate groups focus on tactical targets.

The present structure of al-Qaeda was created when the organization was headquartered in Khartoum, from December 1991 to May 1996. Gradually, the organization developed decentralized regional structures to coordinate its overt and covert global activities. For instance, the Sudanese, Turkish and briefly the Spanish bureaux coordinated clandestine military activities for Europe and North America. The worldwide bureaux have no formal structure with offices or hierarchy, except for the bureau in London, the Advice and Reformation Committee established in July 1994 by bin Laden to disseminate propaganda and coordinate overt activities. There are individuals called the 'person responsible' to carry out entrusted assignments. Dependent on the changing threat, the person – or persons – shifted. After al-Qaeda relocated from Sudan to Afghanistan in May 1996, its bureaux for European and North American operations moved to Turkey. After the September 1998 arrest in Germany of an al-Qaeda leader for Europe, Mamdouh Mahmud Salim, al-Qaeda's bureau in Turkey moved to Spain. Likewise, after the Indonesian dictator Suharto fell from power, al-Qaeda's regional bureau chief Abdullah Sungkar and his deputy Abubakar Ba'asyir moved in 1998 from Malaysia to Indonesia. Similarly, the bureau in Pankishi valley in Georgia moved in 1999 to Chechnia after international security and intelligence agencies discovered that the al-Qaeda-infiltrated International Islamic Relief Organization was funneling US$10 million raised in Europe annually to the al-Ansar Mujahidin in Chechnia led by Khattab, bin Laden's protégé.

At an ideological, organizational and an operational level, al-Qaeda is structured to accommodate rapidly changing reality. Al-Qaeda members, cells, bureaux and leadership tend to gravitate to areas of lawlessness. Al-Qaeda found it difficult to breed when vigorously pursued by law enforcement. Mobility and fluidity will be the guiding principles of al-Qaeda's post-Taliban structure.

Al-Qaeda's North African family (primarily Algerians, Egyptians, Tunisians, Moroccans, Libyans) has responsibility for activities in Europe, al-Qaeda's Southeast Asian family (Malaysians, Indonesians, Filipinos, Singaporeans) has responsibility for activities in the Far East. Al-Qaeda's Central Asian family has responsibility for activity from Turkey across Muslim Central Asia into Xingjiang in China. As a multinational organization, nationalities of a particular region have responsibility for that geographic region. Al-Qaeda's families included Egyptians, Algerians, Moroccans, Libyans, Tunisians, Turks, Kurds, UAEs, Jordanians, Syrians, Palestinians, Lebanese, Somalis, Sudanese, Saudis, Yemeni, Kenyans, Tanzanians, Maurithenians, Chechen, Uigurs (Xingjiang, China), Uzbeks, Tajiks, Turkmens, Kyrgyz, Kazakhs, Pakistanis, Kashmiris, Bangladeshis, Moros (Mindanao, Philippines), Singaporeans and Rohingiyas (Myanmar). Some American Muslims, including African-American Muslims, European Muslims (British, French, Germans, Swedes and Danish), and at least one Australian are in its ranks or associate groups. As a cultural and social network, al-Qaeda members recruited from their own nationalities, families and friends. Al-Qaeda's Emir General Osama bin Laden refers to the head of the September 11 operation as 'Muhammad [Atta] from the Egyptian family.'[2] A member must call another 'brother' and treat him as such. The 'brothers' regard bin Laden as the elder brother.[3]

Al-Qaeda influence on the Taliban largely contributed towards its repressive policy towards Afghan women. Although there are no female members of al-Qaeda, the wives of members nevertheless play an important role in the training camps. They cook, clean and educate the children. Amongst themselves, they meet to study the Koran and discuss religious issues. Some of these women are more radical and committed than the men. While exposed to some decision-making, but never operational, a few associated groups of al-Qaeda have recruited women to important roles. Both the Armed Islamic Group of Algeria and Jemaah Islamiya of Southeast Asia have serving female members.

Al-Qaeda innovatively overcame the problem of cross-cultural barriers and communication by organizing its families regionally and functionally. Libyans managed the documentation and passports office in Afghanistan; Algerians ran fraudulent credit card operations in Europe; Egyptians ran most of the training facilities worldwide; and Palestinian–Syrians ran US charities in the mid-West. A member, for instance, of the Tunisian family, living in or posted to Italy kept contact with Tunisians elsewhere in the European region. Although most of al-Qaeda's European operational cells have been single-nationality based, its US operational cells have always been multinational. Only Algerians staffed the UK cell that planned a sarin attack on the European Parliament in February 2000. An Algerian headed its German counterpart in Frankfurt. In contrast, there have been no single or mono-nationality cells in the USA except in the Midwest where al-Qaeda's Syrian family had a presence, especially in Chicago and Michigan. Like the US cells, European cells are likely to develop a multinational character in the immediate and foreseeable future.

The cells assigned for special missions like 9/11 and the Los Angeles airport attacks are coordinated through an agent-handling system where a single cell leader reports only to his controller or the agent-handler. Most agent-handlers live near the target location or in the 'hostile zone,' meaning in Europe or North America. A number of agent-handlers report to a principal agent-handler who never leaves Afghanistan or Pakistan, or the 'safe zone'. Al-Qaeda's cellular network made it resistant to intelligence penetration. According to Curt Campbell of the US Defense Department, 'When they have a hierarchial system they are much easier for law enforcement to penetrate.'[4] By constantly reviewing past failures, al-Qaeda improves its agent-handling system. The post-Taliban system is likely to be an improvement – more tightly controlled, self-contained, self-reliant and smaller in membership.

Al-Qaeda's lingua franca is Arabic and its terra firma was Afghanistan. Established and dominated by Arabs, Arabs staffed vital positions and controlled key operations. Al-Qaeda refrained from posting non-Arabic speakers to Europe to the critical theater of the 'hostile zone' or to North America. In the Far East, most members speak Malay. Indonesians speak Bhasa, a language akin to Malay. Malaysians, Singaporean Muslims and Filipino Muslims, mostly from Mindanao, speak Malay. Most non-Middle Eastern members, especially the leaders and senior members, learnt Arabic since it was the language of the organization and essential for high command.

What has given al-Qaeda a global reach is its ability to appeal to Muslims irrespective of nationality. It can operate in East Asia, inside Russia, in the heart of Europe, black Africa, the triborder area of Latin America and throughout the USA with equal ease. With the world becoming multicultural with cosmopolitan cities, al-Qaeda's reach and depth has increased. Although the families functioned regionally, members are occasionally handpicked for specialist missions outside the region. For instance 9/11 involved Egyptians, UAEs, Lebanese, Saudis, Yemeni, Iraqis and Moroccans. With the exception of a few members who have communicated by satellite phones with al-Qaeda leaders in Afghanistan and elsewhere, most rigorously observe the cellular system. A cell member reports to his cell leader who, in turn, reports to his area leader who will then liaise with his country leader. Next, the country leader talks to his regional leader who informs Zein-al-Abideen Mohammed Hussein, alias Abu Zubaydah, Head of al-Qaeda External Operations until his capture in Pakistan in March 2002.[5] The al-Qaeda losses included Khalid Sheik Muhammad, the head of the military committee, Abu Zubaydah, the principal recruiting officer, Mustafa Ahmed Hawsawi, the international accountant, and also Ahmed Ressam, the bomber designated to strike the Los Angeles airport during the millennium celebrations. After the USA launched its anti-terrorist campaign in October Mohammed Atef, al-Qaeda's military commander, was killed, in November 2001. Atef was of Egyptian origin and brother-in-law of bin Laden. The al-Qaeda global network also suffered arrests in nearly thirty countries in the first six months after 9/11.

With the loss of Afghanistan, al-Qaeda will increasingly depend on its decentralized structure and on associate organizations. All 'brothers', wherever they serve, belonged to either a support or an operational function. The support network disseminates propaganda, recruits, raises funds, engages in welfare, procures weapons and dual technologies, and transports personnel and supplies. It operates both as open offices and as clandestine cells. In addition to small, medium and large businesses, al-Qaeda has invested in several industrial agricultural and farming projects to deepen its influence worldwide. Support cell members operate through innocuous political, human rights, socio-economic, welfare, humanitarian, educational, cultural and even sports organizations to maintain contact with Muslim communities. To evade paying tax as well as to gain respectability, some of these organizations are registered as non-profit organizations or as charities. Al-Qaeda's operational network engages in reconnaissance or surveillance of future targets and conducts assassinations, bombings, ambushes and other forms of attack. Some al-Qaeda plans to bomb infrastructure targets and to assassinate foreign and local leaders have failed. At least three to four dozen operations have been detected and disrupted by governments or called off by al-Qaeda to meet the changing international political climate.

Al-Qaeda's least studied aspect is its links with several Islamist political parties, guerrilla and terrorist groups. Arabs staff all the key positions of al-Qaeda but bin Laden realized that this could be a weakness and sought non-Arab recruits by forging ties with Islamist parties and groups outside the Middle East. To enhance diversity – essential for a global jihad – al-Qaeda campaigned on a common Shi'a–Sunni platform. Although puritanical, al-Qaeda is practical, continually revising its ideology. Most non-al-Qaeda groups practiced the Salafi and Takfir schools of Islam. To gain strategic depth in new regions, al-Qaeda propagated these potent ideologies beyond the Middle East.

In addition to ideological training, al-Qaeda provided associated and affiliated groups with military expertise. Furthermore, al-Qaeda's 055 Brigade fighting the Northern Alliance in Afghanistan provided critical battle experience for participants before they returned to their home countries where they were the agents of al-Qaeda.

Al-Qaeda's presence in North America, Western Europe and Australasia provided both support and a conducive environment to stage operations. For instance al-Qaeda's founder Abdullah Azzam visited twenty-six American states in the early and mid-1980s. By the late 1980s, al-Qaeda's precursor organization, MAK, had thirty functional offices in the USA. After bin Laden's split with Azzam – and Azzam was murdered – bin Laden wished to take control of MAK's US headquarters at 566 Atlantic Avenue in Brooklyn, New York's Arab district. Al-Qaeda gained control of the MAK infrastructure in the USA in the most deceptive fashion through Dr. Sheikh Omar Abdel-Rahman Ali Abdel Rahman, the spiritual leader of the Egyptian groups. After escaping house arrest in Egypt, the Sheikh traveled to Sudan where he obtained a visa sponsored by a fellow

Egyptian, Mustafa Shalabi, the MAK representative in New York. While the Sheikh was in New York, his followers killed Rabbi Meir Kahane, leader of the Jewish Defense League, in New York in 1990, and also Mustafa Shalabi, the MAK representative, in New York in 1991. Although the Sheikh's follower El Sayyid A. Nosair, an Egyptian, was acquitted of the murder charge, he was convicted of the illegal weapon charge, having trained to kill at the High Rock Gun Club in Naugutuck, Connecticut in 1989. The Sheikh had traveled world-wide including Afghanistan and Pakistan where he met bin Laden and developed a strong friendship. With the loss of Azzam, Osama adopted him as the spiritual leader of al-Qaeda. The Sheikh, blinded by diabetes as a baby, had mastered a Braille copy of the Koran at the age of 11.[6] Born in Egypt in 1938, he is regarded as the Ayatollah Khomeni of Egypt. He was imprisoned in 1970 for describing praying for the late President Nasser as a sin and was placed under house arrest in 1989 for inciting a riot.[7] The Sheikh was in Brooklyn when al-Qaeda trained and financed Ramzi Ahmed Yousef to bomb the World Trade Center in New York in 1993. He lived in Brooklyn until arrested in June 1993 for conspiring to bomb the UN building, road tunnels, bridges, FBI headquarters, government offices, and legislators and officials perceived supportive of Israel. Under an FBI entrapment scheme, a court in New York City found the Blind Sheikh guilty of seditious conspiracy to wage 'war of urban terrorism against the USA' with nine of his followers. The Sheikh was found guilty of the murder of Rabbi Meir Kahane; planning to assassinate President Mubarak of Egypt on a visit to the USA; and of plotting a series of simultaneous attacks on US and UN landmark targets.[8] While one of his other sons, Mohammed, was captured, Abu Asim is believed still to be with al-Qaeda. They fought in Afghanistan and Tajikistan.

The Blind Sheikh was only one of the Islamist preachers who advocated violence against his newly adopted host country. The efficient, swift and harsh US response of arresting the Blind Sheikh, his followers as well as the rendition and extradition of several Islamists from the Philippines, Malaysia and Pakistan for the World Trade Center bombing and the attempted landmark bombings of New York in 1993 deterred further violence inside the USA in the second half of the 1990s. Nonetheless, the USA turned a blind eye to the extremist milieu which was providing personnel and funds to fight several jihad campaigns worldwide. Furthermore, the USA was one of the main centres for al-Qaeda procurement. Operating through a front company, al-Qaeda's representative for the UK Khalid al-Fauwaz procured a satellite phone from Ogara Satellite Networks of Deer Park, New York for US$7,500. The phone number 00–873–682505331 was used by bin Laden to communicate to his network of followers. Another al-Qaeda member Ziyad Khaleel bought batches of 400-minute telephone cards from the company. Essam al-Ridi, al-Qaeda procurement officer and bin Laden's personal pilot, purchased weapons and dual technologies from the USA. Al-Ridi also purchased a T-series plane from Texas, converted it to a personal plane, and flew it via Canada, Iceland and Italy to Khartoum. The American intelligence community never believed that the satellite phone and the airplane would be used to accumulate resources, plan and prepare to target US personnel and infrastructure in East Africa and in the Horn of Africa. US leaders' belief that insulating America from the rest of the world would protect the country gave a false sense of security. The isolationist mentality focused on guarding borders but discounted strategic threats from within the USA or across the ocean. Sheikh Kabbani of the Islamic Council of America declared in January 1999 that Islamists took over 80 percent of the mosques in the United States. Since there are more than 3,000 mosques in the United States, one can conclude that the ideology of extremism has spread to much of the Muslim population, especially youth.

Radicalization of American Muslims by Islamist preachers and penetration of Muslim diaspora and migrants by foreign terrorist groups prompted the FBI to infiltrate some of the Muslim communities. As long as they did not harm the USA, neither the FBI nor other US agencies acted against American Muslims engaged in terrorism. As al-Qaeda was aware that the FBI was monitoring the Muslim communities, they chose to relocate the September 11 operational team away from the Islamic pockets. Al-Qaeda built a network from scratch, independent from al-Qaeda's network in the USA. They were European, Middle Eastern and Asian members who traveled to the USA, trained in the target country and attacked its most prestigious targets symbolic of US military, economic and political power. Using passenger aircraft and crashing them into US targets was, in the words of a former al-Qaeda member, like 'me tightly holding your finger, turning it towards you and poking it into your own eye.'[9]

The coordinated airborne attacks on 9/11 was al-Qaeda's watershed operation. Mohamed al-Amir Awad al-Sayed Atta alias Mohommad Atta, the al-Qaeda operations commander, and four cells conducted the multiple suicide operation. Three of the four aircraft reached their targets, killing nearly 2,900 men, women and children. The fuel-laden Boeing aircraft were as lethal as cruise missiles used by the USA to strike the al-Qaeda leader's home and his infrastructure in Afghanistan.

To launch an operation of this magnitude, al-Qaeda exploited the traditional terrorist technique of entering Western countries. By infiltrating Muslim migrant and territorial communities in Europe and Asia, al-Qaeda used Germany, UAE and Malaysia as launching pads to enter the USA. Even after they were established independently of each other, the cells in Hamburg, Dubai and Kuala Lampur continued independently to assist them.

According to Indian intelligence, al-Qaeda also prepared a backup team to attack the World Trade Center.[10] They were trained on a six-month simulator-training course at the Tyler International School of Aviation in Dallas, Texas.[11]

The September 11 operatives were handpicked for one quality: they were willing to kill and to die for Allah. Recovery of Atta's will in his bag that never reached his flight demonstrated psychological indoctrination to the very end. Moussaoui was arrested three weeks before the operation, yet he refused to compromise. The 9/11 operation demonstrated a leap in operational planning, preparation and execution, suggesting that al-Qaeda is rapidly learning from its past mistakes – such as the failed operation to target the USA on the eve of the millennium – in order to improve its operational effectiveness.

By using passenger airplanes improvised as guided missiles, al-Qaeda introduced a new tactic into the terrorist repertoire. In keeping with the al-Qaeda code, bin Laden and his host Taliban initially denied al-Qaeda's role in the attacks. In October 2001, however, bin Laden praised the September 11 attack, and vowed that the United States would not 'enjoy security' before 'infidel armies leave' the Gulf. Al Zawahiri called on Muslims to join the battle against the USA and Sulieman Abu Ghaith announced that Muslims had a duty to attack US targets everywhere. Although the bulk of Muslims worldwide were appalled by the al-Qaeda strikes, some secretly rejoiced because they perceived them to be justified. The vast majority of the Muslims – Arab and non-Arab – living in the USA do not support political violence, especially terrorism. But they resent the Jewish lobby, the US role in the Middle East and especially support for Israel. Although most Arabs living in the West support al-Qaeda's aims and objectives, they disagree with the tactics adopted by this group to advance its goal. Al-Qaeda's support base in the USA is old and medium in size. However, it is significant because the quality of the support base is high. Unlike the Canadian and the European support bases, the US base consists mostly of wealthy and influential professionals. While spread throughout the USA, it is largely concentrated in New York–New Jersey and in the Midwest where there is a sizable community of Syrian-born Palestinians. As American Arabs are better educated, influential and goal-oriented, they are valued inside al-Qaeda. Like European Arabs and Western converts to Islam, they held or continue to hold important positions or play critical roles in al-Qaeda at home or abroad. Furthermore, they aroused less suspicion crossing international borders. Because they carry US passports, visa requirements rarely applied or were often waived. Al-Qaeda's recruitment policy was to accept the national of any country provided he was a committed Muslim or a convert to Islam. Al-Qaeda made an extraordinary effort to recruit Westerners of Arab origin. There were a few, including retired and serving military personnel who worked or supported al-Qaeda. Ali Abdallah Isa, alias Abu Abdallah, of the US Special Forces trained bin Laden's bodyguards, conducted advance training for al-Qaeda members and designed many of its significant operations. A former member of the Egyptian Islamic Group in New Jersey, Abu Abdallah was of Egyptian origin. He belonged to a fourteen-member al-Qaeda team consisting of retired US military personnel that entered Bosnia through Croatia and trained as well as armed the Mujahidin.[12] Similarly, another American, Abu Musa of Palestinian origin, coordinated the Shia Iranians and the Sunni Arabs who were constantly clashing.[13] American Arab assistance – political, economic and military – to Islamists is a continuation of the support initially triggered by the US government for the purpose of fighting Soviet troops. When the latter withdrew from Afghanistan, the Islamists diverted their praiseworthy support to the Islamists fighting to relieve the suffering Muslims in Bosnia, Kashmir, Mindanao, Chechnia, Algeria, and other conflicts on the escalation. American Arabs could not understand the distinction drawn by Western leaders between fighting the Soviet Union and fighting regimes repressing Muslims. They saw no distinction between one million Muslims killed in Afghanistan versus

100,000 Muslims killed in the Balkans. As MAK harnessed the US Muslim diaspora support during the Soviet period, al-Qaeda tapped the post-Soviet Arab, Muslim and other resources worldwide.

The al-Qaeda support network benefits from its affiliate organizations. These mostly take the form of NGOs and have not been established by al-Qaeda but infiltrated by it. In the USA there are several which raised millions of US dollars and enjoyed charitable status. Since 9/11, US intelligence has stepped up surveillance of suspected NGOs and frozen the funds of Islamic NGOs

From time to time, important al-Qaeda leaders visited the USA, including Muhammad Jamal Khalifa, the brother-in-law of bin Laden. US immigration arrested Khalifa in San Francisco after his luggage and personal effects were searched on 20 December 1994. Among the items recovered was a teaching manual with sections entitled 'Wisdom of Assassination and Kidnapping, Wisdom to Assassinate Priests and Christians, Wisdom to Bomb Christian Churches and Places of Worship, Wisdom for Operations and Martyrdom, Wisdom for Reconciliation with the Enemy and other various methods.'[14] The curricula included extensive discussions on assassination, use of explosives, military training and jihad as well as Islamic organizations, movements and groups such as Hamas and the Palestinian Islamic Jihad.[15] Khalifa was held without bail until 6 January 1995. He was charged for visa fraud, furnishing false information and fleeing to avoid prosecution. He was subsequently extradited to Jordan for financing the bombing of a cinema there in January–February 1994 where he was tried in court but acquitted. As al-Qaeda's chief for Southeast Asia in the first half of the 1990s, Khalifa was responsible for financing Oplan Bojinka, the operation to destroy eleven US airlines over the Pacific, and to assassinate Pope John Paul II and US President Clinton, both of whom were visiting the Philippines in 1994. When arrested in San Francisco and until he was acquitted in Jordan, the US intelligence community did not know Khalifa's role in Oplan Bojinka. After September 11, Saudi intelligence arrested Khalifa in Saudi Arabia.

In comparison with al-Qaeda's North American and Asian network, its European network is one of the newest. In Europe, al-Qaeda established its influence and power by infiltrating existing networks – al-Takfir Wal Hijra, the Armed Islamic Group (GIA) and the Salafist Group for Call and Combat (El Djema Salafiyya Li El Daawa Wa El Qital; Groupe Salafiste pour la Predication et le Combat: GSPC) – as well as establishing its own cells by dispatching operatives and recruiting officers from Afghanistan into Europe

In early 2002, international security and intelligence agencies estimated there to be at least 500 active and dormant members of al-Qaeda and al-Qaeda associate Islamist groups in Europe.[16] Without exception all were elite members, theater-trained in Afghanistan and elsewhere. Although about 150 members have been arrested since September 11, al-Qaeda has a vast strategic reserve of dormant but trained members in Europe to be activated and missioned. The terrorist network functions as an organized crime network or works closely with other organized crime networks. They include the Chechen, Russian, Ukrainian, Pakistani, Nigerian, Turkish and Kurdish networks. These support networks engage in obtaining genuine passports; forging and adapting identity documents needed to obtain passports; adapting passports; smuggling humans, including al-Qaeda recruiting officers and operatives; engaging in credit card fraud and robbery to raise funds; and intimidation. Al-Qaeda and Taliban planned to conduct assassination operations of individuals in Europe but in the wider interest of not disrupting the network for 'more important operations' refrained from doing so.[17]

Al-Qaeda's European network was constantly under the threat of disruption from host governments. Al-Qaeda also faced problems of movement from its European theater to Afghanistan and back. After the East Africa bombings in August 1998, not all al-Qaeda's European recruits could travel to Afghanistan through Pakistan due to the restrictions imposed by the Pakistani government. Although al-Qaeda developed mechanisms to overcome this restriction creatively, many of its recruits traveled to Chechnia, Somalia, Kashmir, the Philippines and Indonesia to receive training. Of al-Qaeda's multilayered network in Europe, the networks in the UK and France have been the oldest. The most robust European terrorist support infrastructure is in the UK where British tolerance of migrants has been abused and misused by two generations of terrorist groups. Even six months after the 9/11 attacks, the key activists of the network remain at large in the UK. Despite the legal proscription of foreign terrorist groups in February 2001 under the Terrorism Act 2000, the UK response to neutralize the infrastructure of al-Qaeda and several other groups active and dormant on British soil has been gravely inadequate. London was clearly al-Qaeda's spiritual hub in the Western world until 9/11.

Khalid al-Fauwaz, a trusted friend of bin Laden, established al-Qaeda network in 1994 in London. Among members, he was also known as Khalid Abdul Rahman Hamad al-Fawwaz, alias Abu Omar, alias Hamad, alias Khalid, alias Abu Mahdi.[18] A former businessman in Saudi Arabia, when he arrived in the UK to establish the network, he was assisted by Dr. Mohammed Al-Massari, an academic, who is also an acknowledged opponent of the Saudi royal family. Osama personally phoned al-Massari and thanked him for his help. Al-Massari is also linked to UK's Al Muhajiroun leader Omar Bakri Mohammed, an Islamist cleric.[19] In addition to its open support for Taliban, al-Muhajiroun recruits have received training in al-Qaeda camps. Al-Fauwaz managed al-Qaeda's media and public relations office called Advice and Reformation Office (ARC) established in an Arab neighbourhood in north London. The ARC office in Beethoven Street, West Kilburn, equipped with state-of-the-art technology, communicated directly with bin Laden and Atef. The ARC provided perfect cover for advancing al-Qaeda interests in Europe and in North America. For instance, ARC arranged the March 1997 meeting between the then CNN journalists and bin Laden.[20] Despite denials, bin Laden established the outfit and the ARC disbursed funds, procured equipment and recruited members. On an ARC letterhead 'Osama M. bin Laden' signed the ARC 'London office' resolution stating: 'The consultative assembly of the Advice and Reformation Committee intending to extend its activity and to ease communication resolves this Monday 11 July 1994: (1) Establish an office in London, U.K. (2) Appoint Mr Khalid al-Fauwaz director of this office.'[21] Al-Fauwaz functioned for five years out of London advancing al-Qaeda aims and objectives before the UK authorities arrested him on 28 September 1998.

Al-Fauwaz's network included a blend of personalities from the political to the militant. Dr. Sassd al-Fagih, another opponent of the Saudi royal family, headed the Movement for Islamic Reform in Arabia (MIRA). A former Professor of Surgery at the King Saud University, al-Fagih managed a state-of-the-art communications office. Unknown to Western security and intelligences services, members of MIRA held key positions in al-Qaeda. ARC and MIRA and similar organizations reached out to the wider world. For instance, MIRA and Committee for the Defense of Legitimate Rights (CDLR) disseminated worldwide the English translation of the twelve-paged Arabic fatwa by al-Qaeda issued in February 1996. In many ways, CDLR endorsed the fatwa because it stated that the 'Al Saud and the American occupation is the source of evil, and they are so intertwined and interconnected that they have become organically connected evil.'[22] The UK took no action to control the use of its soil to disseminate hatred.

Fauwaz and others awaited extradition to the USA for the 1998 East Africa bombings that killed 231 people. The UK bore £428,000 in legal aid, £16,500 in government counsel fees and an estimated £210,000 for their imprisonment.[23] This again illustrates the weakness of the British criminal justice system in the fight against foreign terrorist support networks.

Three Islamist clerics – Omar Bakri Mohammed, Abu Umr al-Takfiri alias Abu Qatada, and Moustapha Kamel, alias Abu Hamza al-Masri, alias Abu Hamza – have supported al-Qaeda and Taliban aims and objectives. After listening to their virulent sermons, at least one hundred British and European Muslims traveled to Afghanistan and received training in al-Qaeda camps. A number of them are in Northern Alliance custody in Afghanistan or in US custody at Camp X-Ray. In addition to preaching in their own mosques, these Islamist clerics attract moderate youth from other mosques throughout the UK. Islamist recruiters conduct the infiltration of mosques of moderate clerics. Richard Reid, the shoe bomber, who attempted to destroy a plane en route from Paris to Miami, and Zacarias Moussaoui, suspected twentieth 9/11 hijacker, worshiped at the Brixton Mosque headed by Imam Abdul Haqq Baker, a moderate cleric. Islamist recruiters targeted these youth. Thereafter, they were exposed to the sermons of Omar Bakri Mohammed, leading al-Muhajiroun in Tottenham, North London, and Abu Qatada, the Palestinian cleric leading the Baker Street Prayer Group. After listening to Abu Qatada, Moussaoui joined al-Qaeda. Moussaoiu was in London when Reid, a British convert to Islam, joined al-Qaeda.

The Finsbury Park Mosque run by Abu Hamza attracted mostly North African Arabs coming from Europe. In addition to Moussaoui, his congregation included Djamel Beghal and Kamel Daoudi. Beghal, an Algerian who acquired French citizenship by marrying a French woman in 1993, joined the Islamists after coming under the influence of an Egyptian Islamist. Before he was recruited and appointed as al-Qaeda leader in France, he lived in London and Leicester where he joined the Takfir Wal Hijra under the influence of Abu Qatada. In late 2000,

Beghal and his family left London for Afghanistan. After leaving his family behind in Pakistan, he visited Afghanistan to discuss a plan to strike US targets in Paris. Although Beghal could not meet bin Laden in Kandahar in March 2001, he met Abu Zubaydah, his principal agent-handler, who presented him gifts from bin Laden as a mark of appreciation. En route to Europe from Afghanistan via Pakistan, Beghal was arrested in Dubai, United Arab Emirates on 28 July 2001. To his interrogators in UAE, he revealed that al-Qaeda deposited funds in a Moroccan bank to bomb US targets in Paris.[24] Al-Qaeda planned to destroy the US Embassy either by crash-diving an explosives-laden suicide helicopter or by explosives strapped to an al-Qaeda member walking into the building. Simultaneously, al-Qaeda planned to destroy the American Cultural Centre by parking an explosives-laden car outside the premises, also in Paris. A few days after Beghal was extradited to Paris on 30 September 2001, he went back on his statement given to the UAE authorities and to the French. He exploited the criminal justice system of a liberal democracy where torture was not permitted.

Beghal's bombmaker was his former flatmate Daoudi, a second generation North African of French citizenship. Daoudi, who escaped the French police, was arrested in Leicester by the British authorities and deported to France at the end of September. Daoudi, also al-Qaeda trained in Afghanistan, was their European specialist on encryption of Internet communication and preparation of code sheets. Beghal's suicide bomber was Nizar Trabelsi, a former football star. Just like some of the September 11 al-Qaeda pilots, Nizar also had used alcohol and cocaine, became a member of al-Takfir Wal Hijra, and believed that a 'martydom' operation would cleanse him of his past sins. After coming under the influence of Abu Qatada in London, he joined al-Qaeda, received training in Afghanistan, and volunteered to kill and die in the planned attack on the US Embassy in Paris. Nizar was highly trusted and respected within al-Qaeda for his commitment – even al-Qaeda's Spanish cell was in communication with him.

With mounting international pressure, the British authorities raided Abu Qatada's West London home and seized £180,000 in different currencies. Until then, he had been fraudulently claiming social security. Abu Qatada, who has political asylum in the UK, was named by the UN as a terrorist suspect. The Spanish authorities have named Abu Qatada as al-Qaeda's spiritual ambassador in Europe. Abu Qatada is also a part of the al-Takfir Wal Hijra leadership, currently headed by Dr. Ayman Zawahiri, bin Laden's deputy. Despite intelligence that Abu Qatada had met Osama in the 1980s, he denies ever having met him. Furthermore, he is wanted by Amman in connection with a series of bombings in Jordan in 1998. When the British authorities developed special legislation in late 2001 to arrest the likes of Abu Qatada, he slipped the net. As of early 2002, he remains in the UK communicating with a few of his trusted associates by email. Another key figure in the UK is an Algerian Abu Doha, who was Ressam's agent-handler. When the British police raided his home, they found forged and adapted passports and instructions on how to make bombs. The intelligence community identify Afghan veteran Abu Hamza as al-Qaeda's link to the two Algerian terrorist groups. Six months after September 11, many of the clerics remain free to preach. This means expansion of the recruitment and support base of Islamist groups including al-Qaeda in the UK. From January 2002 onwards, the UK authorities arrested several al-Qaeda suspects especially Algerians and other Middle Eastern nationals who have been living in Europe. Investigations in January 2002 revealed that the arrested Algerian asylum seekers Baghdad Mexiane and Brahim Benmerzouga were using Leicester as a base to attack targets in continental Europe. So long as the British authorities are unable or unwilling to target al-Qaeda's support network that is disseminating propaganda in London, there will be fund-raising and recruitment for al-Qaeda. Despite arrests in late 2001 and early 2002, the extremist milieu is very much present in London. The continuing threat of Islamist extremism is not native and is exported from the Middle East to the UK. Indeed, the vast majority of British Muslims are very British and detest extreme Islamism. Although those who espoused Islamist extremism is small, it is growing due to British inaction. However, the reluctance of the UK authorities to counter this threat is affecting the peace and security of the vast majority of the peace-loving Muslim community.

The UK is a part of al-Qaeda's European network. In operational planning, preparation and execution, al-Qaeda draws no distinction between the UK and continental Europe. They were considered as one integrated network by the parent organization in Afghanistan. After the USA, al-Qaeda always perceived France as its enemy. However, due to Prime Minister Tony Blair's unconditional support for the USA in the anti-terrorist coalition, the UK too has earned al-Qaeda's wrath.

CONCLUSION

The nature of terrorism has dramatically changed during the past ten years. Instead of resisting globalization, al-Qaeda has aptly demonstrated that its cells are harnessing its forces. Only by developing a multi-pronged, multidimensional, multi-agency and a multinational response can a group like al-Qaeda be defeated.

Intelligence and covert action are key to fighting contemporary terrorism. The knowledge in the US intelligence community of al-Qaeda was gravely weak until the East Africa bombings. Even the best informed in the community believed that the organization headed by bin Laden was 'The Islamic Army' and an alias for it was 'al-Qaeda.' In fact, the 'Executive Order Prohibiting Transactions with Terrorists who Threaten to Disrupt the Middle East Peace Process,' signed by President Clinton on 20 August 1998, listed bin Laden's group as an Islamic Army and with such aliases as 'Al Qaida, Islamic Salvation Foundation, The World Islamic Front for Jihad Against Jews and Crusaders, and The Group for the Preservation of the Holy Sites.'[25] Although it did not list al-Zawahiri, it listed Abu Hafs al-Masri, the military commander and the Egyptian Islamic Group leader Rifa'i Ahmad Taha Musa. By this time, the Egyptians, Jordanians, Pakistanis, Israelis and the French had better intelligence on al-Qaeda. However, within a month of the East Africa attacks, the US agencies realized their weakness and addressed it by cooperating with their better-informed counterpart agencies. 'The US Grand Jury Indictment Against Usama Bin Laden' filed in a US District Court, Southern District of New York, reflect this improved understanding of al-Qaeda.[26] The US capacity to respond improved directly as a result of international intelligence exchange and cooperation. Nonetheless, subscription to excessive secrecy and over-reliance on technical means of intelligence gathering gravely impeded the efforts of the US intelligence community to detect and disrupt September 11. In many ways, it would be wrong to blame the catastrophic failure of the US intelligence community to detect and disrupt September 11. In an age of sharing, the blame should be shared by the international security and intelligence community in general and the AUSCANUKUSNZ – Australia, Canada, the UK, USA and New Zealand – intelligence system in particular. The West is unlikely to develop its human intelligence in the short term. Until then, it will be vulnerable to the threat of Islamist terrorism.

NOTES

1 Abdullah Azzam, al-Qaeda Al Sulbha, *Al Jihad*, principal journal of the Afghan Arabs, MAK, Peshawar, April 1988.
2 Transcript of Osama bin Laden Videotape, Mid-November 2001, transcript and annotations independently prepared by George Michael, translator, Diplomatic Language Services; and Dr. Kassem M. Wahba, Arabic language program coordinator, School of Advanced International Studies, Johns Hopkins University. They collaborated on their translation and compared it with translations done by the US government for consistency. There were no inconsistencies in the translations.
3 Interview, former al-Qaeda member, London, July 2001.
4 Hugh Williamson, Jimmy Burns, Stephen Fidler and Mark Husband, 'A Catastrophic Failure of Intelligence', *Financial Times*, 29 Nov. 2001.
5 'Bin Laden's Martyrs for the Cause', *Financial Times*, 28 Nov. 2001.
6 John K. Cooley, *Unholy Wars: Afghanistan, America and International Terrorism* (London: Pluto Press, 3rd edn, 2002), p. 41.
7 *Jane's World Insurgency and Terrorism* (Jan.–April 2000), p. 290.
8 Ibid.
9 Interview, former al-Qaeda member, London, Sept. 2001.
10 Tactical Interrogation Report of Mohommad Afroz, arrested on 2 Oct. 2001, Intelligence Bureau, New Delhi, India, p. 1.
11 Ibid., p. 2.
12 Abd-Al-Latif Al-Minawi, 'Egyptian Report: Terrorist Links', Cairo, *Al-Sharq Al-Awsat*, 8 Nov. 1998, p. 4.
13 Ibid., p. 3.
14 Muhammad Jamal Khalifa, Arrest in San Francisco, document supplied to the author, undated.
15 Ibid.
16 Based on estimates by military and civilian security and intelligence agencies and national police and law enforcement authorities, Feb. 2002.
17 Interview, al-Qaeda member, March 2001.
18 United States of America Versus Osama Bin Laden *et al.*, Court Reporters Office, Southern District of New York., Day 2 of the trial, 6 Feb. 2001, http://cryptome.org/usa-v-ubl-dt.htm and other sources.

19 Sean O'Neill, 'The Extremist Network That Sprang from "Londonistan" ', *Daily Telegraph*, 3 Jan. 2002.
20 Peter Bergen, *Holy War, Inc, Inside the Secret World of Osama bin Laden* (London, Weidenfeld & Nicolson, 2001), pp. 1–6.
21 Dominic Kennedy, Daniel McGory, James Bone and Richard Ford, 'The Fingerprints of Terror', *The Times*, 24 Nov. 2001.
22 The Ladenese Epistle: Declaration of War (I) 2 Oct. 1996, MSA News ⟨htto://msanews.mynet.net/MSANEWS/199610/19961012.3html⟩
23 Kennedy *et al.*, 'Fingerprints of Terror'.
24 'Man Says He Was Recruited by Bin Laden for Suicide Attack on US Embassy in Paris', Associated Press, 2 Oct. 2001.
25 White House, 'Executive Order Prohibiting Transactions with Terrorists Who Threaten to Disrupt the Middle East Peace Process', Washington, DC, 20 Aug. 1998.
26 USIS, New York, 7 Nov. 1998.

4   Superpower response

The United States of America

Robert Singh

In striking at the 'domestic Tranquility,' 'common defense' and 'Blessings of Liberty' that the US Constitution was established to secure, the terrorist attacks of September 11 not only extinguished thousands of lives but also heralded a dangerous and unprecedented chapter in the 'American experiment.' 9/11 represented the end of what remained of America's post–1991 innocence about the severity of global threats and confirmed the many prior warnings that the question of mainland terror was one of when, not whether, it would occur.

To some observers, the attacks triggered the most sudden and dramatic change in the history of American foreign policy, bringing an abrupt and decisive end to the post-Cold War era.[1] But while many declarations proclaimed a permanently transformed world, American responses instead suggested a remarkable continuity. Rather than initiating a transformation, 9/11 accelerated trends, policies and approaches that were well established. If the attacks' most immediate political effects were certainly dramatic – the Bush administration's approval ratings soared and public confidence in the federal government attained levels unseen since the early 1960s – the dominant features of recent American politics (not least partisan polarization) remained essentially unchanged.

Analogical reasoning in international affairs is as hazardous in theory as it is ubiquitous in practice, hence the question of whether 9/11 will ultimately prove as strategically significant for America as Pearl Harbor, the Cold War or the implosion of the USSR is best left for another day.[2] 9/11 nonetheless proved both that America remains as vulnerable to conventional and unconventional attacks as other nations and that its singular influence renders it an especially inviting target. It also demonstrated, however, that America remains exceptional in its capacity to deploy vast resources and destructive assets on a global scale. The rapid removal of the Taliban regime revealed a hegemonic power with neither peer nor precedent, prompting commentators to compete for adjectival correctness: 'hyper-power,' 'mega-power,' 'behemoth.'[3]

Confronted by such dominance, critics are surely right to caution about the dangers accompanying such unprecedented and (relatively) unfettered power. But commentary on America frequently remains empirically poorly anchored, wrongly conflating official policies with public preferences and embracing stereotypes about (for example) mass aversion to military casualties that resisted close scrutiny long prior to 2001. The reasons why factual accuracy infrequently intrudes on familiar 'truisms' about the USA has received compelling analysis elsewhere[4] but it is in the light of such infrequency that this chapter reviews in turn American perceptions of the terrorist attacks, the responses of the Bush administration and Congress and 9/11's broader significance for American domestic politics and foreign policy.

A CLEAR, PRESENT AND UNPRECEDENTED DANGER

For a nation that experienced almost unbroken economic and military successes from 1991–2001, the shock of 9/11 was profound. The attacks were the most serious on mainland America since 1812, all the more powerful to the public for being – in New York City's case – captured on television. The 'CNN effect' instantly confronted Americans with the grimly disturbing reality that, despite the nation's awesome economic strength and military power in a unipolar post-Cold War world, such resources had failed to guarantee the homeland security long taken for granted. 9/11, and subsequent public and private reactions in many parts of the world, also demonstrated graphically that many people existed – how many remains unclear – who detest the United States.

But America is no stranger to terrorism. Domestic terrorism had come full circle by the 1990s, leftist anti-government extremists of the 1960s (such as the Weathermen) having been eclipsed by those of the radical right. At home, the 1993 World Trade Center attack, the 1995 Oklahoma City bombing and the 1996 Atlanta Olympics pipe-bomb heightened security concerns. Abroad, terrorist attacks on US targets became less frequent but more lethal, from the Khobar Towers bombing in 1996 through the Kenyan and Tanzanian embassy bombings in 1998 to the attack on the *USS Cole* in Yemen in October 2000. Movies such as *Arlington Road* and books such as Richard Preston's *The Cobra Event* popularized terrorist concerns, suggesting that – with 8,633 miles of shoreline, 300 ports of entry and more than 7,500 miles of border with Mexico and Canada – the surprise was not that mainland terrorism occurred but rather that it had remained so rare.

Despite the incidence of increasingly lethal terrorist activities, bin Laden's 1998 declaration of war against America, and explicit warnings of imminent security dangers from the Rumsfeld, Gilmore and Hart-Rudman Commissions during 1998–2001, the Clinton administration had remained myopically focused on economic growth, fiscal restraint and globalization over traditional security concerns. Urgency in defeating al-Qaeda and states that succored it was not a hallmark of the Clinton years as a buoyant Wall Street, declining unemployment and rising profits during a record 107 consecutive months of economic expansion muted the prioritization of national security. Not until 1997–98, under substantial pressure from congressional Republicans, did Clinton acquiesce in substantial increases in the defense budget and subsequently sign the National Missile Defense Act of 1999.

Both prosperity and peace were eroding before 9/11 but the attacks decisively ended the latter, rendering American insecurities not only economic but also physical. The attacks crossed a threshold, occurring without warning against major landmarks and employing symbolic and practical mainstays of American life: commercial airliners transformed into missiles. The anthrax attacks that soon followed provoked widespread fears of further terrorism on a mass scale. Accustomed to believing their nation was invulnerable, 9/11 shattered American sensibilities: most Americans wept or felt depressed in response and substantial minorities reported trouble concentrating and sleeping. Fears and concerns about the likelihood of terrorist attacks – which had been growing since 1991 – increased sharply.[5]

Although some discordant voices were soon heard and silenced (most notably Reverend Jerry Falwell's 13 September typically sober and sensitive declaration that 'the pagans and the abortionists and the feminists and the gays and the lesbians' had 'helped this happen'), to students of American politics, the public's response was unsurprising. As Samuel Huntington has argued, Americans respond to war with near-unanimity only when both democratic values and national security are threatened.[6] Prior to 9/11, World War Two alone met both criteria. While the devastation wrought in New York, Virginia and Pennsylvania offered the clearest evidence of the latter threat, to most Americans the solution to the conundrum of 'why do they hate us?' (however much the attacks were at root the result of 'somebody else's civil war')[7] also provided evidence for the former: revulsion of American values, beliefs and influence.

Popular support for military action in response to terrorism predates 9/11 but, contrary to common non-American perceptions of a bellicose, isolationist and nationalistic nation, mass responses supported a multilateral approach to terrorism, international engagement, a stronger United Nations (UN) role and building goodwill towards America through humanitarian and development aid. The public also rejected the idea of a fundamental clash of cultures between Islam and the West.[8] In short, US opinion was considerably closer to that of Europeans than much media coverage on both sides of the Atlantic suggested.

Ninety-five percent of Americans, for example, agreed that it was important 'for the war on terrorism to be seen by the world as an effort of many countries working together, not just a US effort.' A Harris poll conducted over 19–24 September found 79 percent saying it was 'very' and 16 percent 'somewhat important' to 'build a strong international coalition of many countries to support us.' Eighty-eight percent agreed it was very or somewhat important to 'get the support of as many Arab and Islamic countries as possible.' Whilst 50 percent said military action should occur regardless, 45 percent held that America 'should take military action against terrorist organizations in other countries only if the UN Security Council authorizes it.'

Almost all Americans favored dealing with terrorism through multilateral action. Most preferred including other nations' forces in the Afghan war despite America being constrained by having to make joint decisions. A strong majority supported using international judicial bodies for terrorist trials with a plurality favoring trying bin Laden before an International Criminal Tribunal rather than a New York federal court. The public also showed at least as much support for non-military as military instruments (liquidating terrorist funds, enhancing intelligence, strengthening international law and building goodwill), holding non-military means to be more effective in preventing future terrorism. Most Americans nonetheless agreed that failure to respond militarily to 9/11 would increase the prospect of future terrorist attacks.

An overwhelming majority therefore supported the bombing campaign against Afghanistan. On 6–7 December *Newsweek* found 88 percent approving 'the current US military action against terrorism.' When bombing began, NBC found 90 percent approval. Six percent thought the action was 'too strong' while 76 percent viewed it as 'about right' or 'not strong enough.' Support for military action (including ground troops) was consistently overwhelming and remained so when the possibilities of retaliation, troop casualties and a long war were mentioned.

But while a strong majority also supported military efforts to overthrow Saddam Hussein, only a minority favored this while the Afghan war was continuing or doing so without allied and European support and participation. A 28–29 November Fox poll found 78 percent supported 'having US forces take military action against Iraq to force Saddam Hussein from power' but a Fox News poll conducted on 12–13 December found majority opposition to unilateral action. Although the first sentence of the question inserted a bias towards action ('It is widely acknowledged that Iraq is developing weapons of mass destruction'), 54 percent wanted America 'to develop an international consensus before taking action against Iraq' while only 36 percent said 'the US should take immediate military action.'[9]

Public opinion, then, was markedly less unilateralist and militarist not only than popular non-American perceptions suggested but also than the Bush administration. Its relative lack of influence on official policy stemmed from the most exacting of crisis imperatives powerfully reinforcing the administration's preexisting approach to international affairs.

THE BUSH ADMINISTRATION AND THE 107TH CONGRESS (2001–2)

No American president confronted as grave a national security threat so soon in his administration as George W. Bush. Franklin Delano Roosevelt had been in power for almost nine years when Pearl Harbor occurred. Kennedy went 'eyeball to eyeball' with Moscow over the Cuban missile crisis twenty-two months into his presidency. Bush confronted an actual, not hypothetical, assault on America's mainland involving mass murder on an unprecedented scale just eight months after his inauguration. Unlike all his predecessors, Bush faced not a state but an enemy that was Hydra-headed, only vestigially territorial and – in its semi-corporate hierarchical organization, loosely linked cellular structures and mobile finances – a 'perfect embodiment of globalisation.'[10]

This unique challenge also thrust itself on an administration that, in its initial focus on domestic policy (and despite the continuity of personnel), was a reversal of that of Bush's father. Whether despite or because of the controversy surrounding the disputed 2000 presidential election, Bush had demonstrated a keen grasp of politics 'inside the Beltway.' For five months, the first undivided Republican federal government since 1955–6 governed with a narrow majority in the House of Representatives and an evenly divided Senate. Once Senator James Jeffords (a Republican from Vermont) became an Independent, the Democrats took control of the Senate in June 2001. But 'governing from the center' proved a propitious strategy for a president accustomed to bipartisan bargaining as a governor with weak formal powers in Texas from 1995–2001. Bush's two priorities – a tax cut and education reform – were achieved two months before and after, respectively, the attacks (in a symbolic testament to the domestic focus, Bush was at a Florida elementary school when they occurred). *Congressional Quarterly* recorded his legislative 'success rate' for 2001 at 87 percent – the highest since Lyndon Johnson in 1965.[11]

Bush's foreign policy had attracted extensive critical comment within and outside America. Although relatively few 'pure' unilateralists or multilateralists exist, the first eight months of 2001 saw the administration confirm the latter's worst fears by refusing to send the Treaty establishing an International Criminal Court to the Senate for ratification (January), abandoning the Kyoto Protocol (March), threatening to abrogate the Anti-Ballistic Missile Treaty (May) and withdraw from a UN conference to impose limits on illegal trafficking of small arms (July), rejecting enforcement measures of the 1972 Biological Weapons Convention (July) and withdrawing delegates from the UN conference on racism in Durban (August). In rejecting Clintonian globalism, however, the administration's prioritization of traditional national security concerns gained significant credence – and additional impetus – from 9/11.

Inasmuch as no US government could have eschewed military action after direct strikes on America, the Bush administration's response was a given. But its nature, instruments and duration were shaped by the extensive experience and instinctive hawkishness of most of the foreign policy team. Aside from Secretary of State Powell, the key players – Vice President Dick Cheney, National Security Advisor Condoleezza Rice, Defense Secretary Rumsfeld, Attorney General John Ashcroft and CIA Director George Tenet – shared a basic predisposition towards unilateral action where necessary and feasible to defend American vital interests. Ultimately, the nature of the particular challenge in Afghanistan and the relative success of the military action there substantially advantaged the more hawkish elements within the administration to target not only terrorism but also states acquiring weapons of mass destruction (WMD).

The administration's overall response was unusually disciplined, professional and focused. As one account put it:

> It is hardly surprising that it is tighter-run than its predecessor. The unexpected thing is how successful it has been at moving to the opposite

extreme. The Bush administration focuses relentlessly on a handful of priorities. Most senior officials are self-effacing to a fault. The one media superstar, Donald Rumsfeld, is relentlessly 'on-message.' Leaks are vanishingly rare.[12]

Beyond this, the decision-making process also rejected recent precedents. Under Rice, for example, the National Security Council genuinely acted as the president's advisor, not a policy advocate, while long-abandoned roles of the State and Defense departments were re-established. From Vietnam to Kosovo, the opposition of military chiefs to combat operations that risked US personnel had compelled the State Department to act as the leading advocate of military interventions (for security, peacekeeping and humanitarian missions). In effectively eroding civilian control of the Pentagon – according excessive influence to the military by encouraging military planners to adopt political and diplomatic postures while handing diplomats the task of recommending war plans – such a reversal had served US interests poorly. Powell re-established the State Department's role as one of diplomacy while Rumsfeld presided over a Pentagon offering military options rather than diplomatic obstacles to the president. Moreover, the departments of State and Defense were each compelled – unusually – to speak with one voice.[13]

Rational decision-making was especially important given the profound stakes. Central to internal deliberations were several issues of immense importance, not least the nature of the military response, the public framing of 'war' and reforms to improve mainland security. On each, and despite internal disagreements, the administration reached rapid, clear and decisive conclusions: that it would not distinguish between terrorists and states harboring them (a message directed at Pakistan as much as the Taliban); that, for practical and diplomatic reasons – against the preference of Deputy Defense Secretary Paul Wolfowitz and Defense Policy Board chairman, Richard Perle – Iraq would be relegated to phase two or three of the war; and that, as Bush's carefully calibrated public declarations – in his National Cathedral address, his speech to the joint session of Congress, and 2002 State of the Union message – made clear, the war was likely to be lengthy, global in scope and unprecedented: a perpetual conflict.

The attacks provided Bush with an overarching purpose, transformed his approval ratings and powerfully strengthened the presidency as an institution. Accustomed to being a chief executive, not a legislator, the roles of delegation and final decision-making fitted Bush well. Despite adverse comparisons with 'America's Mayor' Giuliani and derision of his intellect, the president provided focused and measured leadership. By combining a Truman-esque firmness, directness and simplicity of language with a Clinton-esque emphasis on empathy, tolerance and respect, Bush managed to appeal beyond Republicans to Democrats, women and Americans of faith. In the 2002 State of the Union address, for example, Bush declared that 'America will always stand firm for the non-negotiable demands of human dignity, the rule of law, limits on the power of the state, respect for women, private property, free speech, equal justice, and religious tolerance.'[14]

For the first eight months of 2001, Bush won approval ratings in the 50–58 percent range: solid but unremarkable. Not only did 9/11 elevate these to 90 percent but they remained – without precedent – in the 80–90 percent range for several months, and were still over 70 percent in July 2002. Bush's job performance was rated as 'excellent' and 'pretty good' by, respectively, 40 and 39 percent of Americans while Powell received ratings of 47 and 37 percent for the same categories. By comparison, Rumsfeld won 42 and 13 percent while Ashcroft achieved 23 and 42 percent. Republicans and Democrats in Congress, by contrast, received 9 and 49, and 21 and 34 percent.[15]

Crisis imperatives typically re-concentrate power in the executive and 9/11 was no different. Not only did Bush rapidly declare a state of national emergency on 14 September (backdated to 9/11 and still extant in July 2002) and obtain a congressional resolution authorizing the use of all necessary measures to respond to the attacks (with only one dissenting vote in the House) but, in November 2001, Bush issued an executive order providing for alien terrorists to be tried in military tribunal courts with no criminal law or evidential rules of protection. Disclosures of a Continuity of Operations plan involving a 'shadow government,' Bush's appointment of his gubernatorial chief of staff, Joe Allbaugh, to head the federal Office of National Preparedness, and preparations for the establishment of a Homeland Commander-in-Chief together suggested the return of an 'imperial presidency' long thought over.

But such shifts in executive-legislative power invariably entail Congress's active support or reluctant acquiescence. In policy terms, the congressional response to 9/11 was strongly supportive of the president. Bush won a large increase in federal spending to rebuild New York, compensate the families of victims and bail out American airlines. The Justice Department obtained expanded powers to monitor and detain terrorist suspects while the anthrax attacks ensured that the public health system would play a larger role against bio-terrorism. Although its exact authority and powers remained unclear and operational responsibility for homeland security rested more with Cheney, Ashcroft and Allbaugh, the establishment of a new Office of Homeland Security – the first such executive expansion for ten years – offered explicit recognition of the need to rationalize over forty-six agencies with roles in national security (jurisdictional and turf disputes between the State Department, law enforcement and intelligence gathering agencies had, for example, previously allowed terrorists on FBI suspect lists nonetheless to gain entry visas to America). Bush's proposal to create a Department of Homeland Security in June 2002 not only recognized both the imperative and the difficulty of executive branch reorganization – much as Truman had in creating the Department of Defense, Central Intelligence Agency and National Security Council in 1947 – but also shrewdly shared the responsibility for any future intelligence and security policy failures with Congress.

But even here, partisan differences rapidly arose. Sharp conflicts occurred over additional funds, an economic stimulus package, aid for unemployed workers, the airline industry bailout, federalizing airport security staff and efforts to tighten security measures, despite overwhelming public support for each. An ABC News–

Washington Post poll of 29 September 2001, for example, found large majorities (from 69 to 95 percent) supporting additional police powers to combat terrorism with wiretapping, surveillance, admission of foreign intelligence evidence normally deemed illegal in US courts, sharing of grand jury information with intelligence services and allowing the government to detain indefinitely foreigners suspected of terrorist links. Despite the opposition of progressive Democrats and libertarian Republicans, Congress passed the USA Patriot Act in October 2001, giving the government new powers to tap phones, intercept emails and investigate bank accounts.

The acute dilemma for congressional Democrats was the nascent return to a Cold War-type era in which Republican advantages on national security threatened to trump Democratic strengths on domestic policy on a consistent basis. With razor-thin margins in both houses, Bush's deft weaving of security as an economic as well as military issue exacerbated the Democrats' problem until a wave of corporate scandals during the first half of 2002 partially eroded the president's foreign policy-based dominance. By February 2002, Democrats attacked Bush confidant Karl Rove for recommending that Republicans exploit the president's success in the 2002 mid-term elections. In March, Republicans returned the partisan charge with Majority Whip Tom DeLay (a Republican from Texas) denouncing as 'disgusting' Senate Majority Leader Tom Daschle's refusal to let Congress merely 'rubber-stamp' the administration's conduct of the war while US military advisors were despatched to the Phillipines, Georgia and Yemen.

NEW ERAS?

While it remains too early to draw definitive conclusions, one irony of 9/11 may be that its long-term effects could plausibly be greater on nations other than America. Partly, this reflects shifting alignments and balances in the international system but it also represents a function of the stable pattern of constitutional government in America. Without diminishing either the obscene nature of the attacks or the magnitude of the security threat they represent, compared to life on 10 September, the continuities in American domestic politics and foreign policy thus far appear more striking than the disruptions.

Domestically, 'politics as usual' resumed within weeks. A January 2002 poll that asked what 'you and your family are most concerned about' saw 28 percent mention the economy, 15 percent terrorism and national defense, and 10 percent unemployment.[16] 9/11 exacerbated but did not cause the recession that began at the end of 2000 and appeared unlikely to prolong it further than it would otherwise have run (growth in the last quarter of 2001 was 1.4 percent). Nor did the administration's response destroy the federal budget surplus, which had started to shrink during the summer. The parties remained divided over tax cuts, the economy, health care and education, issues that dominated the domestic agenda for over two decades. War remains unlikely to dampen partisanship or discourage Democrats mindful of the fate of a prior war hero (George H. W. Bush) from trudging through the snows of Iowa and New Hampshire: two years in advance, the line-up for 2004 already features Richard Gephardt, John Kerry, John Edwards and Joseph Lieberman. The collapse of Enron, Worldcom and question marks over the finances and ethics of other corporations compounded the sense among Democrats that Bush remained vulnerable.

Admittedly, public attitudes towards government did alter. With few exceptions, declining trust in government was the dominant force in American politics from 1968 to 2001. In the mid-1960s, two-thirds of Americans said they trusted the federal government to do the right thing most or all of the time. By the mid-1990s, that figure had fallen to 20 percent, the lowest of any industrialized liberal democracy. But economic and national insecurities invariably induce calls for government action: an ABC–Post poll in September 2001 found that, for the first time in three decades, most Americans said they trusted the federal government to do the right thing 'just about always' or 'most of the time' – double the percentage of April 2000 and more than three times the proportion of the 'Republican revolution' of 1994.

But the poll also confirmed a longer-standing ambivalence. When asked whether the government solved more problems than it created, the highest-ever proportion of respondents agreed – 42 percent, slightly smaller than the share that held government to create more problems than it solves. When asked to rate the honesty of various professions, only one-quarter gave members of Congress high marks, barely more than in 2000 (and substantially below the 90 percent rating for firemen). That the growth in trust occurred immediately after 9/11 and before the Afghan war suggests it was a function primarily of Americans rallying round the flag. By January 2002, a narrow majority favored a smaller government providing fewer services. Outside economic depression and civil or world wars, the leitmotif of American politics remains 'distrust.' The erosion of a crisis sensibility – admittedly, in the unlikely event that further mainland attacks do not transpire – will plausibly diminish trust in government even as a wartime mood becomes (like the Cold War) a new constant in public life.

Reordering priorities between defense and social programs rather than extending government's scope therefore seems a more plausible shift. But this, too, is a familiar American norm. The federal government's expansion during and after the Second World War was the historical – though not comparative – anomaly.[17] America's post-Second World War self-definition comprised opposition to the USSR and communism and domestic problems compelled politicians to enact laws from civil rights to environmental protection that expanded the federal reach. But with disorder at home and détente abroad, American politics reverted to type from the later 1960s and a steady decline in support for government began (exacerbated by Vietnam, Watergate, and incessant political scandals subsequently), such that it was Democrat Bill Clinton, not Ronald Reagan, who declared the era of big government to be 'over' in 1996.

Moreover, the war against terror appears less likely to enhance government than the Cold War since Americans do not (yet) define themselves in opposition to Muhammad as they did Marx. Unless Huntington's 'clash of civilizations' is realized – by accident or design – and Islam emerges as the functional equivalent of communism, America's asymmetric conflicts with terrorist cells and WMD 'rogue states' is unlikely to yield similar nation-defining qualities. High levels of religiosity combined with increasing levels of tolerance and non-judgmentalism suggest that the support for diversity immediately expressed by Bush after 9/11 will inhibit – but not preclude – the demonizing of Islam in general (it was even ventured that one reason for the inclusion of North Korea in Bush's January 2002 'axis of evil' address was to avoid that list being exclusively Muslim).[18]

Less certain in either duration or magnitude, however, are two shifts that 9/11 did precipitate. First, as noted above, the attacks tilted the domestic balance between security and civil liberties significantly towards the former. A preference for punitive and retributive policies is, however, hardly novel. With few exceptions, American criminal justice policy has increasingly emphasized the quality of just-ice over mercy for three decades. As David Boaz of the Cato Institute observed, 'We've always known that if you put the Bill of Rights up for a popular vote, it would probably lose.'[19]

Second, 9/11 cast question marks over religious and political fanaticism gener-ally. Falwell's grotesquely miscalculated response eroded what limited stock of legitimacy the religious right still possessed among most Americans. On the left, the upsurge of patriotism, nationalism and renewed focus on the shared values and beliefs defining national American identity eclipsed the influence – perhaps vastly overstated anyway by its main academic proponents – of those who view the nation as essentially a collection of ethnic subgroups and hyphenated-Americans. Whether 9/11 represents merely a pause in America's steady 'disunit-ing' or the catalyst for a restoration of a sense of national unity unknown since the Cold War's apex is unclear. But by partially de-legitimizing both the most viscer-ally anti- and pro-government groups, a more tempered public life may yet emerge.

If domestic politics remains mostly familiar, however, two areas of foreign policy shifts are especially noteworthy. In each, however, 9/11's effect was less to induce than accelerate significant changes.

First, US defense expenditures – homeland and abroad – received a major boost. $36 billion dollars were added to the military budget of $328 billion for 2002 and $48 billion for 2003 (a 15 percent increase, the largest since 1981). Defense spending will double that of all the European Union nations combined and, over five years, add another $120 billion to a total defense outlay of approximately $1,700 billion. Bush also requested $38 billion for homeland secur-ity programs for 2003, twice the level of spending for 2002 in a category of expenditure that did not exist in 2001.

But these figures must be qualified. America accounted for almost 40 percent of global military expenditure from 1992–2001 and defense expenditures began to increase (albeit belatedly) under Clinton. At 3 percent of GDP and 16 percent of federal outlays, defense spending amounts to only 14 percent less than the average Cold War year in real terms.[20] Moreover, the additional $48 billion requested by Bush in 2002 is likely to yield only $6–9 billion in additional or new weapons, with the bulk of the monies going to retirement and health packages and other non-weapons requirements. Finally, the overall effect of the increases will likely sharpen rather than blunt civilian and military disagreements (intra- and inter-) on the urgency of national missile defense. Where Democrats tend to see 9/11 as proving its irrelevance, most Republicans view it as confirming the need for all possible defensive measures against those state and non-state actors with both the intentions and capabilities of terrorist attack.

The second major impact is military action, where the Afghanistan campaign reinforced the Bush administration's unilateralist tilt. But this is less a matter of an emboldened public than military necessities. I. M. Destler and Steven Kull have demonstrated the myth of the 'Vietnam syndrome.' Long prior to 9/11, the American public was far more tolerant of military losses than conventionally imagined, providing that the objectives of US operations were supported and their prospects of success were good. Even in instances where Americans disapproved of the operation – Lebanon in 1982, Somalia in 1992 – the public did not demand immediate withdrawals after suffering losses. Crucially, however, foreign policy decision-makers and journalists alike operated on the contrary assumption.[21]

Public attitudes have not substantially changed, then, but the Afghan war illus- trated the extent to which America no longer requires active allied support for military actions (except as bases, fly-over stops and for politically symbolic reasons). Although Powell assembled an impressive coalition, the allied contribu- tion to the Afghan war consisted in providing airbases, over-flight rights and special forces. The war was conducted overwhelmingly by Americans and Afghans. Drawing a central lesson from Kosovo – international friends are always desirable, sometimes necessary but frequently problematic in military terms – the administration waged war on its own terms with US personnel and weapons. With successful predator drone aircraft and targeted bombing (approximately 95 percent of bombs dropped in Afghanistan were precision, compared to 6 per- cent in Iraq in 1991), the war was a notable success for both the American military and US intelligence.[22]

The political difficulty for proponents of multilateralism is that perceptions of where unilateral action is necessary and feasible are now far more widespread within Washington than previously. That is, the Bush administration's pre-9/11 approach has garnered much broader support, to the extent that a 'Bush Doc- trine' of preemptive action against threats to US security (notionally framed with Iraq in mind for 2003 but theoretically applicable on a permanent global basis) had achieved widespread currency by the summer of 2002. With all EU nations bar the UK incapable (technically and logistically), much less politically willing, to deploy substantial forces abroad, operational realities as well as realpolitik strongly condition US policy. Much as the international anti-communist struggle led more through invitation than imposition to an expansion of US influence after 1947, so the war against terrorism has extended and expanded America's singular power. Unless diplomacy, aid and goodwill-building measures sufficiently appease terrorist groups targeting not only America but Europe – strategies that arguably promise few tangible results when faced not only by committed fanatics but broader Muslim and Arab opinion[23] – other nations will likely protest over unilateral action as they free ride on the security benefits of US military interventions.

CONCLUSION

US responses to 9/11 accorded with the Pearl Harbor precedent of a direct assault on American security and values. An administration well versed in histori- cal precedents, keenly aware of America's unprecedented and unmatched power, and instinctively inclined to the necessity and desirability of unilateral action in a unipolar world secured a rapid but partial victory in the first theater of its war on terror. As celebrations of 'the greatest generation' occupied American media attention in 2001, a new generation unaccustomed to mainland mass murder responded with overwhelming approval to the Bush administration's actions. The US response confirmed its international leadership, revived domestic solidarity and left the nation in an unprecedentedly powerful position with a renewed sense of global purpose.

Although the mass media and Hollywood abetted the creation of a wartime sensibility (regularly printing op-eds on the terrorist threat and releasing movies such as *The Sum of All Fears*), most features of domestic politics and foreign policy appeared more enduring than ephemeral in the wake of 9/11. Domestic politics was placed on a strikingly brief hold before familiar features resurfaced: the centrality of economic concerns to a post-industrial workforce in flux; the sharp- ness of partisan conflict between two parties whose electoral coalitions are more closely matched than at any time since the Second World War; and the intractable problems of coordination confronting a supremely fragmented governmental sys- tem. That trade promotion authority ('fast track') should pass by one vote in the House in December 2001 while Enron's collapse prompted Congress's General Accounting Office to sue the Bush administration in February 2002 – the first such occasion in American history – were only the most dramatic confirmations of politics as usual.

Nor did the remarkable success of the Republicans in the 2002 mid-term elec- tions obscure this reality. In regaining a narrow majority in the Senate and main- taining a narrow hold on the House, the elections restored undivided Republican control of the federal government and represented only the third time since 1902 that a president's party gained seats in a mid-term election. But domestic concerns rather than foreign ones dominated the election agenda and most of these races turned, as ever in elections to Congress, on local rather than national – much less international – issues. In particular, the electoral salience of a looming war with Iraq had been diminished when Bush secured bipartisan authorization from Congress for war in October 2002 to disarm its weapons of mass destruction. The Senate voted 77–23 and the House 296–133 to authorize the president 'to use the armed forces of the United States as he determines to be necessary and appropriate in order to defend the national security of the United States against the continuing threat posed by Iraq' (though most Democrats, as previously in 1991, nonetheless voted against authorizing war without a congressional declaration).

In legitimating Bush and easing – though not assuring – passage of his legislative agenda and judicial appointments for the 108th Congress (2003–4), the results nonetheless reflected and reinforced both the priority and preferences of the administration on foreign policy. The unanimous UN Security Council vote in favor of a new resolution on Iraq passed on 8 November, following the prior months' terrorist attacks on Bali and Moscow, augmented not only the administration's warnings on the gravity, scale and multifaceted nature of the threat of international terror but also reinforced the Bush administration's faith in 'pre-emptive' actions against state as well as non-state actors – through coalitions if possible but unilaterally if necessary. Ironically, almost thirty years after Arthur Schlesinger, Jr. had condemned the development of an 'imperial presidency' under Johnson and Nixon, both the enhanced legal authority of the president and the vast reach of American power abroad suggested that it had emerged in an especially potent form by 2003–4.

Implicit in many European responses to 9/11 was the notion that if Americans would only learn more of the Middle East, Islam and global politics, US foreign policy would alter in ways congenial to Europeans and others (the debate here is ultimately less one about excessive or insufficient internationalism but more whether US policies are the ones others favor – a unilateralist America dedicated to enforcing stronger environmental safeguards than Kyoto and dispensing foreign aid to Baghdad and Pyonyang would doubtless win plaudits in Brussels and Berlin). But there is as much reason to infer the opposite. 9/11 powerfully reconfirmed the Bush team's approach: military strength as a necessary but insufficient condition of assuring the national security of a unique nation, political system and people. Only when clear and present dangers from state and non-state actors alike appear decisively more muddied and distant is America's involvement in global affairs likely to be shaped by anything other than the primacy of its own security. For the USA, after saving Europe twice and successfully leading a worldwide anti-communist struggle, another global war is well underway.

NOTES

1 Stephen M. Walt, 'Beyond Bin Laden: Reshaping U.S. Foreign Policy', *International Security*, Vol. 26, No. 3, Winter 2001/02, pp. 56–78. Joseph Nye also asserted that American foreign policy had 'changed dramatically' in 'Seven Tests: Between Concert and Unilateralism', *The National Interest*, Winter 2001/02, pp. 5–13.
2 On the perils of 'real-time' commentaries by academics, see Richard A. Posner, *Public Intellectuals: A Study of Decline* (Cambridge, MA: Harvard University Press, 2001).
3 Paul Kennedy, 'The Eagle Has Landed', *Financial Times*, 2–3 Feb. 2002; Tim Hames, 'Arrogance, Ignorance and the Real New World Order', *The Times*, 15 Feb. 2002, p. 22.
4 Clive Christie, 'US Hate: A Designer Prejudice for Our Time', *The Times Higher Educational Supplement*, 18 Jan. 2002, p. 19.

5 See the summary of opinion survey data collated by the Program on International Policy Attitudes of the School of Public Affairs (PIPA), University of Maryland (http://www.americans-world.org/digest/global_issues/terrorism/terrorism_summary.cfm). Further opinion survey citations in this article are taken from this source.

6 Samuel Huntington, *American Politics: The Promise of Disharmony* (Cambridge, MA: Harvard University Press, 1981).

7 Michael Scott Doran, 'Somebody Else's Civil War: Ideology, Rage and the Assault on America', in James F. Hoge Jr. and Gideon Rose (eds.), *How Did This Happen? Terrorism and the New War* (Oxford: Public Affairs Ltd, 2001), pp. 31–52.

8 PIPA, ibid.

9 http://www.americans-world.org/digest/global_issues/terrorism/terrorism_summary.cfm

10 John Gray, 'Why Terrorism is Unbeatable', *New Statesman*, 25 Feb. 2002, pp. 50–3.

11 *CQ Weekly*, 12 Jan. 2002, p. 110.

12 *The Economist*, 2 March 2002, p. 52.

13 Edward Luttwak, 'Bush Will Go to War Even if It Puts Him Out of Power', *Sunday Times*, News Review, 17 Feb. 2002, p. 4.

14 Cited in William Schneider, 'Long on Character, Short on Details', *National Journal*, 2 Feb. 2002, p. 350.

15 Deborah L. Acomb, 'Poll Track', *National Journal*, 2 Feb. 2002, p. 325.

16 Acomb, 'Poll Track.'

17 H. W. Brands, *The Strange Death of American Liberalism* (New Haven, CT: Yale University Press, 2001).

18 Alan Wolfe, 'The Home Front', in Hoge and Rose, *How Did This Happen?*, pp. 283–94.

19 *Washington Post*, 29 Sept. 2001, p. A1.

20 Kennedy, 'The Eagle Has Landed'.

21 Steven Kull and Clay Ramsay, 'The Myth of the Reactive Public: American Public Attitudes on Military Fatalities in the Post-Cold War Period', chapter 9 in Philip Everts and Pierangelo Isernia (eds.), *Public Opinion and the International Use of Force* (London: Routledge, 2001); Steven Kull and I. M. Destler, *Misreading the Public: The Myth of a New Isolationism* (Washington, DC: Brookings Institution, 1999).

22 Christopher Andrew, 'How We Won the Spy Game', *The Times* (T2), 10 Dec. 2001, pp. 1–2.

23 Of those polled in six Islamic nations 61 percent stated that Arabs were not responsible for the 9/11 attacks. Andrea Stone, 'Many in the Islamic World Doubt Arabs Behind 9/11', *USA Today*, 27 Feb. 2002, p. 1.

5   Loyal ally

The United Kingdom[1]

Andrew Dorman

The devastating attacks on the World Trade Center and the Pentagon, followed
by the subsequent use of anthrax by an as yet unidentified person in the United
States of America, scares in the United Kingdom, and the subsequent war in
Afghanistan and Iraq have had a significant impact within Britain. At the
beginning of September few could have imagined that the British government
would send Royal Marine Commandos on combat operations in Afghanistan or
that Britain would again impose draconian anti-terrorist laws including detention
without trial. Yet these events have happened and September 11, like the death of
Princess Diana and the resignation of Margaret Thatcher, has become a date when
people remember exactly what they were doing when they heard of the attacks.

Yet, opinion within the United Kingdom has been divided, nowhere more so
than within the Muslim community. The majority of people, including those
within the Muslim community, was horrified by the scale of the attack and has
largely supported the government's line (with 74 percent in favor of bombing)[2].
However, there has been an increasing minority opposed to the British response
and a narrow majority against any attack on Iraq.[3] This has resulted in an
inflamed debate about Islam and citizenship.[4] Former Prime Minister Margaret
Thatcher wrote a suitably provocative article in the *Daily Telegraph* entitled
'Islamism is the new bolshevism.' Here she stated:

> The enemy is not, of course, a religion – most Muslims deplore what has
> occurred. Nor is it a single state, though this form of terrorism needs the
> support of states to give it succour. Perhaps the best parallel is with commu-
> nism. Islamic extremism today, like bolshevism in the past, is an armed
> doctrine. It is an aggressive ideology promoted by fanatical, well-armed
> devotees. And, like communism, it requires an all-embracing long-term
> strategy to defeat it.[5]

She went on to demand support from Britain's Muslim community for military
action. There have been equally strident views expressed by other statesmen and
women and tensions have risen between ethnic groups. Multicultural Britain will
not be the same again; although the way it develops post-September 11 is yet to be
fully established.

Similarly Britain has been at the forefront of the US-led response to the attack. Britain was the only other power to deploy forces on the first day of the military strikes on Afghanistan. Subsequently it became the lead power in the international security assistance force (ISAF) deployed in and around Kabul in January 2002. More recently it was to Britain that the United States government turned to supply reinforcements in the wake of Operation Anaconda. As a result, the British government announced the dispatch of 1,700 combat troops including 45 Royal Marine Commando.[6] The British government has also provided strong support for American government concern about Iraq's possession of weapons of mass destruction and provided military forces in support of the American military campaign against Iraq.[7]

Thus the impact of September 11 on Britain as a nation and as a key actor in the international community must be considered when the events of 9/11 are reviewed. To undertake this task this chapter examines the impact of 9/11 from a domestic perspective. It then considers the impact upon Britain's role within the international arena. A review of Britain's involvement in Afghanistan and a discussion of Britain's defense policy then follow.

DOMESTIC REACTION

Britain was one of over eighty countries to suffer casualties from the attack on the World Trade Center. Initial casualty estimates proved overly pessimistic, with fewer than a hundred British deaths, but this still represents the single greatest loss to Britain from a terrorist act. It is far more significant than the Omagh bombing or any other of the bombings in Northern Ireland.

From the beginning the government was clearly aware that the aftermath of September 11 would have a considerable impact on British society and that this needed to be managed. In an unprecedented step the British Prime Minister Tony Blair published on the government's website edited evidence linking al-Qaeda to 9/11.[8] Why was this so? The early establishment of British links to those who carried out the attacks raised a number of issues, such as how integrated multicultural Britain really was. References to Norman Tebbitt's infamous 'cricket test' of national loyalty were again prevalent and the government sought to counter these. For example early on Blair invited members of the various Muslim communities to No. 10 Downing Street for discussions.[9] Subsequently, when the war in Afghanistan began Blair again sought to divorce Islam from the actions of 9/11. In announcing the commencement of military action he stated:

> I wish to say finally, as I've said many times before, that this is not a war with Islam. It angers me, as it angers the vast majority of Muslims, to hear bin Laden and his associates described as Islamic terrorists. They are terrorists pure and simple. Islam is a peaceful and tolerant religion and the acts of these people are wholly contrary to the teachings of the Koran.[10]

In terms of domestic politics there was, not surprisingly, unanimity among the parties. For Iain Duncan Smith, the newly elected leader of the Conservative Party, the timing of the tragedy could not have been worse. The first thing he had to do, as leader of the Conservative Party, was to support the government. To achieve some degree of separation, he sought to take a more hawkish line than Blair. He called for a review of defense and supported the cause of missile defense. He also encouraged the view that the war should be broadened to include Iraq if there was 'compelling evidence' that Iraq was sponsoring or harboring terrorists.[11] As leader of the Liberal Democrats, Charles Kennedy's position was somewhat easier. He could provide support; yet take the moral high ground, holding the government to account over its response to 9/11. Blair has used Duncan Smith and Kennedy's position as Privy Counsellors to keep them updated and, thus by implication, supportive of government action. In releasing some of the information justifying the action in Afghanistan he made this link more overt; he stated:

> much of the evidence that we have is intelligence and highly sensitive. It is not possible without compromising people or security to release precise details and fresh information that is daily coming in, but I hope that the House will find it useful at least as an interim assessment. The Leader of the Opposition and the leader of the Liberal Democrats have seen the full basis for the document on Privy Council terms.[12]

However, the cross-party consensus was put under strain when the Secretary of State for Defense announced in the Commons the dispatch of 45 Royal Marine Commando to Afghanistan without giving acceptable prior warning to the Opposition parties.[13] Nevertheless, support for government action has remained consistent across the front benches. However, grass roots support in all three main parties remained staunchly against any escalation of the conflict to include Iraq, although all three front benches reserve judgment over this issue.[14]

In the Labour Party there was the greatest degree of internal division. There was always a small minority opposed to any military action and under Alan Simpson's leadership they formed 'Labour against the War.' It was noticeable from the start that Blair sought to emphasize a multi-tracked approach to the war in Afghanistan. He downplayed the military campaign, stressed that the military effort was against the al-Qaeda network and its Taliban supporters. Instead, he placed emphasis on an equal commitment to diplomatic and humanitarian efforts. Initially Blair referred to this as a three-pronged approach. However, Tony Blair's own rhetoric has become increasingly more hawkish and with less differentiation from the American view. The result has been that opposition within the Labour Party grew steadily and was clearly most evident in the November 2002 vote in the House of Commons over Iraq. Nevertheless, the initial multilateral line helped ensure that potential critics such as Clare Short remained committed to the Cabinet line. In announcing the commencement of military action on 7 October Tony Blair stated:

On the humanitarian front we are assembling a coalition of support for refugees in and outside Afghanistan, which is as vital as the military coalition. Even before September 11 four million Afghans were on the move. There are two million refugees to Pakistan and one and a half million in Iran. We have to act for humanitarian reasons to alleviate the appalling suffering of the Afghan people and deliver stability so that people from that region stay in that region.[15]

A number of Labour Members of Parliament spoke out during a defense debate in February 2002, as unease about American war aims grew.[16] Bush's quest to expand the war to include the 'axis of evil' has caused many on the left wing of the Labour Party to question their commitment to the party line especially once Secretary of State for Defence, Geoffrey Hoon, adopted similar language.[17] A split began emerging within the party and the preservation of party and Cabinet consensus in the long term appeared extremely doubtful. However, Britain's involvement in the conflict has ceased to be a major news story and other issues have come to the fore for the Cabinet.

As the government sought to deal with the implications of 9/11 four legal issues came to the fore within the wider public debate. First, with the imposition of a new Anti-terrorism, Crime and Security Bill.[18] Second, the issue of extraditing terrorist suspects to the United States. Third, what happens if British forces capture senior al-Qaeda suspects in Afghanistan; and fourth, British prisoners held at Camp X-Ray in Cuba. The initial government response was criticized for being too slow. It was not until 3 October that David Blunkett, the Home Secretary, announced that a new Anti-terrorism, Crime and Security Bill would be put before Parliament. This was to cover money laundering; powers for law enforcement agencies; widening the law to include offenses involving religious hatreds; amendments to the Immigration and Asylum Act to prevent the granting of asylum to those suspected or convicted of terrorist involvement; and complete overhaul of the extradition system.[19]

All these areas caused controversy and accusations that the government was panicking and rushing poorly thought-out and drafted legislation. The new bill was finally introduced on 12 November 2001, two months after the attacks, with the second reading scheduled for a week later. There was much concern expressed about the lack of time for proper parliamentary scrutiny and, in particular, how it related to the European Convention on Human Rights. One aspect in particular drew attention – the effective return of imprisonment without trial (internment), an area of law last dealt with in the 1970s as part of the British attempts to deal with the Provisional Irish Republican Army and thus an issue with a significant political legacy. The Opposition parties were also critical and the bill received a rough ride through Parliament with a number of amendments made. As a result, a number of people were taken into custody without being tried and one has since been released.

The potential extradition of terrorist suspects to the United States raised the issue of the death penalty within some American states. Christopher Meyer, then

British Ambassador to the United States, identified the problem succinctly: 'There is a common [European Union] policy against the death penalty, so I think any attempt to extradite to the United States somebody who might get the death penalty would cause some problems, and we'd have to work this through.'[20] This could therefore result in the failure to extradite suspects to the United States or the government's violation of the European Convention. Either option was a no-win situation for the government and involved some form of political compromise. To date there have been no extraditions, but the problem remains unresolved.

Less controversial in terms of domestic public opinion was the decision that if al-Qaeda suspects were captured in Afghanistan they would immediately be handed over to the Americans.[21] Far more controversial was the issue of British prisoners captured by the Americans in Afghanistan. This area caused a division with the United States administration. The British government, at least in private, would have preferred it if such prisoners were treated as prisoners of war and there was some feeling of discomfort at press coverage surrounding their treatment. Within the national press there were calls for British prisoners to be tried in the United Kingdom. Senior American officials hinted that this was one option. To date none has been returned and such an action would pose problems for the British government. If this had occurred before the adoption of the European Convention on Human Rights then a trial for treason could have led to the death penalty being invoked in the United Kingdom. However, this anomaly was removed from the statute book. The harshest a sentence could be is life. This would pose an interesting challenge to the government, particularly given the divisions within the Muslim community over the war.

The aftermath of 9/11 has had an impact in other areas. Concern has been expressed about the nature of some of the weapons used, with particular attention focused on the American use of cluster bombs. For example, only 51 percent of those polled in November 2001 believed that the use of such weapons was justified.[22] In a sense, this is one of Princess Diana's legacies and the government was forced to defend the American use of these weapons, despite the criticism it subsequently received from various aid agencies.

More long term will be the impact on American defense and how this relates to Britain. Even before 9/11 the Bush administration had already been pushing for the deployment of a national missile defense system.[23] After 9/11 the Bush administration pursued this issue far more and abrogated the Anti-Ballistic Missile Treaty with tacit Russian approval. As homeland defense receives increasing primacy within the USA, the Europeans will no longer be in a position to oppose it. To implement such a capability requires the use of facilities within the United Kingdom at Fylindales and Menwith Hill. The withholding of facilities would be a cause for major tension and one which a British government of whatever persuasion would be keen to avoid. Yet, within the Labour Party, there is a considerable minority strongly opposed to letting the Americans have access to these facilities particularly when such a defense system would not cover the United Kingdom.

9/11 has also had an impact upon the peace process within Northern Ireland. Sinn Fein saw its support within America crumble in the days that followed and has sought to address this by beginning the permanent decommissioning of some of its weapons.[24] International inspectors were able to confirm that some weapons had been permanently disabled and the government hopes that this process will continue. However, Northern Ireland has gone onto the backburner and further progress may be problematic as a result.

More recently the bombing of tourists in Bali, the twin attacks on Israeli targets in Kenya and the fears about a possible chemical or biological attack on the London Underground have reminded the population that the threat posed by terrorism remains. However, all these incidents were newsworthy for only short periods of time and it seems that only a direct attack on the United Kingdom is likely to change public perceptions.

FOREIGN SECURITY POLICY

Historians may conclude that 9/11 witnessed a rebirth of Britain's 'special rela-tionship' with the United States.[25] Commenting on 30 October, James Rubin, a former US Assistant Secretary of State during Clinton's second term, noted:

> What we have seen in these last two months is that the special relationship is not about personalities, it is about policy, and that regardless of who the Prime Minister would have preferred won the election or who is his best friend, the policies of our governments go down so deeply and are on such consonance at deep levels that personalities at the top are really not that relevant . . . Only this government was involved in the initial air strikes.[26]

It was noticeable that at President Bush's address to a Joint Session of Congress nine days after 9/11, it was the British Prime Minister who was the guest of honour and who was publicly thanked. Bush stated that: 'America has no truer friend than Great Britain.'[27]

Tony Blair set out his views on the appropriate response in the debate on international terrorism during Parliament's recall on 14 September. He identified three objectives. First, to bring those responsible for the attacks to justice. Second, to form a common alliance against terrorism and maintain solidarity in support of any action. Third, to rethink the scale and nature of the action the world takes to combat terrorism to make it more effective.[28] Blair promised the US adminis-tration not only strong political support, but also practical cooperation and mili-tary assistance. But before this could take place Blair helped to ensure that there was an appropriate legal case for subsequent actions. The US Ambassador to the United Nations notified the Security Council that they would respond under Article 51 – the right to self-defense. NATO also agreed to invoke Article 5 of the Washington Treaty in the immediate aftermath of the attack with the aim of restoring the security of the North Atlantic area.[29] Despite this agreement the US administration has chosen to build ad hoc coalitions with individual European nations rather than act through the alliance.

As part of the commitment to use military action, Tony Blair linked in the pledge not to abandon Afghanistan and thus to try to hold his own party, country and wider international community together. The pledge also linked into the more idealistic element of Labour's existing foreign policy and can be traced to an important speech Blair made in Chicago in April 1999 during NATO's fiftieth anniversary celebrations.[30] This also led to a divergence in the American–British agenda towards the end of October, as the war appeared to be coming to an end. The question of what would happen to Afghanistan loomed large and the American administration looked disinterested. Blair took the lead in arguing that Afghanistan should not be abandoned but that the international community needed to commit itself to nation building.[31] Britain, perhaps precipitously, deployed a small force from the Special Boat Squadron to take control of Bagram airfield outside Kabul as the forerunner of a much larger force. Following talks in Bonn convened by the United Nations, the British government offered to lead an international force with a UN mandate to provide security for Kabul and possibly elsewhere. Geoffrey Hoon, the Secretary of State for Defence, stated: 'I see every advantage of one country providing the main elements of headquarters of this operation – something the United Kingdom has done very well in the past.'[32]

According to the BBC, the army had suggested providing ground troops and setting up the headquarters for a force of up to 2,000 personnel.[33] However, the planned force was significantly scaled down and the interim government in Afghanistan was forced to accept it, but under a much more restricted mandate.[34] This marked a political upset for Blair's vision. The formation of the international force ran into further political difficulties. The British government's decision to form the force almost entirely out of European countries led the Prime Minister of Belgium to refer to it as a European Union force, much to Blair's embarrassment. Blair quickly issued a rebuttal. Subsequently, further embarrassment was caused by Turkish reluctance to take over as the lead nation for ISAF.[35]

Throughout the campaign the maintenance of the coalition was of primary importance. Consequently there were a number of British visits to Pakistan and the support of Musharraf's government was expressed to a far greater extent than before the conflict. As part of this process, No. 10 used the outgoing Chief of the Defence Staff, General Sir Charles Guthrie, as an important conduit. Guthrie had been a contemporary of Musharraf at the Royal College for Defence Studies and had already been sent to Pakistan when the military had taken control under Musharraf.

The possibility of extending the campaign emerged early in January 2002 when Bush referred to an 'axis of evil.'[36] From the beginning a number of hawks within the US administration argued in favor of dealing with the wider problem of terrorism by targeting states sponsoring terrorism, naming North Korea and Iraq. More recently attention has focused on Iraq, because of concerns about its possession of weapons of mass destruction and suspicion about its links to 9/11. Initially the Blair administration attempted to focus American attention purely on Afghanistan and was less willing to expand the campaign further. Foreign Office Minister Ben Bradshaw told the House of Commons that there was no evidence linking Iraq to 9/11.[37] However, this attitude has begun to change and there have been increasing hawkish statements from Tony Blair and from others within his government. Certainly the maintenance of the air exclusion zones in north and south Iraq have proven too costly, and many analysts have argued that it is only a matter of time before either Britain or America loses an aircraft. In an emergency debate called by the Conservative Opposition in March 2002 Hoon referred to an 'axis of concern' naming four threats: Iran, Iraq, Libya and North Korea.[38] This was a significant change in policy. It indicated a preparedness to extend the war on terrorism, despite the internal opposition within the Labour Party and the apparent opposition in the country. The deployment of 45 Royal Marine Commando marked a move towards a closer association with the Americans and the war-fighting side of the allied response. Thus, it was a move away from the nation-building humanitarian response of the previous autumn.

More recently there was close British involvement in the drafting and successful passage of Resolution 1441 by the United Nations Security Council and in the unsuccessful move towards a United Nations Security Council Resolution authorizing the use of force against Iraq. Ultimately this led to a direct British involvement in the coalition war on Iraq, with the British deploying some 45,000 service personnel and being actively involved in all elements of the war, most noticeably in the southern region of Iraq around Basra.

The other element of British foreign policy has been in its relationship with the rest of Europe. Before the conflict Blair had been strongly pushing for improvements in Europe's defense capabilities after the difficulties encountered during the Kosovo conflict.[39] In conjunction with the French he had pushed for the development of a European Rapid Reaction Force as part of a Common European Security and Defense Policy (CESDP). 9/11 has noticeably put this onto the political backburner and its future direction is the subject of some uncertainty. Blair has clearly become increasingly frustrated with the European response to the ramifications of 9/11, both in terms of the slowness of the response and its lack of substance. A good example of this was the delays in handing over Britain's responsibilities for ISAF. The result has been a marked shift since the turn of the year towards the American agenda and a more pragmatic, less idealistic, approach to CESDP.

BRITISH INVOLVEMENT IN THE WAR IN AFGHANISTAN

From the beginning Blair promised practical and military cooperation to the United States. Preparations for the British military response were made under the codename of Operation Veritas. The coincidental timing assisted these preparations with a major joint warfare exercise in Oman – Exercise Saif Sareea II (Swift Sword) that involved 20,000 service personnel beyond those normally deployed in the region. This greatly assisted the logistical aspects of Britain's preparations. It also allowed the United Kingdom to divert resources from the exercise relatively covertly and thus Britain's involvement initially went largely unseen apart from those areas which the government and/or the Bush administration wished to stress.

British and US military action was initially limited to air strikes and the use of Special Forces. Although Britain's capabilities in the former area were limited, it was particularly noticeable that Britain was the only other country which provided military forces to the United States on the first day, and was the only state with which America was prepared to work. Britain's involvement in the air campaign involved the provision of support aircraft, Tomahawk land attack missiles (TLAM) launched from Royal Navy submarines and the provision of the British base at Diego Garcia in the Indian Ocean as a forward base for operations. Britain lost the ability to conduct long-range air strikes when it phased out its last remaining Vulcan bombers in 1982 after the Falklands War. However, the support aircraft supplied provided important force multipliers to the American effort. For example the aircraft launched from the US aircraft carriers needed to receive additional fuel by mid-air refueling. The system used for this by the US Air Force was incompatible with that used by the US Navy and Britain was able to supply the requisite capability. Likewise, Britain supplied important reconnaissance and command and control aircraft to supplement the American capability. Of less military use, but politically important, was the use of British TLAMs. Britain's arsenal of these weapons was very limited but by also launching strikes Bush could claim that it was a coalition effort, rather than a solely American campaign. The provision of facilities at Diego Garcia was probably the most important asset. It provided a staging post for American bomber aircraft with B-52s and B-1Bs deployed to the base and B-2 Stealth bombers used it as a stopover before their flights home. Not surprisingly, information on the involvement of British Special Forces is sketchy. It is known that both Special Air Service and SBS units were deployed to the region. However, there remains relatively little information concerning their usage.

On 15 November, a 'reconnaissance' party of British troops was deployed to Bagram airport near Kabul. This proved to be a complete surprise for the local Northern Alliance commanders and a period of standoff resulted before agreement was reached in Berlin concerning the interim government arrangements.[40] Geoffrey Hoon formally offered British troops and headquarters on 5 December 2001 during a House of Commons debate.[41] Eventually, a British led ISAF was sent.

DEFENSE POLICY

The use of airliners to attack the World Trade Center was a clear example of what has become known as asymmetric warfare, which the US Defense Advanced Research Projects Agency (DARPA) defines as:

Warfare activities with fewer and less-easily specified objectives [usually involving] smaller numbers of actors and/or force participants, using unconventional tactics that often have high impact (political or material) relative to the force level involved.[42]

Within the Ministry of Defence, Geoffrey Hoon announced that a review of Britain's defense posture and plans would be undertaken[43] but that the basic tenets of the government's 1998 Strategic Defence Review (SDR)[44] remained valid. In other words the government wanted to adapt to the changing situation without being seen to have a follow-on review to SDR or giving significantly more resources to defense.

What this also amounted to was an open acknowledgement that SDR's assumption that, apart from domestic terrorism, there was no direct threat to the United Kingdom was wrong.[45] Hoon admitted that the large-scale reduction of the Territorial Army that formed part of SDR was a mistake and he was grateful that the cutbacks initially envisaged were not put through.[46]

To provide funding for the new defense tasks there have already been a number of defense cutbacks. For example, *HMS Fearless* the navy's only amphibious assault ship and headquarters for a brigade landing was scrapped nine months before its replacement became operational.[47] Likewise the Sea Harrier FA2s are to be phased out of service early and the number of RAF Harriers reduced and shared with the navy. Other cutbacks have included the decision to reduce the RAF's fighter strength while Coningsby is resurfaced, thereby reducing the RAF's ability to protect the UK's airspace against terrorist threats.

The degree to which defense policy will be adjusted has yet to be determined but if there is no significant increase in the defense budget, which seems likely, these changes will, at best, be marginal. So where is it likely to lead? Afghanistan, like Sierra Leone before it, has revealed the requirements for light infantry capable of rapid deployment. In both cases this has fallen upon the Royal Marines deployed offshore and the deployment of a Parachute battalion attached to 16 Air Assault Brigade. The SDR had resulted in the army increasing the size of its armored forces, at the expense of these light forces, and this will need to be reviewed.[48] The logical deduction is to reorder the balance between so-called heavy and light forces, but such a move would be deeply unpopular with the more traditional elements of the army.

The war in Afghanistan also raises questions about European moves towards the creation of its own rapid reaction forces. Britain has been at the heart of the EU's developing Common European Security and Defense Program (CESDP). Progress since the Helsinki Summit announcement in December 1999 has been slow and hesitant with Britain, in particular, becoming increasingly frustrated by foot-dragging. At the same time, NATO has increasingly become more of a political and less of a military alliance, particularly after 9/11. Discussions about further enlargement have proliferated and the US administration has indicated its willingness to include most of the northern hemisphere within NATO. Russia's inclusion in the 19+1 structure will potentially transform NATO's outlook and role. At the same time, whilst NATO invoked Article 5 immediately following 9/11, the coalition that the US administration sought to form involved bilateral discussions between the USA and individual European countries, rather than formally through NATO. The Blair government's attitude towards CESDP has, therefore, changed since 9/11 as it has sought to return to closer links with the US administration. This has been matched by the increasing frustration it has felt with its European allies. The delays and debates concerning the handover of the ISAF command are just the latest example of this. Frustration within the British government has mounted to the extent that CESDP may well go the way of previous European defense initiatives, with no real capability produced, and a political compromise agreed that bears no relationship to the initial requirements set out at Helsinki.

CONCLUSIONS

The full effect of the events of September 11 is yet to be determined as the war continues and threatens to escalate against some, or all, of the so-called 'axis of evil.' However, Britain will certainly not be the same again. Doubts that have been raised about a multicultural Britain may again resurface in the event of significant British military casualties. Everyday life has largely returned to normal; there remains a heightened state of security but the average citizen is relatively unaffected by this. There is also some debate about identity cards and civil rights. Nevertheless, 9/11 has become one of those definitive moments in British history.

More significant has been the effect on Britain's foreign and security policy. The previous pro-European agenda is likely to remain, except in the area of a Common European Security and Defense Policy – the area Britain sought to promote as part of its return to the heart of Europe. How Britain can remain at Europe's heart without it is an interesting issue. This may well help encourage the Blair government to attempt to adopt the single European currency. The crisis has also reaffirmed the 'special relationship' with the USA. 9/11 has helped take the personality issue out of the Blair–Bush partnership and given a greater British say in US decision-making. The flip side of this was the acceptance that should the USA decide to use military force against Iraq, Britain would support the USA and deploy its own forces, as happened.

Three issues remain outstanding. The first is how to continue the war on al-Qaeda and whether to remain in Afghanistan. The second revolves around the aftermath of the war with Iraq and questions of reconstruction. Finally, the question of when Britain itself suffers a successful attack remains. Overall, it can be seen that the ripples of 9/11 continue to spread and their final impact remains to be fully determined.

NOTES

1 The analysis, opinions and conclusions expressed or implied in this chapter are those of the author and do not necessarily represent the views of the Joint Services Command and Staff College (JSCSC), the UK Ministry of Defence or any other government agency.

2 Alan Travis, 'Special Report: Terrorism in the US', *The Guardian*, 18 Sept. 2001; Alan Travis, 'British Do Not See Islam as a Threat to Values', *The Guardian*, 12 Oct. 2001; David Miller, 'Blair Should Read the Polls', *The Guardian*, 3 Oct. 2001.

3 Alan Travis, 'Voters Say No to Iraq Attack', *The Guardian*, 19 March 2002; 'Operation *Enduring Freedom* and the Conflict in Afghanistan: An Update', *House of Commons Library Research Paper 01/81*, p. 87.

4 Euan Ferguson, 'Britain's Defiant Minority', *The Observer*, 7 Oct. 2001.

5 Margaret Thatcher, 'Islamism Is the New Bolshevism', *Daily Telegraph*, 12 Feb. 2002, p. 17.

6 'The Secretary of State for Defence's Statement to the Commons', 18 March 2002, www.mod.uk; Michael Evans and Damian Whitworth, 'Marines to Hunt Mullah Omar', *The Times*, 19 March 2002, p. 1; see House of Commons debate 20 March 2002 called by Conservative Party, www.parliament.gov.uk

7 Philip Webster and Damian Whitworth, 'Blair Urges US to Seek Allies', *The Times*, 11 March 2002, p. 1; Michael Evans, 'Britain May Send Brigades', *The Times*, 11 March 2002, p. 6.

8 'Responsibility for the Terrorist Atrocities in the United States, 11 September 2001', www.number-10.gov.uk

9 'Prime Minister's Meeting with Leaders of the Muslim Communities in Britain', 27 Sept. 2001, www.number-10.gov.uk

10 'Responsibility for the Terrorist Atrocities in the United States, 11 September 2001', www.number-10.gov.uk

11 *Financial Times*, 1 Dec. 2001.

12 House of Commons Debate, 4 Oct. 2001, col.673, www.parliament.gov.uk

13 Bernard Jenkin, House of Commons, 20 March 2002, www.parliament.gov.uk

14 Alan Travis, 'Voters Say No to Iraq Attack'

15 'Prime Minister's Statement on Military Action in Afghanistan', 7 Oct. 2001, www.number-10.gov.uk

16 Alice Miles, 'Blair Would Follow Bush to Baghdad, But Then What?' *The Times*, 6 March 2002, p. 22.

17 Geoffrey Hoon, House of Commons, 20 March 2001, www.parliament.gov.uk

18 See 'The *Anti-Terrorism, Crime and Security Bill*: Introduction and Summary', *House of Commons Research Paper 01/101*, www.parliament.gov.uk

19 Home Office Press Release 236/2001, www.home.gov.uk

20 *Los Angeles Times*, 30 Nov. 2001.

21 www.bbb.co.uk, 9 Dec. 2001.

22 Alan Travis, 'Small Majority in Favour of Bombing', *The Guardian*, 20 Nov. 2001; 'Operation *Enduring Freedom* and the Conflict in Afghanistan: An Update', *House of Commons Library Research Paper 01/81*, p. 23.

23 See www.acq.osd.mil/bmdo

24 'Decommissioning of IRA Weapons – Statement by Prime Minister Tony Blair', 24 Oct. 2001, www.number-10.gov.uk

25 House of Commons Foreign Affairs Select Committee, 'Second Report – British–US Relations', *HC.327*, session 2001–2, 2001, para.16, www.parliament.gov.uk; for a history of the special relationship see John Baylis (ed.) *Anglo-American Relations since 1939* (Manchester: Manchester University Press, 1997).

26 James Rubin, House of Commons Foreign Affairs Select Committee, 'Second Report

  – British–US Relations', op.cit., minutes of evidence 30 Oct. 2001, para. 1, www.parliament.gov.uk
27 George Bush, 'Address to a Joint Session of Congress and the American People', www.whitehouse.gov, 20 Sept. 2001.
28 House of Commons Debate, 14 Sept. 2001, cols. 605–6, www.parliament.gov.uk
29 NATO Press Release (2001) 124, 12 Sept. 2001, www.nato.int
30 Tony Blair, 'Doctrine of the International Community', Chicago, USA, 22 April 1999, www.fco.gov.uk/news/archive.asp
31 James Rubin, House of Commons Foreign Affairs Select Committee, 'Second Report – British–US Relations', op.cit., minutes of evidence 30 Oct. 2001, para. 3, www.parliament.gov.uk
32 Geoffrey Hoon, *Breakfast with Frost*, BBC Television, 9 Dec. 2001.
33 Tim Youngs, Paul Bowers and Mark Oates, 'The Campaign Against International Terrorism', *House of Commons Library Research Paper 01/112*, www.parliament.gov.uk, p. 30.
34 See www.operations.mod.uk/isafmta.doc
35 Amberin Zaman, 'Turks Urged to Take Control of Peace Force', *Daily Telegraph*, 20 March 2002, p. 4; Lale Sariibrahimoglu, 'Turkey Outlines Conditions for Taking Command of ISAF', *Jane's Defence Weekly*, 13 March 2002.
36 George Bush (Jr.), 'State of the Union Address', 29 Jan. 2002, www.whitehouse.gov
37 House of Commons Debates, 27 Nov. 2001, col. 821, www.parliament.gov.uk
38 George Jones and Anton La Guardia, 'UK Warns Saddam of Nuclear Retaliation', *Daily Telegraph*, 21 March 2002.
39 Ministry of Defence, 'Joint Declaration of the British and French Governments on European Defense', Anglo-French Summit, London, 25 Nov. 1999; Moving Forward European Defense, MOD Press Release No.421/99, 25 Nov. 1999; Michael Clarke, 'French and British Security: Mirror Images in a Globalized World', *International Affairs*, 76/4, 2000, pp. 725–39.
40 See www.mod.uk/veritas
41 House of Commons Debate, 5 Dec. 2001, cols. 324–5, www.parliament.gov.uk
42 *Jane's Intelligence Review*, Oct. 2001.
43 'Strategic Defense Review: A New Chapter', Public Discussion Paper, www.mod.uk
44 'The Strategic Defense Review', *Cm. 3999*, 1998, www.mod.uk
45 Bruce George, House of Commons Debate, 19 Oct. 1998, col. 991, www.parliament.gov.uk
46 Carey Schofield, 'Big Cut in TA Numbers Was a Mistake, Hoon Admits', *Daily Telegraph*, 20 Feb. 2002, p. 2.
47 Michael Evans, 'Navy's Oldest Warship Steams Off to Scrapheap', *The Times*, 8 March 2002.
48 Michael Evans, 'Foot-soldiers Steal a March on Elite Troops', *The Times*, 5 Dec. 2001, p. 8.

6 Reluctant moral middle power

Canada

Rick Fawn

9/11 and the war in Afghanistan forced at least four dilemmas onto Canadian official policy and popular views. The largest was the response of the Canadian government and Canadians generally to the attacks that compelled them to join the US-led war-fighting coalition in Afghanistan. This was a reluctant and ambiguous act that contrasted sharply with Canada's self-perception as a non-militaristic international humanitarian assistant. Second, Canada's military unpreparedness and reliance on the USA were underscored and acknowledged. A third concerned the Canadian ethos of multiculturalism and open immigration; after 9/11, these seemingly virtuous policies, so central to Canadian national and political identity, were refashioned by critics at home and abroad almost as aiding international terrorism, to the extent that some even asked if Canada could rightly be targeted by the USA in its war against countries that harbor terrorists. The final dilemma, which compounds the first three, concerns the lasting impact of American measures after September 11, foremost the creation of a North American security 'perimeter,' the implications of which extended across the spectrum of Canadian sovereignty, including the ability to exercise the country's own immigration policy, its own military defense and the management of the flow of economic goods across the world's longest undefended border and the globe's most voluminous trading routes.

REACTIONS TO 9/11

Expressions of Canadian national identity are frequently said to include complaining about, even lamenting, the country's dependence on the USA. Canadians generally seek to differentiate their cultural, political and social values and foreign policy from those of their superpower neighbor. But they also recognize the latter's importance to Canada and also enjoy the tremendous goodwill that exists between them. That the two peoples share the world's longest undefended border and enjoy the world's largest bilateral trading relationship is generally well known, and a source of pride. While Canadians often feel Americans know little of Canada, the similarities in cultural outlook, particularly between (but not only) English-speaking Canadians and Americans is considerable. Expressions of

Canadian respect, even love for the USA are shown in such ways as the singing of 'Irish Eyes' by Prime Minister Brian Mulroney and President Ronald Reagan or, perhaps even more elegantly, in such commemorative publications as the pictorial 'Between Friends' gifted by the Canadian government to the USA on the bicentennial of American independence.

The shock of Canadians at 9/11 was intensified by the closeness, both geographically and culturally, of the two countries; and Canadians responded in tangible expressions of sympathy. It was not just a function of location that Canadian airports immediately took in 224 planes flying within or to the USA; this was seen by the government and the population as an act of friendship. Friendship in need was shown by private Canadians near some of these airports housing the stranded American passengers, and these private measures have become part of the official record of the Canadian response.[1] In turn, Americans established scholarship funds as symbolic repayment.

The events had great security significance because of proximity; fears emerged that Canadian landmarks, such as Toronto's CN Tower, the world's tallest free-standing structure, might itself be targeted. The border between the two states was virtually seamless – casual cross-border shopping was commonplace, and Canadians traveled with ease to the USA with only a driver's license, if even that was requested.

The shock was also great because initial estimates stated that as many as eighty Canadians were killed in the Twin Towers, although at the end of October the Department of Foreign Affairs and International Trade revised the figure to twenty-five casualties, including those in the aircraft. Collective shock and grief were symbolized in memorial services across the country, and especially one attended by over 100,000 people from across the country on Parliament Hill in Ottawa.

Major political figures expressed outrage at the attacks and offered condolences to the US government and people. Official and public overtures were made to assist recovery efforts in Manhattan, including offers to send rescue teams, which were generally declined. A five-hour show on 23 September by leading Canadian musicians called 'Music without borders' raised donations for the New York Firefighters Relief Fund and the Red Cross.

Nevertheless, some statements suggested that American actions or behavior contributed to the attacks. Canadian philosopher John Ralston Saul – a social commentator whose familiarity increased when his wife became Governor-General of Canada and some of whose speeches appear on her official website – wrote in his post-September 11 book *On Equilibrium* 'For forty years now the West has led a rush to balance its trade figures by aggressively selling its armaments abroad. The world is awash in weaponry. You can trace the parallel rising lines of unstable areas slipping into violence as the quantity of weapons on the market increases.' He added, 'To act as if our actions do not have consequences is to pretend that we are without qualities and are naturally passive factors when faced by the actions of others.'[2] The Toronto branch of the Ontario Secondary School Teachers' Federation published an article in its December 2001 newsletter, meant as a teaching aid, entitled *Why America is Hated*.[3] The most remarkable statement came from Prime Minister Jean Chrétien on the first anniversary of the events. In an interview to the Canadian Broadcasting Corporation he explained 'you cannot exercise your powers to the point of humiliation for others.' This provoked furious replies throughout the Canadian media and an American military specialist wrote that Chrétien became 'the hands-down winner of the race to see which Western leaders can say the most shameful and ludicrous things about 9/11.'[4]

Such questioning or dissenting voices, while audible, were nevertheless few. Constructing a tangible response to the attacks, particularly militarily, nevertheless required prompting. *The Economist* magazine contended that no full Cabinet meeting to formulate a Canadian response to the attacks was called for a month, although a Canadian official retorted defensively to the contrary.[5] Regardless, as discussed below, Canadian military policy on Afghanistan appeared belated and deficient to many.

REACTION TO THE WAR IN AFGHANISTAN

Canadian armed forces in Afghanistan were put into a full combat role for the first time since the Korean War a half-century earlier, a mandate conducted under the auspices of the United Nations. Canadian forces, in the form of three naval vessels and twenty-four aircraft, were dispatched to the Gulf War in 1991, but ground troops did not see direct action or enter Iraqi territory. In the 1999 Kosovan war Canadian aircraft flew some missions, but, briefly stated, Canadian opinion was ambivalent about the use of Canadian forces even in an operation presented auspiciously as 'humanitarian warfare.' Canadian personnel, however, contributed to the KFOR, the internationally backed post-conflict peacekeeping operation.[6]

While 9/11 challenged policy-makers worldwide, for Canada the decision to commit troops to combat operations can be construed as a break with previous practice. Unlike British forces in Afghanistan that undertook separate fighting and peacekeeping missions, Canadian personnel were assigned to a combat role. Australian and Canadian foreign policy have often been bracketed together as examples of middle powers, quite apart from the seeming similarities of being predominantly European-settled dominions of former British colonies.[7] Canada presents itself as a peacekeeping nation,[8] and has had over 100,000 personnel serve in over seventy peacekeeping missions. Australia, which readily provided soldiers for Afghanistan, can more easily accept either a combat or peacekeeping role; its overseas history includes both war in Vietnam and the dispatch of armed troops for a humanitarian mission in East Timor.

That said, as part of Operation Apollo, three Canadian warships and 1,000 military personnel were sent to the Arabian Sea on 16 October 2001, and on 19 January 2002 Canada's commitment of additional troops for ground operations in Afghanistan raised its total commitment to about 3,000, making Canadian forces the fourth largest contingent of foreign forces in Afghanistan.

Rather than being an organic Canadian response, however, the decision to contribute combat troops to the US-led operations was in fulfillment of an American request. Perhaps illustrative of the ambiguity of Canadian views on accepting an outright war role was the qualification by Canadian Defense Minister Art Eggleton concerning Canadian military participation in Afghanistan that engendered considerable debate and even ridicule. He said troops would not go where they were not welcome. The Taliban regime and al-Qaeda – implicated by numerous governments in 9/11 – were hardly likely to 'welcome' Western forces, and the American and allied forces equally did not anticipate 'welcome.' Eggleton subsequently qualified his comments by saying that he was referring to what the Northern Alliance would want, but the statement still suggested a distinct reticence by Canadian decision-makers to put military forces in a hostile environment.[9] The disjuncture from the traditional Canadian role of impartial peacekeeper was evident.

Apart from this official ambiguity, opposition politicians ranged from welcoming war in Afghanistan to cautioning about the nature of targeting. On 7 October when the first attacks began, Stockwell Day, a leading right-wing figure and a radical in Canadian politics, effusively declared 'Now is the time to stand together. Today the civilized world struck back against barbarism.' Alexa McDonough, leader of the socialist New Democratic Party, urged restraint, warning 'Justice will not be served by bombing civilian targets such as power plants.' The mainstream press was positive about war: after the Afghan capital Kabul fell the editorial of the *National Post* was entitled 'Dancing in the streets,' and wrote that 'the U.S.-led war has been a resounding military triumph.'[10]

Once Canadian forces were fighting in Afghanistan, support seemed strong. Popular accounts presented by and reflected in mainstream media showed pride in Canadian military action in Afghanistan by the Edmonton-based 3rd Battalion, Princess Patricia's Canadian Light Infantry Group. As part of Operation Harpoon against Taliban and al-Qaeda resistance, Canadian press reported how 'Canadians find al-Qaeda bodies in blasted caves' and discovered and destroyed al-Qaeda weapons.[11] Other accounts wrote: 'Canada's ace snipers right in the thick of battle.'[12] Prominent columnist Richard Gwyn suggested, however, that Canada should return to a more traditional Canadian international role, what could be called 'international social work.' That would be, he continued:

> the best possible way of getting [Canada] noticed, and favourably, in Washington. Militarily, our troops are irrelevant to them. But if we help clean up some of their messes, perhaps even by skilled interventions, help to prevent some messes from starting, we'll be doing the kind of good they [Americans] are bad at. We'd be helping others and be helping the Yanks, and so be helping ourselves.[13]

Popular support for the war effort decreased when, on 18 April, an Air National Guard F-16 dropped, as the official account went, 'one or two' 500-pound bombs on Canadian forces participating in an exercise near Kandahar, killing four and wounding eight soldiers. Canada's Chief of Defense Staff Ray Henault said that to his knowledge the Canadian soldiers restricted their weapons fire to the ground and obeyed all rules of such exercises.[14] The blame appeared to rest entirely with the US pilot, who had received instructions to withhold fire. Canadian grief was exacerbated by reports released the same day by Canadian Press that a similar incident jeopardizing Canadian personnel was avoided by five minutes a month earlier. Some newspaper letters suggested that had Canadian forces killed Americans in error, Americans would have reacted with 'national outrage.'[15]

Anger grew not so much over the incident itself but due to the lack of a response to Canada by American officials, including especially the failure of President Bush to acknowledge it and apologize. Two days later Joint Chiefs of Staff Chairman Richard Myers said the accidental bombing 'was right up there with the worst news I've heard in my career.' An informal web poll by the leading intellectual newspaper *Globe and Mail* asking if Bush 'acted with indifference to the loss of four Canadian soldiers' found 71 percent of respondents in the affirmative.[16] The paper also wrote of the missed opportunities Bush had to make an apology, and of how he showed 'quick dismissiveness' when finally pressed by a Canadian journalist. Even Canadian Deputy Prime Minister John Manley was interpreted as 'implying that the Canadian government felt snubbed' when he stated 'Undoubtedly, it would have been of comfort to the families [of the dead and injured] to hear the President's own words through the media.' The lack of prompt response by Bush was seen to have 'ended up embarrassing' him in Canadian eyes.[17]

Chrétien later told Parliament that Bush had assured him of his cooperation in an investigation into the bombing that had already begun. Joe Clark, a former primer minister and leader of the small opposition Progressive Conservative Party, said that the investigation needed to determine whether the US command of Canadian forces alongside their own was responsible for the tragic outcome.

While Major Jamie Robertson, spokesman for the Canadian Joint Task Force Southwest Asia, admitted, 'This is a nightmare – it is the worst-case scenario when you have fratricide,' Henault said that Canadian forces would continue operations in Afghanistan.

MILITARY UNPREPAREDNESS

Concerns, as in many countries, were made in the media of Canada's lack of preparation for bio-terror. No Western government was prepared for a widespread chemical or biological attack on its population, or indeed of the need to fight a major campaign in such conditions; but this new consideration placed added strain on the ability of the Canadian armed forces to contribute to the Afghan war. Throughout the Cold War Canada had one of the lowest defense-spending rates of NATO countries, and was the second lowest defense-spending member of NATO at the time of the Afghan campaign. The popular expectations for higher defense spending were largely absent, especially with the end of the military posturing of the Cold War.

The cost of the war effort impacted directly upon the ability of Canadian peacekeeping commitments, with plans announced as a consequence to limit operations in the Balkans, and subsequently to use reservists in Bosnia 'to relieve pressure on Canada's over-stretched regular forces.'[18] The armed forces even lacked appropriate uniforms for Afghanistan.[19] The overall cost of the war meant that Finance Minister Paul Martin, committed for years to eliminating Canada's bloated public deficit, said that the federal budget lacked sufficient funds and that new security costs had to be passed onto the public and that no further payments could be made on the national debt of C$547.5 billion.[20]

The significance of the Canadian contribution to the war as a break from the national perception of being a peace-bearing nation was overshadowed by the physical and financial exertion it became. The inability of Canada to sustain its military commitments was only a foretaste of the larger, more profound question of whether Canada could retain sovereignty in the face of the new threats that 9/11 presented to the security of continental USA.

MULTI-ETHNICITY, ACCESS TO CANADA AND NORTH AMERICAN SECURITY

The Canadian government and many Canadians are proud of the country's perceived distinct national identity from the USA, one that includes measures to preserve cultural and political sovereignty as well as a similar but still distinctive foreign policy. Some in Canada began to question collective Muslim identities and intentions after the attacks. A letter to the editor in The *National Post* asked:

> How long, I wonder, will we have to wait for the Muslim leaders of Canada and the United States to come out publicly and condemn the events of Sept. 11 by Osama bin Laden and his al-Qaeda network? They keep saying . . . they need proof. Isn't a confession proof enough? What more do they need? It would appear they are more afraid of offending bin Laden than they are of the truth. I wait with bated breath for their condemnation.[21]

Southam Newspapers asked in an unattributed circulated column that coincided with the Organization of the Islamic Conference meeting in Malaysia in late March 2002: 'Why can't some Muslims agree that killing innocent non-Muslims is unacceptable?' It then quoted Samuel Huntington: 'Wherever one looks along the perimeter of Islam, Muslims have problems living peaceably with their neighbors.' The editorial referred to the 'barbaric standards of the Arab Middle East.'[22] Another editorial in November 2002 noted how the Canadian government refused at that time to outlaw Hizbollah and Hamas and instead of denouncing terrorism, Canadian Cabinet ministers 'give touchy-feely sermons on racial tolerance.'[23] Government support for multiculturalism extended to successful lobbying to have the American government exempt Canadian passport-holders from the new American program of fingerprinting and photographing men of Middle Eastern origin entering the USA.

Popular impressions of Islam and their impact on the Canadian ethos of tolerance and multi-ethnicity aside, the primary long-term effect of 9/11 on the USA – and therefore on Canada – is the provision of 'homeland security.' The practical extension of this is a 'perimeter defense' for North America. Those measures are inevitable for reasons to be mentioned, but they present immense challenges to Canadian sovereignty.

Canada has been seen as a risk to the USA. The official practice of Canadian multiculturalism makes Canada at least as, if not even more, welcoming than the USA to ethnic groups. The porous US–Canadian border allows Canadian residents to gain easy access to the USA. American concern over this vulnerability included in the 1980s fears that Libyan-sponsored assassins of Ronald Reagan would enter the USA from Canada. More recently, and related to the operations of al-Qaeda, Algerian-born Ahmed Ressam, the intended bomber of Los Angeles airport on the eve of the millennium, left for his mission from Canada and only by chance aroused the suspicion of a US Customs officer. Al-Qaeda members have been suspected of operations in Canada; Ressam's Montreal flat contained maps with airports circled.[24] Commentator Gwyn wrote: 'our principle national security concern has now become that of doing everything we can think of to reassure Americans that we are not endangering *their* national security by being too lax, or too generous, about whom we allow into Canada.'[25] American pressure would be for even greater measures to stem the risks of infiltration or attacks against the USA emanating from Canada.

Perimeter defense: Fortress North America and Canadian sovereignty

The perceived danger of access by terrorists to the USA through Canada prompted the US government to seek measures to make secure all of the North American landmass, including Canada. The immediate media expectation was that the Canadian government could not resist American demands. Wrote the large-circulation *Toronto Star*: 'What can [Prime Minister Chrétien] say when the United States begins a concerted push for a continental security perimeter – a Fortress North America? The almost universal answer is that he can't say "No".'[26] But 53 percent of Canadians polled by EKOS Research after 9/11 accepted the idea of a North American perimeter, 'even if' the survey asked, 'it means we must effectively accept American security and immigration policies.'[27] Perhaps both the government and public opinion were acquiescing to the inevitable. The idea of 'Fortress North America' coalesced around preparations for a 'Smart Border,' negotiations for which began 12 December 2001.

The need to ensure the flow of goods across the mutual border was of central importance to Canada. Of the country's exports 87 percent go to the USA, overwhelmingly overland. As a result of the attacks this unparalleled physical flow of goods was halted, with enormous tailbacks of cargo on roads and railways. Sympathetic to the Canadian plight, Michigan Governor John Engler admitted 'things really ground to a halt' after the attacks, and that American trade with Canada was more important than that with Europe and Latin America together.[28] Canada's national newsmagazine observed 'The longest undefended border in the world is under siege.'[29]

Canadian authorities introduced new measures to expedite trade flows, such as the 'Customs Self-Assessment' that started experimentally in April 2002. An American proposal to station armed US Customs officers in Canada prompted Canadian concerns and 'bogged down' the discussions.[30] The perimeter defense preparations extended further than measures to check cross-border cargo and travel, with formal discussions turning to combined military planning. Such measures need to be contextualized by existing US–Canadian defense cooperation – the command of Canadian airspace for security purposes is already held through the North American Air Defense Command (NORAD) agreement, which also has a Canadian as its deputy commander. Coordination of naval operations in Canadian coastal waters is done at NATO headquarters at Norfolk, Virginia.

Nevertheless, popular perceptions in Canada after 9/11 felt that, as a leading newspaper summarized: 'Canada remains an afterthought in defense planning.'[31] Responding to a report commissioned by former Foreign Affairs Minister Lloyd Axworthy which warned that Canadian sovereignty was threatened by US plans for integrated defense, Defense Minister Eggleton replied that the proposed Northern Command was an internal command structure for the US military and that NORAD would 'maintain its high status as a bi-national command.' But Eggleton also said that the Commander-in-Chief of NORAD – always an American – would also be that of Northern Command,[32] a comment unlikely to reassure those concerned with retaining greater Canadian military autonomy.

Few Canadians believe that Canada can defend its expansive airspace and long coastline alone. But Canada's inability to defend itself to any degree makes it entirely reliant on or vulnerable to American defense planning, a threat to sovereignty that received front-page newspaper coverage. Canada's pre-eminent military historian J. L. Granatstein warned in a report issued in June 2002 that 'although terrorism poses a real threat, it is not the most serious crisis.' Instead, he cautioned, 'the danger lies in wearing blinkers about the United States at a time it is in a vengeful, anxious mood' and that 'the Chrétien government seems either oblivious to the danger or else has given up.'[33]

The impending loss of Canadian control over defense and security was further summarized by editorialist Gwyn, who wrote: 'The new geopolitical problem' for Canada was now that 'whichever way the Americans go, we will go too. In the process we could lose our national way.' This implies at least the loss of defense planning or even the integration of Canadian military forces into the American armed services under the proposed North American 'homeland' defense command.[34]

CONCLUSION

While the Canadian government felt and responded to an American obligation to commit troops to the coalition war effort, this represented a departure in Canadian foreign and defense policy. Rather than being an impartial peacekeeper and purveyor of international humanitarian assistance, Canadian troops were in combat. While the justice of that cause was questioned only at the margins of society and otherwise supported throughout the political spectrum, support was dented by American friendly fire and by the realization of the limitations of Canadian military ability, including consequently its capacity to maintain the more typical role as a peacekeeping state.

More important, however, is a constituting element of Canadian national identity – the tremendous influence of the USA over Canada. The American countermeasures to 9/11 will almost certainly hasten Canadian integration into North American-wide security measures. The deep interdependence between Canada with the United States ensures it has little choice. Canadian official reactions to 9/11 could be found to be ambiguous; once adopted, those policies then lacked the physical means to be implemented fully. While Canada was spared direct attack on 9/11, the October 2002 audiotape believed to have been recorded by bin Laden named Canada as one of six countries specifically targeted by al-Qaeda. The Canadian government therefore seems even less likely to be able to avoid making difficult decisions relating to 9/11. Most specifically, the aftermath of 9/11 will have an enormous impact on Canada's economic and security relations with the USA, and thus on Canadian sovereignty.

NOTES

1 These acts are cited in official Canadian government publications on the Canadian response to 9/11. See, for example, 'Canada's Actions Against Terrorism Since September 11th', http://www.dfait-maeci.gc.ca/can-am/~docs/inactive/0003f7.1.–1.htm

2 John Ralston Saul, *On Equilibrium* (Toronto: Penguin (Canada), 2001), p. 321. He also writes that in response to terrorism, 'Concrete action is always necessary. Guilty individuals must be dealt with appropriately' (p. 320).

3 Heather Sokoloff, 'Anti-American Article Decried by School Board', *National Post*, 13 Dec. 2001.

4 Tom Nichols, 'Chrétien's State of Denial is Dangerous', *National Post*, 25 Sept. 2002, p. A22. Nichols is Chairman of the Department of Strategy and Policy at the US Naval War College but wrote in a personal capacity. Chrétien's comments were reported in major media.

5 *The Economist* claimed no full Cabinet meeting was held regarding 9/11 until 10 October. Françoise Ducros, Director of Communications in the Office of the Prime Minister, replied that one was held on 18 September and weekly thereafter. 'A New Face to the Fore' and 'Canada's Response to Terror', *The Economist*, 11 and 18 Oct. 2001. Ducros resigned in December 2002 after referring to President Bush as a 'moron' in earshot of journalists at the Prague NATO Summit the month before.

6 See Kim Richard Nossal and Stéphane Roussel, 'Canada and the Kosovo War: The Happy Follower', in Pierre Martin and Mark R. Brawley (eds.), *Alliance Politics*,

Kosovo, and NATO's War: Allied Force or Forced Allies? (New York: Palgrave, 2000), pp. 181–99.

7 For comparison of Canada and Australia as 'middle powers', see Andrew Fenton Cooper, Richard A. Higgott and Kim Richard Nossal, *Relocating Middle Powers: Australia and Canada in a Changing World Order* (Vancouver: University of British Columbia Press, 1993) and John Ravenhill, 'Cycles of Middle Power Activism: Constraint and Choice in Australian and Canadian Foreign Policies', *Australian Journal of International Affairs*, Vol. 52, No. 3, November 1998, pp. 309–27.

8 Even an editorial that called for more military action by Canadian forces wrote 'it is true that we are traditionally peacekeepers, a role that should remain our primary focus.' 'Our Soldiers Showed Grace under Fire', *Toronto Star*, 27 July 2002.

9 In an official document, he explained:

> the comment that we would not send our forces to Afghanistan if they were not welcome has been misconstrued. It would be absurd to deploy a stabilization force to Afghanistan if the Northern Alliance – which is working closely with our coalition and controls the territory in question – has made it clear that they do not want or need foreign troops for that purpose. While this may change in the future, it certainly would not advance our overall aims and objectives to deploy a stabilization force in the current context.
>
> 'Canada Continues to Act Responsibly and with Conviction in the Campaign Against Terrorism' (Ottawa, Ontario), 29 Nov., 2001 at http://www.dnd.ca/eng/archive/speeches/2001/nov01/29nov01terrorism_s_e.htm

10 *National Post*, 14 Nov. 2001.
11 Stephen Thorne, 'Canadians Find Al-Qaeda Bodies in Blasted Cave', *National Post*, 16 March 2002, p. A15.
12 *Toronto Star*, 9 March 2002, p. A26.
13 Richard Gwyn, 'A Role for Canada in a Changed World', *Toronto Star*, 13 Feb. 2002.
14 See, for example, the coverage in William Walker and Allan Thompson, 'How Could this Happen?', *Toronto Star*, 19 April 2002.
15 Online response by Catherine Taylor of Edmonton, to 'What's Your Reaction to the Deaths of Canadian Soldiers in Afghanistan?', globeandmail.com, posted 18 April 2002.
16 http://www.globeandmail.com/servlet/ GIS . . . dated 20 April 2002.
17 John Ibbitson, 'Never Having to Say You're Sorry', *Globe and Mail*, 22 April 2002.
18 Jon Bricker, 'Part-timers Off to Bosnia to Keep Peace', *National Post*, 25 Sept. 2002, p. A1.
19 In May 2002 it was announced that desert uniforms would be ready by 17 June. Troops meanwhile spattered the wrong uniforms with tan paint. 'Desert Camouflage Ready for Soliders Next Month', *National Post*, 18 May 2002.
20 Robert Fife and Allan Toulin, 'My Budget Has No Fat, Martin Says', *National Post*, 13 Dec. 2001, p. A6.
21 L. A. Bourne, in Letters section, *National Post*, 14 Nov. 2001.
22 Southam Newspapers, 'Arafat's Apocalyptic Creed', *National Post*, 2 April 2002.
23 'Osama's List', *National Post*, 14 Nov. 2002, p. A15.
24 *USA v. Mokhtar Haouari*, S4 00 Cr. 15 (SDNY), Testimony of Ahmed Ressam, 3 July 2001, cited in Peter L. Berge, *Holy Terror, Inc.: Inside the Secret World of Osama bin Laden* (London: Weidenfeld & Nicolson, 2001), p. 152.
25 Richard Gwyn, 'U.S. and Them', *Toronto Star*, 29 Dec. 2001.
26 Tim Harper, 'Tightening the Canada–U.S. Border', *Toronto Star*, 8 Oct. 2001.
27 Cited in Ibid.
28 'U.S. Customs Plans to Clear Bottlenecks', *Toronto Star*, 17 April 2002.

29 Mary Janigan, 'An Open Border?: The Post-Terror Crackdown Intensifies Calls for a U.S.–Canada Perimeter', *Maclean's*, 24 Sept. 2001.
30 Sheldon Alberts, 'Accord Called Step towards North American Perimeter', *National Post*, 13 Dec. 2001, p. A6.
31 See the article of the same name by Hugh Winsor, *Globe and Mail*, 22 April 2002.
32 Graham Fraser, 'Military Merger Not on the Table, Eggleton Says', *Toronto Star*, 27 April 2002.
33 Quoted in Chris Wattie, 'Canada "All But Undefended": Study', *National Post*, 11 June 2002.
34 Richard Gwyn, 'A Role for Canada in a Changed World', *Toronto Star*, 13 Feb. 2002.

7 Support from a bicephalous executive

France

Richard McAllister

This chapter considers the responses of the President, parties and public opinion in France to the events of September 11 and their aftermath. It argues that there was little initial visceral anti-Americanism and little *Schadenfreude*. However, after almost universal expressions of horror and sympathy, across the political spectrum came pleas to 'learn lessons' about the balance of US foreign policy; not to deny 'linkages' to the Middle East; and not to engage in precipitate or disproportionate knee-jerk military responses. That in turn was then balanced by the willingness of most policy-makers to see French involvement on the ground and in the air, in and around Afghanistan. Within French society, tension was evident within the Muslim and the Jewish communities, as well as between them. But it does not appear that views about September 11, the USA and the Afghan war were a major factor in the performance of (anti-American) Jean-Marie Le Pen in the April–May 2002 presidential elections: more troubling to some French voters and many French politicians in 2002, was the Bush administration's 'axis of evil' approach and the prospect of American action against Iraq.

DOMESTIC POLITICAL CONTEXT AND INITIAL REACTIONS

On 13 September, President Chirac, Prime Minister Lionel Jospin and many leading figures attended an ecumenical service in the American Church in Paris. Interior Minister Daniel Vaillant held talks with leaders of the various faiths. At midday on 14 September, much of France was fully involved in the Europe-wide three minutes' silence.

It was noticeable that the traditional semi-automatic reservations to anything American, particularly on the 'intellectual Left' in France, were *initially* to a large degree absent. In *Le Monde*, J-M Colombani's 12 September article was headlined 'We are all Americans'; and *Libération* spoke of strong punishment for those culpable. The mood changed: by spring 2002, many in the French media were expressing concern about the conduct and values of the American '*hyperpuissance.*'

Most public utterances by party leaders began by expressing 'solidarity with the American people.' What then differentiated them was how, and how far, they then went on to add 'however . . .': either to plead that the events should be understood in a wider context in which US foreign policy was itself in question; or to argue against 'precipitate' or 'inappropriate' military response. As *Le Monde* put it, 'both Right and Left reject unconditional support for US actions.'[1]

Domestic context was clearly important: in the pre-election period at the end of the longest *cohabitation* (1997–2002), tensions between gaullist President Chirac and socialist Prime Minister Jospin and his Cabinet were likely to emerge. Yet equally striking was the determination of the French authorities to be seen to be willing to play – within their capacities (an important qualification) – an 'appropriate' military role once operations began in Afghanistan. What caused more furore in the relations of the 'bicephalous executive' than this crisis were the revelations, in October, of tension in the relationship of President and Prime Minister, in the book by the Prime Minister's chief of staff Olivier Schrameck.[2]

There was nonetheless a strange evolution to the relationship between the President on the one hand and Prime Minister and government on the other. Initial sympathy and 'solidarity' with President Bush was obvious; there followed a period in which it seemed each might try to use the situation for their own (electoral) advantage; this in turn was succeeded by a realization that, given the divisions *within* left *and* right, the limitations of French power-projection and US coolness, there was not much to be gained in so doing. At this point (late October), the political class as a whole seemed to settle for 'gesture politics,' combined with a degree of hand-wringing and introspection; and, in particular, slightly envious comparison of the country's role and stance with that attributed to the UK in particular.

President Chirac, hearing the news while on a visit to Rennes, immediately spoke of his 'immense shock,' saying that all the French stood at the side of the American people. He returned to Paris, announcing on the same day the activation of the '*Vigipirate*' security plan; he held urgent talks with the prime minister, foreign, defense, interior and transport ministers.[3] Foreign Minister Védrine, the same day, announced that a crisis unit had already been set up at the Quai d'Orsay. A week later, Chirac flew to Washington for talks with President Bush: the first foreign leader to be so received.

But on 13 September, Chirac gave an interview to CNN. He cited an opinion poll just published, showing that '96 percent of the French people feel total solidarity with the American people . . . I never remember there being such unanimity.'[4] He had, he said, confirmed to Bush that France would join in invoking Article 5 of the NATO Treaty. Reminded of France's role in the Gulf War and Bosnia coalitions, he repeated that France would be at the America's side 'when it comes . . . to punishment for this murderous folly': which did not prevent Defense Minister Alain Richard from reminding listeners that though military action was one means, 'there were others.' Védrine, however, said that the entire world recognized that President Bush was justified in 'legitimate defense': the wording of the Security Council resolution just passed. Asked if the Americans' use of the term 'war' was justified, he replied: 'Even if it's a war unlike any other . . . I don't see what other word one could use.'[5]

Chirac did not immediately summon Parliament: it seemed, as *L'Express* commented, that the 'political chess-board favored a one-man show,' and Chirac's high profile, and acquaintance with the Bush 'clan,' also served to help extricate him from the domestic *scandales* that had mired him.[6]

There was initially near unanimity among the leaderships of the political parties; but less accord between leaders and their 'own' militants. Themes that recurred often as the left debated in mid-September were the 'lessons' of the Gulf War, and the avoidance of a 'clash of civilizations' approach. Even the French Communist Party (PCF) leader, Robert Hue, dropped his traditional anti-Americanism, though he also warned against 'clash of civilisations' simplicities.[7] But journalists soon noted 'some signs of embarrassment' both on the radical left and within the governmental 'plural majority' too, where thoughts went back to the schisms caused by the 1991 Gulf War. Much the same alignments were apparent as then: within the 'governmental plural majority,' J-P Chevènement's *Mouvement des Citoyens* (MDC) and the Greens (*les Verts*) were much more cautious than most of the Socialist Party (PS). Chevènement had resigned over the Gulf War. For *les Verts*, Noel Mamère declared that bin Laden was 'a monster'; though one to whom American foreign policy had given birth. 'The reality is that American foreign and military policy were bound to give rise to forms of terrorism such as we've seen.'[8] Almost hostile was the far-left paper *Lutte ouvrière*: 'You can't unleash wars in the four corners of the world without them catching up with you some day.'[9]

On the right, the predominant line was 'solidarity but no western Crusade.' *Rassemblement pour la République* (RPR) President Michèle Alliot-Marie said she would 'not be shocked' if France helped US reprisals; but France should not assist the 'terrorists' logic' – to create a sort of world war between Islam and the West. Alain Madelin, President of Liberal Democracy (DL), urged that there be none of the subtle equivocations so 'traditional' in such debates in France: total support for the USA was needed.

There was soon discord on the extreme right, caught between Le Pen's *Front National* (FN) denunciation of US 'imperialism' – in language uncannily echoing that of *Lutte ouvrière* and adding for good measure, 'France is not an American protectorate,'[10] whilst taking care to avoid verbal 'slips' about Islam – and Bruno Mégret's *Mouvement National* (MNR) evocation of 'the rise of Islamic extremism' (*islamisme*) and of Islam itself: 'We must stop helping Islam to establish itself on our territory, stop the proliferation of mosques,' he wrote.[11] Mégret managed to stir the pot more when, a few days later, the catastrophic explosion at the AZT factory in Toulouse left some thirty dead and hundreds injured: 'It wasn't an accident but an Islamist attack,' he was reported as saying.[12]

Equally clear was that both right and left refused to give *unconditional* backing to the USA. Alain Juppé (RPR) spoke of treating the 'deep causes of the evil'; and François Hollande (PS First Secretary) wanted France to maintain its 'singularity': 'as for precipitate decisions, or words like "crusade", we should retain our French identity.'[13] And Roland Dumas, foreign minister at the time of the Gulf War, wrote that the attacks on the USA were 'because of the support they bring to the state of Israel' and that common sense demanded that 'one can't separate off this aggression [against the USA] . . . from the situation in the Near East.'[14] These expressions of dissent or of criticism had many roots: *Le Monde*'s correspondent Raphaelle Bacqué specified 'anti-American feeling, still a live force in France'; the scars of division from the Gulf War; anti-globalization; France's historic links with the Arab world; and its large Muslim community. All told, there was a fairly clear 'step back' from the 'we are all Americans' proclaimed and supported only a week earlier.

But would the events be marked by friction or by relative 'solidarity' between the cohabitants? In early October, it was clear that RPR Deputies were 'spoiling for a fight with [Prime Minister] Jospin,' wanting a debate, culminating in a vote as specified in Article 49.1 of the Constitution, on France's backing for the USA; believing that they could show up the 'rainbow majority's' disunity and their own (rare and relative) unity. Chirac had to restrain them. The President warned his troops that nothing was to be gained by gunning for an already 'edgy' Prime Minister who would simply take cover behind Chirac as Head of State: this would just damage France's diplomatic standing.[15]

In the light of this, Jospin's speech at the opening of the annual session of the *IHEDN (Institut des Hautes Études de Défense Nationale)* in Paris on 24 September assumed added significance. He hardly needed to remind that audience that 'the Americans fought with us in the blackest hours in our history'; but France would begin 'at home' (*Vigipirate*) her part in the battle against terrorism; he moved on to the EU dimension and the UN. NATO as such hardly got a mention. The 'no clash of civilizations/crusade' mantra did. Direct military action, he said, would have to be 'proportionate, strategically and militarily justified, and politically coherent . . . The corollary of solidarity . . . is consultation . . . *If* [emphasis added] French forces were to participate . . . Parliament would be consulted and regularly informed . . . as was the case throughout the Kosovo conflict.'[16] This was about as non-commital as possible, and meant to be.

PRESS AND MEDIA COMMENTARY

Immediately after 9/11, the broadsheet press was quick to print appeals to calm and to reason, and appeals against the engendering of hatred based on origin or religion. Sympathy in most of the press did not extend however to 'fall[ing] into the trap of a manicheism dear to those protestant sects who built America,' editorialized *Le Monde*.[17] This was not some 'titanic struggle between Good and Evil,' nor 'clash of civilizations': and one must not demonize a billion Muslims. Targeting the perpetrators, cooperation with others in a protracted struggle, should be the way. Correspondents were sometimes harsher, using such phrases as 'the arrogance of imperial power.'[18] *Le Monde*, however, for a week beginning with its 18 September edition, published a page each day in English straight from the *New York Times*.

Claude Imbert in the liberal *Le Point* editorialized that the shock waves from

9/11 had overturned the chessboard, revealing some strange alliances. France was caught up in the earthquake, but some way from the epicentre: in solidarity with the USA, but far from the Churchillian rhetoric of the 'Anglo-American community'; whilst Britain rediscovered her 'real home' across the seas; whilst Blair pranced around as 'vice-President of an impromptu Atlantic alliance,' France had only a 'hanger-on' part. The Pentagon had called in eighty British officers straight after the events: not one Frenchman! 'Why were we kept at a distance? . . . America regards us as an inconvenient ally, an unreliable one.'[19] He listed the many slights and irritants remembered in Washington. He declared that France should not be content with this marginal role: the fallout was such that she was well placed to contribute, not least through her 'secular' tradition. But the terrorist threat required sticking together with the USA.

The French media immediately cited bin Laden as prime suspect, and prominently mentioned his CIA past, his arms and drugs trade connections, and money-laundering aspects of the hunt. Associates of the major French banking groups were speedily cited;[20] but perhaps more attention was given to British and American banks – the '*sociétés anglo-saxonnes*.'[21]

Then on 6 October occurred the strange, variously-analyzed, and for some shocking events at the France–Algeria football match at the Stade de France. Chirac did not attend: Jospin and several ministers did. The *Marseillaise* was greeted with catcalls and whistles; there was a pitch invasion by a number of *beurs* (offspring of North African immigrants); plastic bottles were thrown at ministers (Elisabeth Guigou was struck); Prime Minister Jospin was visibly shocked; ministers retreated to safety in some panic. Élysée sources put it about that 'their man' would have left immediately upon the insult to the anthem.

The debate raged: was this an indication of sympathy for bin Laden amongst the mainly North African young, or just clear evidence of alienation in the *banlieues* and a failure of the 'integrative project' in France? For most of the press, the verdict tended to the latter.[22] Malek Boutih, President of SOS-Racisme, commented that Islam must take its place within French secularism (*laïcité*).[23]

All the weekly news magazines and the broadsheet dailies, gave extensive space to essays on the nature, and modern evolution, of Islam: Was it inevitably 'political, or it is nothing'? Was it compatible with, or a threat to, French secular republican traditions? Was it 'a self-referential system, immune to self-criticism'? Was it 'inevitably' associated with violence? These were among the questions anxiously debated.[24]

So was the question of linkage or non-linkage to the Israel–Palestine issue: views among the intellectuals ran the whole gamut, from Alain Joxe – 'We must say now, and clearly, that American leadership in the Near East is a serious failure for [the cause of] international peace. If we don't say so now, I don't know when we will be able to say it' – to Pierre Hassner – 'One can have a different view from the Americans, about Israel or elsewhere. But right now, it won't make an impact in the US. For the time being, I don't see any alternative to saying – Yes, we're with you.'[25]

The French weekly press also quickly latched on to two other angles. One was financial: here there was some *Schadenfreude* about the 'Anglo-Saxons'; about the bizarre stock-price movements on Wall Street just before 9/11, in shares related to airlines and insurance and the 'money-trails' that pointed to the City of London. The second was the fate of Afghans with strong French connections: the death, on September 9, of General Massoud (seen as *francophone* and a modernizer) was now seen in a quite new light; and the British connections of his presumed assassins were noted; and Zahir Shah's past was commented upon – readers were reminded that he had studied in France until aged 19. There was anxious debate about the number of suspects with French connections (such as the Daoudi-Berghal faction); and no small anger at the frequency with which the trail led back to the UK, which afforded amazing freedom of movement and access, including financial, it was alleged.[26] London and Leicester were described as the 'ante-chambers of Afghanistan,' even as the British strutted their stuff as the loyal allies of the USA.[27]

PUBLIC OPINION GENERALLY AND REACTIONS AMONG FRENCH MUSLIMS

The 'republican tradition' in France is inimical to census and statistical identification by religious or 'ethnic' background; so there is no officially agreed figure for the number of Muslims or those from 'Muslim backgrounds.' Estimates vary widely – from about 5 million to nearer 8 million – and a main reason is that many from 'Muslim' backgrounds are anything but '*pratiquant(e)s*.' But such figures, roughly 10 to 15 percent of the population, make it the biggest community in Europe of Muslim background. Many are young, alienated in the soulless suburbs of Paris and other towns. Most have adapted to French secularism: but many among the young have not. As *Le Point* put it, 'Before September 11, the young in the suburbs knew nothing of bin Laden. Today, they regard him as a hero.' A 19-year-old said: 'He defended the Palestinians. And if you're a Muslim, you must be on his side.'[28] Others spoke of him 'avenging all the humiliations suffered by the *Arabs* [*sic*].'

In recent years, a divided far right seemed less of a challenge and threat to French Muslims – until the 2002 presidential elections. Also, President Chirac, as Head of State, with his attested dislike of US 'global domination,' was perhaps less enthusiastic in advocating 'wars on terrorism' than major leaders of some other states, which may have contributed to the *relative* lack of 'militant response' in French Islamic circles.

In France, Islam has come to be widely regarded as 'a French religion – like the other religions.' French Muslims are, and for some time have been, less militant than their British co-religionists. *French* Muslims, it seems, are generally reconciled to a secular state; more drawn to a 'non-political' Islam. This may be partly because of the keenly felt echoes of events (albeit reliable information has been so hard to come by) in Algeria since 1992. Yet the number of mosques in France has increased rapidly: Islam has moved 'out of the shadows' of small informal places of worship.

An *Ipsos* poll taken on 14 and 15 September showed 68 percent favouring French participation in military action decided by the USA and NATO; and 21 percent against. But it also showed, once again, that many made a clear distinction between sympathy with the American *people*, and support for the policies of its leaders, especially regarding Arab states.[29]

The opinion survey institute *Ifop* conducted a major poll at the beginning of October, adding these data to earlier research from 1989 and 1994 to give a 'longitudinal' view. The poll distinguished French Muslims from the French population generally, in two samples.[30] Its essential findings were: that French Muslims were open about their affiliation and not worried about declaring it; next, as the general population got accustomed to them, their image with that population improved. However, third, there was clear evidence of a 'community loyalty' that differentiated them from the non-Muslim population, markedly on questions of foreign policy and international morality. Islam continued to have negative associations for many in the general population: 'fanaticism', 'submission', 'rejection of western values' were the three terms chosen most frequently – though all were cited *less* frequently than in earlier polls.

Twelve percent of the Muslim-background sample, but 18 percent of 16–24s, had a 'positive opinion' of Osama bin Laden. Seventy percent (compared with 92 percent of the general population) were positive about French aid to the USA in hunting terrorist networks; but 69 percent (49 percent) were opposed to French participation in a war against states harbouring or assisting terrorists. Sixty eight percent of the Muslim-background sample thought US policy on the Middle East might have 'helped provoke Islamic extremists.' Thirty percent (19 percent) said they detected a change in attitude toward Muslims since the September 11 events. The administrator of the As-Salam mosque in Argenteuil (outside Paris) reported that he and his congregation felt 'scape-goated' by the general population: 'I personally feel an aggressive attitude toward me from non-Muslims; menacing looks' and one imam predicted 'Bush will lead us to disaster and a human catastrophe.'[31]

FRENCH MILITARY INVOLVEMENT IN AFGHANISTAN

The French Constitution, for all its ambiguities, is clear on one point: the president, not the prime minister, is 'responsible for national defense' (Article 21) and 'head of the armed forces' (Article 15): this was recognized by 70 percent of the electorate, as against 3 percent who thought these were the prime minister's responsibility.[32]

In October, many of the journals used such unflattering epithets as '*la France réserviste*' and '*supplétive*' to describe the country's stance. Pierre Lellouche, an RPR defense luminary and close associate of Chirac, roundly criticized France's lack of defense capability. But the Élysée also made clear its view that the lack of commitment reflected lack of political will, not just budgetary constraints. Yet *Le Point* signaled these very budgetary constraints, comparing France's situation with both the USA and UK.

Right at the start, by pure chance, a contrast appeared: the UK's large force already en route for Oman in Operation Swift Sword, was commented upon.[33] Blair was 'Churchillian'; Bush's gratitude to him was noted. France had 'half a *maudit* aircraft carrier', the troubled *Charles de Gaulle*, nowhere to be seen until much later. The government's reference to French 'ships' in the Indian Ocean was a fig leaf, there was one warship, the frigate *Courbet*, and one supply/refueling vessel (the *Var*). There was no real commitment, argued Lellouche, and the reason was because France did not want to get embroiled with the Arab world, nor with its Muslim community: 'In a sort of self-censure, we signal a verbal solidarity, which is not followed up by [meaningful] action.'[34]

Yet, by slow degrees, the French contribution was seen to grow. This followed widespread European disquiet, in late October, at American strategy. At the EU foreign ministers' meeting in Luxembourg on 29 October, Védrine declared the strategy (mainly bombing and special forces) 'isn't working any more.'[35] On 6 November, after meeting Bush to urge more thought about the post-Taliban situation and the involvement of the UN, Chirac disclosed that there were already some 2,000 French military personnel deployed; the UN resolution was passed on 16 November and French forces deployed around Mazar-i-Sharif.[36]

On 3 March 2002, Washington confirmed that French troops, along with troops from Denmark, Norway, Canada, Australia and the USA, were involved in the latest round of military operations in eastern Afghanistan.[37] In the week following, French Mirage 2000-D fighter aircraft participated for the first time in operations in Afghanistan. The sorties were lauched from an airbase in Kyrgyzstan, itself a signatory to the CIS collective security agreement, and thus liable to be a matter of concern to France's 'historical interlocutor,' Russia. Some 200 French troops were also working with US forces at the Manas international airport near Bishkek. On the practical level, France was contributing, albeit modestly.

IMPLICATIONS OF FRENCH REACTIONS FOR EUROPE

Judicial cooperation was obvious from the start. On 17 September, French anti-terrorist judges met with their German, Belgian and Dutch counterparts in Brussels to share information on networks having contact with bin Laden.[38] Justice and Interior Ministers met on 20 September to discuss abolition of extradition requirements – a proposal blocked by France since 1996; on 21 September there followed the 'Extraordinary' European Council on terrorism.

By contrast, little concrete action was proposed to enhance military capability. The draft defense budget was largely pre-empted by personnel costs associated with 'professionalization.' Frustrations deepened over the crucial (for power-projection) Airbus A400M heavy lift aircraft contract, blame for the uncertainities of which were laid at the door of Germany.

IMPLICATIONS FOR RELATIONS WITH THE USA

As did others, the French media from the start questioned whether 'the USA has at its head the President it needs,'[39] adding that he had neither the competence of his father nor the instinct of Clinton. And the US leadership was far from convinced of France's full support: worries only partially assuaged by the Chirac/Védrine visit, which had begun with a brittle exchange with the press corps over the use of the term 'war.'[40]

At the start of the bombing and ground campaign, cautionary notes were struck. In successive editions, *Le Nouvel Observateur* spoke of the 'traps of an inevitable war'; and, discussing American strategy, asked, 'To bomb, and then?' – saying that defeating the Taliban would be the easy part.[41]

The French press and political class anticipated much more difficulty for the Americans in the first 'hundred days' than was the case. Indeed by December the tone was largely eulogistic, speaking of 'Bush's 100-day triumph,'[42] of a campaign 'vigorous, controlled and well-led by the Bush team, giving the lie to a supposed stupidity imputed to it by our *dindonneaux* [young turkeys] of the press';[43] though cautioning that 'bin Laden's head on a platter would not end the war on terrorism.' The main critical tone was, as elsewhere in Europe, over the treatment of suspects taken to Guantanamo Bay.[44]

A singularly rosy picture of the 'results' was painted by centrist politician Alain Duhamel. Under the title, 'the eventide of sovereignty,' he argued that the dissident voices on the far left and far right had been 'marginalized': the presidential 'pre-campaign' had stopped dead in favor of solidarity; France's role, in the UN (as presidency), in NATO and in the EU had been exemplary. The Bush presidency, he averred, had dropped its initial unilateralist temptation and its 'Pontius Pilate' approach to the Near East. The episode showed the unwinding of sovereignty; the end of parochial reactions; 'more terrorism brings more unity.'[45]

Rather more cynical was Catherine Pégard: it was just as well, for Chirac and Jospin, that the Americans had not asked too much of France militarily because both men found the deployment of diplomacy and historic links more congenial; *cohabitation* worked all the better because up to then, in November, there 'had been no hard decisions to take' . . . 'paradoxically, the *insignificance* [emphasis added] of our participation . . . guarantees our [internal] cohesion.'[46]

Bush's 'axis of evil' speech on 29 January 2002 reawakened a good deal of anti-Americanism. Even normally sympathetic sources such as *Le Point* expressed concern: contrasting 'good and evil' was not a suitable 'method for conducting foreign policy'; 'France [*sic*] is completely opposed to any unconsidered widening of the Afghan theater of operations'; 'on Iraq, French analysis differs *radically* from that of the USA.'[47] *Le Nouvel Observateur* opined: 'What's new is not that the USA is the only superpower . . . but that it realises it, and has decided, in the face of the rest of the world, to cash in on the dividends of its success'; and it sourly reported a senior Pentagon official as summing up: 'We [the USA] fight; the UN feeds; the Europeans rebuild.'[48] This might infuriate Europeans, but, said many French sources, the remedy lay in their own hands: if they did not wish to be 'snivveling satellites' of the USA, European defense capabilities would have to be greatly enhanced.[49]

The last word should perhaps go to Pierre Beylau writing in *Le Point* that Bin Laden's sanctuaries were not just in Pakistan and Saudi Arabia: 'The third sanctuary has been established in the core of our industrialised societies, in the hearts and minds of young kids psychologically and culturally far removed from Afghan redoubts. They have broken with the traditional Islam of their parents . . . to take on a sort of improvised Islamic trotskyism bent on universal revolution.' This was a planetary broth where geopolitics, religion, social ills and uncertainty about identity all played.[50] It was not a happy prospect for France; and not one where its 'internal cohesion' would be easy to sustain, whatever courses of action the country decided to follow.

Following the presidential and legislative elections in spring 2002, power returned completely to the centre-right. President Chirac had a fresh mandate. As the temperature rose over Iraq, France concentrated its efforts on intense diplomatic advocacy of the 'two stage' strategy in the UN Security Council, before finally participating in the unanimous vote for the one resolution in early November. This 'two stage' approach was widely shared by most Europeans, but again put France at odds with the USA. In October 2002, asked whether there was 'a direct link between the Iraqi affair and . . . the bin Laden issue,' the reply was that 'no evidence has been found, or at any rate officially reported' of such a link, but that 'we can't rule out terrorist groups using the Iraqi affair as a pretext' for new activities.[51]

NOTES

1 *Le Monde*, 18 Sept. 2001, p. 17.
2 Olivier Schrameck, *Matignon Rive Gauche* (Paris: Edition du Seuil, 2001); see press reports 16 and 17 Oct. 2001.
3 French Embassy London: *Statements*, 01/172, 11 Sept. 2001.
4 French Embassy London: *Statements*, 01/181, 13 Sept. 2001; *Le Monde* 15 Sept. 2001, p. 10.
5 *Le Monde*, 18 Sept. 2001, p. 13.
6 *L'Express*, 27 Sept.–3 Oct. 2001, p. 16.
7 *Le Monde*, 15 Sept. 2001, p. 10.
8 *Le Monde*, 18 Sept. 2001, p. 17.
9 As reported in *Le Monde*, 15 Sept. 2001, p. 10.
10 *Le Monde*, 23–4 Sept. 2001, p. 21.
11 Cited in *Le Monde*, 16–17 Sept. 2001, p. 10.
12 *Le Monde*, 23–4 Sept. 2001, p. 21.
13 *Le Monde*, 18 Sept. 2001, p. 17.
14 *Le Monde*, 18 Sept. 2001, p. 17.

15 Catherine Pégard, in *Le Point*, 12 Oct. 2001, p. 11.
16 French Embassy London, *Speeches and Statements*, 01/205, 24 Sept. 2001, pp. 1–7; *Le Monde*, 25 Sept. 2001, p. 3.
17 *Le Monde*, 15 Sept. 2001, p. 17.
18 *Le Monde*, 15 Sept. 2001, p. 19.
19 Claude Imbert, *Le Point*, 12 Oct. 2001, p. 5.
20 See, for example, *Le Nouvel Observateur*, 4–10 Oct. 2001, p. 19.
21 See, for example, *Le Monde*, 15 Sept. 2001, p. 4.
22 See, for example, *Le Point*, 19 Oct. 2001.
23 *L'Express*, 4–11 Oct. 2001, p. 16.
24 See, for example, *Le Nouvel Observateur*, 4–10 Oct. 2001, pp. 9ff. and 27.
25 *Le Monde*, 23–4 Sept. 2001, pp. 12–13.
26 *Le Point*, 2 Nov. 2001, p. 54.
27 *L'Express*, 28 Feb.–6 March 2002, pp. 8–11.
28 *Le Point*, 12 Oct. 2001, p. 66.
29 Reported in *Le Monde*, 18 Sept. 2001, p. 17.
30 This summary of findings is based on reports in *Le Point*, 5 Oct. 2001, pp. 69–74.
31 *Le Monde*, 23–4 Sept. 2001, p. 9.
32 According to a 1999 Sofres poll, reported in *L'Express* 2621: 27 Sept.–3 Oct. 2001, p. 16.
33 Jacques Isnard in *Le Monde*, 18 Sept. 2001, p. 16.
34 *L'Express*, 4–11 Oct. 2001, pp. 14–15.
35 *Le Monde*, 31 Oct. 2001, p. 2.
36 *Le Monde*, 8 Nov. 2001, pp. 1–2; and 16 Nov. 2001, pp. 1–2.
37 *Financial Times*, 5 March 2002, p. 13.
38 *Le Monde*, 19 Sept. 2001, p. 4.
39 *Le Monde*, 15 Sept. 2001, p. 1.
40 *Le Monde*, 20 Sept. 2001, p. 5.
41 *Le Nouvel Observateur*, 11–17 Oct., pp. 28–9; and 18–24 Oct. 2001, pp. 26 and 32.
42 *L'Express*, 13–19 Dec. 2001, p. 50.
43 Claude Imbert, *Le Point*, 21 and 28 Dec. 2001.
44 See, for example, *Le Point*, 25 Jan. 2002, pp. 46–8.
45 *Le Point*, 5 Oct. 2001, p. 51.
46 *Le Point*, 16 Nov. 2001, p. 32.
47 *Le Point*, 8 Feb. 2002, p. 12.
48 *Le Nouvel Observateur*, 14–20 March 2002, p. 36; see also *L'Express*, 7–13 Feb. 2002, p. 5: 'The Giant and the Dwarfs', on the 29 January Bush speech.
49 *L'Express*, 7–13 Feb. 2002, p. 5.
50 *Le Point*, 5 Oct. 2001, p. 57.
51 French Embassy London: *Statements*, 02/281, 16 Oct. 2002.

8 Redefining its security role

Germany

Adrian Hyde-Price

The German response to 9/11 was conditioned by the Federal Republic's role as a strategic partner of the USA and reflected the public sense of shock and horror at these atrocities. This sense of shock deepened when it was discovered that a number of the terrorists had lived and worked in Hamburg. Speaking to the Bundestag on the day following the terror attacks, Chancellor Schröder spoke for most Germans when he declared that 'yesterday, September 11, will go down in history for all of us as a black day.' The atrocities in New York and Washington, he noted, were directed against the 'civilised international community' as a whole. Consequently the Federal Republic would extend 'unconditional – I repeat – unconditional solidarity' to the United States, including the deployment of military forces.[1]

Two days later it appeared as if the shock of events had given way to concern about the implications of the US-led war on terrorism, and that the German government might distance itself from military action. Defense Minister Rudolf Scharping said that 'I hope we all remain calm and do not now speak of a state of alarm. We do not face a war. We face the question of what is an appropriate response.'[2] However, in his speech to the Bundestag on 19 September, Chancellor Schröder praised the 'level headed attitude of the American Administration' and declared Germany's willingness to give the US military support in its anti-terror campaign. Schröder argued that the struggle against terror had nothing to do with a putative 'clash of civilisations' or 'a war against the Islamic world either,' but was directed against those who threatened the very basis of civilized international society. He also argued that UN Security Council Resolutions 1368 and 1373, along with NATO's activation of Article 5 of the Washington Treaty, gave a clear legal base for military action against the perpetrators of terrorism and countries harbouring them.[3]

Schröder's call for 'unconditional solidarity' with the USA was endorsed by all parties in the Bundestag on 19 September with the notable exception of the former East German communist party, the PDS (Party of Democratic Socialism). By 565 to 40, the Bundestag approved a resolution which agreed to 'make available appropriate military facilities' to the USA and its NATO allies. The breadth and depth of support for the government's position reflected the widespread shock and revulsion in Germany at the attacks on the American people and their institutions. The decision of the PDS not to align themselves with the anti-terror coalition was in part a function of the knee-jerk anti-Americanism that pervades their 'anti-imperialist' ideology. It also reflected a conscious political strategy to position themselves as the only 'anti-war' party in Germany, hoping thereby to win support from disaffected Greens and left-wing social democrats and facilitate the difficult task of building a political basis in the Western *Länder*. Thus at the party's Federal Party Conference (*Bundesparteitag*) in Dresden (6–7 October 2001), the PDS federal organizer, Dietmar Bartsch, declared that 'the PDS is and remains *the* peace party in Germany.'[4] This pacifist stance proved popular with many young and first-time voters, and contributed to the electoral success of the PDS in Berlin in the 21 October local elections (where the party achieved its best ever result with 22.6 percent of the vote). Nonetheless, it is important to note that the PDS at federal level was keen to distance itself from some of the more extreme expressions of anti-Americanism and *Schadenfreude* (pleasure in the suffering of others) evident in sections of the party (the Hamburg PDS *Land* Committee being one example). The *Bundesparteitag* stressed in its resolution on September 11 that 'terror is terror' and could not be justified by references to 'injustice and exploit-ation' or the 'north–south conflict.' Similarly Gregor Gysi emphasized that the capture of the perpetrators of the attacks was an essential element in the fight against terrorism, but nonetheless maintained that this was 'at its core a police action,' and should not be the excuse for massive military retaliation by the USA.[5]

GERMAN DIPLOMACY

In the initial period following the terrorist attacks, one of the key roles of Ger-many was to contribute to the creation and consolidation of the international alliance against terrorism. A central role in this diplomatic offensive was played by Joschka Fischer, the Foreign Minister and leader of the Green Party. His import-ance, however, was not limited to his foreign policy role. He was influential in mobilizing and consolidating the support of the 'soft left' around the government's policy of 'unconditional solidarity.' Like Schröder, Fischer was also sensitive to the implications of September 11 for race relations in Germany's increasingly multicultural and multi-faith society, and called for a constructive 'debate' between Christianity and Islam to help build better understanding and tolerance.

Nonetheless, Fischer's primary role was in the diplomatic arena. Fischer embarked on an intense round of shuttle diplomacy around the Middle East in an effort to mediate between the Israelis and Palestinians,[6] and also visited Central Asia and Pakistan in order to strengthen the international coalition against terror-ism (in part, through offers of financial aid). He also worked assiduously to build a common EU diplomatic response to the terrorist attacks and encouraged a prom-inent role for the United Nations in the anti-terror campaign.[7] Foreign Minister Fischer's efforts were complemented by those of Chancellor Schröder, who also played an important role in garnering diplomatic support for the anti-terror coalition. In early November, for example, Schröder traveled to the Far East, visiting China, New Delhi, Islamabad and, on his return flight, Moscow. His message was that the military campaign in Afghanistan had to continue, despite mounting calls at home from Green Party members for a halt to the bombing.[8]

Another important contribution made by German diplomacy to the anti-terror campaign was the organization and funding in Bonn of a UN-sponsored conference on the creation of post-Taliban interim regime. The conference began on 27 November with an opening address given by Foreign Minister Fischer, and involved representatives from four Afghan groups.[9] Despite significant differences between them, they eventually agreed to the creation of a temporary transitional government that would give way to a more representative two-year administration after six months. The 'Bonn Accords' were signed on 5 December, and established a twenty-nine-member interim government led by Hamid Karzai.

The war on terrorism exposed a tension at the heart of German diplomacy that had been increasingly evident in the 1990s. This was the balance to be struck between inclusive diplomacy conducted through multilateral institutions, and more exclusive diplomacy operating through informal groupings (usually involving major powers). This tension was already evident in the Balkans with the Contact Group on the one hand, and the EU's Common Foreign and Security Policy (CFSP) on the other. In the case of the conflict in and around Afghanistan, Germany was involved with an informal summit meeting of the 'Big three' (UK, France and Germany) prior to the October EU Council meeting in Ghent, Belgium. A similar meeting planned for London on 4 November was enlarged to include other member states and EU officials after criticism from Italy and other member states that felt excluded.[10]

Indications of serious differences of opinion between the German government and the USA over the anti-terror campaign only really appeared in January 2002 in the wake of President Bush's controversial 'axis of evil' speech. In his State of the Union address to a joint session of the two houses of Congress on 29 January, Bush argued that 'our war against terror is only beginning' and declared that the USA would act against an 'axis of evil' formed by Iran, Iraq and North Korea. These countries were accused of developing weapons of mass destruction and, in the case of Iraq and Iran, of harbouring and directing international terrorists.[11] The USA, he argued, 'would not wait on events while dangers gather.' This apparent threat to extend the 'war on terrorism' to these three countries was widely condemned in the German media, and Foreign Minister Fischer subsequently expressed his disquiet with this suggestion. There was a clear distinction, he argued, between the war in Afghanistan (which had been justified under Article 51 of the UN Charter) and attacks on other countries. The USA also came in for widespread criticism in Germany in official and unofficial circles for its treatment of al-Qaeda and Taliban detainees captured in Afghanistan and transferred to Camp X-Ray in Guantanamo Bay, Cuba. The USA refused to grant these captives the status of prisoners of war under the 1949 Geneva Convention, and classified them instead as 'unlawful combatants' or 'battlefield detainees.' Relations between Germany and the USA were particularly strained after the release of photographs showing shackled detainees forced to sit on the floor wearing face masks and blindfolds.

DOMESTIC SECURITY

The attacks on New York and Washington raised understandable concerns in Germany about domestic security and the country's vulnerability to similar terrorist threats.[12] These concerns were fuelled by a wave of hoax anthrax letters in Germany and – more worryingly – evidence that Osama bin Laden's al-Qaeda network had put down deep roots there. Not only had a number of the September 11 terrorists lived in Germany, it became increasingly clear that al-Qaeda had a substantial financial and logistical base in Germany (with Frankfurt, intelligence sources suggested, providing the principal center of the terrorist network). In addition, informed estimates suggested that Germany might be home to up to 31,000 members or supporters of militant fundamentalist Islamic organizations, some of them having contact with al-Qaeda.[13] In this context, therefore, it was essential for the Red–Green government to act quickly and decisively to address public unease about domestic security, whilst assuring rank-and-file members of the coalition parties that fundamental civil liberties would remain sacrosanct.

Responsibility for tackling this sensitive but important agenda of domestic security fell on the shoulders of Otto Schily, the Federal Interior Minister. From the very start, his calm but forceful approach provided a reassuring image to the German public, and helped diffuse some popular concerns about law and order. Pledging that the government would display 'absolute toughness' against radical Islamists operating in Germany, Schily moved swiftly to introduce a series of measures designed to strengthen internal security. After a short but intense debate, 'Security Package I' (*Sicherheitspaket I*) was adopted by the Cabinet on 19 September and subsequently passed by the Bundestag.[14] This changed the *Vereinsrecht* (the Law on Associations) by banning religious groups that were deemed to be extremist and introduced a new Section 129 b in the existing anti-terror paragraph of the criminal code (introduced in the 1970s to tackle the problem of left-wing terrorism). This revision gave the police the power to pursue suspected terrorists residing in Germany but plotting against other countries. The federal authorities also moved to improve air safety by more rigorous checking on the background of airport employees and monitoring their subsequent behavior; improving baggage checks; and having security staff placed on selected flights of Lufthansa, the national airline. In addition, Security Package I toughened banking security regulations; bolstered security for public buildings (especially American and Israeli); and allowed the police to gain access to personal information gathered by government agencies, thereby breaking a long-held taboo. These measures were underpinned by the provision of DM 3 billion for the fight against terrorism.[15]

The need to give more urgent attention to the issue of domestic law and order was underlined by the unexpected electoral success of Ronald Schill's '*Partei Rechtsstaatlicher Offensive*' (the PRO, or 'Law and Order Offensive Party') in the

Hamburg *Land* elections on 23 September 2001. The northern Hanseatic city-state of Hamburg had long been a social democratic bastion, but Schill's party, campaigning on a law and order ticket and capitalizing on popular concerns about domestic security in the wake of September 11, won a staggering 165,000 votes (approximately 20 percent of the total). His calls for more police and tougher sentencing chimed with the popular mood, especially after revelations that three of the hijackers had lived and studied in Hamburg. This domestic political earthquake resulted in the end of forty-four years of SPD rule in Hamburg and the formation of a CDU–PRO–FDP coalition, with Ronald Schill as the new *Land* Interior Minister.[16] The Red–Green federal government in Berlin responded to the electoral success of the Schill party and continuing public concern about domestic security by introducing 'Security Package II.' This was much more far-reaching in scope and intent than the first batch of proposals, and raised sensitive issues about the balance between security and civil liberties.[17]

Otto Schily's proposals involved the revision of a number of laws related to government agencies in order to coordinate the government's anti-terrorism policy more coherently and effectively. In particular, the Federal Office for the Recognition of Asylum Claimants and *Länder* offices dealing with asylum applications were instructed to report evidence of extremist activities on the part of asylum seekers to the Office for the Protection of the Constitution. It was also proposed that in order to give the security and law enforcement agencies more reliable information, fingerprints or other biometric characteristics should in future be included in identity cards, passports and visa applications. These proposals led to an intense debate within the Red–Green government about the implications of such measures for civil liberties. In both governing parties, there was considerable concern about the dangers of an excessively 'transparent citizen' (*gläsender Bürger*) resulting from increased police surveillance and intelligence gathering. In the end, the revised package – which was formally approved by the cabinet on 7 November – specified that compulsory finger printing of all visa applications would not be introduced by decree (as Schily proposed) but by legislation subject to parliamentary scrutiny. In addition, it was agreed that the Federal Criminal Investigation Office (BKA) would not be authorized to investigate suspects without a prior judicial indictment (again, as Schily had suggested).[18]

It is quite evident that 9/11 has changed the terms of the debate on law and order in Germany. Public concerns about crime and domestic security had been rising for some time in Germany as in many other European countries, but had always been balanced by a vocal and influential civil liberties lobby (especially strong in the Green Party and amongst the left more widely). September 11, coupled with the electoral success of Schill's PRO in Hamburg, has however shifted the balance further towards tougher internal security controls and a more 'transparent' citizenry.[19] The most sensitive issue is how to tackle the core of Islamic fundamentalist militants in the Federal Republic without harming community relations in Germany's increasingly multicultural society. Another controversial issue is whether or not to use the Bundeswehr to defend nuclear power plants in Germany. Many Greens have been vehemently opposed to this, whereas

Chancellor Schröder has insisted that 'we need action in civil defense and disaster procedures,' and that the constitution did allow 'the deployment of Federal Armed Forces in situations where it is meaningful and necessary.'[20] The security measures drawn up after September 11 were finally given Bundestag approval in December, and led to an immediate crackdown on radical Islamic groups. Over twenty such groups were banned on 12 December, at the same time as police launched early morning raids on mosques and other premises in seven *Länder* during which two men were arrested and numerous documents seized.[21]

One other area where the German authorities can and have made a valuable contribution to the anti-terror campaign is in identifying and rooting out the financial and organizational network of al-Qaeda and cognate groups. Already by 2 October 2001, German banks had frozen approximately DM 8 million in 214 accounts suspected of being linked to terrorist groups. This action was followed by Finance Minister Hans Eichel's announcement on October 5 that all 44 million bank accounts in Germany would be subject to government scrutiny for unusual cash flow patterns, although actual transactions would remain confidential.[22] Hans Eichel also worked closely with his colleagues in the G7 and Russia on a comprehensive action plan on combating terrorism and money laundering, aimed at drying up the financial roots of international terrorism. This was approved at a meeting of the G7 in Washington on 6 October (a meeting originally scheduled for September but postponed after the terror attacks). The campaign to eradicate the financial roots of terrorism received an important fillip on 28 November, when German police arrested a 27-year-old Moroccan national, Mounir Motassadeq. He was suspected of having controlled a bank account of the 'Hamburg cell,' responsible for planning and executing the 9/11 terror attacks.[23]

German government initiatives to tighten up domestic security have been accompanied by strenuous efforts to deepen European cooperation in combating terrorism. The federal government pushed hard for this at special sessions of the European Council in Brussels (20 September) and Ghent (19 October). The main thrust of these discussions was to introduce a European arrest warrant, to strengthen links between anti-terrorist experts in Europe and to optimize transatlantic policy cooperation with the USA.

THE MILITARY CAMPAIGN

On 7 October 2001, the USA launched its long-expected military campaign against the infrastructure of al-Qaeda and its Taliban hosts in Afghanistan. 'In this situation,' Gerhard Schröder declared in the Bundestag four days later, 'active solidarity and responsible action are expected of Germany – and they will indeed be forthcoming. Our solidarity must be more than mere lip-service. And we must pursue a policy which is in keeping with Germany's responsibility in the world, as well as the Federal Government's responsibility for people in Germany.' Germans, he argued, had been able to overcome the consequences of two world wars and achieve freedom and self-determination with the help and solidarity of their

American and European friends. Now they had an obligation and an opportunity to repay these past debts and to demonstrate their willingness to shoulder their new-found responsibilities for international peace and security. 'Let there be no mistake,' he continued, 'this expressly includes participation in military operations to defend freedom and human rights, and to establish stability and security.'

As the military campaign against al-Qaeda and the Taliban regime unfolded, however, a growing number of critical voices were raised, not just on the pacifist and anti-American left, but also within the ruling coalition parties, especially the Greens.[24] Doubts were raised about the effectiveness of aerial bombing and the feasibility of avoiding collateral damage. It was also clear that forging a coalition of the Pashtun tribes and strengthening the military capabilities and political cohesion of the Northern Alliance was proving more difficult than initially expected. As the Muslim religious festival of Ramadan approached, a growing number of critics within the Green Party and the SPD called for a pause in the bombing campaign. For example Claudia Roth, the co-chairperson of the Green Party, caused considerable consternation in the government by calling on 15 October for a halt to the bombing and questioning the legality of the use of cluster bombs.[25] By late October, ten out of sixteen Green Party organizations at *Land* level had called for a pause in the bombing so that humanitarian aid could be delivered during the Ramadan holiday period. Public opinion polls also suggested that 55 percent of the population were critical of the bombing campaign and America's conduct of the anti-terror war.[26] In addition, some within the German foreign and security policy community voiced concern that the USA was bypassing NATO and building alternative coalition networks (for example with Pakistan, Uzbekistan and Tajikistan) in order to maximize its room for maneuver. The danger with this, it was felt, was that it indicated a declining American interest in the transatlantic alliance. This in turn reflected the fact that many in the USA felt that Germany – along with most European NATO countries, with the limited exception of the UK – lacked the resources, training or equipment to make a significant contribution to their military operations.

Nonetheless, as the difficulties of the campaign in Afghanistan became increasingly apparent – particularly after the failure of Operation Anaconda – and in order to broaden the political basis of the anti-terror alliance, President Bush made a formal request to the German government on 5 November for military support.[27] Chancellor Schröder was quick to respond by offering 3,900 troops in support, arguing that this decision was made 'in a solidarity that I have expressed again and again since the September 11 attacks on New York and Washington.' However, this led to further rumblings of disquiet from pacifist elements in the Green Party.[28] On 6 November, Foreign Minister Fischer threatened to resign when he failed to persuade enough members of his Green parliamentary group to back the proposed Bundeswehr deployments. Faced with the potential threat to the effectiveness of this coalition government, Chancellor Schröder decided to up the political stakes by linking Bundestag approval for the military requirement (a legal and constitutional obligation) to a confidence vote, rather than relying on the support of the mainstream opposition parties. This was only the fourth time this procedural device has been used in the history of the Federal Republic, and underlined the seriousness of the threat to the government's stability. The crucial vote was held on 16 November, with the government needing a majority in the 666 seat legislature (or 334 votes). The government coalition had 341 seats in total, but on 11 November, eight Green deputies announced their intention to vote against the military deployment, threatening to bring down the government.

In the end, Schröder's motion was supported by 336 to 326 in the vote, the eight dissident Greens having decided to split their vote with four registering their opposition, and four voting for the confidence motion. The Bundestag vote disguised both the much broader cross-party support for Bundeswehr participation in the war against terrorism, and the fragility of this support within the ruling coalition. Schröder subsequently admitted that he had 'underestimated' the opposition to the military deployments within the parliamentary groups of both the Greens and SPD.[29] Whilst pacifist elements in the Greens were more vocal in their opposition, after the vote had been held fifteen SPD deputies declared that they too would have voted against, had it not been for the confidence motion. The political difficulties of the coalition were seized upon by the opposition, with Friedrich Merz, the CDU parliamentary leader, accusing the Chancellor of 'playing thoughtlessly with foreign policy because you cannot manage your domestic policies, in a last-ditch effort to save your government.' Chancellor Schröder, however, insisted that 'for a decision of such consequences, it is absolutely necessary that the Chancellor and the government relies on a majority from their own coalition.' He also underlined the historic nature of the vote: 'Today's decision on the military deployment will certainly be a turning point: for the first time soldiers will be readied for armed deployment outside the NATO region.'[30]

GERMANY'S CHANGING FOREIGN AND SECURITY POLICY

September 11 marks a further stage in the post-Cold War redefinition of German foreign and security policy. This was clearly signaled by Chancellor Schröder in his Bundestag speech of 11 October 2001. 'Following the end of the cold war, the re-establishment of Germany's unity and the restoration of our full sovereignty,' he argued, 'we must shoulder international responsibility in a new fashion.' The Federal Republic, he insisted, 'must assume a measure of responsibility which is in keeping with our role as a key European and transatlantic partner, as well as that of a strong democracy and strong economy in the heart of Europe.' He further stated that,

> Only ten years ago no-one would have expected more from Germany than secondary assistance, i.e., infrastructure or funds, in the international efforts to safeguard freedom, justice and stability. As I pointed out immediately after September 11, this era of German postwar politics is over once and for all. Particularly we Germans, who were able to overcome the consequences of

two world wars and achieve freedom and self-determination with the help and solidarity of our American and European friends, now have an obligation to shoulder our new responsibilities in full. Let there be no mistake: this expressly includes participation in military operations to defend freedom and human rights, and to establish stability and security.[31]

Chancellor Schröder's attempt to charter a new course for German foreign policy in the twenty-first century has important consequences for defense expenditure. If Germany's new-found obligation to shoulder its responsibilities is to include military operations, then the Bundeswehr needs both structural reforms and sufficient finance. 'The Bundeswehr,' one analyst has noted, 'must overcome its founding charter as a non-interventionist, conscript-based territorial defence force.'[32] Throughout the 1990s, defense expenditure was repeatedly cut in an elusive search for the 'peace dividend,'[33] whilst far-reaching military reform was repeatedly postponed. In May 2000, the Red–Green government finally committed itself to a process of defense restructuring, but there are doubts whether this will give the Bundeswehr a significant capacity to respond to security challenges requiring force projection and out-of-area military crisis management. The public admission in the spring of 2001 that the Bundeswehr was no longer fully operational and no longer capable of fulfilling all its alliance obligations underlines the distance Germany has to travel if it is to be able to shoulder its 'new responsibility in full' and participate 'in military operations to defend freedom and human rights, and to establish stability and security.'[34]

The Red–Green government has used 9/11 further to 'normalize' German foreign and security policy, specifically in terms of the use of military force. Chancellor Schröder made this clear in his interview with *Die Zeit* when he declared that his aim was to remove the taboo on the use of military force (*Enttabuisierung des Militärischen*) and to build a 'permissive consensus' for the use of military force as a legitimate instrument of foreign policy. Arguing that 'September 11 has changed the world situation,' he also noted that the Bundeswehr's participation in the war on terrorism marked a clear watershed. Earlier interventions by the German military were focused on Europe, he argued, whereas the current deployments were to take place outside Europe. 'That is a qualitative difference, but one which arises from the changed role of Germany in the world and the expectations of its partners.' However, with reference to the continuing legacy of Germany's civilian power strategic culture, and the fact that approximately 60 percent of the population opposed the participation of their soldiers in a ground war,[35] Schröder remarked that 'I would much prefer to have a society that is so "civilian" in nature that a government has difficulties justifying the use of the military, to one characterised by a hurray-patriotism.'[36]

The Chancellor has also sought to redefine the conceptual assumptions underpinning social democrat and green approaches to foreign and security policy by arguing that although the Red–Green government 'has always said that our main focus must be on crisis prevention and management . . . This has never been an excuse not to take military action if need be.' Germans, he argued, are 'to the fore in taking resolute action to both safeguard peace in the world and create and maintain stability based on respect for human rights and human dignity.' He also noted that the German government 'has long since been working on comprehensive concepts of stability and security,' involving material security, social security, legal security, 'and, of course, but only in this context: military muscle.' This he argued, was a concept 'which we have already proposed and, as far as possible, implemented in the Balkan conflicts,' and which was 'a genuinely European concept.'[37]

CONCLUSION

9/11 will without doubt go down as a defining moment in the history of the early twenty-first century. For Germany, a country that has long prided itself on enjoying a close and beneficial alliance with the USA, this will give added importance to the elements of security, intelligence and defense cooperation in their bilateral relationship. Germany can draw on its own experience of combating terrorism in the shape of the Red Army Fraction (aka the 'Baader-Meinhof gang'). The fact that some of the al-Qaeda terrorists were based in Germany prior to launching their attacks has given greater urgency to the task of strengthening US–German counter-terrorist cooperation, in the context of improved transatlantic cooperation between the USA and the EU. The EU's 'Third Pillar' (Justice and Home Affairs) will also now become a much more important aspect of the European integration process, reflecting a growing domestic concern in member states with law and order issues.

The primary significance of the 9/11 terrorist attacks for Germany is that they generated a further stimulus to the ongoing process of redefining Germany's post-unification role in the world. Building on the experience of its participation in the Kosovo war, this will involve a greater willingness to use military force.[38] 'The readiness to make a military contribution to security,' the Chancellor noted, 'is an important commitment to Germany's alliances and partnerships. However, it is not just that. The readiness to live up to our greater responsibility for international security also implies that Germany has a new perception of its foreign policy.'[39] The opposition leader of the Free Democrats, Guido Westerwelle, underlined the importance of the decision to contribute German troops to the anti-terror campaign by arguing that 'this is an hour that will find its way into the history books,' and one that represented 'a qualitatively new level in foreign and security politics.'[40] Schröder's declaration of 'unconditional solidarity' with the United States, and the government's twin-track approach of strengthening domestic security and supporting the US-led war on terrorism, has won broad approval in the Bundestag and amongst the public more widely. Nonetheless, there are strong German reservations about extending the anti-terrorist campaign to target the 'axis of evil,' and continuing worries about unilateralist tendencies in US foreign policy. Domestically, the terrorist attacks have led to the introduction of new anti-terrorist and 'homeland security' legislation, and increased public concern about law and order issues more widely. At the same time, there are countervailing pressures arising from concerns about the erosion of civil liberties. Naturally, September 11 has not had as profound an impact on Germany as it has had on the USA, but it has forced many Germans to confront the dilemmas and uncertainties of international security in an age of globalization.

NOTES

1 'Regierungserklärung von Bundeskanzler Schröder vor dem Deutschen Bundestag zum Terrorakt in den USA', 12 Sept. 2001, http://www.bundesregierung. de/top/dokumente/rede/ix 55757.htm

2 See *Keesings Record of World Events*, Vol. 47, No. 9 (Sept. 2001), p. 44, 336.

3 'Regierungserklärung von Bundeskanzler Schröder vor dem Deutschen Bundestag zum Terrorakt in den USA', 19 Sept. 2001, http://www.bundesregierung. de/top/dokumente/rede/ix 56381.htm://template=singleid=55757

4 Wilfried Schulz, ' "Unerwartet Harmonisch": Dresdner Bundesparteitag der PDS', *Deutschland Archiv*, Vol. 34, No. 6 (Nov.–Dec. 2001), pp. 924–8 (p. 924).

5 Ibid, p. 924.

6 Wolfgang Proissi, 'Kommentar: Grenzen Deutscher Aussenpolitik', *Financial Times Deutschland*, 29 Oct. 2001.

7 'Rede von Bundesaussenminister Joschka Fischer vor dem Deutschen Bundestag, 18.10.2001', http://www.auswaertiges-a . . . /ausgabe_archiv/archiv_id=2239 &type _id=3&bereich_id=. See also 'Rede von Bundesaussenminister Fischer vor der 56 Generalversammlung der VN in New York am12. November 2001', http://www. www.auswaertiges-a . . . /ausgabe_archiv?archiv_id=2292&type_ id=3&bereich_id=

8 'Germany Defends Action Amid Unease', http://europe.cnn/2001/WORLD/ asiapcf/south/10/29/gen.india.schröeder/index.html, 1 Nov. 2001.

9 'Mit Afghanistan-Konferenz beginnt "Post-Taleban-Prozess" ', http://text.bundes regierung.de/nurtext/dokumente/Artikel/ix_63104_1499.htm

10 'Treffen des Bundeskanzlers mit Europäischen Staats- und Regierungschefs in London', http://www.bundesregierung.de/dokumente/Artikel/ix_61744.htm; 'Guess Who Wasn't Coming to Dinner?', *The Economist*, 10 Nov. 2001, pp. 31–2; and Lionel Barber, 'Europe's "Great Powers" Break Rank', *Financial Times*, 5 Nov. 2001.

11 For a transcript of the address see appendix, *Keesings Record of World Events*, Vol. 48, No. 1 (Jan. 2002), pp. 44,591–3.

12 'Wie der 11. September Deutschen verändert hat', *Focus*, 29 Dec. 2001, pp. 44–8.

13 Joachim Krause, 'The Consequences of September 11 2001 for Transatlantic Relations', *Newsletter, Issue 05 (11.23.01) German Foreign Policy in Dialogue*, http://www.deutsche-aussenpolitik.de/publications/newsletter/issue5.html, pp. 4–6.

14 BMI 2001, Sicherheitspaket 1, http://www.bmi.bund.de/dokumente/Pressemit-teilung/ix 61828.htm (12 Nov. 2001).

15 For an example analysis of these measures see Sebastian Harnisch and Wolfgang Brauner, 'The German Response to the September 11th Terrorist Attacks: A Shift in the Domestic Political Debate and Party Politics?', *Newsletter, Issue 05 (11.23.01) German Foreign Policy in Dialogue*, http://www.deutsche-aussenpolitik.de/publications/newsletter/issue5.html

16 For details see Hans-Georg Golz, 'Machtworte', *Deutschland Archiv*, Vol. 34, No. 6 (Nov.–Dec. 2001), pp. 921–4.

17 Jost Müller-Neuhof, 'Innere Sicherheit: Augenmass', *Der Tagesspiegel*, 27 Oct. 2001.

18 *Keesings Record of World Events*, Vol. 47, No. 10 (Oct. 2001), p. 44,417.

19 See for example Walter Schilling, 'Germany after September 11', *Transatlantic Internationale Politik*, Vol. 3, No. 1 (Spring 2002), pp. 81–3.
20 'Statement by the German Chancellor, Gerhard Schröder, to the German Bundestag, 11 October 2001 in Berlin', *Transatlantic Internationale Politik*, Vol. 2, No. 4 (Winter 2001), pp. 150–4, at p.152.
21 *Keesings Record of World Events*, Vol. 47, no. 12 (Dec. 2001), p. 44,519.
22 Ibid. no. 10 (Oct. 2001), p. 44,417.
23 Ibid. no. 11 (Nov. 2001), p. 44,471.
24 Steven Erlanger, 'Schröeder's Coalition Split over Bombing', *International Herald Tribune*, 12 Oct. 2001; Anton-Andreas Guha, 'Am Bombenkrieg in Afghanistan Scheiden Sich Die Geister: Friedensforscher fordert neue Sicherheitspolitik', *Frankfurter Rundschau*, 5 Nov. 2001.
25 *Keesings Record of World Events*, Vol. 47, No. 10 (Oct. 2001), p. 44,393.
26 Mary Elise Sarotte, 'German Troops to Join War Effort', *The Guardian*, 7 Nov. 2001, p. 6.
27 'Bundeskabinett beantragt die Zustimmung des Bundestages zum Einsatz der Bundeswehr im Zampf gegen den internationalen Terrorismus', 8 Nov. 2001, http://www.bundesregierung.de/dokumente/Artikel/ix_61919.htm
28 'Der Krieg duldet keinen faulen Frieden', *Die Zeit*, 47/2001, http://www.zeit.de/2001/47/Politik/print_200147_gruene.html
29 'Bundeskanzler Gerhard Schröder im Gespräch mit den ZDF-Redakteuren Thomas Bellut und Klaus Bresser im ZDF am 16 November 2001', http://text.bundes regierung.de/nurtext/dokumente/Rede/ix_62937_1499.htm
30 'Schröder wins Confidence Vote as France Deploys Troops', http://news.independ ent.co.uk/world/europe/story.jsp?story=105288
31 Schröder, *Transatlantic Internationale Politik*, pp. 150–4 (p. 153).
32 Mary Elise Sarotte, *German Military Reform and European Security*, Adelphi Paper 340 (Oxford: Oxford University Press for the IISS, 2001), p. 12.
33 In an interview in November 2001, Foreign Minister Fischer argued that the notion of a 'peace dividend' was a 'major mistake', because 'peace was not to be savored without investing in it in the shape of crisis prevention measures.' Interview von Bundesaussenminister Joschka Fischer, *Westdeutschen Allgemeinen Zeitung*, 1 Nov. 2001.
34 Sarotte, *German Military*, p. 62.
35 Kate Connolly, 'German Troops to Join War Effort', *The Guardian*, 7 Nov. 2001.
36 'Eine Neue Form der Selbstverteidigung: Bundeskanzler Gerhard Schröder über die Bedrohung der westlichen Zivilisation und Deutschlands Rolle in der Welt', *Die Zeit*, 43/2001, http://www.zeit.de/2001/43/Politik/200143_schröeder.html
37 Schröder, *Transatlantic Internationale Politik*, pp. 153–4.
38 Adrian Hyde-Price, 'German Perceptions', in Mary Buckley and Sally Cummings (eds.), *Kosovo: Perceptions of War and Its Aftermath* (London and New York: Continuum, 2001), pp. 106–21.
39 *Ibid*, p. 153.
40 Steve Erlanger, 'Germany Offers Troops to Help US', *International Herald Tribune*, 7 Nov. 2001.

9 Leadership seeking greater legitimacy

Italy

Philip A. Daniels

As in the rest of the world, the terrorist outrages of 9/11 provoked deep dismay and condemnation in Italy. The unfolding crisis in the weeks following the attacks presented the Italian government with a difficult political challenge. Only installed in office in the summer of 2001, the government of Silvio Berlusconi had had a difficult baptism. Even before the election victory of May 2001 a number of leading international newspapers and journals had questioned whether Berlusconi was fit to govern given the outstanding corruption charges against him and the potential for conflicts of interest given his vast personal wealth and business concerns. His right-wing coalition government that included the populist Northern League and the post-fascist National Alliance had also attracted criticism from some of Italy's European partners worried about the rise of xenophobia in European Union member states. The G8 summit in Genoa in July 2001 was emblematic of the government's inauspicious first weeks in office. Despite months of planning, the summit was the scene for terrible violence, including the death of a young demonstrator shot by a police officer and allegations of unprovoked attacks by the security forces. Italy was widely criticized both at home and abroad for its handling of the summit and the Berlusconi government saw its international standing fall further. The international crisis provoked by the 9/11 attacks, however, gave Berlusconi a new opportunity to use the international arena as a vehicle for the legitimation of his government.

ITALIAN GOVERNMENT POLICY

The Cabinet convened an emergency meeting on 11 September to express its condemnation of the attacks and to pledge Italy's solidarity with the USA. In the weeks that followed, government policy was characterized by inertia, confusion over Italy's role in the 'war on terrorism' and strained relations with both its European partners and the United States. The tone for the government's rather inept handling of the crisis was set on 12 September when Berlusconi proposed the convening of an extraordinary G8 meeting to discuss the international response to terrorism. Other member governments showed little interest in this proposal since the G8, often criticized as an exclusive club for the rich, was hardly an appropriate forum for the building of a broad international coalition against terrorism. In addition, the anti-globalization riots that had marred the G8 summit in Genoa in July were still fresh in the mind.

While the Berlusconi government was quick to pledge its solidarity with the United States, in the first weeks of the crisis there was no clear indication of the role Italy would play in the war on terrorism. The mixed messages coming from Renato Ruggiero, the minister for foreign affairs, and Antonio Martino, the minister for defense,[1] were indicative of the problems at the heart of the Italian government. Italy's low profile in the international arena and the apparent inertia of Italian diplomacy provoked widespread criticism from the opposition and the press, including from sections generally supportive of Berlusconi and his government. In particular, Berlusconi's lack of visibility and his failure to go immediately to Washington, as both Prime Minister Blair and President Chirac had done, was seen as damaging to Italy's standing in the Western alliance.[2]

The government's mishandling of the crisis came to a head on 26 September. At a press conference in Berlin, following a summit meeting with Chancellor Schröder of Germany and Prime Minister Putin of Russia, Berlusconi was reported to have declared the 'superiority' and 'supremacy' of Western civilization over Islamic civilization. The ill-judged comments provoked an international outcry. The Arab League condemned the remarks as 'racist' while the USA and Italy's European allies quickly dissociated themselves from comments that threatened to undermine all their efforts to ensure that the 'war on terrorism' was not misrepresented as a religious war or a 'clash of civilizations.' Two days after Berlusconi's gaffe, Raymond Forni, President of the French National Assembly, showed his disgust by canceling a meeting fixed for 9 October with Marcello Pera, President of the Italian Senate. For his part, Berlusconi said his remarks had been misunderstood and blamed both left-wing journalists for deliberately misrepresenting him and the domestic opposition parties for trying to make political capital out of the ensuing crisis. This disingenuous rebuttal did not convince, however, for Berlusconi's remarks had been widely reported[3] and were entirely consistent with his habit of making ill-judged, off-the-cuff comments at press conferences. In the Italian Senate on 28 September, Berlusconi declared himself innocent of the allegations and therefore, in his view, no apology was required. He took the same line on 2 October at a reception for Arab ambassadors in the Prime Minister's offices at Palazzo Chigi. The ambassadors made clear, however, that they were dissatisfied with Berlusconi's earlier statement to the Senate. The Prime Minister expressed his regrets for what had happened but denied that he had provoked it. In the end, the ambassadors accepted a form of words without an apology but also without any references to a conspiracy by the left and the press. Berlusconi's gaffe and his rather inept attempts to repair the diplomatic damage further undermined Italy's credibility in the international arena and isolated it, at least temporarily, from its principal allies. This sense of isolation deepened in early October when the war in Afghanistan began and Italy was not mentioned by President Bush in his tribute to 'friends' fighting alongside the United States.[4]

Italy's diplomatic shortcomings during the early weeks of the crisis served to confirm a longstanding national sentiment that the country did not punch its weight and was undervalued in the international arena. Decades of unstable and ineffective national government had undermined Italy's position in international diplomacy and left it with a reputation as an unreliable partner. Although successive Italian governments had pursued a more assertive, active and interventionist role alongside their allies since the early 1990s (for example, in the Gulf War and in the Kosovo crisis), the feeling persisted that Italy did not enjoy the same international standing as the other large states in the European Union (Britain, France and Germany). This sense of being relegated to the sidelines was confirmed at a European heads of government summit in Ghent on 19 October. On the eve of the summit, President Chirac convened a meeting with Prime Minister Blair and Chancellor Schröder to discuss the international situation. The meeting revived traditional Italian fears that an informal European Union *directoire*, excluding Italy, was in the process of being established. Berlusconi was furious that he had not been invited to the meeting but President Chirac justified the decision on the grounds that Italy had not assumed any direct tasks in the war in Afghanistan. Italy was again snubbed at the beginning of November when Blair arranged a dinner at Downing Street with Chirac and Schröder. In response to opposition criticisms blaming him for Italy's isolation, Berlusconi accused the parties of the left of being 'anti-patriotic.' Blair attempted to play down the importance of the proposed meeting, saying that its purpose was solely to inform Chirac and Schröder of the results of his recent visit to the Middle East. Italy had not been invited, according to Blair, because on his way back from the mission he had stopped off in Genoa to speak to Berlusconi about the outcomes. Despite these reassurances, Berlusconi was adamant that he should be invited to the Downing Street meeting in order to bolster his image as an important international player and to head off domestic political criticism that he was responsible for Italy's isolation. In addition, he was concerned that if he were to be excluded, it would make it more difficult for him to get parliamentary approval on 7 November for the government's decision to commit Italian military forces to the war in Afghanistan. Following intense diplomatic activity, Italy, along with Belgium and Spain, secured an invitation to the Downing Street meeting. The timing was particularly important for Berlusconi because on the same day as the meeting in London (4 November 2001) the Bush administration accepted the offer of an Italian military contribution to operation 'Enduring Freedom.'

The international image of Italy was further damaged in the post-September 11 period by two pieces of legislation passed by the Berlusconi government. The first, introduced by decree on 25 September, permitted the re-entry of capital without fiscal sanctions even if it had been taken out of the country illegally in the first place. The second limited the use of international interrogatories as evidence in judicial investigations and trials. Critics of the government, at home and abroad, argued that both measures were inappropriate at a time when the Western allies were emphasizing the need for international cooperation and strict fiscal regulatory regimes in the fight against international terrorism. These criticisms were partly tempered by the government decree of 12 October setting up a

Committee for Financial Security that would have the task of identifying and blocking flows of money tied to the networks of international terrorism.[5]

POLITICAL PARTIES AND PUBLIC OPINION

The outrages of 9/11 drew condemnation from parties and leaders across the Italian political spectrum. There was much less consensus, however, on how the US government should respond to the attacks. Berlusconi's right-wing governing coalition was unequivocal in its support for the Bush administration's decision to wage war on terror. The opposition parties of the center and left were, however, more divided on the American military response. The official position of the principal center–left opposition alignment, the Olive Tree, was to support the international coalition's war on terror and for Italy to participate fully in the military action. Massimo D'Alema, the President of the Left Democrats, the leading opposition party in the Olive Tree alliance, described the attacks as 'against the whole of humanity and not just against the USA.'[6] He warned, however, against 'a blind reaction which would feed a spiral of violence and play into the hands of the terrorists.' In his view, 'the struggle against violence and terrorism is not only and principally a military battle.'[7] He called for Italy to play a full role in the international coalition to ensure that its voice would be heard in the development of political and humanitarian initiatives. Francesco Rutelli, leader of the centrist *Margherita* (Daisy) grouping within the Olive Tree alliance, promised 'the full political commitment of the opposition at the side of the government' but, like D'Alema, cautioned against a response that could worsen the situation. Other components of the Olive Tree alliance, however, refused to give support to a military solution to the threat of terrorism: the Greens, with a strong tradition of pacifism, argued that the crisis called for a political, not military, response; the Party of Italian Communists took a similar line, arguing that the focus of policy should be on a negotiated settlement of the Palestinian question.[8] Communist Refoundation, not part of the Olive Tree alliance, condemned the terrorist acts as 'a blind, destructive inhumanity'[9] but took a strong anti-war position. The roots of the opposition to military action from some sections of the left could be found in a strong pacifist tradition and in a continuation of hostility towards the United States and NATO among the remnants of Italian communism.

These divisions among the parties of opposition intensified in the weeks following the attacks. The annual peace march from Perugia to Assisi on 14 October 2001 became the setting for a very public dispute. Pacifist groups participating in the march warned that center–left party leaders who had supported the American intervention in Afghanistan would not be welcome. Those that did attend, including D'Alema and Rutelli, were jeered by demonstrators. In their view, however, there was no contradiction between support for Italy's allies in the war on terror and their own participation in the march.

The divergence of views within the opposition parties also became clear in the parliamentary debates and divisions on the military intervention in Afghanistan.

On 9 October the opposition Olive Tree alliance voted with the parties of the governing majority in support of the American action in Afghanistan. The Greens and the Party of Italian Communists, however, defied the official position of the Olive Tree alliance and voted against the military response. In a further parliamentary vote on Italian military intervention on 7 November President Ciampi invited the majority and opposition parties to give an image of compactness to Italy's international allies and to reassure the Italian armed forces that a united Parliament and country was behind them. Rather than vote a common document, both the majority and the opposition presented their own resolutions incorporating shared principles: these included the recognition of the legitimacy of American intervention in Afghanistan, the requirement that military action should be targeted against well-defined objectives and the commitment to make the maximum effort to avoid civilian casualties. Using the same parliamentary tactic employed in 1999 when Italian forces intervened in the Kosovo crisis, the majority voted for its document with the abstention of the opposition, and then the opposition voted for its document with the abstention of the majority. In this way, the overwhelming majority of Parliament voted for a set of common commitments without agreeing to a common resolution. Once again, however, the Greens and the Party of Italian Communists dissented from the official position of the Olive Tree alliance and voted against the commitment of Italian forces to the war in Afghanistan; in total, sixty-one senators and deputies belonging to the alliance voted against. The center–left's internal divisions over the war caused much bitterness within the Olive Tree alliance because it threatened to undermine the leadership's efforts to project an image of a credible alternative government.

The overwhelming parliamentary endorsement for Italian intervention in the conflict was not representative of a more ambivalent Italian public opinion. According to opinion surveys, the majority of Italians was in favor of a military response to the terrorist threat but hesitant about the participation of Italian forces in a war. A poll conducted immediately after the terrorist attacks showed 81 percent in favor and only 11 percent against NATO's alignment with the USA.[10] Subsequent survey findings indicated, however, that Italians were unaware of, or chose to ignore, the military obligations this placed on Italy as a NATO member. A poll conducted on 15 September 2001 found that 53 percent of respondents thought that an American military response was right while 36 percent rejected this course of action. The same poll, however, showed 49 percent of respondents were against Italian participation alongside the United States in an armed action against the terrorists while only 44 percent were in favor.[11] Once the shooting war began, the percentage opposed to Italian participation increased: a poll conducted on the eve of the parliamentary vote on Italian military intervention found that 55 percent of respondents were against active Italian participation in the conflict while 43 percent were in favor.[12] The Italian public's misgivings about the war were also shown in mid-October 2001 when an opinion survey showed 72 percent in favor of a 'humanitarian pause' in the bombing to allow aid to reach Afghan civilians.[13] The reluctance on the part of many Italians to see their armed forces drawn into the war in Afghanistan almost certainly reflected the unease about the conduct of American foreign policy: for example an opinion survey found that 45.9 percent of respondents thought that Americans were in part responsible for the tragedy of September 11; 44.6 percent attributed the responsibility exclusively to the terrorists.[14]

THE VATICAN AND CATHOLIC OPINION

The opposition of much of the Italian public to the war in Afghanistan is explained, in part, by their adherence to the pacifist tradition rooted in Catholic moral doctrine. The Vatican, an important moral authority that has played a significant though declining role in postwar Italian politics and society, was quick to stress that the conflict was not a religious war of Christianity against Islam. In a papal visit to Kazakhstan and Armenia in late September 2001, Pope John Paul attacked the fanaticism and hatred that 'desecrate the name of God and disfigure the authentic image of man.'[15] The Pope called for dialogue and a search for peace, emphasizing that 'the spiral of hatred and violence should not prevail'[16] and that the Western governments' desire for justice should not be transformed into indiscriminate revenge. Within the non-monolithic Catholic Church, however, a variety of divergent positions emerged in the weeks following the attacks on New York and Washington. At one end of the spectrum of Catholic opinion, the hardliners supported a strong military response by the West.[17] At the opposite end of the spectrum, the pacifist Catholic groups associated with the Liliput network rejected any military solution to the terrorist threat. The largest part of Catholic opinion was aligned, however, with the prudent response of the Pope who rejected the 'spirit of revenge' while accepting the right of the USA to punish those guilty of the terrorist atrocities. According to this view, the response of the American government had to be proportionate and targeted against the culpable rather than an excessive and indiscriminate military reaction that might provoke a wider conflict with the Islamic world. The USA's legitimate right to self-defense was reiterated, though qualified, by the Pope in his 2002 New Year message in celebration of World Peace Day. He spoke of 'a right to defend oneself against terrorism,' a right which must, however, be consistent with 'moral and juridical rules in the choice of both objectives and means.'[18]

CONCLUSION

The crisis provoked by the atrocities of 9/11 caused significant difficulties for the Italian government. Disagreements among senior ministers in the governing coalition, delays in formulating a coherent policy response and a frequently clumsy handling of diplomatic relations conveyed the image of an inexperienced administration. Prime Minister Berlusconi, in particular, did little to enhance his international standing in the early weeks of the crisis.

In the domestic political arena, there were significant disagreements about the war in Afghanistan and the role that Italian forces should have in it. The main opponents of the war came from Catholic pacifist groups, the Greens and sections of the communist left. These groups had little parliamentary strength, however, and the government could count on support from the principal parties of the center–left opposition grouped in the Olive Tree alliance. This alliance was keen to achieve a bipartisan consensus over the issue of war and, at the same time, to enhance its credibility as a potential alternative government. The center–left's support for a military intervention in Afghanistan was not, however, unconditional. It had deep misgivings about the foreign policy of the Bush administration and called for a greater emphasis on political and diplomatic initiatives to address what it saw as the issues, particularly the Palestinian question, at the heart of the problems of international terrorism. Much of the Italian public shared this unease about the effectiveness and the morality of the military response targeted on Afghanistan and opinion polls showed majorities against the intervention of Italian armed forces.

Doubts and divisions in Italy over the direction of US foreign policy became more pronounced following President Bush's reference to an 'axis of evil' in his State of the Union address in January 2002. In common with the majority of its EU counterparts, the Italian government was very reluctant to see an extension of the military action to encompass other states viewed by the Bush administration as sponsors of terrorism. The opposition parties of the center and left in Italy were hostile to military action against states such as Iraq on the grounds that it could not be justified in international law and that it would undermine the international coalition against terrorism. The Italian government's difficulties in the face of US and European divisions over widening the military campaign were clearly illustrated in August 2002 when Antonio Martino, Defense Minister, announced that Italy would be ready to take part in military action against Iraq if there were proof that it was developing weapons of mass destruction.[19] Other members of the government called for prudence, arguing that such an attack would require a UN resolution.[20] Lamberto Dini, Minister for Foreign Affairs in the previous center–left government, warned that Italian government support for a US attack on Iraq would distance Italy from the majority of its EU allies.[21]

Aside from the domestic political divisions over the issue, the government's reaction to the crisis highlighted subtle shifts in the foreign policy priorities of Italy under Berlusconi. The ideological affinities with President Bush and the emphasis on deregulated capitalism in the United States had encouraged Berlusconi on taking office to develop a special relationship with Italy's transatlantic ally. At the same time, the Berlusconi government, Italy's most Euro-skeptical in the postwar period, has given the European arena a lower priority and has been involved in a series of damaging disputes with its European allies.[22] In this context of a conscious reorientation of Italy's foreign policy it is ironic that the Italian government's rather inept handling of the post-9/11 crisis succeeded in distancing it from both its American and European allies.

NOTES

1 For example, Martino's rather casual suggestion on 20 September that a NATO operation involving Italy could begin without the prior approval of Parliament provoked a
   strong reaction from the opposition. Berlusconi confirmed the following day that
   Parliament would decide on any Italian intervention.
2 Berlusconi finally visited the United States on 15 October 2001 several weeks after the
   visits of Blair, Chirac and Shroeder.
3 *L'Unità*, 27 September 2001, reported his comments as follows: 'we must be aware of
   the superiority of our civilization, a civilization that constitutes together a system of
   values and of principles that has given great well-being to the populations of the
   countries that practise it, a civilization that guarantees the respect of human, religious
   and political rights.' All translations from Italian original by author.
4 In an attempt to demonstrate solidarity with the United States Berlusconi announced
   that his party, Forza Italia, would hold a USA Day in Rome on 10 November 2001.
   Critics dismissed it as something of a cheap stunt. An estimated 40,000 people
   attended the demonstration, around half the number who turned out for an anti-war
   rally in Rome on the same day.
5 A further decree law of 18 October introduced the crime of 'international terrorism'
   and made it easier for magistrates and police to carry out searches and phone-tappings.
6 *Il Sole–24 Ore*, 10 Oct. 2001, p. 7.
7 *L'Unità*, 13 Sept. 2001, p. 15.
8 *L'Unità*, 16 Sept. 2001, p. 9.
9 *L'Unità*, 12 Sept. 2001, p. 12.
10 A national sample of 946 respondents was asked: 'Article 5 of the NATO Treaty
   defines armed aggression against one member state as an attack on the whole alliance.
   Therefore NATO has aligned with the USA. Do you agree with this decision?' Survey
   conducted by CIRM Market Research, 13 Sept. 2001. Source: http://www.istituto-
   cirm.com/indice/130901.htm
11 A national sample of 946 respondents was asked: 'America is preparing a military
   action against the terrorists. In your opinion is this the right response to what happened
   on 11 September in Manhattan?' Survey conducted by CIRM Market Research.
   Source: http://www.istituto-cirm.com/indice/150901(3).htm. A second question
   asked: 'Are you personally in favor or against the participation of Italy in an armed
   action alongside the USA against the terrorists?' Survey conducted by CIRM Market
   Research. Source: http://hwww.istituto-cirm.com/indice/150901(2).htm. A survey by
   PEOPLESWG produced similar findings: 61 percent of respondents agreed that the
   9/11 attacks justified an American military reaction (28 percent disagreed); 49.4 percent of respondents favored an economic embargo or sanctions against countries suspected of harboring terrorists while only 29.6 percent saw military action as the most
   acceptable response. Survey for *Famiglia Cristiana*. Source: http://www.swgbologna.it/
   ricorda/USA_terrorismo.html
12 A national sample of 1,046 respondents was asked 'Are you personally in favor or
   against active Italian participation alongside Anglo-American forces in the war against
   terrorism in Afghanistan?' Survey conducted by CIRM Market Research, 5 Nov. 2001.
   Source http://www.isitituto-cirm.com/indice/051101.htm
13 While 18 percent opposed a pause. A national sample of 1,006 respondents was asked
   'Are you personally in favor or against a "humanitarian pause" in the bombing to allow
   aid to reach the stricken Afghan population?' Survey conducted by CIRM Market
   Research on 12 and 13 Oct. 2001. Source: http://www.istituto-cirm.com/indice/
   131001.htm
14 Survey conducted by PEOPLESWG. Respondents were asked: 'In regard to the tragedy that has hit New York, some argue that the responsibility for the attack should be

attributed exclusively to the terrorists, while others think that the Americans should bear a part of the responsibility for the policy they conduct in the world. Which of these two positions do you largely share?' Source: http://www.swg.bologna.it/ricorda/USA_terrorismo.html

15 *L'Unità*, 25 Sept. 2001, p. 4.

16 *L'Unità*, 13 Sept. 2001, p. 12.

17 This position was represented, for example, by Alessandro Maggiolini, Bishop of Como, who was reported to have said that 'St. Francis, although an example of saintliness, cannot substitute for a minister of defense.' *Corriere della Sera*, 16 Sept. 2001, p. 20.

18 From the message 'Non c'è pace senza giustizia, non c'è giustizia senza perdono' (There is not peace without justice, there is not justice without forgiveness), 1 Jan. 2002. Cited in A. de Guttry and F. Pagani, *Sfida All'Ordine Mondiale: L'11 settembre e la risposta della comunità internazionale*, Rome, Donzelli, 2002, p. 25.

19 *La Repubblica*, 2 Aug. 2002, p. 9.

20 Alfredo Mantica, under-secretary of Foreign Affairs. He went on to say that 'this is not the first time that the Defense Minister has come out with declarations of this type.' *La Repubblica*, 2 Aug. 2002, p. 9.

21 *La Repubblica*, 2 Aug. 2002, p. 9. An opinion poll published in *La Repubblica* (p. 9) on the same day indicated a majority of respondents against Italian participation in an attack on Iraq: 58 percent of respondents were opposed while 33 percent were in favor.

22 In the final months of 2001 Italy clashed with its European partners over a number of issues including the Berlusconi government's decision to buy an American military transport plane rather than the A400M being developed by the European consortium and its initial unwillingness to agree to the adoption of a European arrest warrant. At the beginning of January 2002, the strongly pro-European Foreign Minister, Renato Ruggiero, resigned over the government's increasingly negative stance on Europe.

ical Islamist state and
..lar Arab nationalism

..n and Iraq

Roland Dannreuther

The terrorist attacks of 9/11 on the USA shone an immediate international spotlight on Iran and Iraq. These were both countries which were potential suspects for the attacks and whose recent history was one of considerable hostility towards the USA. As the perpetrators were identified as the al-Qaeda group and the Taliban in Afghanistan, Iran and Iraq's geographical proximity and potential religio-political links with these groups increased their international exposure. When President Bush's spokesperson set up the challenge that 'this is the time for nations to choose whether they are with the United States and the free world against terrorism or they are not,' it had a particular salience and urgency for Iran and Iraq.[1] Leaders of both states knew that, if they failed the test, they opened themselves to be the next target in the US-led war against terrorism. As 2002 progressed, it became clear that Iraq was destined to be the next target with the Iraqi President Saddam Hussein enjoying less and less room for maneuvre or escape.

This chapter analyzes the manner in which the government and people of Iran and Iraq adapted to this new challenging environment in the aftermath of the events of 9/11 and the war in Afghanistan. It first sets out to give a broad assessment of the principal features of the Iranian and Iraqi states, their foreign policy priorities and their specific relations with the United States, and the degree to which it is appropriate to treat the two states in similar categories, such as the tendency to call them 'rogue states.' It then moves on to examine in more detail the reactions in Iran and Iraq respectively.

ROGUE STATES?

The tendency to place Iran and Iraq in the same category is, to a large extent, driven by the policy approach and framework adopted by successive US administrations. During the Clinton period, Iran and Iraq were defined as 'rogue states' or, as the category was later refined, 'states of concern.' A broader policy was adopted for the Gulf region which included the notion of a 'dual containment' of Iran and Iraq. This tradition has continued under the Bush administration and was given a new twist at the President's Union address to the Congress on

29 January 2002 when he included Iran and Iraq, along with North Korea, as countries representing an 'axis of evil.'[2]

The reasons why the US government has tended to place Iran and Iraq in the same category are driven by three main factors. First, and most significantly in the light of 9/11, Iran and Iraq have been consistently designated by the State Department as states which sponsor terrorism. In the Department's report on *Patterns of Global Terrorism: 2000*, Iran was characterized as 'the most active' state sponsor of terrorism in the light of its continued moral and material support to Lebanese and Palestinian Islamist groups, in particular Hizbollah, Hamas and Palestinian Islamic Jihad. The report recognized that Iraq's ability to use terrorism had declined due to international pressure but that Iraq still 'continues to plan and sponsor international terrorism.'[3]

The second factor is that Iran and Iraq are also judged by the US administration to be developing and producing weapons of mass destruction (WMD) and their means of delivery. In the immediate aftermath of the 1990–1 Gulf War, Iraq committed itself to implementing UN Security Council Resolution 687 which demanded a full, complete and verifiable destruction of all such WMD capabilities. Over a decade later and Iraq has not succeeded in satisfying the UN Security Council that it has fulfilled its obligations and has thus remained under a UN-mandated sanctions regime. The unanimous vote for UN Security Council Resolution 1441 in November 2002, which made a further and more forceful demand for disarmament, represented the frustration of both the United States and the international community at Iraq's non-compliance. The US government is also convinced that Iran is similarly engaged in developing WMD capabilities and Congress has legislated for a unilateral sanctions regime on Iran as set out in the Iran–Libya Sanctions Act (ILSA).

The final factor is the perceived hostility of the Iranian and Iraqi regimes to core US interests in the Middle East and beyond. Iran and Iraq are viewed in Washington as direct threats to stability in the Persian Gulf region which has been the main rationale for the 'dual containment' policy. Likewise, Iran and Iraq are viewed to be hostile to US efforts to promote an Arab–Israeli peace settlement through adopting a rejectionist anti-Israeli stance and in supporting radical groups which seek to undermine any potential moves to a workable settlement.

However helpful in terms of simplifying the policy-making process towards a complex part of the world, there are dangers that placing Iran and Iraq into the same category obscures the many differences between the two countries and can lead to oversimplistic policy prescriptions. Although Iran and Iraq have been identified as 'rogue states' for over a decade, it is notable that this has not led them to become allies or partners. Despite occasional hints at a rapprochement, their bilateral relations remain characterized by extreme levels of distrust which is the legacy of a brutal and destructive war between the two countries from 1981 to 1988. Since the end of the war, no lasting peace settlement has been reached and there remain disputes over such issues as the return of prisoners of war. The engrained hostility between Iran and Iraq is also a reflection of the ideological and ethnic differences between the two states. Formally, both the Iranian and

Iraqi regimes present themselves as revolutionary, but Iran defines itself as a radical Islamist state, while Iraq remains committed to a secular Arab nationalism as defined through adherence to Ba'athist ideology. The Iraqi government's proud assertion of its essentially Arab identity, despite the large Kurdish minority in the country, is likewise in conflict with Iran's majority Persian ethnic identity.

The differences in the composition of the Iraqi and Iranian states are paralleled by significant divergences in terms of political systems and regimes. The Iraqi regime, under President Saddam Hussein, is a highly dictatorial quasi-totalitarian regime, where dissent is brutally repressed, no substantive opposition is permitted, and popular acquiescence is secured through a mix of patronage and state-imposed terror.[4] Iran's government, though far from democratic by Western standards, is an oasis of pluralism and liberalism when compared with Iraq. The foundations of the Iranian political system remain firmly tied to the legacies of the 1979 Revolution and Khomeini's religio-political ideology but, despite these constraints, there has emerged an increasingly free and vibrant policy debate and the growth of competing factions and parties. Broadly speaking, there is currently a 'reformist' grouping, which is supported by President Khatami, a majority in the *Majlis* (Parliament) and more broadly in Iranian civil society, and a 'conservative' grouping which finds its main support in a number of the most powerful Islamist revolutionary institutions, such as the Islamic Revolutionary Guards, the Council of Guardians and the judiciary.[5] The Supreme Guide, Ayatollah Khamenei, who is the official head of state and Khomeini's successor, attempts to take a mediating position between these two factional groups but whose general predilection is to support the conservatives.

In relative terms, the political system is far more liberalized in Iran than in Iraq. In Iran, elections take place regularly, political debate is permitted, and mechanisms for peaceful political change are potentially available. Certainly, the political system remains deeply flawed with unaccountable individuals and institutions wielding disproportionate powers and continually undermining the reforms which the popularly elected bodies, such as the Presidency and Parliament, are committed to implementing.[6] But, despite these flaws, the most significant challenges to the government come primarily from those working within, and accepting the essential legitimacy of, the political system rather than from those who seek to subvert the system from without. This is not the case in Iraq where there is no practical opportunity legitimately to oppose the government. As a consequence, the most significant challenges to the Iraqi government come from exiled groups or those Iraqis living in territory not under the central government's control, most notably the various Kurdish parties who have maintained a degree of autonomy in Northern Iraq. The London-based Iraqi National Congress (INC), which loosely gathers together all the most significant exiled opposition forces including the Kurdish parties, is the symbolic manifestation of this principally external challenge to Saddam Hussein's rule.

These significant differences in the type and nature of the political systems in Iran and Iraq inevitably have an impact on policy-making. In the aftermath of the 'axis of evil' speech, even US officials were compelled to differentiate US policy by noting that the administration was seeking a 'regime change' in Iraq and not in Iran. European allies of the United States have pursued a more consciously differentiated approach, engaging in a 'constructive dialogue' with Tehran, criticizing the US-imposed unilateral sanctions on Iran, while generally supporting the UN-mandated sanctions policy towards Iraq.

In any assessment of Iranian and Iraqi relations with the perpetrators of 9/11 – al-Qaeda and the Taliban – a similarly nuanced approach is required. In practice, neither state had much in sympathy with these groups. The nationalist Iraqi regime has been in continual conflict with Sunni extremist Islamist groups and had no special affinity with Osama bin Laden, whose original split from the Saudi royal family came after his offer to use the Afghan Mujahidin to liberate Iraqi-occupied Kuwait was rejected. For Iran, al-Qaeda and the Taliban represented a far more direct and significant threat. Both groups embody ideological challenges to Iran's Islamist credentials, espousing a Sunni Islamist ideology which is consciously anti-Iranian and anti-Shi'a. The Taliban and al-Qaeda were also based in a country immediately bordering Iran where Iran's national interests were directly engaged. In 1998, Iran mobilized over 200,000 troops on its border with Afghanistan in response to the Taliban's capture of Mazar-e Sharif and the subsequent slaughter of nine Iranian diplomats and thousands of the minority Afghan Shi'a Hazara community. For Iran, therefore, the issue of the Taliban and the al-Qaeda has been a much more significant issue in terms of core national and regional interests than for Iraq. It is this country which is therefore assessed first.

IRAN: THE COST OF AMBIVALENCE

The initial response of the Iranian leadership to 9/11 generated considerable optimism that Iran might seize the opportunity to improve relations with the United States and further enhance its international respectability. President Khatami stated on the day of the events that 'I condemn the terrorist operations of hijacking and attacking public places in American cities which have resulted in the death of a large number of defenseless people.'[7] More significantly, the conservative forces, in the guise of the substitute Friday prayer leader for Tehran, Ayatollah Muhammad Emami-Kashani, also condemned the attacks.[8] For the first time since the 1979 Revolution, the ritual chant of 'Death to America' was not heard at the meeting. It is true that Emami-Kashani continued his address to stress that 'Israel and the usurper Zionist regime are the number one state terrorists' and that the United States was deeply implicated through its support of Israel. A number of newspaper articles at the time also suggested that US intelligence services and/or Zionists were behind the attacks.[9] But, in general, there were clear indications that Iran was officially seeking to dissociate itself from the terrorist attacks. Candlelit vigils in a number of squares in Tehran in commemoration for the victims of the attacks also suggested a degree of popular pro-American sentiment.

The official US response to this was supportive but also cautious. Colin Powell noted that 'Iran made a rather positive statement for Iran' but added that 'we have serious differences with the government of Iran because of their support for terrorism.'[10] The potential for an opening in US–Iranian relations and for gaining the involvement of Iran in the anti-terrorist coalition was, however, seized upon by a number of European and other allied countries who sent a succession of high-level intermediaries. The most prominent of these was the British Foreign Secretary Jack Straw who arrived in Tehran on 25 September. Britain, having successfully obtained a resolution over the Fatwa against Salman Rushdie which had permitted the reestablishment of diplomatic relations, sought to explore whether a similar compromise could be reached over conflicting US and Iranian approaches to terrorism.[11] It was not expected that the Iranian leadership would have to withdraw support from their Islamist allies in Lebanon and Palestine, such as Hizbollah, Hamas and Palestinian Islamic Jihad. At a minimum, they would have to dissociate themselves from those acts by these organizations which could be considered to be 'terrorist' in that they deliberately target innocent civilians.

Such a compromise did not, though, find political support in Iran. On 26 September, Ayatollah Khameini asserted his political supremacy by chairing a Supreme National Security Council meeting and enforcing a hardline position rejecting any rapprochement with the United States. The next day, he stated clearly that 'we shall not offer any assistance to America and its allies in this attack on Afghanistan.'[12] President Khatami, whose position is constitutionally inferior to that of Supreme Guide, was brought into line when he also criticized the United States for its arrogance in thinking that it 'can distinguish between good and evil.'[13] The core substantive issue which undermined the prospects for compromise was Tehran's refusal to shift from its conviction that Israel should be considered a terrorist state and that the Palestinian uprising, including the role played by the Islamist groups, represents 'a natural, legal and firm reaction against the criminal actions of the occupying Israelis.' In Khameini's speech, he argued moreover that the aim of the US anti-terrorism coalition was not only 'to settle scores with anyone who defended the oppressed people of Palestine' but also to establish itself as the dominant power in Central Asia, Afghanistan and Pakistan.

Khameini's uncompromising stance undermined any potential for a radical breakthrough in Iran's relationship to the United States or its willingness to support the military action in Afghanistan. The conservative elements in Iran, whom Khameini has increasingly tended to support, saw no practical advantage in a change of policy towards the USA since it would only undermine their position and status in the political system. In addition, the conditions set for Iran joining the anti-terror coalition touched on the core ideological foundations of the Islamic Republic – anti-Americanism and anti-Zionism. To question these foundations would potentially threaten to undermine the legitimacy of the Iranian political system itself. Within Iran, there had also been no national debate over qualifying support for the Islamist groups in their struggle against Israel. It was an area of unquestioned ideological commitment which even the reformist groups were not in a position to challenge fundamentally, especially when their hold on the real structures of power in Iran was so weak.

The dilemma that the Iranian government now faced was how, given this rejection of any official cooperation with the United States, it could still ensure that Iran's core national and regional interests would be promoted in the upcoming military campaign in Afghanistan. In reality, there was a considerable convergence in interests between Iran and the anti-terror coalition, since Tehran would also welcome the overthrow and elimination of the Taliban and al-Qaeda. There was also a clear concern that Iranian interests should be taken into account in any post-Taliban Afghanistan. More generally, Iranian leaders were anxious to promote their international credentials by demonstrating their constructive and moderate role in the international response to 9/11. The Iranian regime had faced a similar type of dilemma with the anti-Iraq coalition formed during the 1990–1 Gulf War; a coalition whose core objectives had also been in Iran's national interest. During that war, Iran had adopted a strictly neutral position which had ultimately not produced the political dividends that had been expected. In the coming war in Afghanistan, the Iranian leadership was committed to adopting a more proactive role which protected Iran's core interests but without undermining its ideological commitments.

The strategy that Iran adopted to satisfy these conflicting objectives was to work actively and energetically with the United Nations. Iranian officials made clear that they would be willing to join an anti-terrorism coalition but only if it was under the aegis of the United Nations.[14] To secure such a UN-based coalition, Iran first sought to get the United Nations to support a definition of terrorism which would reject the US version by making a distinction between freedom fighters and terrorists which would absolve the Palestinian and Lebanese Islamist groups. Support for this initiative was first sought by Iranian diplomats in the wider Muslim world and particularly through the Islamic Conference Organization (OIC). But, when the OIC met to decide on this issue, its Arab and Muslim leaders passed the buck to the UN to determine the definition of terrorism. When the UN convened in early October, there was similarly a failure to define terrorism, in both the Security Council and the General Assembly, despite resolutions firmly condemning the phenomenon. Iran's diplomatic efforts had thus failed to achieve its initial objectives.

When the campaign started in Afghanistan in early October, Iranian leaders sought to define a new approach which would balance its ideological commitments with its pragmatic interests. Thus, the US-led operations were dutifully condemned by the Iranian political leadership, including both Khameini and Khatami. But, at the same time, a secret message was sent to Washington, which was subsequently confirmed by Powell, stating that Iran would rescue any American military personnel who landed on Iranian territory.[15] Although the significance of this message tended to be exaggerated in the international media, it was nevertheless an indication from the Iranian leadership that, while it did not support the US intervention, it would not seek actively to undermine it. In calibrating its response, Iran also differentiated its condemnation of the United States from its continued moral and material support for the Northern Alliance, its traditional ally in the internal Afghan political scene, despite the Alliance's collaboration with US forces. Thus, when Kabul was finally overrun in November, Iran fully praised the victory of the Northern Alliance and celebrated the defeat of the Taliban, while still condemning the United States.

Iran's careful balancing act was also maintained in the delicate negotiations for a post-Taliban settlement in Afghanistan. Again, so long as these negotiations were undertaken within the auspices of the UN, the Iranian government consciously adopted a moderate and consensual stance. Iran welcomed the efforts of the UN special envoy for Afghanistan, Lakhdar Brahimi, and supported his initiatives for a multi-ethnic interim government. So long as Iran's core interests were protected, most notably by an Afghan government which would protect the Shi'a Hazara community and be supportive of Iran's regional role, Tehran demonstrated a willingness to compromise and to seek constructive solutions. Discussions with President Musharraf of Pakistan resulted in a broad bilateral agreement for the composition of any interim government. At the Conference in Petersberg, Germany, in late November, which brought together the various Afghan factions, Iran played a similarly constructive role and welcomed the decision to make Hamid Karzai the head of the interim administration in Afghanistan. The positive role played by Iran was recognized by US State Official Richard Haas who noted that 'they have a lot of influence with the Northern Alliance, and to the best of my knowledge, they have used that influence constructively to bring about some sort of compromise that we saw in Bonn.'[16]

By the beginning of 2002, Iranian diplomacy appeared successfully to have managed the difficult balancing between condemnation of the US 'war against terrorism' and constructive support for a stable post-Taliban political order in Afghanistan, which could embellish Tehran's claims for international respectability. A number of events conspired, though, to undermine this. First, Israel intercepted a boat on 3 January with arms shipments to the Palestinian Authority which, it was alleged, had originated from Iran. Then, unnamed sources in the Pentagon and State Department made increasingly frequent claims that Iran was providing refuge to fleeing al-Qaeda fighters and that it was arming local Afghans, particularly in the Western provinces adjoining Iran, to undermine the new interim government.[17] Despite the confirmation during a visit to Tehran by UN Secretary General Kofi Annan that Iran was in full cooperation with the United Nations, George Bush explicitly included Iran in his 'axis of evil' speech on 29 January as a country which 'aggressively pursues [WMD] weapons and exports terror, while an unelected few repress the Iranian people's hope for freedom.' On 3 February, Donald Rumsfeld added that 'we have any number of reports that Iran has been permissive and allowed transit through their country of al-Qaeda members. We have any number of reports, more recently, that they have been supplying arms in Afghanistan to various elements in the country.'[18]

The Iranian response to the Bush speech was predictably hostile and saw a closing of ranks between the conservative and reformist forces. On the occasion of the twenty-third anniversary of the Revolution, over 100,000 Iranians took to the streets and condemned the USA. Although the speech extinguished any hope of a US–Iranian rapprochement, in reality this was never seriously on the cards. In addition, it is arguable whether the hardening of the US stance strengthened the conservative forces or even whether it had a significant impact on the continuing internal reformist–conservative struggle. The focus on 'unelected officials' in Bush's speech actually provided the reformist groups with a useful weapon to promote their cause. The Rumsfeld claims were more problematic but, rather than immediately denying their validity, some reformist Iranian officials requested the US government to share the intelligence which would substantiate these claims.[19] In general, what emerged is not so much a transformation in the balance of power between the conservatives and reformists but that struggle being translated into the differing policies which were being pursued by the competing factions in Afghanistan. As 2002 progressed, the internal struggle only increased in intensity as Khatami appeared finally to lose patience with the conservative stranglehold on power and sought to put forward legislation that would curb the powers of the judiciary and the veto-wielding Council of Guardians.[20]

The fact that US attention during 2002 became increasingly focused on Iraq relieved some of the external pressures on Iran. Both Iran and the United States sought to find a mutual accommodation which would stabilize their relations as the preparations for a military confrontation became more imminent. For the Iranian leadership, there was a fine balancing act between formal condemnation of US unilateralism and the threat of the use of force with an implicit support for the US goal of 'regime change' in Iraq. For its part, the US administration reassured Iran that it would not be the next target, relaxed some of the earlier rhetoric, but without fundamentally shifting from its hardline position towards the Iranian regime. As in the immediate aftermath of 9/11, this strictly limited accommodation demonstrated that neither the USA not Iran were yet in a position to forge a new and more cooperative relationship. Iran's political progression had not gone sufficiently far to be able to undermine the core underpinnings of the Islamic revolution – its ideological commitment to opposition against the USA, its abhorrence of Israel and its unqualified support for those Palestinian groups seeking to overthrow Israel. For the USA, these continuing ideological convictions meant that no substantive change in policy towards Iran was politically feasible.

IRAQ: SEEKING TO AVOID THE INEVITABLE

The challenges facing Iraq were significantly different from those facing Iran. First, the Iraqi regime had no practical opportunity to use 9/11 to improve its standing with the USA, not least because Iraq, unlike Iran, was initially one of the prime suspects for the attacks. Second, the Iraqi regime did not face significant internal challenges to its rule but rather the activities of opposition groups outside its control and which enjoyed varying degrees of support from the United States. Third, the Iraqi regime, like the Iranian, had no particular love of al-Qaeda or the Taliban but, unlike Iran, had no particular stake over developments in Afghanistan due to its physical separation from the country and its traditional disinterest in the regional competition for power in Afghanistan. For Iraq, the main challenges of 9/11 were more simply defined – to avoid becoming itself a military target of the 'war against terrorism' and to continue to pursue its core objectives of securing a lifting of sanctions without having to eliminate its residual WMD capabilities.

Saddam Hussein's response to these challenges was, characteristically, to take the diplomatic offensive and to seek to use 9/11 to burnish his anti-American credentials. As in the past, Hussein targeted his message specifically for the Arab masses, seeking to gain their popular support by highlighting his heroic willingness to stand up against the United States in contrast to the other meeker and more compromised Arab and Muslim leaders. By so doing, he hoped to produce a popular groundswell which would undermine the willingness of Arab governments to support US intervention into Iraq. He thus became the sole voice amongst all the Arab and Muslim leaders not to condemn the 9/11 attacks and to argue that the USA essentially got what it deserved since 'he who does not want to reap evil should not sow evil.'[21] Over the next few months, the rhetoric only became more virulent, reaching its culminating point or perhaps nadir with Saddam's son, Uday, praising the 'daring operations carried out by Arab Muslim youths.'[22] These verbal attacks were combined with a number of dramatic gestures, such as Hussein's call to establish a 7 million 'Jerusalem army' to liberate Palestine and the initiation of a campaign for all Iraqi citizens to pay into a fund supporting the Taliban.[23] During the military operations in Afghanistan, and when it was clear that Iraq had avoided being the target of the first phase, the aggressive rhetoric against US allies in the region also increased with, for example, calls for reincorporation of Kuwait into Iraq.

The various groups in opposition to the Iraqi regime quite naturally generally strongly supported the US anti-terrorist campaign. These groups sought also to find justifications for why the US administration should extend the campaign to target directly the regime of Saddam Hussein. Thus, the Iraqi National Congress went to considerable lengths to demonstrate to the US administration that there was a direct link between Iraq and the 9/11 attacks. The INC leadership provided evidence that senior Iraqi intelligence officers had been in contact with al-Qaeda and that one of the most senior of these officials had met Muhammad Atta, who died in, and was one of the masterminds of, the operation.[24] For their part, the Kurdish parties which have a substantial degree of autonomy in Northern Iraq, sought to demonstrate their commitment to the anti-terror coalition by engaging in a confrontation with a small splinter Islamist Kurdish group, the Jund al-Islam, which it was claimed included al-Qaeda fighters and was working with the Iraqi regime.[25] Even the main Shi'a opposition group, the Supreme Council for an Islamic Republic of Iraq (SCIRI), whose close support and base in Iran has meant no official connection with the USA, came out in favor of a US attack so long as it targeted the 'terrorist regime' rather than the Iraqi people.[26]

The Bush administration was certainly supportive of these overtures by the

Iraqi opposition groups, since it included senior officials, most notably Deputy Secretary of Defense Paul Wolfowitz, who had long argued for closer US ties with these groups and greater efforts towards the overthrow of the Iraqi regime.[27] However, the failure to find the 'smoking gun' which directly implicated Iraq with 9/11 resulted in a consensus behind the more cautious approach adopted by Powell who advocated focusing the first phase of the campaign on Afghanistan and leaving the Iraqi dossier until after the successful execution of that campaign. Thus, Iraq survived the initial military intervention which was limited to attacks on Afghanistan.

However, the increased US pressure and focus on Iraq was not indefinitely but only temporarily postponed. Once Kabul had fallen in November, the US administration intensified its campaign against Iraq. On 18 November, Condoleezza Rice stated that Iraq's President 'poses a danger to his people, to his region and to us because of his insistence on possessing weapons of mass destruction.'[28] With a new UN Security Council resolution on Iraq passed on 3 December, President Bush issued an uncompromising demand that Iraq accept UN weapons inspectors. In answering a question as to what would happen if Saddam Hussein fails to comply with this demand, he stated that 'he'll find out.'[29] The US policy was clearly and explicitly defined. It was now essentially unquestioned in Washington that, in Bush's words, 'the Iraqi regime has plotted to develop Anthrax, and nerve gas and nuclear weapons over the decade' and that the only way out of its predicament was for Iraq to allow UN inspectors in. Although there remained a continuing debate between hawks and moderates over what should be done about Iraq, a consensus had been formed that Iraq would have to accept the return of the weapons inspectors unconditionally and that, failing this, a campaign to ensure a 'regime change' would follow. The divisions were no longer over the question of 'if' but the 'when and how' of a campaign to replace the Iraqi regime.[30]

Under this renewed and focused US pressure, the Iraqi regime did engage in more intensive regional and international diplomatic activity to undermine US objectives. As usual, it sought to gain the support of its main allies on the UN Security Council, Russia and China. However, the reception in Moscow and Beijing was not as warm as prior to September 11, as both countries sought to capitalize on improved relations with the USA through their support for the anti-terror coalition. Iraq sought to compensate this weakening of its international support through a more energetic attempt to improve its regional standing. It attempted to galvanize support in the Arab world against any US attack and secured a visit by the Secretary General of the Arab League, former Egyptian Foreign Minister, Amr Musa. The Iraqi leadership indicated to Musa that it was also willing to overcome the rift with Kuwait and Saudi Arabia, who had consistently refused to reestablish diplomatic relations, by engaging in a dialogue over continuing unresolved bilateral disputes.[31] A similar but more high-level overture was made to Iran which involved a visit by Iraqi Foreign Minister Naji Sabri to Tehran in late January and who promised to deal with outstanding humanitarian issues. Finally, Iraq also adopted a more conciliatory attitude to the UN which resulted in its offer of a dialogue with the UN over the issue of weapons inspectors. The first meeting on this issue between the Iraqi Foreign Minister and Kofi Annan had taken place on 7 March.

By the spring of 2002, the framework for the confrontation between the USA and Iraq had been well established. For the US administration, the failure to find a clear link between Iraq and the 9/11 attacks did not weaken the claim that Iraq should be a target of a 'war against terrorism.' Rather, the evidence that Iraq continued to possess and develop WMD was itself seen to be a sufficient justification for extending the campaign against Iraq. A strong consensus behind this had emerged not only in the US administration but in Congress as well. For Iraq, the challenge was to use its tried and tested diplomatic machinations, in combination with clear economic incentives, to insure a sufficient regional and international consensus for the lifting of sanctions and in opposition to any US-led military action. Iraq had survived phase one of the war against terrorism but there were real questions whether it could indefinitely avoid its inclusion in phase two.

By late autumn 2002, Iraq's room for maneuvre had become even more constrained. The US administration, adopting the approach recommended by Powell and British Prime Minister Tony Blair, sought to obtain an international consensus on policy towards Iraq through seeking an agreement within the UN Security Council for more forceful action to disarm Iraq. Despite all Iraq's attempts to persuade its traditional allies, whether Russia, China or other Arab states, to support its stance, the dynamic towards a common position became unstoppable and resulted in the unanimous passing of UN Resolution 1441 in November which provided a strict timetable for Iraq's full compliance with the demands for disarmament. The choice facing Saddam Hussein now appeared stark – either disarm or face war. Iraq's friends as well as enemies warned that there was no other alternative. However, Saddam Hussein's continuing predilection for brinkmanship was revealed in an interview just prior to the passing of the resolution when he confidently confirmed that 'Time is in our favor, and we have to buy more time hoping that the US–British alliance might disintegrate because of the presence of public opinion.'[32] Whether this showed strategic foresight or rather a critical misjudgment, the test of wills between Iraq and the United States appeared to be reaching its final stage.

CONCLUSION

In retrospect, both Iran and Iraq faced a difficult challenge to turn 9/11 to their advantage. The problem was that the terrorist attacks in the United States had made the government and people much less forgiving of countries, such as Iran and Iraq, which had been consistently portrayed as in the forefront of supporting terrorism and developing WMD capabilities. The Iranian government sought to deflect this through presenting a moderate face in its constructive support for an Afghanistan free of the Taliban and al-Qaeda and its de facto support of the removal of Saddam Hussein's regime. But, the Iranian leadership was not willing to compromise the core ideological commitments of the revolution which, in essence, forestalled any prospect of a rapprochement with the United States. For Iraq, the strategic options remained essentially unaffected by the events of September 11. What had changed was the degree of US determination to ensure a final end to the regime under Saddam Hussein. As has been the case over the past ten years, Saddam Hussein's hope and expectation was that the combination of Arab hostility, European prevarication and Israeli–Palestinian bloodshed might again prove insurmountable obstacles to a large-scale intervention. 9/11 had, though, significantly transformed the strategic environment, strengthened and invigorated US resolve and determination, and significantly reduced Iraq's options and escape routes.

NOTES

1 Press Briefing by Ari Fleischer, 26 Sept. 2001, in www.whitehouse.gov/news/briefings
2 George W. Bush, 'President's State of the Union Address', 29 Jan. 2002 at www.whitehouse.gov/news/releases/2002/01/20020129-11.html. For an analysis of the speech, see 'US Redefines Middle Eastern Geopolitics', 1 Feb. 2002 in stratfor.com
3 United States State Department, *Patterns of Global Terrorism: 2000* at www.state.gov/s/ct/rls/pgtrpt/2000
4 Kanan Makiya, *Republic of Fear: The Politics of Modern Iraq* (Berkeley: University of California Press, 1998); Amatzia Baram, 'Saddam Husayn Between his Power Base and the International Community', *MERIA Journal*, Vol. 4, No. 4, Dec. 2000; and Charles Tripp, *History of Iraq* (Cambridge: Cambridge University Press, 2000).
5 David Menashri, *Post-Revolutionary Politics in Iran: Religion, Society and Power* (London: Frank Cass, 2001); and Daniel Brumberg, *Reinventing Khomeini: The Struggle for Reform in Iran* (Chicago: University of Chicago Press, 2001).
6 For example for the problematic role played especially in the electoral process by the Guardians Council, see A. William Samii, 'Iran's Guardians Council as an Obstacle to Democracy', *Middle East Journal*, Vol. 55, No. 4, Autumn 2001.
7 *Iranian State Television*, 11 Sept. 2001 translated by FBIS.
8 *Voice of Islamic Republic of Iran*, 14 Sept. 2001 in BBC Monitoring Middle East – Political.
9 For a good survey of not only Iranian but also Arab newspapers' responses to 9/11, see Cameron S. Brown, 'The Shot Seen Around the World: The Middle East Reacts to September 11th', *MERIA Journal*, Vol. 5, No. 4, Dec. 2001.
10 *Boston Globe*, 18 Sep. 2001.
11 Charles Recknagel and Azam Gorgin, 'Iran: What Was behind Straw's Dramatic Visit', Radio Free Europe/Radio Liberty, 26 Sept. 2001.
12 *Iranian State Television*, 26 Sept. 2001 translated by FBIS. See also Jim Muir, 'Hostile Neutrality', *Middle East International*, 12 Oct. 2001.
13 Quoted in Bill Samii, 'Iran Will Not Assist "America and its Allies" ', *Iran Report*, Radio Free Europe/Radio Liberty, 1 Oct. 2001.
14 See the interview with Mohsen Rezaie, Secretary of Iran's Expediency Council, in *Financial Times*, 15 Oct. 2001.
15 *New York Times*, 16 Oct. 2001.
16 Bill Samii, 'Tehran Welcomes Afghan Accords and Interim Chief', *Iran Report*, Radio Free Europe/Radio Liberty, 17 Dec. 2001.
17 Jim Muir, 'Iran: Bush Stirs the Nest', *Middle East International*, 8 Feb. 2002.
18 *ABC Television*, 3 Feb. 2002. Rumsfeld's comments are also quoted in Breffni O'Rourke,

'EU: Harsh U.S. Criticism of Iran and Others Makes Allies Wonder What's Next', *Weekly Report*, Radio Free Europe/Radio Liberty, 4 Feb. 2002.

19 For example, see the request made to the US to provide such information by Foreign Minister Kharrazi in *Iranian News Agency* (IRNA), 5 Feb. 2002 in FBIS.

20 Guy Dinmore, 'Iran's Top Leader Enters Political Fray as Crisis Mounts', *Financial Times*, 14 Nov. 2002.

21 *Reuters*, 12 Sept. 2001.

22 *Al-Sharq al-Awsat*, 10 Feb. 2002. Uday was reported to have stated this in a meeting with Ali Kilani al-Qadhafi, who supervises Libya's radio stations.

23 *Arab Press* (AP), 1 Oct. 2001 for a report on the 'Jerusalem Army'.

24 David Nissmann, 'INC Claim Saddam Linked to Bin Laden Network', *Iraq Report*, Radio Free Europe/Radio Liberty, 5 Oct. 2001.

25 *Kurdistan Newsline*, 19 Sept. 2001.

26 David Nissmann, 'SCIRI Welcomes US Strikes at "Terrorist" Regime', *Iraq Report*, Radio Free Europe/Radio Liberty, 29 Nov. 2001.

27 Phyllis Bennis, 'Iraq: Next on Washington's List', *Middle East International*, 25 Jan. 2002.

28 *Ibid.*

29 Reported in Sana Kamal, 'Iraq: Bracing Itself', *Middle East International*, 7 Dec. 2001.

30 For this shift in the debate, see Patrick Clawson, 'Focusing on Iraq: The Question is How, Not Whether', *Policy Watch*, Washington Institute for Near East Policy, 29 Nov. 2001.

31 *Middle East International*, 25 Jan. 2002.

32 *Al-Usbu'a*, 3 Nov. 2002.

11 Support with qualification
Syria

Raymond Hinnebusch

The reaction of Syrian leaders to 9/11 must be contextualized in their broader policy environment. Syria's state formation put the country on an Arab national-ist foreign policy tangent that has endured countless leadership changes. The loss of the Golan Heights to Israel in the 1967 war locked it into a struggle to recover this territory which recently took the form of a proxy war in Lebanon. However, with the end of the Cold War option to balance between the superpowers, the Syrian regime began to 'bandwagon' with – that is, appease – the US hegemon, partly in order to balance the greater threat from Israel. Hence, it joined the Gulf coalition and the Madrid peace process which brought Syria and Israel close to a 'land-for-peace settlement.' At the same time, the stagnation of the state-dominated economy, as oil prices and aid to Syria declined, required an opening to the world capitalist market and an influx of investment which would only be forthcoming after a peace agreement.

It was widely expected that these developments, combined with the leadership change upon the death of President Hafiz al-Asad, might be the watershed that released pent-up pressures for change. Bashar al-Asad was seen as representative of a new generation with a vision of 'modernization' which entailed economic liberalization, a reduction of rent-seeking corruption and an opening to the West. Bashar was, however, constrained by the old guard inherited from his father and refrained from directly challenging the stranglehold on the economy of the rent-seeking alliance of security barons and the regime-supportive bourgeoisie that effectively deterred new private investment. Moreover, the failure of the Syrian–Israeli peace process at the 26 March 2000 Clinton–Asad Geneva Summit, the consequent deterioration of relations with the USA, the outbreak of the second Palestinian intifadah and the rise of the hardline Sharon government in Israel soured the foreign policy context for reform. With a peace settlement off the agenda and with it the prospect that economic liberalization might rescue the economy, Bashar's regime opted to pursue alternative alignments, notably the enhanced strategic priority given to relations with Europe and, above all, the opening to Iraq from which the regime hoped to secure the resources to stabilize the economy. However, the events of 9/11, in stimulating a new and assertive American interventionism in the area, makes this strategy much more risky than hitherto and threatens to abort the regime's main strategy for securing its survival.

OFFICIAL VIEWS

Syrian officialdom has, so far as can be detected, responded to 9/11 with one voice, although some of the President's young advisors may be more keen to take advantage of the crisis to widen relations with the West while the old guard harbors a deep distrust of Washington.

President Bashar al-Asad sent a letter of condolence to President Bush in the aftermath of the attacks.[1] Syria underlined its adherence to the side of 'international legitimacy' which it sees as a crucial protective barrier in its struggle with Israel. Syrian leaders stressed that they, too, had been victims of Islamic terrorism in the 1980s when the Muslim brotherhood mounted a violent insurrection. Bashar declared: 'In Syria, we are very familiar with this issue, and we were the first in the world to deal with terrorist movements that threatened the regime.'[2] Syria reputedly provided the USA with intelligence information.

Syrian officials indicated that they were prepared to cooperate in the American war on terrorism, but not unconditionally, and indeed they had more reservations than most other countries about the 'war on terrorism.' They rejected the American insistence that if a country was not totally with Washington it was against it; rather, Syria sought a third way. Syria was 'unwilling to enter into a coalition whose goals, outcomes, means, and final date were not defined' except by Washington.[3]

Terrorism, officials argued, had to be defined through the UN or by an international conference and the war against it waged under the authority of the UN, not at the discretion of the USA. Damascus apparently denied that the USA had a legitimate right to launch war unilaterally on Afghanistan on the grounds of self-defense (Belgian Foreign Minister Louis Michel remarked on a visit to the Middle East that 'except for Syria, no country has opposed the US's right to respond, provided that the response is justified and its targets defined').[4]

In fact, official Syrian views of what constituted terrorism and how to deal with it were substantially different from the dominant Washington view. Syria argued for a distinction between terrorism and the armed resistance of national liberation movements which, it insisted, was legitimate under the UN charter. Hizbollah was a legitimate movement resisting the Israeli occupation of Lebanon while Hamas and Islamic Jihad were resistance movements against the Israeli occupation on the West Bank/Gaza. Bashar stated: '[We] must not allow the charge of terrorism to be slapped on the resistance movements fighting the occupation, both in Lebanon and in Palestine.'[5] On the other hand, Syria insisted that the violent repression being carried out by Israel in the West Bank/Gaza was state terrorism for which Israel had to be held accountable.

Syria's view of the proper *means* for fighting terrorism also differed from that of the USA. The Syrian government indicated its willingness 'to participate in political and security actions provided that these security actions do not involve participation in assassinations, but [only] investigations and exchanges of information, to be followed by legal action.'[6] However, Syria absolutely refused to participate in military actions which 'would incite to terrorism and harm civilians.'[7] Bashar told visiting Prime Minister Tony Blair that the attack on Afghani cities was unacceptable to Syrians and reputedly told American officials that he considered the war to be mere revenge.

Syrian officials stressed that fighting terrorism required dealing with the conditions that generated the resentment in which terrorism could thrive. Bashar insisted that an effective war on terrorism meant dealing with the injustice that breeds it. Syrian commentators argued that '[U]surping and sucking the resources of the helpless third world countries' was a source of the resentment and frustration that generated terrorism. So was 'undermining other cultures' values, and trying to impose on them specific dictates.' More than any other root cause, 'occupation stands as the main cause for hating the occupier and whoever supports it.'[8] In other words, Syria was arguing that the behavior of the United States' Israeli ally in continuing its violent suppression of Palestinians and occupation of Palestinian land in defiance of international law, was the root cause of much terrorism. By implication, if the United States wished effectively to deal with the roots of terror, it had to change its Middle East policy.

PUBLIC OPINION

The view that the actions of the US government had brought 9/11 upon its people was widely held across the Arab world, including in Syria. Syria was quiet after the events, with no demonstrations of joy in the streets. However, an editorial by Syrian Arab Writers Association chairman 'Ali 'Uqleh 'Ursan, in the association's journal, *al-Usbu' al-Adabi* about his feelings after the terror attacks in the USA, is, although reflective of an illiberal regime-connected element, perhaps not unrepresentative of the immediate wider reaction:

> The deaths of the innocent pain me; but the eleventh of September . . . reminded me of the many innocents whose funerals we attended and whose wounds we treated . . . I remembered the funerals that have been held every day in occupied Palestine since 1947 . . . I remembered Tripoli [Libya] on the day of the American–British aggression, and the attempt to destroy its leader's house as he slept; then, his daughter was killed under the ruins . . . I remembered the oppression of the peoples in Korea and Vietnam . . .
>
> The symbolism of penetrating the Pentagon . . . is greater by far than the fact that it continues to exist, and continues its aggression against the peoples, and its threats against Afghanistan and bin Laden . . . [This attack means that] if the peoples awake, if they have this kind of will and . . . if they choose to resist arrogance and imperialism . . . what will happen then? . . . Something collapsed in the US, and I maintain that this is the beginning of the collapse of the US as the only dominant superpower in the world.[9]

Once the war in Afghanistan began, Syrians were chiefly alarmed at the apparently unrestrained way in which Washington seemed able to use its power against those it deemed to be enemies. Hostility to the US 'anti-terrorism' campaign cut across all groups and classes from the ruling elites to Westernized opposition-oriented intellectuals to the Islamic-oriented petite bourgeoisie. Nobody believed bin Laden had acted alone and almost all Syrians believed he was being used as a pretext by the USA to impose its will on behalf of Israel and to settle old scores in the region. US behavior was seen to have removed America's mask of civility to reveal the malign intentions of the complex of Zionists, oil interests and militarists at the heart of the Bush administration. All feared Iraq and possibly Syria would be the next targets.[10]

SYRIAN POLICY BETWEEN REGIME NEEDS AND WASHINGTON PRESSURES

The 9/11 events, in precipitating a much more assertive and intrusive US 'war against terrorism' in the Middle East, have sharply contracted the Syrian regime's freedom to manipulate the wide-ranging relations it needs to protect its vital interests. On the one hand, it has vital investments in new relations with Iraq, in Lebanon, where it is a major supporter of Hizbollah and in its role as a champion of the Palestinian militants who are based in Damascus. On the other hand, it cannot afford to antagonize Washington which it needs to restrain Israel and restart the peace process, which can obstruct its access to the international economy and the Iraqi market, and which, in a worst case scenario, could target Syria militarily. Syria is attempting to walk a thin line between these conflicting needs and demands.

Potential Syrian–US disputes crossing a whole range of issues predate 9/11. Indeed, in a brief discussion in October 2000 when then Secretary of State Madeline Albright first met President Bashar al-Asad, he reportedly rejected her requests to rein in Hizbollah and to cease flights to Baghdad.[11] After 9/11, Syria faced a Washington regime dominated by highly unsympathetic leaders and interests which were trying to use the old 1980s image of Syria as a terrorist state to justify pressure on or action against it. Indeed, Syria had never been removed from Washington's original 'terrorism' list because of its continued support for Hizbollah and its hosting of Palestinian militant organizations. Yet, Damascus seemed determined not to be stampeded into acquiescing to American demands. When asked about the US terrorism list, Syrian Foreign Minister Faruq al-Shara; replied, 'We do not believe in this list. Many countries do not believe in it, because we have all been fighting terrorism for years.'[12] Bashar warned against Arab and Muslim countries simply succumbing to American pressures. The regime seemed to be calculating that Syria could outlast the crisis until American fury subsided or international constraints on its unilateralism were repaired.

A major bone of contention with Washington was the presence of so-called rejectionist Palestinian factions in Damascus. Syrian hosting of these groups symbolized its claim to champion the Palestine cause which is a key to domestic legitimacy and a reserve card in any future diplomatic bargaining with Israel. The

Bush administration is insistent that the Damascus offices of Hamas and Islamic Jihad, responsible for suicide bombings in Israel, be closed, even though all they get is safe haven, not operational bases. While there was an early expectation that Bashar would phase out Damascus' role as such a haven and the militant factions were themselves anxious about it, in fact, at the Doha Islamic summit in November 2000, Bashar solicited funds for them.[13] Moreover, on the first anniversary of the second Palestinian intifadah in late September 2001, Syria hosted a conference attended by leaders of all the organizations considered pariahs in Washington but which Syria deemed liberation movements: Hizbollah Director-General Hassan Nasrallah, Hamas Political Bureau head Khaled Mash'al, Islamic Jihad leader Ramadhan Abdallah Shalah, PFLP-General Command Director-General Ahmad Jibril, and PFLP Overseas Command chief Maher al-Taher. Deputy Secretary-General of the Syrian Ba'ath Party Abdallah al-Ahmar, told the conference that 'as in the past, and present, Syria will in the future continue to be a haven for those struggling for liberation, and for the restoration of honour and holy sites.'[14]

Another point of contention was Hizbollah, a major Syrian ally in Lebanon, which is seen by Israel's Washington friends as a terrorist movement and is remembered by the Republican party rightwing for terrorism and hostage taking aimed at the USA during the 1980s. Widely seen in Syria and the Arab–Islamic world as a liberation movement which almost uniquely scored a major success against Israel in forcing its withdrawal from southern Lebanon, Syria's association with Hizbollah enables it to share in this prestige and any Syrian move against it would be deeply damaging to regime legitimacy. Moreover, Hizbollah pressure on Israel's northern border was one of the few ways Syria could impress on Israel that it could not have peace while retaining Arab territory although Sharon's retaliatory attacks on Syrian targets in Lebanon raised the risks and costs of this tactic.

Initially, Syria was heartened that Hizbollah was not included in the first terrorism list drawn up in Washington after 9/11 but was dismayed when Hizbollah was added to the second list followed by demands on the Lebanese government to freeze its financial assets and extradite Islamic militants involved in terrorism in the 1980s. But Hizbollah, far from being a terrorist group, is a major political party, representative of the Shi'a community in Parliament and with an extensive social welfare network. Beirut can hardly comply without sacrificing its own stability but defiance could carry undetermined costs and threats to a Lebanese order in which Syria is deeply invested.[15] Syria can urge Hizbollah to dampen tensions on the Lebanese border with Israel and purportedly acceded to an EU request to do so. Reputedly also, it stopped the transfer of arms from Iran to Hizbollah across Syrian territory. The only Lebanese Islamist movement to have links with Osama bin Laden, the small Isbat al-Ansar, was long regarded as an opponent by both Beirut and Damascus and has been the focus of police action by both.

Another point of tension with the USA is Syria's deepening rapprochement with Iraq after decades of conflict. An Iraqi official announced in July 2001 that Baghdad would give priority to Syria in awarding import contracts under the UN oil-for-food program in return for help in opposing US and British proposals to impose 'smart' sanctions on Baghdad. Syrian Prime Minister Mustafa Miro, in the first visit by a Syrian premier since ties were broken off in 1980, delivered a letter from Bashar to Saddam, stressing the 'support of the Syrian people for Iraq and its solidarity with the fight to lift the unjust embargo' on Iraq.[16]

The Syrian–Iraqi rapprochement has geopolitical significance. Bashar spoke enthusiastically of Iraq as Syria's strategic, economic and scientific depth. Syrian–Iraqi military cooperation in the event of an Israeli attack on Syria was also reputedly discussed during a visit by Qusay Hussein to Damascus. If Syrian–Iraqi hostility, a regional constant for decades, is replaced by a new strategic alignment, this, together with the Syrian–Iranian alliance, could transform the region's power balance to Israel's great detriment. The relation is, however, even more a matter of geo-economics. Its centrepiece was the reopened oil pipeline from Iraq to Syria's Mediterranean port of Banias through which Damascus was said to receive about 200,000 barrels per day of Basra Light crude at below market prices for processing in local refineries, while exporting an equivalent amount of Syrian Light crude at much higher international prices. The pipeline could produce up to $1 billion a year in revenue for the Syrian government, about 5 percent of Syria's gross domestic product. There are also plans to build a new pipeline to Iraq. On top of this, increased trade with Iraq was considered a critical element in reviving Syria's stagnant economy and giving Syrian business a foothold in the Iraqi economy at a time when an end to the sanctions seemed on the horizon. A huge cross-border commerce developed while contracts to provide Iraq with goods under the food for oil program, which increased from $57 million in 1997 to $2 billion in 2001, allowed the private sector to export goods that might not be competitive on the free market. The pipeline revenues accrue to the cash-strapped state and the monopolies acquired in the Iraqi market by the regime's business clients service its patronage networks. While this will not solve the wider crisis of the Syrian economy, it may be enough to preserve the regime while relieving pressures to conform to the neo-liberal demands of 'globalisation.' This goes against Bashar's longer-term vision of modernization but the failure of the peace process and regime survival interests make it unavoidable.[17]

The Iraqi pipeline became an issue with the USA and a political lever Syria tried to manipulate against Washington well before 9/11. After the *Los Angeles Times* reported that Syria was facilitating the sale of Iraqi oil outside the oil-for-food regime,[18] US Secretary of State Colin Powell visited Damascus to coordinate pressure on Iraq in March 2000. He reported that he had won Bashar's agreement to allow the UN to monitor the pipeline, to refrain from violating international sanctions on Iraqi oil and to put proceeds from Iraqi oil in UN escrow accounts. In reality, Iraq oil is largely bartered for Syrian goods shipped to Iraq, short-circuiting such escrow accounts. Ibrahim Hamidi reported that Powell mistakenly understood that Syria intended to include the existing oil pipe in the framework of the UN resolutions, while the Syrian President had referred to the new pipeline Syria plans to lay down. Syria claims it merely assured Powell that it was committed to 'all UN resolutions' and international legality, implying that its full compliance was contingent on Israel's compliance with such resolutions.[19] The Syrians also tried to balance between Washington and Baghdad regarding the American proposed 'smart sanctions.' On the one hand, they did not want officially to oppose them and only expressed 'great caution' about them. Yet Syrian Foreign Minister, Faruq Al-Shara' refused to discuss the Iraqi issue with an American envoy on the grounds that there must first be 'firm positions regarding the Israeli aggression against the Arabs.'[20] Syria hoped to make the price of cooperation in keeping Iraq isolated, at the expense of its own economic interests in Iraqi ties, significant. The fact that Syria still did not have full diplomatic relations with Iraq (which even Jordan does) suggests that, for Damascus, Iraq was viewed as a geopolitical card that it can play in return for concessions from the USA.[21]

However, 9/11 raised the stakes of Syria's Iraq policy. Alignment toward Iraq increased the risk that Syria would become the focus of American hostility. In this environment, Syria could not afford to be outside 'international legitimacy' especially after it was elected to the UN Security Council in 2001. Yet, unabashed, Syrian leaders went so far as to announce that an American attack on Iraq would be considered an attack on all the Arabs. Syria greatly fears such strikes would be part of an attempt to install a pro-American regime in Iraq, which would encircle it with unfriendly regimes. As insurance against this possibility Syria has simultaneously consolidated its links to Baghdad while continuing to cultivate its older ties to the opposition – the communists, anti-Saddam Ba'thist and Kurdish factions – so as to be in a position to retain or increase its influence in a post-Saddam Iraq, together with Iran, which has close ties to the Shi'a opposition. Syria hopes that any change in regime can be made to serve its, rather than Washington's, interests.

The Syrian government seeks to shelter its interests from Washington's hostility by tightening its relations with Europe and the Arab world. Syria puts great hopes in the capacity of Europe – which it sees as having a more sophisticated and sympathetic understanding of the Middle East – to restrain Washington. Ibrahim Hamidi reported that the Syrian leadership considered the Europeans to be a 'bridge between the American culture and the Arabic–Islamic culture.'[22] However, there was disagreement during talks between the Syrian leadership and a European delegation, as Belgian Foreign Minister Louis Michel acknowledged in a joint press conference with Syrian Foreign Minister Faruq al-Shara: 'I cannot agree with the definition of terrorism of my [Syrian] colleague, and I do not think that he agrees with my definition.'[23]

As regards the Arab world, Syria's close relations with US allies, Egypt and Saudi Arabia, may help shelter it. Syria has tried to get the Arab states to stand together in dealing with Washington, both in rejecting any attack on Iraq and in insisting that the USA end its support for Sharon's repression of the Palestinians. But Damascus has also been disappointed by the readiness of the Arab states to appease rather than bargain with Washington. Bashar has argued that Washington needs cooperation from the Arabs:

[W]e in Syria do not think that the Arab and Islamic situation is weak; on the contrary, the Americans need the Arab and Islamic countries in order to forge the American coalition, and woo them . . . the Americans desire to woo these parties, because they need them for the battle . . . all [we] need is patience.[24]

According to Syrian Information Minister Adnan Omran, the Arabs should play the cards they have: it is incumbent on the Arab states to discuss with the USA the 'imbalanced relationship' wherein Arab friendship is met by American support for Israel's violations of international law.[25]

CONCLUSION

Syria's stand on 9/11 has been among the least receptive to American demands. Its instinctive reaction to such threats is to balance against the threatening power, not bandwagon with it–as most other Arab states have done. The reason for this is, above all, that Syria remains a dissatisfied power as long as the Golan remains under Israeli occupation and Washington is the main backer of its Israeli antagonist. But Syria also has a strong interest in limiting American intrusion into the region which could frustrate the relations with Iraq that it badly needs on geo-economic grounds. Finally, the Syrian government's stand is undoubtedly congruent with Syrian public opinion and, indeed, arguably closer to that of much of the Arab and Islamic world than are the attempts of other Arab governments to appease Washington. The two new and perhaps conflicting foreign policy initiatives of Bashar's government, the simultaneous openings to both Europe and to Iraq, show how far the regime seeks to keep its options open and to widen its freedom of action by balancing between a multitude of powers.

Whether Syria can sufficiently manipulate these variegated alliances to sustain its policy in the face of Washington's assertive new interventionism in the Middle East depends in great part on factors outside its control. These would include whether the climate of American domestic politics continues to support such interventionism, whether international constraints on it are repaired and whether the ongoing conflict in Palestine facilitates or obstructs it.[26] But Syria's own diplomacy can also make a difference, especially whether it can find protective cover in a wider Arab coalition including US allies, Egypt and Saudi Arabia. Also important would be whether it can disarm its enemies in Washington by being seen as a responsible power, which, if its interests are respected, can be a part of the solution to international terrorism.

NOTES

1 *Al-Hayat* (London), 25 Sept. 2001.
2 *Al-Safir* (Beirut), 25 Sept. 2001.

3 *Al-Hayat* (London), 1 Oct. 2001.

4 *Al-Hayat* (London), 29 Sept. 2001; *Al-Hayat* (London), 1 Oct. 2001.

5 *Al-Safir* (Beirut), 29 Sept. 2001.

6 *Al-Hayat* (London), 1 Oct. 2001.

7 *Al-Hayat* (London), 1 Oct. 2001.

8 *Syria Times* (Damascus), 30 Sept. 2001.

9 *Al-Usbu' al-Adabi* (Damascus), 15 Sept. 2001 in *Special Dispatch No. 275*, Middle East Media Research Institute, 25 Sept. 2001.

10 Informal discussions, Damascus, Dec. 2000–Jan. 2001. Such anecdotal evidence is the best available in the absence of formal survey data. However, Syrian opinion is unlikely to be substantially different from the findings of such surveys of opinion in similar countries. A Gallup poll of 10,000 people in Indonesia, Iran, Jordan, Kuwait, Lebanon, Morocco, Pakistan, Saudi Arabia and Turkey reported in *The Guardian*, 28 Feb. 2002 found that only 11 percent believed Arabs were responsible for the Trade Center attack and 61 percent did not, with the 'not' percentage highest in Kuwait (89 percent) and Pakistan (86 percent); the USA was overwhelmingly described as 'ruthless, aggressive, arrogant and biased,' with over 54 percent having an unfavourable view of the USA and 22 percent a favourable view. Bush was disliked by 58 percent and liked by 11 percent. The Afghanistan war was thought morally unjustifiable by 77 percent and justified by 9 percent.

11 Alan Markovsky, 'Syria's Foreign Policy Challenges U.S. Interests', *Policywatch*, No. 513, 19 Jan. 2001, The Washington Institute for Near East Policy, www.washingtoninstitute.org

12 *Al-Hayat* (London), 29 Sept. 2001.

13 Anders Strindberg, 'Growth with Strength: Syria's Hardline Reformer', *Jane's Intelligence Review*, Feb. 2001, p. 33.

14 *Al-Hayat* (London), 28 Sept. 2001

15 *Middle East International*, 23 Nov. 2001, pp. 15–17.

16 AFP, 'Iraq and Syria Turn New Page after 20 Years of Broken Relations', 12 Aug. 2001.

17 Gary C. Gambill, 'Syria's Foreign Relations: Iraq', *Middle East Intelligence Bulletin*, Vol. 3, No. 3, March 2001, www.meib.org; STRATFOR.COM Weekly Global Intelligence Update 18 Oct. 2000, http://www.stratfor.com/; Beth Flynn, 'Iraq: From Rogue State to Free Trader', *Middle East International*, 5 April 2002, pp. 25–6.

18 *Middle East International*, 9 Feb. 2001, p. 12.

19 Yotam Feldner, 'Escalation Games: Part II: Regional and International Factors Between Washington and Baghdad: Iraq'. Middle East Media Research Institute, 25 May 2001, www.memri.org

20 Yotam Feldner, 'Escalation Games: Syria's Deterrence Policy Part I: Brinkmanship', Middle East Media Research Institute, 24 May 2001, www.memri.org

21 Ibrahim Hamidi, 'Syria Collects "Cards" to Secure Her Regional Role', *Daily Star* (Beirut), 14 Dec. 2001.

22 *Al-Hayat* (London), 1 Oct. 2001.

23 *Al-Hayat* (London), 29 Sept. 2001.

24 *Al-Safir* (Lebanon), 27 Sept. 2001.

25 *BBC Summary of World Broadcasts*, 7 Jan. 2002.

26 Washington seemed bent on increasing the pressure on Syria with the introduction into Congress in September 2002 of the so-called Syria Accountability Bill, which would place travel, trade and financial penalties on Syria for its 'support of Hizbollah . . . its continued occupation of Lebanese territory . . . and its acquisition of weapons of mass destruction and ballistic missile programs.' See 'Syria Faces Terrorism Accusations', *Daily Star* (Beirut), 9 Sept. 2002, http://www.dailystar/com.lb

12 Conflicting pressures

Saudi Arabia

Gwenn Okruhlik

The reaction to 9/11 from Saudi Arabia has been complex and pained. Saudi Arabians had to confront the harsh reality that fifteen of the nineteen hijackers came from within their borders, prompting an unprecedented period of critical self-examination.[1]

Two repercussions stand out: first, though meaningful reform was studiously avoided for the past two decades, there is now an undeniable need for serious structural change in Saudi Arabia. The reform process that began slowly in late 1998 must be accelerated, in politics, economics and society. Second, there is a new strain in the United States–Saudi Arabian partnership. There are critical political disagreements between the countries that can no longer be submerged under the imperatives of money and oil. The regime in Saudi Arabia must respond to multiple domestic constituencies – clergy, intellectuals, 'Wahhabis', nationalists, women, Shi'a, Sunni and the business community – with competing interests.

To understand the reactions to 9/11, we must appreciate the internal crises in 1979 and 1991 and the diversity of the population. Instituting major structural reforms in the midst of fierce domestic debate may ultimately prove more difficult than a military campaign against terrorists or the reorganization of intelligence organizations.

POLITICS AND ISLAM: CRITICAL MOMENTS IN 1979 AND 1991

Tumultuous events occurred in 1979. The Islamic Revolution in Iran toppled the Shah's government. In nearby Saudi Arabia, the oppressed minority Shi'a community in the Eastern Province organized open demonstrations in several towns. That same year, a Sunni Islamist rebel, Juhaiman al-Utaibi, and his followers forcibly took control of the Great Mosque in Mecca and tried to oust the ruling family, claiming that its members had deviated from the path of Islam. The regime responded to these events by instituting ever-tighter controls over social and political life. A narrow and intolerant interpretation of Islam came to dominate the national discourse. A Saudi scholar explained that 'Different groups ended up competing with fundamentalists over who can appear more conservative in the public eye.'[2] The power of the radical religious right grew during this time (known inappropriately in the West as 'Wahhabism'). The response of the regime unfortunately produced two decades of political paralysis.

The Gulf War of 1990–1, and particularly the stationing of US troops in Saudi Arabia, then ushered in a decade of turmoil. Opposition groups took shape in the country and abroad largely under the rubric of Islamism.[3] With the war, what was a private and social resurgence of Islam was transformed into an explicitly political movement; that is, many Wahhabi believers became Salafi activists. Mostly, there was a convergence of dissent for the first time.[4] Whether male or female, urban or rural, rich or poor, Sunni or Shi'a, ordinary Saudis grew weary of ad hoc and arbitrary governance. People shared in common a desire for the rule of law. The decade was a time of crisis made more tense when King Fahd suffered a stroke in 1995.

Finally, in late 1998, after a strenuous struggle over succession during Fahd's illness, Crown Prince Abdullah began to consolidate his position among familial contenders to the throne. Once secure, he initiated a series of small reforms that began to respond to the grievances of dissidents. At the same time, the radical right remained potent, as 9/11 made evident. Saudi Arabia's response to the international effort against terrorism must be placed in the context of the regime's effort to balance competing social forces at home.

IMMEDIATE RESPONSES TO 9/11

In the immediate aftermath, the government condemned the attacks, expressed its condolences to the families and friends of victims, and lent its support to the US-led 'war on terrorism.' Saudi Arabia immediately cut diplomatic ties with the Taliban, which it had long supported in finances and ideology. Abdullah, now the de facto ruler, immediately initiated the shipment of extra oil to the USA to ensure that the economy was not disrupted.

At the same time, Saudi spokesmen postured awkwardly as they came to terms with the fact that their youth, largely from the mountainous southwestern Asir Province, had perpetrated the atrocities. The utter shock and alarm was first expressed as denial. Prince Nayf, Minister of the Interior, repeatedly distanced the Kingdom from the act saying that there was no proof of Saudi involvement. There were cautious warnings against hasty retaliation. Prince Turki bin Faisal later acknowledged this, saying that 'September brought a great upheaval. At first we all went into denial, saying that Saudis could not have taken part in such acts since they are contrary to our principles. Then came contemplation: Who are we? How could such a thing happen after years of development and contacts with the outside world?'[5]

Public sentiment in the international press, particularly out of the UK and USA, grew increasingly strident. Angry editorials were published with dramatic titles such as 'Our Enemies the Saudis'; 'The Saudi Terror Subsidy'; 'Nuke

Mecca'; 'The Saudis – Friend or Foe'; and 'They're Rich, They're Spoiled.' Many argued for a severance of diplomatic ties and oil purchases, though the latter was clearly not feasible. Passion was directed especially against Islam, the Saudi educational system, and the oil relationship. The media bashing was so intense and unrelenting that it provoked a defensive reaction in Saudi Arabia. Abdullah responded by saying it was designed to drive a wedge between Saudi Arabia and the USA.[6] Fearful for their safety, hundreds of Saudi students in the USA returned home to continue their studies. Saudi Arabia and Iran, leaders of the Sunni and Shi'a communities in Islam, issued a joint statement in defense of Islam as a belief system that promotes peace and tolerance. The national education system was declared sound. Saudis, in the elite and in society, could not comprehend the vitriolic nature of the bashing. Their perception was that they had, after all, been close allies with the USA for decades, a relationship that predates even the US relationship with Israel. It was the Saudi advocacy of moderate and stable prices that had ensured a steady supply of affordable oil to the Western economies for so many years. Saudi Arabia had often increased production to lower oil prices in the international economy, even as that policy decreased its own national revenues. Now, to many Saudis, decades of cooperation seemed fruitless as the country as a whole was blamed for the actions of fifteen young men. It was perceived to be collective punishment for the actions of a few.[7]

THE INTERPLAY OF DOMESTIC AND INTERNATIONAL POLITICS

Official responses: the ruling family and government

A close partnership with the USA in the current crisis would only fuel further domestic opposition, something that had finally begun to lessen in the period before the attacks. Abdullah is relatively unblemished by charges of corruption or decadence. He is a devout Muslim and a critical thinker; he has a strong nationalist voice and pan-Arab sentiments. All of this coloured his response to 9/11. While Abdullah reaffirmed his commitment to and friendship with the USA, he remained sharply critical of US policy in the region. He cooperates with American efforts to trace the money supply to terrorists, yet remains cognizant of the need to maintain national dignity in the face of overwhelming power.

Prince Waleed al-Talal offered New York City Mayor Rudy Giuliani, a $10 million donation to help the families of the victims. This photo opportunity of solace amid the pain quickly fell apart, however, when an aide of Prince Waleed distributed a statement that said it may be time for 'the US government to re-examine its policies in the Middle East and adopt a more balanced stand towards the Palestinian cause.' What was obvious to him and most of the world was not at all evident to a grieving nation. The gift was pointedly declined on the spot. This exchange exacerbated tensions even further.

Prince Nayf often denied Saudi involvement in the plane crashes.[8] He insisted on concrete evidence from the US government, which apparently was slow in coming. When it was finally presented, Nayf also distanced the actions of a few men from the good intentions of his country. But there were also unconfirmed reports of sweeping arrests in Saudi Arabia in the months following the attacks. And in June 2002, Saudi Arabia announced the arrest of eleven of its own citizens (plus a Sudanese and an Iraqi) for suspected links to al-Qaeda.

The Council of Ministers and the Saudi Arabian Monetary Authority worked closely with US investigators and Interpol.[9] All bank accounts in the country were scoured and the Bush administration reported that the government froze the assets of more than sixty-six individuals, companies and charities who were under suspicion of channeling funds to terrorism. New laws to protect against money laundering in the Kingdom were instituted in cooperation with the Paris-based Financial Action Task Force. The investigation into Islamic charities was especially difficult because the country's leadership role in the Islamic community mandates that the al Saud, on behalf of the country, fund organizations throughout the international Muslim community. Alms-giving to the less fortunate is not a choice in Islam, but an obligation of faith. All believers must contribute a percentage of their wealth to the needy. The al-Saud simply could not prohibit charity. The delicate balancing act the regime faced was to assist the USA and yet to protect its religious obligations.

Societal responses: people, clerics and media

The horror of the endlessly played television footage left people shocked. They mourned innocent deaths with the rest of the world and, at the same time, people comprehended the grievances long articulated by opposition groups. Internal grievances concern repression, maldistribution of wealth and, primarily, the US military bases on Saudi soil. External grievances are about US support for repressive regimes, US sanctions on Iraq and the uncritical US support for Israel. Ordinary Saudis abhorred the violent strategy of 9/11 but the grievances resonated broadly across the country.

The events initiated a period of public self-scrutiny in the Kingdom. Saudis came openly to question developments in their country, particularly since 1979. Debate is most evident in the media and in clerical statements. The media, traditionally tightly controlled by government censors, voiced critical opinions. The staid government-owned stations now competed with dynamic talk shows on regional and international satellite television broadcast across the country. Coming to grips with 9/11 ushered in a period of greater openness and accelerated pressures for domestic reform. A businessman in Riyadh grappled with the dilemma, 'September 11 didn't come out of nowhere. The question for America is: Why are you so hated in the Arab world? The question for us is why 15 of our people participated in this act.'[10] Socio-political debate now permeates Saudi society. There were simultaneous reports of rising anti-Western sentiment (a car bomb killed a British banker in Riyadh in June, 2002) and pleas for dialogue with the West.[11]

There are multiple clergy (ulema) in Saudi Arabia, and they argued about the proper Saudi response to the war on terrorism through a series of religious opinions (fatwas). The official clergy are appointed by the regime and regularly issue religious opinions that support state policy. Popular-level clergy preach in the mosques and schools throughout the country. Their opinions do not carry official weight but sometimes receive more popular support than their official counterparts. After 9/11, fatwas were the site of contestation in Saudi society.

The radical clergy are the violent rightist elements that support bin Laden. Prominent among them was Sheikh al-Shuaibi who issued an important fatwa in October 2001 that expanded the idea of jihad from fighting foreign infidels to fighting unjust domestic regimes. He effectively justified struggle against the al Saud family in religious terms. Other clerics also called for people to fight US aggression in Afghanistan. These opposition opinions were countered by official fatwas from the Council of Senior Ulema that stated that killing non-Muslims was not permissible under Islam. Other official fatwas deplored suicide bombings.[12] At the Grand Mosque in Mecca, Sheikh al-Sudais urged wisdom, reason and self-control.[13]

Interestingly, the clerics called 'radical' before 9/11 turned out to be the 'reformists' after it. For example Sheikh Salman al-Awdah, a fiery opposition preacher who spent five years in a Riyadh prison after the Gulf War turmoil, denounced the attacks and admonished Saudi youths against heeding calls for jihad. Rather than calling for the overthrow of the al-Saud, he now calls for 'more avenues for people to express their opinions, and more opportunities available . . . to engage in fruitful and constructive dialogue.'[14] Sheikh Safar al-Hawali, out of jail for three years, also now speaks of reforming the system rather than overthrowing it. He also released a six-page, single-spaced 'Open Letter to President Bush' in October 2001.

The government now allows the Islamist reformists (formerly thought to be radicals) to speak with relative freedom in the media. The al-Saud realized, too late, that exclusion promotes radicalization; inclusion may moderate political positions. It is incumbent upon the al-Saud to allow for political expression that is critical and vibrant in order to provide an alternative to the militant fringe. Bin Laden's attraction was artificially enhanced by the absence of viable alternative ideologies. For meaningful reform to blunt the call of the radical flank, it requires that the regime allow a vibrant political space to grow. There must be an alternative to royal authoritarianism and the radical religious right.

IMPACT OF 9/11 ON US–SAUDI ARABIAN RELATIONS

Saudis have traditionally been careful to distinguish between the values of the American people (many of which are embraced) and American foreign policy (which is disdained). Broad consensus exists across Saudi Arabia that American foreign policy in the region is critically flawed.

Even though the strong relationship between the USA and Saudi Arabia was reaffirmed in official statements, it was actually being tested long before the attacks. In 2000, anti-US sentiment intensified alongside the Israel–Palestinian War. Abdullah called for the USA to show more even-handedness and warned of instability if the violence was not defused and peace negotiations restarted.[15] The *USS Cole*, part of the post-Gulf War US military presence, was attacked off the coast of Yemen. The attack coincided with anti-US and anti-Israel demonstrations in Saudi Arabia. By summer 2001, Abdullah declined an invitation to visit the United States and warned of the possible eruption of regional war if Israel were not restrained. Like many Arabs, Abdullah wants the USA to use its enormous economic leverage to restrain Israeli aggression. The steadfast US refusal (or inability) to do so was viewed as the major stumbling block to a two-state solution to the turmoil.[16] A high-level Saudi military delegation canceled a meeting with their US counterparts the day before the planned event. Finally in August, in apparent exasperation, Abdullah reportedly sent a letter to Bush in which he stated that there comes a time when nations must part ways. 'You go your way, I go my way. From now on, we will protect our national interests, regardless of where America's interests lie in the region.'[17] It should be read as a diplomatic warning that the status quo was unacceptable. Again, ten days before the attacks, Abdullah exchanged letters with Bush that said US policy towards Israel and Palestine was now untenable. His persistence and exasperation reflect the sentiment in Saudi Arabia and the wider Middle East. His anger over US policy towards Palestine is palpable and real.

In the face of opposition to US foreign policy in the Middle East and to the seemingly permanent stationing of US bases in Saudi Arabia, the government eventually limited the use of those bases in the country to command, control and communication. The high-tech bases fomented such intense opposition that they could not be utilized for directly launching strikes against Afghanistan from Saudi soil. Clerics and journalists in the Kingdom decried the slaughter of innocent civilians in the war. This tension culminated in January 2002 with reports and denials that the US troops in Saudi Arabia were being transferred to neighboring states where opposition was less intense.[18] It was confirmed in April 2003 that they would be moved to Qatar. President Bush's apparent intent to bomb Iraq only fueled the tension – tension that rose still further when the war actually began. Repeatedly, the Saudi government informed the Bush administration that they would not be allowed to use the bases in Saudi Arabia to launch attacks on Iraq, though, in fact, there was some level of cooperation. In August, the alarming text of a briefing given to the Defense Policy Board the previous month by a RAND Corporation analyst was released. The author called Saudi Arabia 'the kernel of evil,' 'the most dangerous opponent of the US,' and 'the prime mover' in world-wide terrorism.[19] Though the US and Saudi governments both distanced themselves from the report, it fomented still more rhetoric about militarily taking over the oil fields of Saudi Arabia. Tensions escalated further in August 2002 when the families of victims of 9/11 filed a trillion dollar lawsuit in US courts seeking damages from Saudi individuals and institutions.

The likelihood is that some facets of the US–Saudi relationship will continue relatively unchanged. Oil is important to both countries. Though Saudi oil only comprised about 15–17 percent of US imports, it constituted 60 percent of Japan's oil needs and a substantial portion of the European Union's. Even at the meeting between Crown Prince Abdullah and President Bush at the Bush ranch in Texas, Saudi Arabia was careful to rule out the possibility of using oil as an instrument to protest US policy towards Israel and Palestine. Other trade also continues, as do the many joint business ventures that the countries share in common. The US exported $8 billion to Saudi Arabia in 1999. US corporations have $4.1 billion in direct investment in Saudi Arabia, more than in Egypt and Israel. By mid-2002, the government reopened the shaky negotiations with international oil companies for lucrative participation in the $25 billion gas projects. What may be re-evaluated in the relationship is American hegemony in the region: the utility of US bases in Saudi Arabia and US policies towards Palestine, Israel and Iraq.

In sum, the domestic contest between reformists and the radical religious right reverberated in policy in the year following 9/11. The result was a two-level diplomatic approach in which Saudi Arabia cooperated in money laundering clean-ups and the freezing of bank accounts while it hesitated openly to confront its radical religious movement or to allow the USA fully to utilize the bases.

CONCLUSIONS: CONFRONTING THE DANGERS WITHIN

The contestation between different domestic constituencies has an impact on national policy even under a hereditary monarchy. A formidable challenge before Abdullah is to contain the radical religious right in Saudi Arabia as he institutes reforms. He must move quickly enough to satisfy the many disgruntled elements in the country yet with enough sensitivity to prevent a far-right backlash. This is no easy task given that the al-Saud base their right to rule on Islamic legitimacy. The tragic explosions at the Riyadh housing compounds in May 2003, however, highlight the urgency of immediate structural reforms.

In March 2002, there was a fire at a girl's school in Mecca. It appears that the building's exits were locked from the outside and the windows barred in order to prohibit contact with males. Fifteen young girls died in the blaze. A flurry of anger and criticism exploded through the Kingdom. A cleric was sacked; educational bureaucracies were reorganized so that the same authority now administers male and female education. Control over girls' education was one of the last bastions of unfettered religious authority. It may be that this incident was so heinous and indefensible that it actually provided Abdullah the space to reign in the radical religious right.[20] The devastating combination of the World Trade Center and the girl's school fire accelerated internal debate over the proper relationship of religion and politics.

The domestic debate indicates that there is indeed an important opening in Saudi Arabia. But it is not yet institutionalized. In the end, the new leniency is dependent on the person and leadership of Abdullah. If reforms are to endure, they must be made structural. The reform effort may backfire if not handled with sensitivity and if not institutionalized. As a Saudi remarked, 'We are capable of identifying the problems. But solving them will require more than a reform-minded sovereign. It will require an army of reformers'.[21]

More than in any other country, 9/11 has driven home the need for structural domestic reforms. It is not that Saudis are clamoring for a full-fledged, party-based competitive democracy. They are, however, clamoring for freedom of expression and assembly. Contentious voices resonate because of the exclusionary nature of governance. Political institutions and the sprawling religious bureaucracy must be reformed to incorporate different ethnicities, religious branches and regions. Stringent norms that mandate gender segregation, the covering of women and, sometimes, their seclusion in the domestic realm, must be addressed. Abdullah, a champion of women's rights within the Saudi context, must grant women greater mobility and rights while avoiding a backlash from the religious right. Reforms that were underway since Abdullah consolidated his position in 1998 have been accelerated in media, law, education, economy and gender roles.

The tragedy of 9/11 brought intense self-examination throughout all levels of Saudi Arabian society. Foreign Minister Saud al-Faisal said that, 'It is always good to take stock, and we are taking stock. Standing still is the last thing that any government would wish for, least of all our government.'[22] Islam will continue to be a part of public life in Saudi Arabia. The key reform is an emphasis on tolerant, plural Islam. No one practice of Islam has a monopoly on the word of God. 'Wahhabi' doctrine will continue to be important among parts of the population, though return to its social and religious expressions rather than explicitly political expressions. For example in education, the government cannot simply delete religion from the curriculum but it can mandate inclusion of the richness and diversity of Islam. Abdullah cannot distance himself from Islam if he is simultaneously to promote meaningful reform and contain the religious right. Rather, to be effective, Abdullah will likely wrap himself in the mantle of tolerant, plural Islam – the Islam of most Saudis.

Abdullah must create political space and allow political voice for the millions of Saudis who simply want the rule of law. The only way for the al-Saud to retain their position is to broaden their 'right to rule' to include meaningful representation of the diversity of the people and the protection of civil rights. Ordinary Saudis want to participate in the development of their country, particularly in meeting the demands of a young, booming population for education, health and employment. Millions of Saudi Arabians hope that the tragedy of 9/11 accelerates meaningful and difficult internal reforms, as well as a careful re-evaluation of US foreign policy in the region.

NOTES

1 For a fuller explanation of the sources of dissent before 9/11, see Gwenn Okruhlik, 'Networks of Dissent: Islamism and Reform in Saudi Arabia', *Current History*, Jan. 2002,

pp. 22–8 (posted at www.ssrc.org/sept11/buildingpeace/okruhlik) and 'Understanding Political Dissent in Saudi Arabia' at www.merip.org PIN 73

2 Sulaiman al-Hattlan, 'Saudis' Problem of Extremism', *Arab News*, 20 May 2002.

3 Madawi al-Rasheed, 'Saudi Arabia's Islamic Opposition', *Current History*, Jan. 1996, pp. 16–22 and Mamoun Fandy, *Saudi Arabia and the Politics of Dissent* (New York: St. Martin's Press, 1999).

4 On the relationship between oil and opposition in Saudi Arabia, see Gwenn Okruhlik, 'Rentier Wealth, Unruly Law, and the Rise of Opposition: The Political Economy of Oil States', *Comparative Politics*, Vol. 31, No. 3, April 1999, pp. 295–315.

5 Alain Gresh, 'Death in a Girls' School Changes National Tone', *Le Monde Diplomatique*, 12 May 2002.

6 'Saudi Says US Media Attacks Aim to Undermine Ties', Riyadh, Reuters, 5 Nov. 2001.

7 To counter media bashing emanating from the United States, Saudi Arabia launched a counter-offensive in May 2002. It hired a powerhouse public relations firm, Qorvis Communications, to rehabilitate the image of Saudi Arabia in the minds of Americans through a campaign of commercials and advertisements. It seems not to have been a sustained effort.

8 'It is true that Saudis were on the planes, but who can be certain whether they were behind the attacks? Until now, no one has found me any proof of this', *Der Spiegel*, Hamburg, 16 Dec. 2001.

9 For an official report from Saudi Arabia on its role in the war on terrorism, see 'Initiatives and Actions in the Fight Against Terrorism', Aug. 2002, Royal Embassy of Saudi Arabia. Available at www.saudiembassy.net

10 Abdul Aziz al-Dukheil in Barbara Slavin, 'Shaken Saudis Take a Hard Look at Society', *USA Today*, 25 April 2002.

11 In April 2002, over 120 Saudi intellectuals signed a letter, 'How We Can Coexist', that was a response to a letter from American conservative intellectuals called 'What We Are Fighting For.' The text is posted on www.islamtoday.net. For both letters, see www.americanvalues.org

12 Roula Khalaf, 'Saudi Rulers Seek to Counter Calls for Jihad', *Financial Times*, 26 Oct. 2001.

13 'Saudi Cleric Urges Non-Violent US Attack Response', Dubai, Reuters, 28 Sept. 2001.

14 Douglas Jehl, 'After Prison, A Saudi Sheikh Tempers His Words', *New York Times*, 27 Dec. 2001.

15 Susan Sachs, 'Saudi Prince Urges Reform', *New York Times*, 4 Dec. 2000.

16 Public opinion surveys are a recent development in Saudi Arabia. Shibley Telhami has conducted some of the earliest polls. For his work, see www.bsos.umd.edu/sadat/publications/op-ed/Polling

17 Robert Kaiser and David Ottoway, 'Saudi Leaders' Anger Revealed Shaky Ties', *Washington Post*, 10 Feb. 2002. Accounts of this letter vary slightly.

18 CNN, 'Saudis Ask US to Reduce Forces, White House Admits', 28 Jan. 2002.

19 Thomas Ricks, 'Briefing Depicted Saudis as Enemies – Ultimatum Urged to Pentagon Board', *Washington Post*, 6 Aug. 2002.

20 After the fire in the girls' school, a newspaper editor in Riyadh implores, 'When will we ever be ashamed of our attitude towards women? We ascribe all of society's ills to them, as if they were the sole intermediaries between men and vice.' Turki al-Sudairi, editor of *al Riyadh*, in Gresh, May 2002.

21 Fahd al-Mubarak in Gresh, May 2002.

22 In Slavin, 'Shaken Saudis'.

13 The consequence or the cause?

Impact on the Israel–Palestine peace process

David Newman

9/11 had a number of direct and indirect impacts on the Israel–Palestine peace process. The direct relevance was expressed in two main areas: the fight against terrorism, and the degree of involvement, or re-involvement, of the USA in the peace process. This chapter first explores how 9/11 was interpreted by both Israelis and Palestinians and the extent to which these interpretations were used by them to influence US policy in the Middle East; and second, examines how American policy was influenced by events in the region and the way in which these events were connected to the 9/11 discourse. Finally, the chapter discusses the impact of 9/11 on domestic Israeli discourse and the way in which these events were exploited by the Israeli government in implementing a hardline retaliation policy against the Palestinians for their increased use of terror against Israeli civilians.

ISRAEL, THE USA AND THE GLOBAL ANTI-TERROR COALITION

The initial attempts by President Bush to assemble a global anti-terror coalition were partially hampered by the US position on the Israel–Palestine conflict.[1] Both Israel and the Arab world immediately pointed to the linkages between their own situation and the events of 9/11, albeit from two diverse and contrasting perspectives. Islamic countries of the Middle East attempted to focus on the Israel–Palestine conflict as an underlying reason behind 9/11. Initially, they conditioned their support for the anti-terror coalition group of countries with a stated change in – what they perceived as – America's unconditional support of Israel. As such, Israel was not included categorically as one of the countries in the coalition for the fight against global terror. For its part, Israeli politicians and citizens from throughout the political spectrum rejected this stance, arguing that is was no more than an excuse to deflect the guilt from the root cause of Islamic fundamentalism. The Israeli government proposed its own linkage with 9/11, arguing that it must include the Palestinian fundamentalist organizations, such as Hamas and Jihad, who were responsible for attacks on Israeli civilians, and that these organizations should be included in the list of terrorist organizations to be targeted by the USA.

9/11 was viewed initially in Israel as a vindication of claims that the root cause of renewed violence in the region was the Palestinian terror organizations and their attacks on Israeli civilians. It was naturally assumed that the world would 'wake up' and come to sympathize with Israel, if only because they too had now experienced terror of a type previously unknown. Immediately following Bush's declaration of a global war on terror, it was almost taken for granted that Israel would be the first, and major, partner of the USA, and that Palestinian organizations, such as the Hamas, the Jihad and the Tanzin, would be prominent amongst the list of terrorist organizations.

It therefore came as a shock to many Israelis when it was made very clear by the Bush administration that Israel would not be an active partner in the war against terror, not least because the desired coalition partners included such states as Pakistan and Iran, whose leaders would categorically not agree to join a coalition with Israel. The list of terrorist organizations to be targeted omitted any Palestinian ones, including those responsible for the suicide bombings inside Israel.

The Israeli government reacted quickly to the Arab and Islamic arguments that the foundational reason for 9/11 was American policy towards the Israel–Palestine conflict and, in particular, perceived US bias in support of the Israeli position. This was later placed on the website of the Israel Foreign Ministry, which merits reading in its entirety. It includes: 'Any attempt to connect the September 11, 2001 terrorist attacks to US policy towards Israel is not only factually wrong, but also a shameful exploitation of that tragedy for political gain.'[2]

Israeli Prime Minister Ariel Sharon went as far as warning Washington 'not to appease the Arabs at our expense' and compared such appeasement policies with those made by British Prime Minister Neville Chamberlain in 1938. Israel, Sharon stated, 'would not be Czechoslovakia', a remark he was made to retract following pressure from a furious Bush administration.

Israel was not alone amongst the international community to dismiss this apology for the terrorist outrage, but while any form of linkage was rejected firmly by Israel, the rest of the international community gradually accepted the existence of a linkage, not as a justification for 9/11 but in understanding the suspicion displayed by the entire Islamic–Arabic world to the USA in its attempt to include them in the anti-terror coalition against one of their neighbors and cultural, if not political, allies. There was an acceptance that, if the Middle East was to become terror-free, and if there was to be the beginning of a rapprochement between the USA and the Islamic world, then the Israel–Palestine problem would have to be addressed as part of a longer-term and wider-ranging policy, which would include the implementation of a just and equitable solution, in addition to the all-out war against global terror. An enforced solution to the Israel–Palestine conflict would have to consist of a clear guarantee of Israel's security, coupled with the end of occupation and the establishment of a Palestinian state. For as long as such a solution was not forthcoming, the USA would continue to be seen as an ally of Israel and, as such, would never be able to influence, or become acceptable, across the Middle East.

That the Hamas and Jihad organizations, responsible for the attacks on Israeli civilians, in the West Bank settlements and in Israel proper, at bus stations, shopping malls and discotheques, would not be included amongst the list of terror groups to be targeted by the USA, was unacceptable to the Israeli government and public. Arab leaders emphasized the distinction between the 'terrorist' groups against whom they were prepared, even if begrudgingly, to join in the American campaign, and the 'freedom fighters' or 'militants' struggling for independence and an end to occupation. The fact that innocent civilians were being killed was not, in their view, a sufficient factor to turn these groups into targeted terror groups, not least because Israeli retaliation brought about a much larger number of fatalities and casualties amongst the Palestinian population – including innocent civilians. Had Bush insisted on including these groups on the list of targeted organizations, the chances of putting together the regional coalition would have been even more difficult, perhaps impossible.

It was also clear to the Palestinian leadership that, despite the fact that the increased Hamas and Jihad activity of the past year signaled a dissatisfaction with the path of negotiation undertaken by Arafat because of the failure to deliver a Palestinian state and an evacuation of Israeli settlements, it was not in its interests to go along with an American decision to include these movements in their list of organizations to be targeted, even if the activities undermined the leadership of Arafat and his Fatah organization. Since the failure of the Camp David negotiations and the eruption of the al Aqsa Intifada, popular support was ebbing from Arafat and any attempted return to the negotiations in favor of the radical and violent campaign against Israel. Contrary to what may have initially been perceived by the outside world, any decision to include these organizations on the American list would have been perceived as tacit agreement by Arafat to curb his own internal opposition and, as such, would likely have lost him further support. Palestinians would have interpreted any agreement to such a move as acquiescence to outside powers, particularly the USA, in helping quell internal opposition when, in their view, it was these internal groups which were now waging the 'true' war against Israeli occupation.

Equally for most Israelis, the failure of Arafat to clamp down on Hamas and Jihad was a clear indication that the renewed violence was taking place with the tacit approval of Arafat. Both Sharon and his Defense Minister, Ben Eliezer, argued that had Arafat wanted to, he could have used his own security forces to insure that terrorist activity ceased and that perpetrators were imprisoned. While this may have been true at the beginning of the al-Aqsa Intifada, by 9/11, a year after the renewal of violence, Arafat lacked total control over all the Palestinian factions and he would have been unable to prevent every suicide bombing. Again, Arafat looked to his internal constituency. Most Palestinians viewed Hamas and Jihad activities as a legitimate response to the failure of a negotiated solution and to the continuation of settlement expansion, and also as a response to Israel's own military retaliations, including the targeting of specific Hamas and Jihad leaders. Palestinian researcher Khalil Shikaki has shown from his surveys among Palestinians that the renewed violence was approved by a growing number of what he terms the 'young guard,'[3] even if it was in defiance of Arafat's preferred policies (and it is by no means clear that it was) and that any serious attempt by Arafat to use his own forces to limit the activities would be interpreted as a surrender to Western and foreign powers in the fight against occupation. Shikaki showed that support amongst the Palestinians for the peace process dropped from 44 percent in 1995/96 (when Peres was Prime Minister after the assassination of Rabin), to 30 percent under Netanyahu, to 24 percent under Barak and to only 11 percent after Sharon came to power. By July 2001, the popularity of the Islamist and nationalist opposition groups surpassed that of the Fatah and the Palestinian Authority for the first time.[4]

The Palestinian cause was not helped by footage of Palestinians dancing and rejoicing in the streets of West Bank towns after 9/11. Recollecting the disastrous consequences for Palestinians in Kuwait after they had supported the Iraqi invasion in 1990, the Palestinian police promptly ended these public demonstrations and ensured that more pictures did not reach the world media. Had the Palestinian authorities not acted so quickly, it is likely that they would have found themselves the target of American wrath, regardless of attempts by the rest of the Arab world to place the Palestinian struggle in a different category to that of other Islamic terrorist groups.

The Bush administration had to maneuver between these two contrasting narratives. It could not accept the simplistic explanation that the roots of 9/11 were due to US policy towards the Israel–Palestine conflict, not least because it did not perceive itself as being the dishonest broker that the Arab world suggested. However, Bush was unable completely to dismiss the Israel–Palestine arena as irrelevant to the wider regional events, especially with the increased terrorism and retaliation between the two combatants. In terms of the US major objective – the eradication of al-Qaeda, the capture of bin Laden and the end of the Taliban government – instability in another part of the region only complicated the task. Despite repeated American requests for both Israel and the Palestinians to implement a ceasefire while the Taliban was being defeated, no adequate response was forthcoming. If anything, violence increased as Arafat and Sharon tested the boundaries of what could be achieved while the USA was engaged elsewhere. Hamas and Jihad terrorism reached new peaks, as did Israeli retaliations, leaving the USA no option but to intervene yet again in a conflict from which the Bush administration had sought to distance itself.

AMERICAN INVOLVEMENT

Of all American international intervention, none has taken as much energy or resources for as lengthy a period of time as the Arab–Israel conflict.[5] Every US administration has been active in the region, often reaching new heights during crises, such as the wars of 1956, the Six-Day War of 1967, the Yom Kippur War of October 1973, as well as in negotiations such as the insistence of the first Bush administration in 1991 to convene the Madrid Peace Conference, and later active involvement under Bill Clinton in promoting and advancing the Oslo Accords and the subsequent rounds of negotiations throughout the 1990s.

That Clinton was able to continue with his efforts at reaching a final and negotiated solution to the conflict up until the last days of his administration was a clear indication of Bush's desire to exclude the conflict from his own political agenda. Clinton could not have continued to be so actively involved in the negotiation process without the tacit approval of the incoming president. Despite intense efforts on the part of the outgoing administration and, in particular, Middle East envoy Dennis Ross and the US Ambassador to Israel, Martin Indyk, all attempts to broker an agreement between Israel and the Palestinians ended in failure.

At the very most, the Bush administration attempted to find a way to implement the Mitchell and Tenet Agreements[6] which were no more than attempts to arrange a ceasefire and return the situation to where it had been less than a year before. Given the extremity of the situation that was developing in Israel–Palestine, this was minimal intervention, and far less than would have been forthcoming under the previous administration.

Paradoxically, the one country in the region which was prepared to give its unconditioned support to the USA after 9/11 was the state which was perceived by the rest of the region as being one of the sources of the problem, namely Israel. It became clear to Bush's administration that any attempt at a long-term solution to terrorism and at rapprochement with the Islamic world would involve the Middle East again. Although traditionally America has not been perceived by the Arab world as constituting an honest broker because of its continued unconditioned support of Israel, from the outset, the Bush administration was perceived by both protagonists as potentially less favourable towards Israel, not least because of the Bush family oil interests, the influence of former Secretary of State James Baker (who had filled that position under the previous Bush administration at the time of the Gulf War and the subsequent Madrid Peace Conference and who had openly clashed with Israeli leaders), and the fact that Bush did not share the same close connections with the American Jewish community as did Clinton. This was to prove to be an erroneous assessment, as the Bush administration gradually took on a categorical pro-Israel and anti-Arafat (not to be confused with an anti-Palestinian) position.

On 13 September, Sharon compared Arafat to bin Laden, but the Bush administration was not yet prepared to go along this road. On 19 September, Bush forced Sharon and Arafat to agree to a ceasefire and it was announced that if the ceasefire held for 48 hours, Foreign Minister Shimon Peres would reopen peace talks with the Palestinian leader. Sharon was weakened by the US government because Bush could not assemble an international coalition without Israel agreeing to withdraw its forces from the West Bank, while Arafat's position was greatly weakened by media pictures depicting Palestinians cheering the attacks on the World Trade Center. But the Islamic Jihad refused to recognize the ceasefire, sporadic violence continued, and by 23 September Sharon defied US and European pressure and canceled all ceasefire talks with the Palestinians.

In addition, there was the European factor. Few issues unite the foreign policy making of all EU countries as does the Israeli–Palestinian conflict. Europe has been trying to get its foot in the door of the Arab–Israel conflict resolution process, but this has been resolutely rejected by consecutive Israeli governments who view the European position as being pro-Arab.[7] Neither does the USA have an interest in allowing the EU to become a full partner in the efforts to negotiate a Middle East peace, preferring to maintain its own monopoly and influence.[8] But the EU began to test the waters. EU Foreign Minister Javier Solana, British Prime Minister Blair and Foreign Minister Jack Straw and German Foreign Minister Joschka Fischer all made several important visits to the Middle East, including to Syria and Iran, thereby increasing their credibility in the region. Israel viewed this European intervention as justifying its own claims that Europe was continuing pro-Arab policies, while the Bush administration (despite gratitude to Blair for his assistance in getting the coalition in order) suspected the EU of trying to muscle in to the region as an alternative mediator.

It did not take long for American Secretary of State Colin Powell to announce the appointment of a new special envoy to the Middle East, retired General Anthony Zinni, which was greeted with much cynicism by both Israelis and Palestinians. He was relatively unknown and had not previously been involved in the complexities of the Israel–Palestine arena. But it was the appointment per se, rather than the person, which indicated the active reinvolvement of the USA. There was a clear link between the appointment of the special envoy and the need for the American administration to show the shaky anti-terror coalition that it would seek an equitable solution to the Israel–Palestine conflict. The appointment signaled the beginning of the second phase of the post-9/11 events, coming as it did in the week when the Northern Alliance, with American aid, completed its defeat of the Taliban regime. However, Zinni's visits to the region were always greeted by an increase in terrorism, a retaliation by Israel, and the creation of immediate situations which made it impossible for him to accomplish even minor initial objectives.

In retrospect, we can distinguish two main phases in American policy towards the Israel–Palestine arena during the twelve months following 9/11. The first was the reticence to include Israel in the anti-terror coalition, the initial refusal to include fundamentalist Palestinian organizations in the list of terror organizations, and the continued demands that Israel meet its obligations to withdraw from the Occupied Territories and to continue towards a negotiated settlement. The second, commencing in the spring of 2002, saw a backing off on the part of the USA in openly opposing Israel's strong military retaliation, and even partial reoccupation of Palestinian Authority autonomy areas, after increased terrorism and suicide bombings inside Israel. This reached a peak following the Passover massacre in the seaside resort of Netanya, following which Israeli troops began to enter West Bank towns, destroying terrorist and civilian infrastructure. The Bush administration adopted a much tougher stance towards the Palestinian leadership, especially towards Arafat, demanding substantial changes in the former's structure, the holding of elections, and evidence that the leadership would help stamp out the terrorist activities of Hamas and Jihad.

The decision by the Israeli government to reoccupy parts of the West Bank, including most of the major urban centers, was met with only meek approval from the US administration which now equated Palestinian terrorism with the atrocities of 9/11. Sharon visited the USA on a number of occasions in a successful attempt to convince Bush that they faced a common enemy – namely fundamentalist forms of terrorism – and that certain Palestinian militant organizations should be added to the terrorist list. Through the spring and summer of 2002, the Israeli government was given carte blanche by the USA to deal with the threat of terrorism. The US administration also demanded the introduction of significant regime changes to the Palestinian Authority in an attempt to forge what it perceived as a more moderate leadership, although it did not yet demand the removal of Arafat, despite Sharon's statements to the effect that Israel no longer recognized Arafat as a legitimate partner for future peace negotiations.[9]

The two distinct phases are probably reflected best in two major speeches of Powell and Bush. Powell's, delivered a few weeks after 9/11, focused on the need for an equitable solution, in which the principles of the failed Camp David negotiations were reiterated: territorial withdrawal on the part of Israel, the establishment of a Palestinian state, an end to violence and terrorism, and a guarantee of Israel's security. The nuances had clearly changed when Bush finally spoke on Israel–Palestine in July 2002. Reiterating all the basic conditions, Bush emphasized the need to end the violence directed against Israeli civilians and also called for Palestinian leadership change. While Bush still made it clear that Israel should withdraw from the Occupied Territories and allow a Palestinian state, the changes were clearly pro-Israel. It was joked in some circles that the reason it took Bush so long to make a public statement on the Israel–Palestine conflict was because there was no one in the White House who could translate the speech from Hebrew into English.

By October 2002, Israeli military control of the West Bank was almost complete, while the international debate was diverted from the Israel–Palestine arena to the expected American invasion of Iraq. Here too, the USA and Israel demonstrated close cooperation. With the exception of Blair, Israel was the only country to support unequivocally the American determination to bomb Iraq, notwithstanding the fact that this could potentially result in Iraqi missiles being fired against Israel. At the White House, Sharon was promised advance notice of any such American attack. He also tried to persuade the administration to give him a free hand to respond militarily to any Iraqi missile attacks on Israel – unlike the case ten years previously when the previous Bush administration had put strong pressure on the Shamir administration not to respond to Iraqi provocations during the Gulf War. The US administration did not exert heavy pressure on Sharon not to retaliate in such an eventuality, but the consensus within Israel was that the government would not hold back as it had done ten years previously, if only that it should not be interpreted as weak by other Arab countries in the region.[10]

THE ISRAELI DOMESTIC SCENE

9/11 had a major impact on the vibrant debate inside Israel. Israelis of all political persuasions identified with the US tragedy. The American fight against terror became translated into the Israeli fight against terror and the military incursions into the West Bank were justified not only because of the Palestinian terror, but because it was now legitimate to use all means at the disposal of the state to eradicate organizations or persons linked to terror activities. There was no criticism of the American attack on Afghanistan, nor were there many voices raised against the Israeli incursions into the West Bank. The cooptation of the left-wing Labor Party into Sharon's government of national unity had already served to silence any serious opposition some months before 9/11. The use of 9/11 terminologies to justify Israel's own fight against terror made it even more difficult, almost impossible, for these political or media voices to raise any questions about Sharon's policies, thus silencing any serious political debate over the future of the peace process. Some voices of dissent were raised amongst the Israeli–Arab community in Israel[11] but these were muted as they were simplistically accused of being pro-terror. In other words, the debate around the conflict and the failure of the peace process was deflected by the government to the anti-terror debate.

The sentiments expressed by the Israeli public after 9/11 were shown in the monthly public opinion survey conducted for that month by the Steinmetz Peace Research Center at Tel Aviv University. Results reveal that 57 percent indicated that Israel's exclusion from the anti-terror coalition would benefit Israel's national interest. However, 32 percent thought that American policy omitting Israel from the coalition harmed Israeli interests. Eighty-three percent said no differentiation should be made between the attacks on the USA and those by the Palestinians and only 10 percent thought there was an ethical difference.[12] In October 2001 survey data showed that 51 percent of Israelis supported the American war in Afghanistan and 62 percent said all means, including those not legally sanctioned, should be employed.[13]

The same poll showed different attitudes among Palestinian–Arabs. Only 3 percent supported further US bombings, while 52 percent opposed them, mainly for humanitarian reasons. Only 9 percent of Israeli Arabs thought ideological terror could be defeated by military means.[14] The Palestinian–Arab citizens of Israel have always been in an unenviable position. While they are citizens of Israel, making up approximately 20 percent of the population, their national identity is Palestinian. Although they are represented in the Knesset, many Israelis view them as constituting a 'fifth' column in that they identify more strongly with Palestinian and Arab national aspirations than they do with the state of which they are citizens. Rather than constituting a bridge between the Arab world and Israel, they are perceived with suspicion on both sides and this is reflected in their response to the public survey questions. The fact that they had suffered thirteen fatalities in demonstrations held in solidarity with their Palestinian co-nationalists soon after the outbreak of the al-Aqsa Intifada in September 2000, meant that they too were increasingly identifying with the Arab–Islamic position in response to the events of 9/11, strongly contrasting the position held by the state and the majority Jewish population.

The fight against terror also resulted in a virtual paralysis of open governmental debate inside Israel. The Labor Party was criticized by many of its supporters for leaving the way open for the government to follow Sharon's policies without any adequate or meaningful parliamentary opposition. This situation was exacerbated following 9/11 and the further increase in Palestinian terror against Israeli civilians in the first half of 2002. Within the Israeli discourse, 9/11 was inherently linked to every Palestinian suicide bombing and the means of countering such terrorist activity were immediately compared to the American war against al-Qaeda and Afghanistan, a cause which virtually all sectors of the Israeli populace – from the left and right of the political spectrum – supported. As such, it became even more difficult for the Labor Party to leave the government, in opposition to the cessation of negotiations or what was seen in some quarters as an overzealous Israeli army response. That Defense Minister Binyamin ben Eliezer was elected as the new leader of the Labor Party diminished the distinction between the policies of the two major parties. Ben Eliezer refused all pressures, even from members of parliament of his own party, to leave the government, arguing that the fight against terrorism was a national cause and that he fully supported Sharon's policies in this respect.[15] In the face of criticism, both Sharon and Ben Eliezer pointed to the American war in Afghanistan, arguing that this was the only alternative.

As in all situations of war, internal criticism of the government's policies were few, especially in the aftermath of terrorist atrocities. The media, which had been under constant attack during the previous two years for bias towards the left-wing pro-Oslo positions and for socializing the public into supporting the peace agreements without making them aware of the dangers of renewed violence, underwent their own shift after 9/11. With the exception of the liberal *Ha'aretz* newspaper, all major media outlets turned to the centrist-right hard line security positions,[16] while the major English-language newspaper, the *Jerusalem Post* – read by much of the foreign affairs and diplomatic community – moved from right-of-center to extreme right wing, blindly supporting Sharon's position and policies, with the majority of its writers forging a strong link between the US and Israeli all-out wars against terror. The *Post* was in the forefront of the campaign aimed at delegitimizing the Oslo peace process for constituting what it termed as: naive, unrealistic and, in the words of Charles Krauthammer, a bad case of false messianism.[17]

Criticism of the government's policies, even mild criticism that the military incursions into the West Bank and the destruction of the civilian infrastructure of the Palestinian Authority was an overreaction, were often met by a barrage of right-wing and governmental critique that stated that there should be solidarity during a time of war and criticism of government was unacceptable.

This switch in the public discourse partially explains the almost total silence of the Israeli peace movements after 9/11. They had been on the decline since the collapse of the Camp David talks and the return of street violence.[18] But the attack on terror and the military incursion into the Palestinian Authority areas in the spring of 2002 was supported by most Israelis, including many who had been previously active in the pro-peace organizations. Apart from the work of some small splinter factions, the overall peace movement found itself unable to resume its large-scale activities when the violence returned and threatened the existence of the Oslo process. After 9/11 and the growth in terrorism and suicide bombings, the peace movements were unable to challenge the legitimacy of the hardline military response, including the destruction of the civilian infrastructure of the Palestinian Authority. Had they resumed their public activities in favor of an immediate return to the negotiations table, they would have been accused of siding with the terrorists. They did attempt to organize some mass demonstrations in Tel Aviv, but no more than a few thousand people appeared for a rally which in the past would have had 20,000 to 30,000 supporters. There were attempts by some small splinter groups, such as Ta'ayush, to help alleviate the plight of the Palestinian civilians who were under siege and did not have access to medicines, fresh food and other basic life necessities, but these activities were the exception rather than the rule. Given the intensity of the terrorist attacks, few Israelis were prepared to become involved in such activities, laying the blame on the critical social and economic conditions of the Palestinians and on their inability to stop the terrorism from within. The legitimation afforded the hardline military response by the Bush administration was acceptable to the vast majority of Israelis, sickened by the continual scenes of human carnage after each successive suicide bombing in restaurants, buses and shopping centers, including many who had been involved in the activities of the pro-peace movements in the past.

CONCLUSION

9/11 had direct impact on the Israel–Palestine conflict, but changed over time in its effects as the initial American reticence to focus on the linkages between Afghan–Taliban terror and Palestinian Hamas and Jihad actions, gradually became transformed into American support for Israel's anti-terror actions, even where they exceeded their initial brief and caused havoc to the civilian population. This was best summed up in the cynical comments of Israeli security officials who, shortly after the events of 9/11, were reported as stating that:

> For Israel, September 11 was a 'Hanukkah Miracle,' Israeli political and security officials recently told the newspaper *Ha'aretz*. Thousands of American fatalities are considered a godsend—in this cynical world—simply because their deaths helped shift international pressure from Israel onto the Palestinians, while allowing the Israeli government to pursue its regional objectives unobstructed. And indeed, in the past months, the United States has unfalteringly supported all of Israel's actions.[19]

This change was partly due to Israel's unequivocal support of all American actions, but more so because of increased intensity in Palestinian suicide bombings and the realization that the fight against terror was a common cause to both states, regardless of the reasons underlying the different terrorist operations. As such, the fallout of 9/11 strengthened US–Israel relations, despite the fact that the Bush administration had initially been expected to be less friendly towards Israel than the previous Clinton administration, and despite the fact that a right-wing Sharon government was not expected to gain much support amongst Israel's traditional friends in the Western world. The peace process halted almost completely, the fight against terror took on new dimensions of a mini-war, and it remained for a cessation of violence on the part of the Palestinians for the USA, and its Western allies, to bring new pressures on Israel and the Palestinian Authority to renew negotiations. Within Israel, support for Sharon remained strong throughout 2002, resulting in his resounding success at the general elections held in January 2003, in which he almost doubled the seats of his ruling Likud Party.[20]

NOTES

1 A. Ben Zvi, 'The Bush Administration and the Middle East: In the Shadow of September 11', Occasional Papers, Jaffee Center for Strategic Studies, Tel Aviv University, Vol. 4, No. 4, Feb. 2002.

2 The website of the Israel Foreign Ministry is to be found at: www.Israel-mfa.gov.il/

3 K. Shikaki, 'Palestinians Divided', *Foreign Affairs*, Jan./Feb. 2002.

4 Details of the Shikaki survey material can be found on the website of the Palestinian Center for Policy and Survey Research: http://www.pcpsr.org

5 See S. Spiegel, *The Other Arab–Israel Conflict; Making America's Middle East Policy, from Truman to Reagan.* (Chicago: University of Chicago Press, 1985); William B. Quandt, *Peace Process: American Diplomacy and the Arab–Israeli Conflict since 1967* (Berkeley: University of California Press and Brookings Institution Press, 2001 (Revised edition)).

6 The Mitchell and Tenet Agreements were by two American officials, the former a US Senator who had helped negotiate the Good Friday Agreement in Northern Ireland, the latter the head of the CIA. Both Agreements were negotiated during 2001, following the coming to power of Sharon but prior to 9/11. In neither case were these Agreements implemented.

7 During 2001/2, Israel became increasingly anti-European and this was reflected in numerous statements by both government officials and the media.

8 This is now being played out with the renewed American efforts to implement the Road Map towards Palestinian Statehood.

9 This policy had changed by 2002/2003 with the US demand for the removal of Arafat. In May 2003, a new Palestinian prime minister, Mahmoud Abbas (Abu Maazer) was appointed and was immediately visited by US Secretary of State Colin Powell on his post–Iraq war visit to the region.

10 Caroline Glick, 'PM: PA Escalating Terror Ahead of US War on Iraq: Israel will Attack Iraq if Harm is Done', *Jerusalem Post*, 26 Sept. 2002.

11 Arab–Palestinian citizens of Israel constitute approximately 20 percent of the total Israeli population, as distinct from the non-citizen, stateless Palestinian population of the West Bank and Gaza Strip.

12 Steinmetz Center, Peace Index, Sept. 2001. See: http://www.tau.ac.il

13 Ibid., Peace Index, Oct. 2001.

14 Ibid.

15 In November 2002, Ben Eliezer had finally taken his party out of the National unity government. It was expected that new elections would be held soon and, at the latest, by autumn 2003. Most public opinion polls predicted a victory for the right-wing Likud Party of Prime Minister Ariel Sharon with an even larger majority.

16 David Newman, 'The Myth of the Left Wing Media', *World Press Review*, Aug. 2002.

17 Edgar Legkowitz, 'Krauthammer: Israel Has Abandoned Oslo Messianism', *Jerusalem Post*, 11 June 2002.

18 David Newman, 'Why the Israeli Peace Movements Collapsed', *New York Times*, 30 Aug. 2002.

19 Neve Gordon, 'The Enemy Within: Israel's Gravest Danger Is Not the Palestinians', *In These Times*, 22 Dec. 2001.

20 See David Newman 'Change or continuity? The Israeli elections, January 2003', Mediterranean Politics, Vol. 8 (1), 2003, pp. 143–50.

14 A vulnerable continent

Africa

David Kenda Adaka Kikaya

The events of 9/11 brought radical changes to the expectation that terrorism is generally a domestic issue and resulted in considerable attention to issues of relative stability and peace. Africa was dragged into a war that had distant significance but a massive impact on it. It seemed to confirm that 'When America sneezes, Europe catches a cold but Africa suffers pneumonia.' This chapter focuses on reactions in West, East, North and South Africa, and offers an assessment of the terrorist attacks in Kenya in November 2002.

COLLECTIVE VULNERABILITY AND ECONOMIC FALLOUT

Africa joined the international community in expressing condolences to the USA and, in particular, to the bereaved families. Delegates at the fifty-sixth United Nations General Assembly (UNGA) in New York, of whom I was one, tried to come to grips with the disaster that had befallen their host. It changed the entire atmosphere of this collegiate annual conference. German Minister of Foreign Affairs Joschka Fischer relayed what leaders in many countries felt: 'We now live in the terrible knowledge that no country in the globalised world is invulnerable to terrorism.'[1]

Many African leaders of ailing economies felt themselves to be worst hit from the economic fallout. In Kenya, the important tourism sector slumped by 20 percent, while tourism in the fourteen African nations from Namibia to Madagascar which constitute the Southern Africa Development Community (SADC) declined on average by 10 percent within three months of 9/11.

The situation further deteriorated when security in major airports and US embassies was tightened, drastically restricting traveling. Immigration personnel behind heavily padded partitions became uncooperative and indifferent to applicants, adversely affecting prospective tourists, students and business people. These frustrations aggravated what would otherwise have been a somber reaction by Africa.

Western media strongly advocated retaliation against the perpetrators – a media seen by many Africans as biased.[2] This approach was not new to Africa since, over the years, the continent had received more than its fair share of negative coverage which gave the impression that it was ravaged by instability and savagery.[3] Writers from Africa have persistently accused the Western media of fanning animosity between warring groups.

African leaders thus interpreted this event as yet another opportunity for donor countries and Bretton Woods institutions to continue the marginalization of the continent as a recipient of economic assistance due to their heightened priority of combating terrorism.

Many Africans supported the coalition against terrorism, but emphasized that war should be carried out under UN conventions.[4] This was echoed in March 2002, during the Commonwealth Heads of Government Meeting (CHOGM) held at Coolum, Australia, which pledged to eradicate terror by focusing on its root cause. The CHOGM agreed that all member states adopt the report of the Commonwealth Committee on terrorism and a pledge to assist small and lesser developed countries to meet their obligations under the UN Security Council Resolution 1373 which condemned the attacks and expressed determination to prevent 'all such acts.'[5] There was lack of unanimity, however, about a wholesale condemnation of the Taliban or al-Qaeda.

AFRICA ON THE ALLIED COALITION

President George Bush's address to the UNGA on 6 October 2001 was dismissed by some critics as a headmaster's inaugural speech at a high school morning assembly. These delegates, especially from Africa, took exception to his 'chest thumping' assertion that, '*Governments have to choose whether they are with us or the enemy.*' Delegates argued that there was no unanimous agreement on who the enemy was.[6]

Bush's statement went down poorly with many leaders, including some who ordinarily warm up to the USA. A Ghanaian delegate mused on how condescending the statement was, describing it as being indicative of how President Bush's mentality lagged behind contemporary support for collective action and common solutions to worldwide problems of poverty, HIV/AIDS and terrorism in a globalized post-Cold War world.[7]

Iraq's statement to the UNGA seemed to sum up the views of the radical extreme:

> The entire world needs to save itself from a bottomless chasm towards which it might be pushed by USA . . . in fact, the United States, given what we know about how its leaders behave in crises, needs to be saved by the World as the World saves itself rather than being pulled down by the weight of the US as it falls into a fathomless pit from which there is no emerging.[8]

In fact, Bush's outlook was interpreted as one eager for a justification to infiltrate the Muslim world, especially those states which were not its trusted allies, not only in the Middle East but in Africa and elsewhere.

Some African delegates saw Afghanistan as the USA's first direct victim after which other suspect countries, such as Sudan and Somalia, would follow. Consistent with 'the enemy of my enemy is my friend,' US leaders recruited the assistance of the Northern Alliance to help topple the Taliban.[9] The installation of Hamid Karzai as interim leader to the new government raised eyebrows especially as it was later perceived that he and Zalmay Khalizad, the Kabul government's current delegate to Washington, were exclusively there to serve US interests, given their long connection with the USA.[10]

African countries became tense during the bombing, particularly Sudan, Somalia, Libya and Algeria. The tension intensified when CIA reports indicated that terrorist camps had been set up in Afghanistan and that approximately 50,000 to 70,000 militants from fifty-five countries had trained there in recent years, some of whom came from Africa.[11] Divisons within Africa fell into two categories. First, some people in Muslim-dominated countries took a religious stand by sympathizing with al-Qaeda, whilst their governments condemned the attack. Second, Muslims distanced themselves from Christians whom they perceived as pro-American, as riots in northern Nigeria illustrated.

It did not take long before investigations focused on some African countries that had benefited from Osama bin Laden's finances, such as the construction of a factory for pharmaceuticals in Khartoum.[12] Reports held that bin Laden and his allies found it relatively easy to enter African countries with Islamic affiliations and lax border security. Internationally acclaimed terrorists exploited these weaknesses to hibernate in Africa and conduct their clandestine missions. One such example is the Kurd, Abdullah Ocalon, who was arrested in Kenya in 1998 and long sought by the Turkish government for what it called terrorist activities.[13]

Bush's statements against such countries as Iraq, Iran, North Korea, Sudan and Somalia was interpreted as arrogance in Africa. Critics saw this as a way of avenging unsuccessful missions in these countries years ago.[14] To most Africans, this vengeance brought back fresh memories of the humiliation that US soldiers suffered in 1993 in Somalia where some were butchered while others were publicly dragged along the rough dusty roads of Mogadishu, by poorly equipped Somali soldiers.

To Africans, the Bush administration showed no intention of fulfilling its promises about assisting the continent. Contrast was drawn between the $30 billion voted by the US Congress immediately after the Trade Center attacks to the paltry $200 million given to the UN in 2001 to fight HIV/AIDS that claim high casualties in Africa.[15] African leaders queried why the disaster in the USA demanded considerable attention when AIDS kills 8,000 Africans weekly.[16] Although this could be dismissed as a rather far-fetched and unfair accusation, it underscored the disquiet that pervades the continent on America's perceived disdain for Africa.

It was widely felt that the September 11 attack helped refocus the world's attention to the Middle East.[17] Branding the Palestinians as terrorists, the Israelis had over the years unleashed brutality in a move to contain them.[18] The suicide bombers therefore were viewed by many in Africa as freedom fighters struggling against Israeli occupation of their territory.[19] Many Africans readily identified themselves with the Palestinians since it was the only response left to them, similar to independence struggles like Tanzania's 'maji maji' and Kenya's 'Mau Mau.' Parallels were drawn with many other freedom fighters on the continent, including the Algerian 'Front for National Liberation' against the French government; Nelson Mandela's 'Inkatha' freedom fighters of South Africa against the Boers; and Robert Mugabe's 'Patriotic Front' against the British-backed regime of Ian Smith's 'Unilateral Declaration of Independence' (UDI) in the then Rhodesia.

WEST AFRICA

One of the strongest reactions came from Senegal's President Abdolaye Wadde. He condemned the perpetrators for associating their assault with Islam and applauded the US anti-terrorist coalition. He none the less preferred concerted UN involvement to a unilateral approach. He was critical of the comparatively mild reaction given to the tragedy of August 1998 that befell Africans when American embassies in Kenya and Tanzania were bombed killing over 400 and injuring more than 5,000. Addressing the fifty-sixth UNGA in his capacity as Chairman of the African Union (AU), President Wadde lamented that 'the conflict caused by international terrorism affirmed they are advanced and strong and therefore all governments globally should equally join to show their solidarity in addressing security, stability and peace of all nations.'[20] President Wadde called on the global body collectively to address the root cause of terrorism. In particular, the AU Chairman urged African heads, through the AU, to convene and expeditiously address the problem of terrorism on the continent.

Wadde stated that Africa should not wait for first world countries to solve their problems. This was prompted by the lackluster response towards his joint financial initiative 'The New Partnership of African Development' (NEPAD) with Presidents Thabo Mbeki of South Africa and Ollesegun Obasanjo of Nigeria, which failed to attract substantial donor funding. The African Development Bank (ADB), which wanted funding to finance programmes to combat poverty, sought US$2.6 billion for the next three years.[21]

In West Africa there were also widespread riots. Islamic groups demonstrated in favor of bin Laden and al-Qaeda – whom they saw as a David fighting the American Goliath – and clashed with Christians mistakenly identified as American sympathizers. Nigeria was particularly hit when religious clashes between Muslims and Christians ensued immediately after September 11, reportedly killing over 500 people and injuring more in the Central Nigerian city of Jos, with wanton property destruction.[22]

Muslims regarded bin Laden as a hero who had destroyed the untouchable twin towers, which metaphorically symbolized the USA as a superpower. Many Muslims believed that the West was fundamentally anti-Islamic and therefore bin Laden's attempts were perceived as the only way to get back at the 'arrogant' West and, in particular, the USA.

As an Islam-dominated country, Nigeria has withstood many religious and ethnic clashes but the terrorist attacks aggravated the tensions. Reports indicated that the introduction of Sharia law in the populous northern state of Zamfara, had managed to contain radical Muslim opinion. But the widespread riots and destruction suggested otherwise.

Nigerian Christian bishops had condemned the government for adopting Sharia law, saying it would only escalate religious and ethnic violence. They complained that this was a violation of human rights of non-Muslims in the country's multi-religious society. It was known that some in the government hoped that Sharia law would be banned.

Oil-rich Nigeria is a powerful ally of the USA with a vast consumer market in a turbulent continent. Washington was quick to announce debt relief without the usual stringent conditions.

EAST AFRICA

Ironically, East African countries that genuinely deserved debt relief were not to receive it. The 1998 terror attacks in Kenya and Tanzania had massively damaged their already ailing economies and infrastructure. For a long time, there was pressure on the World Bank, IMF and other donors to waive significant debts from these poor countries.[23] Instead, during the anti-terror war, Pakistan was granted $1 billion in aid and sanctions imposed in 1998 for nuclear tests were waived. Pakistan had also been isolated for violations of democracy by its military regimes, including by current President General Pervez Musharraf.[24]

Most African leaders saw this as a rare opportunity to benefit from America. When focus shifted to the continent, several heads of state sought to be noticed as being ready to assist the Americans.[25] President Daniel arap Moi of Kenya led a pro-American, anti-terrorism demonstration in Nairobi. It did not take long before such opportunism was noticed for what it was. Baroness Valerie Amos, British Minister for Foreign Affairs, accused Moi of taking advantage of the situation to regain international aid.[26]

This brought a scathing attack from the East African elder statesman who said his actions in response to the 1998 bombing that had exposed his and Tanzania's subjects to terrorism, had been humane. However, columnists in the local media believed that the government had placed the country in a precarious position when the President, together with his Cabinet, senior government and party officials, had led the anti-terrorism demonstration.

This demonstration irked Muslims who in turn spilled onto the streets to condemn America's brutality, which had brought untold harm to East Africa.[27] The problems between the central government and Muslims escalated when security services from America descended on Kenya's Muslim-populated coastal region, ostensibly seeking members of al-Qaeda. Muslims protested their harassment at the hands of the foreigners.[28]

The matter was deemed political by its critics when an opposition activist in

Mombasa was put under house arrest under suspicion of having links with al-Qaeda. Resentment worsened when an imam was among eighteen suspects arrested in the north-eastern region of Kenya although he was later released on grounds of mistaken identity. The release occurred, however, only after violent demonstrations in this region, which borders one of Washington's target 'enemies' – Somalia.[29]

Kenya's ailing economy was recovering from a recession and desperately needed aid, which donors suspended nearly ten years ago. Earnings from major agricultural exports like tea, coffee and flowers declined by an average of 20 percent after the terror attacks.[30] Furthermore, Kenya Airways immediately incurred a loss of Kshs 35 million (US$500,000) over a period of two months in lost passenger and cargo business due to booking cancellations. Worse still, the airline projected a fall in its pre-tax profit by Kshs 300 million (US$4.8 million).[31]

Investigations into al-Qaeda seemed to bear fruit when local media reported that three suspects were arrested 400 kilometers west of Nairobi. Security personnel refused to disclose details, but it was possible that they had been flown to an undisclosed American location.[32]

Somalia reappeared in the limelight as the FBI and CIA suspected bin Laden was funding some radical groups there.[33] With no legitimate government in place and marred by conflicts instigated by clan warlords, the country was susceptible to infiltration. Fear of a possible US military strike heightened when the FBI discovered radio communications equipment hidden in caves. Reports indicated that Taliban members fleeing US bombardment in Afghanistan had already moved from Pakistan via Somalia to Mozambique.[34]

Visits by Britain's Secretary of Defence Geoffrey Hoon to Kenya caused speculation of military attacks on Somalia. This gained credence when US naval vessels with 3,000 personnel landed at Mombasa on the Kenyan coast. Forces from Britain and Germany later joined them in the guise of a joint military exercise on the border with Somalia. This was the largest joint military exercise ever conducted in the region or indeed, continent. Military analysts viewed this as an inevitable preparation for strikes on Somalia.[35]

This caused panic among Kenyans, especially those on the coast who felt they were being exposed to repeat terror attacks, which reverberated southwards to Tanzania's coastal city of Dar es Salaam, prompting more anti-American demonstrations. Muslim leaders accused the Kenyan government of hosting hostile foreigners reminiscent of colonialists, and urged the foreign troops to look for another base since it was illegal for a member state in the AU to be used as a base for attacking another member state. Muslims threatened to disrupt the lucrative tourism business on the coast in the event of an attack on Somalia.[36] The government, however, reassured them saying that the military forces were there temporarily and would not be involved in any military offensive.[37]

It was also rumoured that US security personnel had infiltrated Somalia and met warlords. They had held talks with leaders of the Rahanweyn Resistance Army, discussing possible cooperation in the intended military strikes.[38] It later emerged that the warlords were united in opposition to the USA's military. Media reports suggested that Ethiopians were training some Somali fighters to serve as proxies on the side of the Americans in the impending war against Somalia, similar to the cooperation with the Northern Alliance in Afghanistan.[39] Somalia's interim government panicked and quickly convened in Mogadishu, pleading with the USA to hold fire.

Somalia's interim President Abdigassim Sald Hassan accused Western media of falsely calling the country a haven for terrorists.[40] He was strongly backed by the Inter-governmental Authority on Development (IGAD), a regional organization which warned the USA against any military strike.[41] Political analysts queried whether this military move was an act of vengeance after the Somalian militia of General Mohammed Aideed killed US Rangers in Operation Restore Hope.

By contrast, Sudan was a country bedraggled by conflicts. Its leadership saw a golden opportunity to please Washington by handing over secret files on bin Laden who had lived there in the early 1990s.[42] Abu-Anas al-Liby, described as one of the twenty-two most dangerous terrorists in the world, was held in Sudan's capital Khartoum and implicated in the 1998 embassy bombings in Dar es Salaam and Nairobi. He was handed to the Americans in return for restoration of diplomatic relations and associated trappings.

The coalition against al-Qaeda that spilled over into the continent of Africa revealed dubious deals by US companies which were discovered by the US government. The Tanzanian government then realized it was losing millions of dollars in revenue from an illegal trade involving a rare gemstone, Tanzanite, that was selling on the US market, netting approximately $300 million. The government of Tanzania was surprised because the trade had been banned and only $16 million in earnings for the state were recorded. Enraged Tanzanian parliamentarians saw this as yet another of America's unashamed exploitations of Africans; they had earlier been infuriated by the small compensation for the August 1998 terrorist attacks.[43]

Political analysts predicted that authoritarian regimes on the continent would take advantage of the generalized phobia against terrorism to rid themselves of opponents. The Ugandan government passed an anti-terrorism bill that gave the government power to add any suspicious group to its terrorist list. This was seen as a way to suppress opposition parties and rebel groups opposed to Uganda's President Yoweri Museveni.[44]

NORTH AFRICA

Reactions from the North of the continent were contrary to expectations given that it is a predominantly Muslim region which has long lived with Islamic fundamentalists who have brought terror to its doorstep. It has also been enmeshed in the Israeli–Palestinian conflict and interpreted 9/11 as an escalation of the same. The Algerian government made a surprising move when it handed over to US intelligence classified information on Islamic organizations accused of terrorism.

In Egypt, there were attempts to eliminate groups associated with terrorism by capturing and imprisoning them. Those who escaped were suspected of joining bin Laden.[45] This gained credence when bin Laden's second in command, an Egyptian named Ayman al-Zawahri who was said to 'have Osama's mind,' was allegedly rejuvenating al-Qaeda movements on the borders of Afghanistan.[46]

Libyan President Colonel Muammar Gaddafi, a consistent thorn in the flesh of the West, declared himself on the side of the campaign against terrorism. This perhaps was bearing in mind America's threat against states harbouring terrorists. Many analysts perceived the move as an attempt by Gadaffi to avoid Western aggression.

SOUTH AFRICA

Southern Africa, which is predominantly Christian, with a small Muslim population, was not affected much other than by the revival of Qibla, a radical Muslim movement that risks being banned.[47] In spite of these threats, there were pro-bin Laden demonstrations by Muslims in the streets of some of South Africa's cities. Most were largely peaceful but sent out a strong message of support to other Muslims.

These sentiments seemed to receive backing from President Thabo Mbeki who condemned the US refusal to stop what he saw as indiscriminate bombings. UN Secretary General Kofi Annan, the World Bank President Wolfson and Mbeki jointly regretted that the war was not only waged against a poor, rugged country but also against dwellers of poverty-stricken third world countries. Mbeki advised that, 'this necessarily breeds a deep sense of social injustice, social alienation, despair and a willingness to sacrifice lives among those who feel they have nothing to lose.'[48]

THE MOMBASA ATTACKS

Terrorism revisited Africa when Kenya was hit for a fourth time by well-coordinated attacks on 28 November 2002, twenty-five kilometers north of Mombasa City. It was claimed that the car that rammed into the Israeli-owned Paradise Hotel was packed with 200 kilograms of explosives, killing sixteen people. A rocket was also fired at a departing Israeli passenger jet. Kenyan media emphasized similarities to the 1998 attack that destroyed the US embassy in Nairobi when a vehicle laden with 800 kilograms of explosives killed 212 people. In both incidents Kenyans were the majority of casualties.[49]

Kenyans were numbed with shock but tension also emerged. Tension because many thought that the 1998 attacks had formed a passing wave. Foreign troops from Germany, America, Britain and India were still deployed along the Kenyan coast after 9/11. There was some bitterness because the incident brought back fresh memories. Although Kenyans were not the targets, many became the victims. In 1998, the bereaved families encountered difficulties in getting compensation from the US government. Some families affected by the Mombasa attack accused Israel of failing to help them. The Kenyan government released Kshs 3 million (US$38,000) to pay for some expenses.[50]

Rather than Kenya being considered unsafe to visit, the indigenous press and authorities contended that the Mombasa attacks were targeted incidents, not an ongoing instability. While the British government warned its nationals against making visits, the German government insisted that it would not deter its citizens from visiting.

Speculation about Kenya's insecurity, nevertheless, persists. Many deem the country's foreign policy to be ambiguous, especially on the Middle East conflict. At the same time, Kenya has been left vulnerable by being an ally of the USA and a commercial partner of Israel. Laxity by the Kenyan security has also drawn criticism as investigations show that they had knowledge of the possible attacks eight months in advance. But Kenya is also in a difficult position, sharing long borders with both Sudan and Somalia – countries believed to have strong connections to al-Qaeda. That said, partnership between Kenya and Western governments in the fight against terrorism can be expected to continue. On 5 December 2002, Bush welcomed Moi to the White House and stated that the Mombasa attack reinforced his resolve to pursue, apprehend and punish those bent on such acts.

CONCLUSIONS

To many in Africa, this crisis made clear the hypocrisy of Western countries in attempting to placate Africa and to imply that their problems would be considered a priority this century. September 11 served to push the continent lower down the list of Western priorities as the USA and its coalition concentrated on world terrorism.

9/11 also prompted Africans to relive the 1998 attacks on US embassies. In fact, Kenya had suffered its first serious terrorist attack in 1981 when a historic hotel, The Norfolk (known euphemistically as 'The House of Lords' during the colonial period), was blown up by a massive bomb blast, in retaliation to Kenya's alleged logistical support and ground refueling facilities for the Israeli planes involved in the famous 'Entebbe raid.'[51] It demonstrated how much more vulnerable and defenceless are countries with weaker economies. Responses expressed at the subsequent UNGA of October–December 2001 were predictable.

Comparisons were made to the new law that has been passed by the Bush administration in which the American victims were getting $11 billion compensation while their Kenyan counterparts were given only $3.4 billion. In explaining this away, the Bush administration argued that it was anyway doing the country a favor through the compensation.[52]

Whereas African leaders were in broad agreement about combating terrorism, they were reluctant to be drawn into what was perceived as Washington's unilateral crusade. They preferred a collective approach by the UN. Most felt strongly that the root cause of terrorism was in the Middle East and needed to be addressed if effective measures were to contain it and serious attention paid to the plight of disenfranchised Palestinians. This line of thought seemed to win the day and it remains to be seen if the USA will be sober enough to embrace this collective opinion in a globalizing world.

Financial aid to Africa through the Monterey agreement of March 2002, the NEPAD initiative and the results of the G8 meeting in Canada are welcomed by a continent that is ravaged by poverty, HIV/AIDS and indebtedness. It was none the less perceived to some extent as a means of placating Muslims and of reducing anti-Western sentiment.

NOTES

1 The fifty-sixth session of the Annual United Nations General Assembly met in New York from October to December 2001.
2 Edwards Herman, 'Collateral Damage: Is It Ever Justifiable?', *Kenya Times*, 21 Feb. 2002, p. 14.
3 John Pilger, 'Media's Strange Role in the War against Terror', *Kenya Times*, 21 April 2002, p. 12.
4 Interview with former South African President Nelson Mandela by the Chinese News Agency *Xinhua*, *Kenya Times*, 24 Feb. 2002, p. 12.
5 Communiqué of the Commonwealth Heads of Government Meeting, March 2002.
6 Confirmed by Ms Njeri Rugeni, a journalist from the *Daily Nation*.
7 Personal communication after the speech during informal discussions in the corridor.
8 Iraqi government delegate, paper on 'Complete Disarmament', 56th UN General Assembly.
9 John Mula, 'The Letter from Washington', *East African Standard*, 27 Jan. 2002, p. 19.
10 Eduardo Galeano, 'The Economic Dynamism of Fear', *East African* 4, 10 March 2002, p. 30.
11 *Daily Nation*, 26 Jan. 2002, article by Reuters, p. 26.
12 Simon Denyer, 'New FBI East African Link to Bin Laden', *East African Standard*, 27 Sept. 2001, p. 1.
13 VPPU, 'We Support War on Terrorism, says VP', *East African Standard*, 19 Feb. 2002, p. 5.
14 Magesha Ngwiri, *Daily Nation*, 9 Dec. 2001, p. 9.
15 Chinese News Agency *Xinhua*, 'Terrorism Was to Cost $30 Billion This Year', *Kenya Times*, 27 Feb. 2002, p. 12.
16 *New People Magazine*, March–April 2002, p. 1.
17 John Knight, 'Sinn Fein Ilk Do Not Deserve Crowning', *East African Standard*, 27 Jan. 2002, p. 19.
18 'Israel Calls Off Crucial Talks with PLO Leader,' *Daily Nation*, 24 Sept. 2001, p. 13.
19 *Kenya Times*, 15 April 2002, Chinese News Agency *Xinghua*, p. 18.
20 Address by the President of Senegal in his capacity as Chairman of the African Union to the 56th UN General Assembly.
21 Moussa Awuonda, 'Africa Loses as Donors Invest in Anti-terror War', *Kenya Times*, 11 Feb. 2002, p. 21.
22 *Daily Nation*, 24 Sept. 2002, p. 14.
23 Chris Johnson, 'Debt Relief in Africa' in *'Guide: Africa' Foreign Policy Association-Africa/Africa* http://www.fpa. . ./newsletter section- debt
24 *Daily Nation*, 24 Sept. 2001, p. 3.
25 *Daily Nation*, 18 Dec. 2001, p. 7.

26 This undiplomatic exchange was widely carried by the local Kenyan media and reported on the BBC World Service.
27 Mohammed Hyder, 'Third Class Citizens', *BBC Focus on Africa*, Jan.–March 2002, p. 17.
28 Simon Denyer, 'FBI in East Africa', *East African Standard*, 27 Sept. 2001, p. 1.
29 *Daily Nation*, 10 Dec. 2001, p. 1.
30 *Daily Nation*, 12 Dec. 2001, p. 15.
31 *East African*, 19 Feb. 2002, p. 12.
32 *People's Daily*, 18 Feb. 2002, p. 1.
33 Dennis Onyango, 'No Links with Osama: UN Moves to Save Al Barakaat', *East African*, 29 April–5 May 2002, p. 22.
34 Edward Malei, 'Enemies Everywhere', *New People Magazine*, March–April 2002, p. 3.
35 Commentary by TV journalist, Joe Ageyo, on prime KTN (Kenya Television Network) news, closely associated with CNN, 4 Feb. 2002 at 9.00 p.m.
36 Evelyn Kwamboka, 'American Ambassador Meets Muslims in Mombasa', *East African Standard*, 3 April 2002, p. 1.
37 Mohammed Affay, Assistant Minister Foreign Affairs and International Cooperation, 'Foreign Troops Not Hostile', *East African Standard*, 18 April 2002, p. 19.
38 *Daily Nation*, 11 Dec. 2001, p. 14.
39 *Daily Nation*, 11 Jan. 2002, p. 6.
40 *Daily Nation*, 14 Jan. 2002, p. 9.
41 *Daily Nation*, 15 Feb. 2002, p. 5.
42 Richard Dowden, 'Africa's Ground Zero', *BBC Focus on Africa*, Jan.–March 2002, p. 9.
43 Alfred Ngotezi, 'Tanzanite and Terrorism', *East Africa*, 4–10 Feb. 2002, p. 18. This matter came to the fore when the CIA alerted the Tanzanian leadership that Osama bin Laden's al-Qaeda terrorist group had suspected links with this lucrative Tanzanite trade.
44 *Daily Nation*, 18 March 2002, p. 14.
45 David Bamford, 'View from the North', *BBC Focus on Africa*, Jan.–March 2002, p. 23.
46 *Daily Nation*, 26 Jan. 2002, p. 15.
47 Farouk Chothia, 'Dousing the Flames', *BBC Focus on Africa*, Jan.–March 2002, p. 26.
48 Magesha Ngwiri, 'Who'll Defeat Third World Countries?', *Daily Nation*, 16 Dec. 2001, p. 9.
49 *Daily Nation*, 2 Dec. 2002, p. 1.
50 The Nation Team, 'State to Pay All Bills for Bomb Victims', 2 Dec. 2002, p. 3
51 During Uganda's reign by dictator Iddi Amin Dada, a plane on which the majority of passengers were Jews was hijacked to Uganda's International Airport – Entebbe. Kenya allegedly provided logistical and refueling facilities to the Israeli Entebbe raid rescue mission. Hence the revenge attack on this hotel in Nairobi.
52 *Daily Nation*, 2 Dec. 2001, p. 36.

15 Political Islam in Southeast Asia and the US–Philippine alliance

James Putzel

Within hours of the attacks of 9/11, President Gloria Macapagal-Arroyo joined many others around the world in condemning the atrocities.[1] However, the President went further than many other leaders pledging the Philippines' 'all out support' to the United States.[2] Within ten days it was clear that the USA was preparing a strike on Afghanistan and members of the Macapagal-Arroyo administration were quick to say they would aid the effort and even send troops if asked to do so.

Without doubt the reactions in the Philippines to 9/11 were linked to the battle of the central state with its Islamic minority. However, in this chapter I argue that the government's enthusiasm to join the US alliance represented the action of a weak state and, while offering potential short-term gains, it risked a deepening of the longstanding violent conflict with Islamic separatists. I look first at the contrast between Philippine reactions and those of others in the region. I then examine briefly the roots of the conflict with separatists in the south and suggest that the central state attempted to gain leverage out of September 11 in its battle with Islamic organizations. I argue that these events have coincided with the agendas of both the US and the Philippine governments to revive military cooperation, concluding with an assessment of the risks involved in waging a war against terrorism rather than addressing the causes of terrorist action.

THE PHILIPPINE RESPONSE IN A COMPARATIVE SOUTHEAST ASIAN PERSPECTIVE

The enthusiastic support for the USA expressed by the Philippine government after 9/11 stood in sharp contrast to the reaction of other members of the Association of Southeast Asian Nations (ASEAN), who, while condemning the terrorist attacks, were much more circumspect about giving their full endorsement to any US countermeasure. Dr. Mahathir Mohammad, Prime Minister of Malaysia, gave his support to the US effort to hunt down terrorists, including those operating in Southeast Asia, but he opposed the strikes against Afghanistan.[3] Mahathir's government was intent on maintaining a positive relationship with the USA, in order to continue to attract investment and ensure access to US markets, while not antagonizing the member states of the Organization of Islamic Conference (OIC). Thailand was even more hesitant to announce unconditional support for the USA, worried that Washington might request use of its military bases, while Singapore, no doubt feeling extremely vulnerable, was uncharacteristically slow in endorsing US military action.[4]

In Indonesia, home of the world's largest Islamic population, reactions to 9/11 and subsequent strikes against Afghanistan were perhaps the most polarized in the region. President Megawati Sukarnoputri, on a trip to Washington only a week after the attack, expressed strong solidarity with the USA, seeking a reversal of the US Congressional ban on support for the Indonesian armed forces. However, after the strikes on Afghanistan, her foreign minister asked the UN to replace the USA in leading the fight against terrorism, saying military action in Afghanistan was causing 'deep concern in Jakarta.'[5] Megawati was torn between, on the one hand, using the opportunity of the US-led anti-terrorist drive to gain international support and approval of Jakarta's own battle with armed separatists in Aceh and Irian Jaya, and, on the other hand, keeping her distance from the USA in order not to give political ammunition to the moderate and radical Islamic organizations which constitute the most potent opposition to her government.

Megawati had assumed the presidency just three months before September 11, when the veteran Islamic leader Abdurrahman Wahid was forced out of office on corruption charges. She was a compromise between Muslim leaders and the armed forces, which continued to play a key role in brokering power in Jakarta even after the transition to formal democracy. In April 2001, under pressure from the armed forces, Jakarta stepped up its military campaign against the Free Aceh Movement (GAM). By January 2002, Megawati seemed to abandon efforts for a peaceful resolution of the war when she labeled GAM an 'enemy of the state.' By July she appeared to be giving her generals a free hand to punish 'sternly' the guerrillas.[6] There have been accusations that Aceh militants received weapons through networks stretching from Afghanistan and Pakistan to the Philippines and Malaysia.

However, while hoping to gain support for the fight against Islamic and other armed movements at home, the Jakarta government was not eager to move against Islamic political movements in Jakarta, said to be linked to Osama bin Laden. Megawati's hold on power in Indonesia remained fragile as neither she nor her secular party, the Indonesian Democratic Party of Struggle (PDI Perjuangan), commanded significant authority among the Muslim population. After US strikes were launched against Afghanistan, Vice President and leading Muslim politician Hamzah Haz called for an end to the bombing and questioned the 'proof' the Bush administration said it had that Osama bin Laden was responsible for the 9/11 bombings. Activists of his United Development Party (PPP), the largest Muslim party in the country, staged anti-US demonstrations.[7] Outside the government, the Islamic Defenders Front (FPI), headed by Muhammed Rizieq, vowed to hunt down Americans and Britons in the country.[8] The Islamic Youth Movement (GIP) reportedly signed up volunteers to fight in Afghanistan, following the example of Islamic militants who had fought alongside the mujahideen against the Soviet occupation in the 1980s.[9]

Even before 9/11 US authorities had claimed Indonesia as a center of terrorist activity connected to bin Laden's al-Qaeda network. The Java-based Laskar Jihad, possessing a sizable militia, did not hide its links with Taliban forces in Afghanistan, though its leader Ja'far Umar Thalib disowned Osama bin Laden.[10] In January 2002, Singaporean authorities announced that they had arrested militants of *Jemaah Islamiyah* (Islamic Community), said to be a network stretching throughout Southeast Asia with its base in Jakarta. Singaporean and Philippine authorities backed by the USA claimed that Jemaah Islamiyah was linked to al-Qaeda and was directed by Abubakar Ba'asyir, a Muslim cleric and leading member of the Indonesian Mujahidin Council (*Majelis Mujahidin Indonesia* – MMI).[11] While Ba'asyir professed his admiration for bin Laden, Indonesian authorities interrogated the Muslim leader in February, reporting no evidence of links to al-Qaeda and also denying Singaporean claims that Indonesian intelligence services had provided a report purportedly written by the cleric outlining terrorist plans.[12]

The position of Megawati's government radically changed after the bombing of a nightclub in Bali on 12 October 2002, which killed at least 180 people, three-quarters of whom were foreigners. The attack coincided with another explosion close to the nearby US consulate and a third in the mainly Christian area of Manado, the capital of North Sulawesi, just in front of the Philippine consulate. The bombing in Bali was targeted for maximum political and economic impact, virtually bringing to a standstill the tourist industry on which the struggling Indonesian economy remained heavily dependent. While a quarter of those killed in Bali were Indonesians, most were from the non-Muslim communities.

Speculation was rife that this was the work of Jemaah Islamiya and Malaysia, Singapore, the United States and Australia put severe pressure on Megawati's government to take action. Within days the government arrested Abubakar Ba'asyir and other leading Islamic radicals and passed a presidential decree increasing police powers to fight terrorism. The decree allowed detention of suspects without charges, stiffer penalties including the death penalty for those involved in terrorist action and less rigorous evidentiary requirements for arrest. Mindful of the distrust of the military among opposition Islamic organizations and the general public, the President's decree allowed some judicial review of detention orders, rejected the establishment of a special anti-terrorist commission and, most importantly, left the police rather than the armed forces (TNI) in charge. Since many of the Islamic militants and clerics targeted as sympathizers with al-Qaeda were persecuted during the Suharto years, including Ba'asyir, and since they contributed to the fight to oust the dictator, Megawati had to avoid turning them into martyrs.

The bombings in Bali and Sulawesi, followed by new attacks in the Philippines, suggested that Islamic radicals across the region were coordinating activities. They clearly shared goals of establishing communities on the basis of Islamic law, a common disgust over Western inaction on Palestine and a common approach to engaging in terrorist action. However, it remained far from certain that Jemaah

Islamiyah ever existed in an organized form. Just before his arrest, Ba'asyir denied
again any knowledge of the organization and blamed the bombings on US intelligence operatives. In fact, the only evidence that Jemaah Islamiyah was more than
a loosely knit network of contacts was provided by state prosecutors during the
trial of Ba'asyir under the Suharto regime and it is not deemed credible.[13]

By looking at the threat as one emanating from a unified organization, governments of the region could, in the short term, gain more legitimacy for deploying draconian security measures against home-grown Islamic radicals. However,
there was a risk that the tactic could backfire in the longer term by both empowering repressive and unaccountable military forces, thus weakening the possibilities
for democratic consolidation, and giving the Islamic radicals more legitimacy –
perhaps making their 'regional reach' a self-fulfilling prophecy.

Malaysian, and more reluctantly, Indonesian authorities attempted to placate
the USA by taking a harder line on home-grown Islamic radicals and, in fact,
joined the Philippines in justifying more draconian security measures by participating in the international war against terrorism. However, they both remained
critical of US war plans against Iraq, while US authorities hesitated to intervene
directly in either country presumably for fear of precipitating a political crisis.
The situation in the Philippines was very different.

Indonesia's Megawati was facing an Islamic opposition increasingly radicalized
in the face of problems in the transition to democracy. Similarly Dr. Mahathir's
United Malay National Organization maintained its authority in Malaysia by
beating back democratic opponents, leaving the Parti Islam SeMalaysia as the
only viable challenger to its position. With Muslim majorities in both countries,
leaders could not appear to be too enthusiastic about a US campaign, which,
despite assurances of being anti-terrorist rather than anti-Muslim, nonetheless
was focusing its sights on Islamic countries. In the Philippines, Muslims make up
only a minority of the population.

WAR WITH ISLAMIC MOVEMENTS IN MINDANAO

Nothing demonstrates more clearly both the nature of the fight between Islamic
organizations and the central government and its intractability than the observa-
tion that the Muslim communities of the Philippines have become a minority in
their own territory. The provinces in which Muslims live have among the worst
poverty rates in the country. Of the twenty-three provinces that made up Mindanao and the Sulu islands in 1998, only four had less than 50 percent of all
households living below the poverty line, while at the same time they encompass a
huge resource for development in the future.[14]

In 1903 Muslims made up 76 percent of the population of the southern island
of Mindanao, the traditional homeland of Muslims in the archipelago. By 1990, a
century of Christian settlement had reduced the Islamic community to only
19 percent of the population.[15] While the Spanish colonial authorities never succeeded in bringing the sultanates of Mindanao fully under their control during

more than 300 years of colonial rule, an aggressive policy of settlement was pursued from the outset of US colonial authority at the start of the twentieth century, which led to the marginalization of Muslim communities.

This forceful reduction of the Muslim population to a minority in its own territory means that demands for autonomy, or for separation, could never be realized through democratic means. In fact, in referenda held in 1989 and 2001 in the provinces that comprise the historic territory of Muslim Mindanao, Sulu and Palawan, the percentage voting in favor of autonomy mirrored very closely the division of the population between Muslims and non-Muslims. Thus, only the five provinces with a Muslim majority elected to join the Autonomous Region of Muslim Mindanao (ARMM), which emerged from these plebiscites.[16]

With normal democratic means denied them and suffering from chronic poverty, it is not surprising that Islamic communities turned to violence to seek redress for historic claims to their homelands. Open warfare broke out between the Muslim communities and the central government in 1971 when the Moro National Liberation Front (MNLF) under the leadership of Nur Misuari, launched its first military operations. The move to open armed struggle was the result of a confluence of factors: the passing of an old generation of Muslim leaders who had participated in elite politics along clan lines bringing little improvement to increasingly marginalized Muslim communities; the intensification of conflicts over land and the rise of vigilante groups among Christian settlers with open support from the government of President Ferdinand Marcos (1965–86) and the Armed Forces of the Philippines (AFP); the radicalization of a younger generation inspired both by left-wing ideas garnered as students in Manila and radical religious ideas through studies in the Middle East and Pakistan; and the move towards much more repressive and intrusive actions by the Marcos government, which would culminate in 1972 with the declaration of martial law.[17]

The MNLF grew in strength quickly with both military and political support from the OIC. However, it remained weakly integrated, with its leader, Misuari, defending a secular nationalist position, and others, like Hashim Salamat, more devoted to the establishment of an Islamic state. A peace agreement struck with the Marcos dictatorship in 1976, brokered by Libya in Tripoli, fell apart within a year, but not without aggravating tensions within the MNLF over whether the movement would settle for autonomy rather than independence. In 1984, Salamat's faction broke away and established the Moro Islamic Liberation Front (MILF).

The armed Muslim organizations flourished in a context where the central government had failed both under democratic and authoritarian structures of government to deliver sustained development in Mindanao and the Sulu archipelago. State weakness discredited both the idea of an integrated Philippines, as well as democratic and authoritarian versions of secular government. The central government had little control over large parts of the archipelago, which allowed the Muslim organizations to receive significant amounts of aid from the Islamic countries and their leaders to move freely abroad. In the 1980s, young members of the MNLF and MILF gained battle experience as part of the international force that fought against the Soviet occupation of Afghanistan.[18]

After the Marcos regime collapsed in February 1986, it took a further ten years before President Fidel Ramos secured a full peace agreement with the MNLF. Ramos offered to establish a non-elective Southern Philippines Council for Peace and Development (SPCPD), which would encompass all the provinces within historically Muslim territories in a special zone for development and he offered Misuari both the chair of this council and the government's support in the next election for governorship of the the ARMM. MNLF troops would be integrated with the AFP and the Philippine National Police. At the same time, the Ramos government stepped up military pressure on the MILF. In 2000, the administration of President Joseph Estrada unleashed a major military campaign against the MILF.[19] While the MILF's firepower was decimated, the sheer ruthlessness of the military campaign unleashed by a presidential office riddled with corruption probably did more than any MILF propaganda could do to win the hearts and minds of Muslims to the organization's call for an alternative state run on Islamic principles. This was reinforced by poor performance of the ARMM and the SPCPD under Governor Misuari. The MILF, while beleaguered, was stronger, with many communities particularly in their home base in Maguindanao, practicing Islam under the authority of religious leaders committed to preserving a Muslim way of life.

From the early 1990s, another force appeared in the battle between Muslim communities and the central government. Abu Sayyaf, translated as 'Father of the Executioner,' was apparently established in 1990 or 1991 in Basilan by Abdurajak Abubakar Janjalani, an Islamic scholar who had studied jurisprudence in Saudi Arabia, undertaken military training in Libya and fought in Afghanistan.[20] Janjalani appeared committed to the establishment of an Islamic state very much in the model of the Taliban's state in Afghanistan.

Some saw Abu Sayyaf as part of an international fundamentalist movement linked to Osama bin Laden, others as a group manipulated by the Armed Forces as a kind of agent provocateur, while others condemned it as no more than a bandit gang intent on amassing funds through kidnapping for ransom. Most likely, it was a combination of all three. Most of the sources dealing with Abu Sayyaf are journalistic and speculative, making it difficult to ascertain what information has been planted by security forces bent on discrediting and defeating the organization and what may reflect something of the truth.[21] While there is no doubt that Abu Sayyaf was a loose coalition with some groups more committed to banditry than the pursuit of Islamic goals, key leaders of the organization represented a new radical Islam that gained considerable support throughout Basilan and the Sulu archipelago. They could not have survived for two years in the face of intensive military pursuit without local support. Disillusionment with compromise, the hostility of Christian elites in Mindanao and the sheer brutality of government offensives, clearly made local communities and fighters within the MNLF and MILF somewhat sympathetic to the message of the Islamic clerics that founded Abu Sayyaf.

Even if the appeal of Janjalani and the other cleric leaders in Abu Sayyaf (most of whom had been killed by July 2002) was a sign of what is yet to come in Mindanao, in the short term, Eric Gutierrez's argument that the sheer weight of local warlord and bandit politics subsumed Abu Sayyaf was probably right.[22] In June 2001, Galib Andang, alias Commander Robot, a maverick member of Abu Sayyaf in Sulu told the *Philippine Daily Inquirer* that Osama bin Laden had helped the organization at the outset through his brother in law, Jamal Khalifa, but ironically added, 'Khalifa does not trust us anymore, because these people just steal the money' – it would seem Philippine political corruption defeated even Osama bin Laden.[23]

MACAPAGAL-ARROYO SEIZES THE OPPORTUNITY OF 9/11

When Macapagal-Arroyo assumed the presidency in January 2001 after Estrada was forced to leave office facing charges of corruption, her government adopted a three-pronged strategy to deal with the Islamic movement in the south. First, the administration moved to revive peace talks with the MILF.[24] Second, the administration threw its support behind a faction of the MNLF that had challenged Governor Nur Misuari's leadership and endorsed first the holding of a new referendum on autonomy in August 2001 and then elections within the Autonomous Region to follow in November, both of which were opposed by Misuari. Third, her government declared 'total war' against the Abu Sayyaf expressing its determination to bring the kidnapping crisis to an end and to wipe out the 'terrorist group.'

After little more than eight months in power, her strategy appeared to be coming apart. Despite a ceasefire with the MILF, hostilities continued. Misuari demonstrated his determination to hold onto the MNLF leadership, calling for a boycott of the new referendum and even presiding over a congress that called for an independent Bangsamoro Republic. At the end of May, Abu Sayyaf staged a spectacular new kidnapping of twenty hostages, including three Americans, from an island resort in Palawan and efforts by the military to track them down proved futile.

The events of September 11 offered the Macapagal-Arroyo administration an opportunity to gain some leverage in its fight with the Islamic movements on these three fronts. While the President concentrated the public eye on the pursuit of Abu Sayyaf, her government attempted to place the rest of the Islamic movement on the defensive lest they be condemned as part of the target in the international war against terrorism. When the President declared her unconditional support to the USA in its fight against international terrorism, there were few protests coming from the MILF and rival factions of the MNLF.

The MILF, in an attempt to distance itself from Abu Sayyaf and position itself as the emerging legitimate representative of Muslims in Mindanao, publicly rejected Taliban leader Mullah Mohammed Omar's call for a jihad against the

United States. The MILF said it supported US efforts to punish those responsible for September 11, as long as innocent Muslims would not be subjected to attack or persecution.[25] This drew the line short of any military action against Afghanistan.

Even when US strikes against the Taliban regime began and protests were launched by Muslim communities in the cities of Mindanao, the MILF took a cautious approach. In Marawi City a crowd of about 10,000 gathered to denounce the US action. Hadji Abdulah Dalidig, founder and chair of the Marawi-based Islamic Movement for Electoral Reform and Good Government, said hundreds were willing to go to Afghanistan to fight alongside the Taliban. But MILF military chief Al-haj Murad said his forces were more concerned with Mindanao than Afghanistan and that while they fought Russians in Afghanistan, they would not be going this time.[26]

Not only did the events of September 11 allow the Macapagal-Arroyo government to put the Islamic movement on the defensive, but by linking the actions of Abu Sayyaf to an international network of terrorists they made the government's own impotence in ending the group's activities more acceptable both at home and abroad. They ensured, as well, that Islamic countries, both neighbours and other members of the OIC, would tone down or end support for all Islamic organizations pursuing their political objectives through armed means. Most importantly, the events of September 11 provided the political opportunity for the Macapagal-Arroyo administration to seek and receive the direct assistance of the United States in bringing Mindanao under control.

A NEW ALLIANCE WITH THE USA

Just ten days after the tragic events in New York and Washington, National Security Advisor Roilo Golez confirmed that the government was seeking US assistance to fight Abu Sayyaf.[27] On 23 September, Defense Secretary Angelo Reyes said that US forces and coalition partners fighting 'the war against global terrorism' could use Clark and Subic bases, as well as the Benito Ebuen Air Base in Mactan, Cebu.[28] Three days later, President Macapagal-Arroyo announced a 'Fourteen Point Plan' to combat terrorism. In it she said Executive Secretary Alberto Romulo would head a Cabinet oversight committee on internal security – mimicking the Bush-created 'Office of Homeland Security.'[29]

In mid-October a high-level US military team arrived in the country and traveled to Mindanao and Basilan to assess the country's needs in fighting Abu Sayyaf.[30] Shortly afterwards it was announced that the annual military exercises carried out between the two countries under the Visiting Forces Agreement would be modified, with some training taking place in Basilan close to the front line with the Abu Sayyaf. By late February, 660 US soldiers started arriving in the country with 160 Green Berets heading for Basilan.[31] The joint 'exercises' were underway by early March. Still Abu Sayyaf proved elusive and the first major achievement by the US-backed Philippine forces took several months, when the last of the hostages were freed, with one of the Americans killed in the process, in June 2002.

Active US involvement in the fight in Mindanao coincided with what was arguably a common agenda in the two countries aimed at renewing close ties between their armed forces. This had been pursued by successive administrations ever since the Philippine Senate had taken the historic decision in 1991 not to allow the USA continued access to its bases in the country.

The United States appeared to have several objectives in its intervention in the Philippines following 9/11. First, involvement in supporting Philippine troops fighting Abu Sayyaf allowed US forces to open a 'second front' beyond Afghanistan in the 'war against terrorism,' which strategists appeared intent on doing, perhaps to secure early and demonstrable victories against 'the enemy.' Second, from the US government's point of view, the weak state in the Philippines was a porous point for international networks operating beyond the pale of the law and it was intent on getting the Macapagal-Arroyo administration to cooperate in closing down some of the networks that Islamic organizations might be using. Finally, from their own previous support of Islamic networks mobilized to fight Soviet forces in Afghanistan, US intelligence agencies knew that networks in Southeast Asia were extensive and they likely wanted a Philippine entry point to attack those networks, particularly since it was still politically impossible for the USA to get directly involved in either Malaysia or Indonesia.

Greater US involvement in the Philippines also served the objectives of the Macapagal-Arroyo administration. First, US involvement offered the possibility that the AFP might finally make some progress in fighting the Abu Sayyaf. Second, US involvement would provide much needed military assistance, which would shore up the AFP's support for the administration – always a worry as the military had become so politicized since the Marcos years. Third, the events of September 11 meant that the Philippines could invite closer US involvement in its own war without unduly provoking its more independent minded neighbours in ASEAN. Finally, 9/11 allowed the Philippine government to increase cooperation with the USA while keeping the nationalist movement at bay.

In the absence of 9/11, inviting a more active US role in the fight with Abu Sayyaf would have provoked an immediate and powerful nationalist reaction at home. Not only was the nationalist response muted, but there was positive public support for increased US involvement.[32] Of course, there were voices on the right and the left that criticized the quick decision to invite closer US involvement. Senator Gregorio Honasan, who had led a bloody right-wing coup attempt against President Corazon Aquino in 1989, cautioned that greater US involvement 'might endanger the lives of our people and affect our ability to survive any global conflict.'[33] With the first talk of allowing the USA renewed use of Subic and Clark, some on the left did not hesitate to condemn the administration calling it a 'supreme act of puppetry.'[34] Most activists on the left were careful to condemn the bombing of the World Trade Center, while opposing direct US military involvement in the Philippines as well as its actions in Afghanistan.[35] However, their protests appeared feeble, while public opinion polls showed overwhelming approval for US involvement in the fight against Abu Sayyaf.[36]

While mainstream nationalists were cautious in opposing a renewal of military relations with the USA, they were not altogether silent. Vice-President and Foreign Secretary Teofisto Guingona made his reticence clear. Guingona had been one of the Senators who had voted ten years earlier for an end to US military bases in the country. By July 2002, his differences with the president over greater US involvement forced him to relinquish his control over the Department of Foreign Affairs. Although the nationalist movement was muzzled, there were important risks both to the United States and to the Philippine state in increasing US military involvement in the war with Islamic movements in the country.

RISKS AND OPPORTUNITIES IN THE WAKE OF 9/11

Soon after the tragic events in New York, Macapagal-Arroyo became an even more enthusiastic supporter of the US 'war against terrorism' than the British Prime Minister. In doing so she hoped to shore up her administration and gain an advantage in the longstanding unresolved war with Islamic separatists in the south. The United States hoped to gain a deeper foothold in Southeast Asia, in order to combat what it perceived as the greatest threat to its security, the rise of Islamic militancy throughout the world.

While the Macapagal-Arroyo administration may have perceived gains in tying itself so closely to the USA, not the least of which would be the bolstering of the President's domestic and international position in the lead-up to elections in 2004, joining the US crusade posed some real dangers. The rise of terrorist action among Islamic militants in various parts of the world has emerged from three factors: a perception of the marginalization of Islam; the failures of weak secular states – whether organized on democratic or authoritarian lines – to deliver a better life for deprived communities; and the cynical exercise of Western power internationally. The USA and its allies appeared intent on making Samuel Huntington's 'clash of civilizations' a self-fulfilling prophecy by uncritical support for Israeli intransigence towards the Palestinian people's effort to achieve security in their homeland and by first neglecting Afghanistan's plight under the oppressive regime of the Taliban and then responding to 9/11 by unleashing the full might of the US military machine against a war-ravaged country.[37]

Similarly, in the Philippines, intransigence towards the aspirations of Muslim communities, coupled with a singular failure to improve the historical inequities born of aggressive Christian settlement in Islamic homelands, was contributing to the rise of increasingly orthodox and intransigent Islamic opposition. Aside from having to contend with Abu Sayyaf and the MILF, by mid–2002, the government was facing a renewed armed struggle by supporters of Nur Misuari's MNLF in Jolo.[38] Counting on the USA to bolster its fight with the Islamic movements could open the opportunity for Islamic militants to seize the nationalist mantle and thus legitimize increasingly violent means to redress historic wrongs. If this happens there will be little prospect for any sustained peace. Elsewhere in Southeast Asia, if efforts to consolidate democracy are not coupled with socio-economic improvement and the bolstering of state authorities in the face of rapacious private elites, then there too those pursuing political action by violent and even terrorist means may well gain support among ordinary people.

NOTES

1 *Philippine Daily Inquirer*, 11 Sept. 2001. Citations to the *Philippine Daily Inquirer* refer to the date of the article's appearance on the website and can be found in the newspaper's electronic archive: http://www.inq7.net/archive/index.htm

2 'PGMA's Letter to U.S. President George W. Bush regarding Terroristic Attack in the U.S.A.', Palace Guest House, Malacanang, 12 Sept. 2001. http://www.opnet.ops.gov.ph/speech–2001sept12a.htm

3 Craig Francis, 'Malaysia Opposes Air Strikes', *CNN*, 8 Oct. 2001 (Posted: 4:44 a.m. EDT, 0844 GMT). http://www.cnn.com/2001/WORLD/asiapcf/southeast/10/08/attack.malaysia.reax/

4 *Far Eastern Economic Review*, 4 Oct. 2001.

5 *Indonesia Post*, 14 Oct. 2001. http://www.indonesia-news.com/

6 John McBeth, 'Give War A Chance', *Far Eastern Economic Review*, 25 July 2002.

7 *Indonesia Post*, 14 Oct. 2001.

8 Achmad Sukarsono, 'Jakarta Braces for Anti-U.S. Protests', *Reuters*, 12 Oct. 2001, 3:45 p.m.

9 Suaib Didu, leader of the GIP, cited in Achmad Sukarsono, 'Jakarta Braces'.

10 Andrew Marshall, 'The Threat of Jaffar', *New York Times*, 10 March 2002.

11 Marshall, 'Threat of Jaffar'. US Department of State, 'Patterns of Global Terrorism 2001' (Washington, DC, May 2002) http://www.state.gov/s/ct/rls/pgtrpt/2001/

12 *Jakarta Post*, 14 and 21 Feb. 2002.

13 International Crisis Group, 'Al-Qaeda in Southeast Asia: The Case of the "Ngruki Network" in Indonesia', *Indonesia Briefing*, Jarkarta/Brussels, 8 Aug. 2002.

14 'Family Income and Expenditure Survey, 2000', National Statistics Offices, 17 Oct. 2000. S. Lourdes and Fermin D. Adriano, 'Is There Hope for Mindanao's Development: Achieving Sustainable Peace and Development for Mindanao', part of *Yellow Paper II, Beyond EDSA: The Post-Erap Reform Agenda*, n.d., mimeo.

15 W. K. Che Man, *Muslim Separatism: The Moros of Southern Philippines and the Malays of Southern Thailand* (Quezon City: Ateneo de Manila University Press, 1990), p. 25; *1990 Census of Population and Housing* (Quezon City: National Statistic Office).

16 These were Lanao del Sur, Maguindanao, Sulu, Tawi-Tawi and Basilan. *1990 Census of Population and Housing*; Commission on Elections, 'National Canvassing Results, August 14 Plebiscite' as of 22 Aug. 2001 (COMELEC website, June 2002 http://www.comelec.gov.ph/results/armmpleb2001.htm) and B. R. Rodil, *Kalinaw Mindanaw: The Story of the GRP–MNLF Peace Process, 1975–1996* (Davao City: Alternate Forum for Research in Mindanao, 2000), p. 90.

17 On the history of the modern Islamic movement in the Philippines see: Che Man, *Muslim Separatism* (Quezon City and Oxford: Ateneo de Manila University Press and Oxford University Press, 1990); Patricio N. Abinales, *Making Mindanao: Cotabato and Davao in the Formation of the Philippine Nation State* (Quezon City: Ateneo de Manila University Press, 2000); Peter Gowing, *Muslim Filipinos: Heritage and Horizon* (Quezon City: New Day Publishers, 1979); Cesar Abib Majul, *Muslims in the Philippines* (Quezon City: University of the Philippines Press, 1973); Eric U. Gutierrez, 'Re Imagination of the Bangsa Moro: 30 Years Hence', Quezon City: Institute for Popular Democracy, 2001 (downloaded from: http://www.ipd.ph/pub/wip/reimagining_bangsamoro-e_gutierrez.shtml)

18 Admitted by MILF military chief, Al-haj Murad, among others. *Philippine Daily Inquirer*, 9 Oct. 2001.

19 General Angelo Reyes, Chief of Staff of AFP, at Rotary Club, 16 Nov. 2000, Manila Hotel.   http://www.rcmanila.org/Archives/General_Angelo_Reyes/body_general_angelo_reyes.html

20 *Manila Chronicle*, 10 April 1995 and Fe B. Zamora, 'Al Harakatul al Islamiya: The Beginnings of Abu Sayyaf', *Philippine Daily Inquirer*, June 2001. http://www.inq7.net/specials/inside_abusayyaf/2001/features/formative_years.htm

21 For a review of the more credible journalistic accounts see Graham J. Turbiville, Jr., 'Bearer of the Sword', in *Military Review*, Command and General Staff College Fort Leavenworth, Kansas. Downloaded in June 2002
    (http://www-cgsc.army.mil/milrev/english/MarApr02/turbiville.htm)

22 Eric Gutierrez, 'From Ilaga to Abu Sayyaf: New Entrepreneurs in Violence and their Impact on Local Politics in Mindanao', paper prepared for the Fourth European Philippine Studies Conference organized by the University of Alcala and the Spanish Pacific Studies Association (AEEP), 9–12 Sept. 2001, Alcala de Henares, Madrid.

23 *Philippine Daily Inquirer*, 24 Sept. 2001.

24 *Philippine Daily Inquirer*, 16 April 2001.

25 *Philippine Daily Inquirer*, 16 Sept. 2001.

26 *Philippine Daily Inquirer*, 9 Oct. 2001.

27 *Philippine Daily Inquirer*, 22 Sept. 2001.

28 *Philippine Daily Inquirer*, 24 Sept. 2001.

29 *Philippine Daily Inquirer*, 26 Sept. 2001.

30 *Philippine Daily Inquirer*, 12 Oct. 2001.

31 *Philippine Daily Inquirer*, 13 Feb. 2002.

32 *Philippine Daily Inquirer*, 25 Feb. 2002.

33 *Philippine Daily Inquirer*, 16 Sept. 2001.

34 *Philippine Daily Inquirer*, 16 Sept. 2001.

35 This was the reaction of Sanlakas, the National Democratic Front and Akbayan (*Philippine Daily Inquirer*, 17 and 18 Sept. 2001).

36 *Philippine Daily Inquirer*, 29 Sept. 2001.

37 Samuel P. Huntington, *The Clash of Civilizations and the Remaking of World Order* (London: Simon & Schuster, 1996).

38 Misuari fled Jolo to Malaysia where he was detained and later turned over to Philippine authorities and imprisoned on charges of rebellion.

16 Unexpectedly at center stage

Pakistan

Samina Yasmeen

9/11 brought Pakistan to the center stage of global politics. Instead of being marginalized as a failed or failing state bordering on economic bankruptcy and implosion, Pakistan has emerged as central to the US-led coalition against terrorism. In return, it has received political and economic support from several major states, ending its diplomatic isolation. The transition in its status, however, has not been smooth. While dealing with a significant regional and international change, the Pakistani government has had to grapple with domestic resistance to joining the US-led 'war on Terrorism.'

This chapter argues that a multiplicity of views on Pakistan's identity and place in the post-Cold War world provides the context in which Pakistan's responses can best be understood. 9/11 sharpened the division between these views. While General Pervez Musharraf's action reflected the primacy of a liberal approach to domestic and foreign policy, Islamists viewed the situation in and around Afghanistan as a clash of civilizations. This divergence created conditions in which the Pakistani government resorted to the use of 'Islamic language' to explain its decision to terminate support for the Taliban regime and to participate in the US-led coalition. Meanwhile, Islamabad had to readjust to the changed realities in Afghanistan and explore a new foreign policy posture which has benefited Pakistan to some extent. The simmering resentment among the Islamists, however, risks undermining Pakistan's stability.

SECURITY AND IDENTITY: DIVERGENT PERSPECTIVES

Since its creation in August 1947, notions of identity and perceptions of threat to its security have influenced the security discourse in Pakistan. The debates on identity have centred round the place of Islam in the state: for some it is a state for Muslims whereas others emphasize its persona as an Islamic state. The debates around threat perceptions, on the other hand, are linked to the question of the conditional or unconditional nature of Indian hostility. Against the background of variations in the nature of USA–Pakistan relations, the security discourse also centres on the issue of American reliability or unreliability.

The interplay between these different dimensions has resulted in the creation of relatively three distinct schools of thought on Pakistan's foreign policy in the post-Cold War era. The orthodox school generally conceives of Pakistani identity in terms of its distinctness vis-à-vis India. Pakistan is seen as a state created for Muslims and hence different from the essentially 'Hindu' India. The history of Indo–Pakistan relations has convinced those subscribing to this school of Indian unconditional hostility. The cessation of American support for Pakistan soon after the Soviet withdrawal from Afghanistan also renders this group skeptical of American reliability. Hence those subscribing to the orthodox school have argued in favor of an independent foreign policy posture. Translated into action, it means developing a nuclear capability to counter the perceived Indian threat, and supporting groups engaged in 'freedom struggle in Indian occupied Kashmir.'

Islamists view Pakistan as an Islamic state, and not just a state for Muslims. While they were always present in the society, their numerical strength has increased in the 1980s when General Zia introduced a policy of Islamization to legitimize his military rule. These Islamists subscribe to the thesis of civilization clash. For them, the world is divided into Muslims and non-Muslims. The Christian United States (and the West) is seen as being aligned with Jewish Israel, and Hindu India. This alliance is seen as being targeted against the Muslim Ummah in the international system. Pakistan is perceived as being particularly at risk due to its nuclear program and its status as a significant Muslim state. To counter this perceived civilizational threat, the Islamists favor turning Pakistan into a 'true Islamic state,' establishing alliances with other Muslim states, and supporting Islamic causes around the world. The list includes supporting Islamic groups in Chechnia, Palestine, Bosnia and Kashmir.

Liberals and moderates question the validity of these views and prescriptions. For them, Pakistan's identity exists independently of the Indian reality, as a state for Muslims and not as a theocratic Islamic state. For them the Indian hostility is essentially conditional. Judging the US policies on reliability or in civilizational terms appears illogical to them. Opting for the notion of comprehensive security, they favor moderate policies that would attract the necessary political and economic support to strengthen Pakistan internally. This involves engaging the USA irrespective of its India policy, and establishing a correct, if not a cordial, relationship with India.

The multiplicity of views on Pakistan's identity and the appropriate approaches to ensuring Pakistan's security is paralleled in civil society. This has been most obvious in relation to the emergence of Islamists in Pakistan's society. In decision-making circles, their rise dates back to the Islamization process initiated by General Zia in the 1980s. A number of administrative and legislative changes, the modified educational system, the introduction of the 'language of Islam' and the preference given to those obviously practicing Islam meant that Islam came to occupy the center-stage in official discussion of the country's identity. These ideas filtered into the larger society in the wake of the Soviet occupation of Afghanistan in 1979, and the American–Pakistan alliance to 'roll the Soviets back.' The CIA and the Inter-Services Intelligence Agency (ISI) of Pakistan introduced the language of jihad against the Soviet occupation. A number of religious schools (*madrassahs*) were opened in Pakistan to indoctrinate and provide military training to Afghans and others willing to join in the jihad. The Soviet withdrawal from Afghanistan convinced both the supporters and students of these *madrassahs* of the validity of an Islamic approach to world politics. The result has been the emergence of groups in Pakistan that have internalized the notions of Pakistan's Islamic identity while questioning modernity, secularism and liberal Islam. In extreme cases, they opt for Islamic militancy in the name of 'practising true Islam.'

Against the background of weakening state structures, failures in democratic processes and worsening corruption, this diversity of views has paved the way for linkages between similar schools of thought in decision-making circles and in civil society. This, in turn, has created contradictions in Pakistan's foreign policy behavior. While moderates opted for a relatively cautious foreign policy in the 1990s, the orthodox and Islamist groups used their connections in government to push Pakistan in the direction of adventurism. This trend was most obvious in relation to developments in Afghanistan.

Participation in the US-led campaign to push Soviet troops out of Afghanistan had caused some sections of the Pakistani government to view Afghanistan as providing Pakistan with a 'strategic depth' in its adversarial relationship with India. For others, it validated the relevance of Islamic concepts to contemporary world politics, and suggested the need for some of a close relationship between Pakistan and Afghanistan. Since this was contingent upon a pro-Islamabad government being in power in Kabul, these groups actively became involved in determining the future course of political developments in Afghanistan. The ISI emerged as a dominant player in this context. Predominantly as a coalition between anti-Indian and Islamist elements, it controlled the direction of Pakistan's Afghanistan policy.[1]

The rise of the Taliban to power in September 1996 reinforced the ISI's dominant role in Pakistan's Afghanistan policy. Meanwhile, the Taliban's extreme orthodox interpretation of Islam and their designation of Afghanistan as an Islamic state attracted sympathizers from civil society. A large number of students educated in the value of jihad in *madrassahs*, accepted and supported the Taliban's aim of setting up the first truly Islamic state. They were encouraged and supported by the ISI and other Islamic groups in the process.[2] They were recruited and trained as jihadis to fight against perceived oppression of Muslims around the world. Kashmir came to occupy a special place in this context. 'Freedom fighters' were trained in Afghanistan to fight in the Indian part of Kashmir. This coordination created a 'triangulation of jihad' which undermined the efforts of the moderates to engage the USA and to reduce the level of hostility with India.

Liberal and moderate elements in Pakistan did not support this new Afghanistan policy. The Foreign Office, for instance, opposed the unreserved support for the Taliban regime which flouted international norms and pursued policies that tarnished Pakistan's reputation. Liberals in civil society also feared that support for the Taliban would encourage 'Talibanization' of Pakistan and change Pakistani society. Their ability to alter the course of Pakistan's Afghanistan policy, however, remained limited as the Benazir Bhutto and Nawaz Sharif regimes avoided offending Islamists for fear of losing their support. General Pervez Musharraf noted the concerns of the liberals when he assumed power in October 1999. However, given the support extended to him by Islamists within the military, his ability to alter the level and nature of support for Afghanistan was severely circumscribed.[3] Pakistan effectively remained hostage to its Afghanistan policy.

THE TERRORIST ATTACKS AND PAKISTAN

9/11 brought tensions between opposing Pakistani views on security and foreign policy into sharper focus. The focal point was developments originating from, and responses to, the nexus between the Taliban regime and al-Qaeda. As one of the three states to have recognized the Taliban, the Pakistani government needed to decide if it could continue to support its Afghan protégé and also whether Islamabad should join the US-led 'Coalition against Terrorism,' and what its nature should be.

The moderates and liberals, led by Musharraf, viewed the situation as having pushed Pakistan to a critical historical juncture. Having supported the Taliban with limited ability to control its behavior, Pakistan now ran the risk of paying for its support of terrorist acts as well. US President Bush's declaration to punish both 'the terrorists and those who harbor them' made it apparent that continued support for the Taliban could incur American retaliation against Pakistan as well, which could extend to the destruction of its nuclear installations.[4] Pakistan's existence was deemed to be at risk as an indirect consequence of its support for the Taliban. Moderates believed that supporting American moves to build a coalition against terrorism could only avert the risk. It was seen as the only rational and available option to guarantee Pakistan's existence as a viable state.[5]

The orthodox elements supported the liberals due to the manner in which New Delhi had responded to 9/11.[6] The Indian government strongly condemned the terrorist attacks but also used the occasion to draw attention to Pakistan's support for terrorism. Washington was urged not to draw a distinction between the support for terrorism in Afghanistan and Pakistan. To substantiate the need for such an approach, Indian intelligence agencies handed over incriminating evidence against Osama bin Laden and the details of training camps in the Pakistani part of Kashmir.[7] New Delhi also offered the US government the use of its defense bases and refueling facilities for air attacks against the Taliban and al-Qaeda. From Islamabad's perspective, it indicated a concerted Indian effort to enlist American support for neutralizing Pakistan as a viable state.[8] It was also seen as ending any possibility of Pakistan securing a 'fair' resolution to the Kashmir dispute.

The need to ensure Pakistan's existence and to deny India strategic advantage prompted Islamabad to adopt a dual-track policy. Participation in the US-led coalition was a dominant part of this policy. Soon after the news broke, Musharraf issued a statement strongly condemning the attacks and assured the US government of Pakistan's support. He also urged Pakistani-Americans to extend their full support to the host state.[9] But more importantly, the Pakistani government engaged in high-level discussions on how Pakistan was to participate in the anti-terrorist coalition. Bush and Powell had presented Musharraf with a list of 'concrete actions' that they expected Pakistan to take in moves against bin Laden and the Taliban. It included a demand for sharing intelligence and the use of Pakistani airspace for possible attacks on Afghanistan.[10] Musharraf agreed in principle to 'respond positively to any of the international plans aimed at Afghanistan-related terrorism.'[11] The exact nature of this cooperation, however, was decided after he had held detailed consultations with his military commanders, followed by a joint meeting of the federal cabinet and the National Security Council on 14 September.[12] The Pakistani government acquiesced to the US demands for intelligence sharing, logistical support and access to airspace for any actions in Afghanistan. American forces were provided access to facilities in Pasni, Dalbandin and Gwadar in Baluchistan. However, Islamabad made it clear that no American ground troops could be stationed in Pakistan.[13] Nor were Pakistani troops to participate in any attack on Afghanistan.[14] Pakistan also demanded that Israel and India would not be a part of any international military coalition forces that might be stationed in Pakistan.[15]

The participation in the anti-terrorism coalition also had a significant domestic impact in Pakistan. Against the background of the links established since the early 1980s, a number of Pakistani Islamic groups had raised funds for the jihad and the Taliban in Afghanistan. Other international groups with a declared objective of supporting the Muslim Ummah and some notables on their boards had also been operating in Pakistan to support the Taliban regime. Some of these had been providing channels for transferring funds to Islamic militants across the world. Following the request and information from the American government, the Pakistani government banned several groups, including the Al-Rasheed Trust.[16] It also targeted the *Hundi* or *Havala* system[17] which had traditionally enabled terrorists and others alike to transfer funds across national boundaries without relying on the established banking channels.

Engaging and convincing the Taliban regime to cooperate with Washington emerged as the second major plank of Pakistan's policy. This was a direct result of an interest in ensuring that the Islamists within the government and society did not view participation in the coalition as a 'sell-out' to the USA. The Pakistani government urged the US government to furnish evidence of bin Laden's complicity in the terrorist attacks. Meanwhile, it sent a series of delegations to Taliban leader Mullah Omar, urging him to cooperate with Washington. The first delegation included the head of the ISI, General Mahmood, who had been a staunch supporter of the Taliban.[18] Having been stranded in the USA on 9/11, he held meetings with the US Deputy Secretary Richard Armitage and Pakistan's Ambassador, Maleeha Lodhi. On his return he was assigned the task of securing Mullah Omar's support. A few days later, Musharraf sent another delegation of Islamic leaders along with Mahmood to suggest that the Taliban could extradite bin Laden to a neutral country where his complicity could be assessed.[19]

These moves did not attract unanimous support from within the military establishment. The Islamization policies introduced by General Zia had affected the outlook of the military in Pakistan. As in the wider society, a division of opinion also emerged in the military along the lines of liberal, orthodox and Islamic ideas. By October 1999, this had resulted in a number of Islamists rising to senior positions in the army. Of these, Mahmood, General Aziz and General Usmani had been instrumental in bringing Musharraf to power. Although Musharraf undertook steps that reflected his liberal outlook soon after taking power, the Islamists continued to wield influence on Pakistan's Afghanistan and Kashmir policies. Their commitment to supporting the Taliban, therefore, naturally constrained them from supporting the change in Pakistan's policy following the terrorist attacks. However, given Pakistan's military tradition of not openly questioning the Chief of Army Staff, they did not voice their criticism openly.

The Islamists in society were not encumbered by the demands of institutional discipline. From the outset, therefore, they raised objections to Pakistan altering its Afghanistan policy. The Defense of Afghanistan and Pakistan Council, with membership from a number of Islamic groups and parties, led the process of questioning and opposing the government's decision.[20] Their concerns revolved round bin Laden's innocence, the threat posed to the Islamic regime in Afghanistan and US strategic designs on Pakistan. They argued that the Bush administration had not provided any credible evidence implicating Osama bin Laden. In their opinion, 9/11 was masterminded by a highly organized Jewish and/or anti-Muslim group. The claim to bin Laden's innocence was based on his portrayal in Western media as a terrorist during the 1990s.[21] Since the bombings of the US embassies in East Africa and the American reprisal attacks, this portrayal was paralleled in the mythologization of bin Laden in Pakistan and Afghanistan as a true Muslim leader who had forsaken his elitist background to help oppressed Muslims worldwide. His 'true commitment to Islamic principles' was also perceived as the explanation for his condemnation of the links between oppressive Muslim governments and Washington, and his opposition to the stationing of American forces in Saudi Arabia. Such courageous stands were seen as attracting the wrath of the USA which was looking for opportunities to rein in and/or kill the only true Muslim leader. By accepting his culpability in the absence of credible evidence, the Islamic groups argued, the Pakistani government was becoming a pawn in the US war against bin Laden.[22]

A similar line of argument was taken on the Taliban. For the first time, the Islamists argued, a truly Islamic state had been established in Afghanistan. The Taliban, under Mullah Omar, were implementing Islamic law in line with a correct interpretation. Their Islamic outlook also determined their relationship to the outside world. They were not prepared to submit to US dictates, nor to condone oppressive US policies against other members of the Muslim Ummah. By providing sanctuary to bin Laden, and by permitting establishment of training camps on Afghanistan's soil, the Islamists argued, the Taliban was questioning international norms. More importantly, it was engaged in jihad and fighting for Islam. Hence, it was incumbent upon all Muslims to support the Taliban's struggle against 'Judeo–Christian–Hindu conspiracies.' The Pakistani government's decision to participate in the anti-terrorism coalition was, therefore, viewed as an un-Islamic act. The demands made by the Musharraf regime that the Taliban hand over bin Laden to a neutral state were criticized as being unrealistic and not deserving of the support of the Ulema or religious leaders.[23]

Finally, the Islamists argued against Musharraf's alliance with Washington on the basis of their analysis of American motives in South and West Asia.[24] The USA was portrayed as committed to a strategy of influence and control over the region due to its geostrategic and economic significance. Driven by the need to secure oil and gas supplies, and to neutralize Pakistan's nuclear capability, the Islamists argued, Washington had wanted to establish a large military presence. 9/11 had provided Washington with the excuse to realize its goals. By using bin Laden and the al-Qaeda–Taliban nexus as an excuse, the US government was prepared to establish a permanent presence in Pakistan. They pointed to the stationing of US troops in Saudi Arabia and Kuwait after the Gulf War of 1991. Any participation in the US coalition against terrorism, therefore, was tantamount to compromising Pakistan's long-term national interest, including its nuclear capability.

Such a multilayered analysis of the causes and implications of US policies in the region caused the Islamists to demand a reversal of Pakistan's policy of supporting Washington's agenda. Failure to do that, they suggested, would elicit 'a resolute response' from committed Muslims. These veiled threats were accompanied by a call to the Muslim Ummah to help bin Laden and the Taliban in their hour of need. Islamic groups used mosques and Friday sermons to mobilize masses to engage in jihad alongside the Taliban and al-Qaeda. Public rallies were organized and the Pakistan and US governments were regularly castigated for their plans. Militant groups including Jaish Mohammad, Harkatul Mujahedeen and Harkatul Jihad also actively encouraged potential jihadis to cross the Afghan–Pakistan border. Students enrolled in approximately 20,000 *madrassahs* became the obvious recruits for this religious duty. According to some reports from the Chaman border post alone, up to 300 students crossed daily into Afghanistan to participate in the jihad on behalf of the Taliban and bin Laden.[25] Tribes along the Pakistan–Afghanistan border also declared their support for the Taliban and opposed any demands for unconditionally surrendering bin Laden. To this end, they shifted their weapons to the mountain areas between Pakistan and Afghanistan.[26]

The call to jihad by the Islamists also drew supporters from some with liberal or orthodox perspectives. Concerned about US policies, and particularly the developing relationship with India, they sympathized with the analysis presented by the Islamic groups. Also critical of the military regime taking the decision without due consultation, they sided with militant groups. Many individuals left for jihad in Afghanistan at very short notice.

The preponderance of jihad-related discourse prompted the Pakistani government to respond by using 'the language of liberal Islam.' Pakistan's policy options were explained and justified in terms of the principles enshrined in the

Holy Koran and *Sunnah* (Prophetic practices). This recourse to Islamic language was most obvious during a televised speech by Musharraf on 19 September.[27] Islam, he emphasized, enjoins its followers to make rational and wise decisions that ensure the continued viability of their state. Drawing upon the examples of agreements signed by the Prophet Muhammad with Jews in Medina and the Mekkans, he pointed out that Muslims needed to consider the prevailing balance of power and form appropriate alliances. The Pakistani government's support for US actions was presented as evidence that the military regime was following established Islamic practice. The UN Security Council's resolution passed on combating terrorism and the US moves against terrorists were presented as representing the will of the international community. Islamabad's support for these views was evidence of its identity as a good international citizen. Musharraf claimed that Pakistan was ensuring the safety of its nuclear program, the viability of the state and ensuring that India could not exploit the situation to harm Pakistan.

A large proportion of liberal and moderate opinion supported Musharraf's policy and justification. For them, US moves had created space for liberals in Pakistan who had been feeling harassed and pressured by the 'street power' of the Islamists. Ending support for the Taliban was also seen as a way to prevent the 'Talibanization' of Pakistan.[28] Unlike their Islamist counterparts, however, the moderate elements essentially remained silent. Their reluctance to voice support for the changed policy was linked to the fear of what might happen once the USA launched its attacks on Afghanistan.[29] Many feared that an alliance between Islamists in the government and society with drug traffickers and smugglers who had amassed wealth by abusing agreements on transit trade could lead to a civil war in Pakistan. Moderates remained both nervous and silent about the unfolding situation at home.

THE AMERICAN ATTACKS ON AFGHANISTAN

US attacks on Afghanistan on 7 October escalated tensions between Islamists and liberals. Having been informed of the impending bombings, General Musharraf moved to neutralize the Islamists in his regime. Generals Mahmood, Usmani and Aziz were either dismissed or sidelined.[30] The changes did not necessarily eliminate pro-Taliban sentiments in the ISI and other sections of the government, but it reduced the chances of the Musharraf regime and the ISI working for two different partners. Islamists in society could not be sidelined. The US attacks were seen as proof that Washington was determined to implement its agenda against Islam, Muslim leaders and Islamic states. They viewed the regime's active support for Washington as an un-Islamic act. Islamist discourse on combating US strategy was widened on lines similar to opposition against the Saudi monarchy and other pro-American regimes in the Middle East. The Musharraf regime was portrayed as colluding with the USA in the latter's nefarious designs and, therefore, deserved to be condemned and overthrown. Some of them called on Pakistan's military personnel to remove the 'un-Islamic regime' and install a truly Islamic government. At the same time, the Pakistani masses were urged to wage a jihad in both Afghanistan and Pakistan.[31]

The negative portrayal of the Pakistani government's participation in the US strategy was heightened by the arrival of refugees at the Pakistan–Afghanistan border. Having accommodated nearly 3 million Afghan refugees since 1978, the Pakistani government had been reluctant to let still more enter its territory. The prospects of al-Qaeda and anti-Pakistan elements entering the country as refugees hardened its approach. The government sealed the 1,400-kilometer border with Afghanistan and refused to let the refugees enter Pakistan. Some refugees managed to bribe their way in, but the majority remained languishing in Afghanistan. Refugees' stories of destruction caused by US bombing added to resentment among the Islamists. It also created a sense of communal guilt in Pakistan: ordinary citizens with no strong opinion felt that they were conspiring with the US government to kill innocent Afghan Muslims. This resulted in a sudden increase in the frequency of protests against the Musharraf regime. Compared to previous demonstrations, the number and scale of protests was insignificant.[32] The demonstrations in the Punjab, North-West Frontier Province and Baluchistan failed to attract large crowds in opposition to the governmental policies. However, they did demonstrate the schism between the liberal regime and the Islamist elements.

Simultaneously, differences emerged between Washington and Islamabad's approach to the appropriate strategy in Afghanistan. The US government had conveyed a sense of inclusivity by informing the Pakistani government in advance of impending attacks. In Islamabad it seemed that Washington would take Pakistan's sensitivities into account. Given the anticipated response from a constellation of Islamists, smuggling and drug trafficking interests, the Pakistani government was anxious that the attacks should finish quickly. This was reinforced as US attacks provoked larger demonstrations. The sense of identification with Muslims, present even among the relatively liberal and secular sections, combined with the fast approaching month of Ramadan, prompted Musharraf to underscore that the campaign be finished before the start of Ramadan. Such a prescription did not sit well with the US government which intended to continue the attacks until its objective of eliminating al-Qaeda was completed. Hence, President Bush was quick publicly to refute Musharraf's comments that the 'military action [was] . . . expected to be short.'[33]

More significant divisions, however, emerged over the government of Afghanistan after the bombing. From the outset, the Pakistani government was keen to ensure that the Taliban not be replaced by Northern Alliance domination.[34] This stemmed from its concern that the links between New Delhi and the Alliance would possibly lead to Pakistan facing an 'Indian threat' from the east and west. Hence, Islamabad drew a distinction between hard-core and liberal Taliban and suggested that the support of the latter group could be secured to rule Afghanistan. Islamabad also explored alternative Pushtun leadership including Commander Haq (who was executed by the Taliban) and Pir Syed Gilani. The US government had also explored alternatives to the Taliban, with overtures to the former King Zahir Shah. Concerned about American policy which envisaged an active political role for the Alliance, the Pakistani government voiced its opposition to the choice of a predominantly non-Pushtun alliance but soon realized the limits of its influence on the American Afghan strategy.[35] The process was eased by the speed with which the Northern Alliance defeated the Taliban and occupied Mazar-i Sharif as well as Kabul.

The end of the Taliban also affected the nature of domestic opposition to Musharraf's policies within Pakistan. The speed with which Taliban fighting units retreated or shifted loyalties created a sense of disillusionment among Pakistani Islamists. That the Islamic regime had lost power so quickly raised questions about their ability to fight for Islam.[36] More importantly, the news that retreating Taliban units had left Pakistani and other jihadis to fight and be massacred dampened enthusiasm for supporting the 'true Islamic regime' in Afghanistan.[37] Like the war in Afghanistan, opposition to Islamabad's participation in the alliance came to an abrupt and quick end.

PAKISTAN AFTER THE TALIBAN

9/11 and its aftermath marked a watershed in Pakistan's history. Previously, Pakistan was increasingly identified as a failed or a failing state. Fears were expressed about Pakistan imploding under the pressure of mounting lawlessness, sectarian strife and near economic bankruptcy. Frequent changes of democratically elected governments, rampant corruption and the subsequent military coup in October 1999 had all contributed to Pakistan's diplomatic isolation. The terrorist attacks and Pakistan's participation in the US-led coalition suddenly altered the situation. Within just a few days, Pakistan emerged from its isolation to be identified as a major participant in the war against terrorism.

The impact was most obvious in the changed nature of Pakistan's relations with the USA. The USA had moved to an obviously Indo-centric approach to South Asia during the Clinton administration. In addition to high-level contacts, Washington was entertaining ideas of lifting sanctions imposed on India after its nuclear tests of May 1998. Pakistan, largely ignored by the USA, was not to enjoy similar treatment, subjected to the sanctions imposed due to its nuclear program, the nuclear tests of May 1998 and the military takeover in October 1999. All this changed with 9/11. The USA came to identify Pakistan as a 'frontline state' and accord it a major role as a 'liberal Islamic regime' in the international campaign. It began exploring ways in which it could strengthen Pakistan's nuclear command and control structure and prevent terrorists from having access.[38] All sanctions, except those related to democracy, were lifted within four weeks.[39] Washington moved to provide economic assistance to Pakistan which totaled US$746 million for 2001–2.[40] The US government also agreed to deferring loan repayments with an effective value of US$1 billion for Pakistan.[41]

Taking cue from the USA, a number of states including Canada, Japan, Britain and Norway, pledged aid. The total volume from developed states amounted to

US$1–1.2 billion by April 2002. International Financial Institutions also provided loans.[42] Meanwhile, non-resident Pakistanis have deposited more than US$1.4 billion in Pakistani bank accounts for fear of it being confiscated by their respective governments, including in the United States, Britain and other European states.[43] Pakistan's foreign exchange reserves increased from US$1.106 billion by the end of February 2001 to more than US$5.566 billion by 1 June 2002.[44]

Pakistan's emerging de facto alliance with the USA could have impacted upon its relationship with China as it supported US plans without consulting Beijing. But Musharraf tried to control the damage by visiting China soon after the attacks on Afghanistan subsided. He has been keen to ensure continuity in Pakistan's relations with Beijing.

The attacks have also impacted upon Pakistan's regional policy. The end of the Taliban prompted Pakistan to revisit its Afghan strategy. During the Bonn meeting it was trying to influence the course of events by continuing to suggest alternatives. But once the interim arrangement was agreed, the Pakistani government opted for a 'hands-off policy.' Its only involvement revolves round willingness to assist Afghanistan economically. To some extent this is linked to a realization that the reconstruction agenda would benefit Pakistan directly or indirectly. This approach was evident during Musharraf's visit to Kabul on 2 April 2002. He emphasized that the main purpose of his one-day visit was to 'assure assistance to my brother Karzai' in the reconstruction. He acknowledged the strains between them but stressed the longer history of friendly relations.

The changed Afghan policy has also affected links with Iran. The Iranian government had viewed Pakistan's influence in Afghanistan with concern. The military regime had attempted to reassure it by suggesting tripartite discussions on Afghanistan's future. But alliance with the USA rekindled Teheran's fears. Aware of these concerns and its limits in shaping post-Taliban developments, Pakistan has avoided conveying its continued strategic interest in Afghanistan. This, in turn, has created the possibility of lessening tensions between Pakistan and Iran.[45]

The most obvious change, however, has occurred with respect to Pakistan's Kashmir policy.[46] Pakistan's participation in the anti-terrorist coalition took away the rationale for its direct support for groups engaged in waging jihad in the Indian part of Kashmir. The defeat of the Taliban also ended the triangulation of Pakistan's Kashmir policy. No longer can Islamic militant groups be trained in Afghanistan and sent to Kashmir with tacit support from sections in the Pakistani regime. At the same time, taking advantage of the changed environment and the attacks on the Indian parliament on 13 December, General Musharraf has banned a number of Islamic militant groups that had led the struggle in Kashmir. This has not ended Islamabad's *declared* support for the Kashmiri 'freedom struggle.' In the interest of retaining the support of orthodox groups, the military regime has continued to emphasize the need to resolve the issue, possibly with American help. Nonetheless, in the changed scenario, Pakistan is unlikely to return to the days of active support for the Kashmiri 'freedom fighters.'

The positive developments coexist with the possible negative impact of Pakistan's membership of the anti-terrorist coalition. The suppression of the Islamic militants and the recourse to the language of 'liberal Islam' has temporarily resulted in the victory of the moderates in Pakistan. The Islamists have been concerned at the turn of events without an open clash with the military regime. But they have indirectly raised the question of bias in media reporting and have claimed that the Taliban had not forsaken their Pakistani and Arab supporters. They also emphasize the positive contribution made by *madrassahs* in educating the poor masses. At the same time, they apparently seem willing to follow the liberal Islamic agenda and change the curriculum of the *madrassahs*. This accommodating attitude, however, conceals a sense of unhappiness with the change in the government's domestic and foreign policy. The Islamists, including the militant groups, are lying relatively low with an avowed commitment to return at an 'appropriate time.'[47]

This return may become possible if ordinary citizens do not share in the benefits of Pakistan's alliance with the USA, or if the military regime continues to revise the 1973 Constitution. The manner in which Islamic groups have reacted to the presidential referendum and the introduction of a 'constitutional package' in Pakistan since April 2002 already indicates such a possibility. Alternatively, radical/militant Muslim groups may gain ground in Pakistan due to an apparent sign of the US government reassessing the level of its support for Pakistan in the post-Taliban era. The domestic reaction in Pakistan to the Americans' cautious and somewhat pro-Indian stance on the Indo–Pakistani tension, has shown that such a reassertion of radical Islamists is possible. The resulting dissatisfaction would provide an easy avenue for the Islamists to argue that the Pakistani government had joined in a war against other Muslims but only to benefit a select group of 'colluders.' The struggle between moderate and Islamic views on Pakistan's foreign policy may reappear.

US foreign policy towards Muslims in general can also trigger negative attitudes among the Pakistani public. President Bush's identification of Iran and Iraq as part of the 'axis of evil' has already reinforced feelings among ordinary citizens that Washington is using the 'war on terrorism' as a means of 'subjugating' Muslims globally. President Bush's resolve to remove Saddam Hussein, and the war in Iraq in 2003, are viewed by many in the world as part of a larger picture in which the US government is pursuing an essentially anti-Muslim policy. The beleaguered Islamic militants are likely to exploit these moves as further evidence that the Musharraf government has joined hands with an essentially anti-Muslim American administration in Washington. The implications of such portrayals and the attendant strengthening of the position of Islamists may be far more serious than in the past. This is especially so as al-Qaeda members and former Taliban are known to have entered Pakistan and found sanctuaries. The government and liberal elements in society will need to ensure that they do not lose the balance of power in favor of the militant, orthodox interpretations of Islam.

NOTES

1 Interviews conducted with Pakistani officials and journalists, Jan. 2002.
2 See, for example, Anjum Choudhury, 'Jihad Jar rahey Gaa' (Jihad will continue), *Jaish-e-Mohammad*, Vol. 2, No. 12, Sept. 2001, pp. 17–18.
3 This was apparent in his failed moves to change the Blasphemy Law due to the opposition from the Islamic groups.
4 Arshad Ahmed Haqqani, 'Harf-e-Tamanna: Sadar Musharraf sey Eik Mulaqat' (A meeting with President Musharraf), *Jang* (Lahore), 18 Sept. 2001.
5 Interviews with Pakistani officials, Jan. 2002.
6 Interviews with Pakistani officials, Jan. 2002.
7 Ajay Suri, 'India Arms FBI with Osama Tapes, Papers', *Indian Express*, 15 Sept. 2001; and Sanjay Singh and Srinjoy Chowdhury, 'India Offers USA Use of its Military Bases', *The Statesman* (New Delhi), 15 Sept. 2001.
8 Interview with a Pakistani journalist, Dec. 2001.
9 *Dawn*, 12 Sept. 2001; *The News* (Islamabad), 13 Sept. 2001.
10 Similar demands for 'fullest cooperation' were conveyed to Pakistan's Ambassador to the USA, Maleeha Lodhi, and the Chief of the ISI, General Mahmood, who had been on an official trip to the USA. Tahir Mirza, 'Pakistan Gets USA List of Demands', *Dawn* (Islamabad), 14 Sept. 2001.
11 Kamran Khan, 'Parameters for Cooperation Fixed', *The News* (Islamabad), 15 Sept. 2001.
12 Faraz Hashmi, 'Decision on USA Demands Today', *Dawn* (Islamabad), 15 Sept. 2001.
13 Amir Mateen, 'USA Planning to Minimise Use of Pakistani Bases', *The News*, 4 Oct. 2001.
14 Statement by Pakistan's Foreign Minister, Abdul Sattar; Faraz Hashmi, 'Pakistan Not to Join Operations beyond Borders', *Dawn*, 16 Sept. 2001.
15 Aslam Khan, 'India, Israel Not to be Part of Coalition Forces', *The News*, 17 Sept. 2001.
16 See, for example, Mubashir Ziadi, 'Charity or Terrorism?', *Herald* (Karachi), Oct. 2001, pp. 46–7; *The News*, 13 Oct. 2001; 'Action on Bank Accounts of Al-Rashid Trust and Harkatul Mujahideen Taken to Avoid Negative Impact on Business', Foreign Office Spokesman, 28 Sept. 2001, http://www.pak.gov.pk/terrorist-attack-america/Terrorist-28.htm#5
17 The *Hundi* and *Havala* system involves exchange of money across national boundaries by using informal channels. Individuals normally get a slip with instructions from country A for the relevant person in country B who provides the required amount on the guarantee that the equivalent will be paid to its contacts in country A by the relevant persons.
18 Ahmed Hassan, 'Kabul to be Told to Hand Over Osama to USA', *Dawn* (Islamabad), 17 Sept. 2001.
19 'Kandahar Talks Prove Fruitless', *Dawn* (Islamabad), 29 Sept. 2001.
20 'A Gathering Storm: Fundamentalists Marshal their Forces to Protest against USA Intent to Attack Afghanistan', *Newsline* (Karachi), Oct. 2001, pp. 45–6.
21 See, for example, 'A Gathering Storm', pp. 45–6.
22 See, for example, statements by Islamic news media in, 'The War of Words', *Newsline* (Karachi), Oct. 2001, p. 54.
23 'Up in Arms', *Newsline* (Karachi), Oct. 2001, pp. 49–50.
24 Azmat Abbas, 'War of Words', *The Herald*, Oct. 2001, pp. 32d–33.
25 Naziha Syed Ali and Massoud Ansari, 'Mission of Faith', *Newsline* (Karachi), Nov. 2001, pp. 42–5.
26 'Up in Arms', *Newsline* (Karachi), Oct. 2001, p. 50.
27 'Text of President Musharraf's Speech, 19 September 2001', (Pakistan High Commission, Canberra).

28 Interview with Begum Sarfraz Iqbal, Islamabad, Dec. 2001.

29 Samina Yasmeen, 'The War for Muslim Hearts', *Australian Financial Review*, 26 Sept. 2001, p. 59.

30 Christopher Kremmer, 'Musharraf Muzzles Islamic Sympathisers', *Sydney Morning Herald*, 9 Oct. 2001.

31 Nadeem Iqbal, 'War Comes Home', *Newsline* (Karachi), Nov. 2001, pp. 22–5.

32 Interview with Suzannah Price, BBC Correspondent in Pakistan, Jan. 2002.

33 'I do not know who told the Pakistan President that. Generally, you know, we do not talk about military plans,' said President Bush. *Dawn*, 11 Oct. 2001; and for text of President Musharraf's speech, see, 'Only Terrorist Camps Targeted', *Dawn* (Islamabad), 9 Oct. 2001.

34 As early as 25 September 2001, Pakistan's Foreign Minister Abdul Sattar had warned that military assistance to the Northern Alliance 'would be a recipe for disaster.' *Dawn* (Islamabad), 26 Sept. 2001.

35 In some ways, the US Ambassador to Pakistan, Ms Wendy Chamberlain, acknowledged Pakistan's acquiescence to American strategy. *Dawn*, 7 Nov. 2001.

36 Information based on interviews conducted in Islamabad and Lahore during December 2001 and February 2002.

37 Sarfraz Iqbal, 'Islami Mulq sirf Afghanistan Hey?' (Is Afghanistan the only Islamic state?), *Ausaf* (Islamabad), 12 Nov. 2001; and Iqbal Khattak, ' "Taliban Let Us Down . . ." Say Pakistani Volunteers', *The Friday Times* (Lahore), 23 Nov. 2001.

38 'USA Aid to Pakistan to Cement Anti-terror Alliance', *Jane's Defence Weekly*, 10 Oct. 2001.

39 'USA Lifts Democracy Sanctions on Pakistan', *The Nation* (Islamabad), 5 Oct. 2001.

40 'Bush Seeks More Aid for Islamabad: WB Chief Visiting Next Month', *Dawn*, 23 April 2002.

41 Tahir Mirza and Masood Haider, 'Musharraf, Bush Oppose Alliance's Takeover', *Dawn* (Islamabad), 12 Nov. 2001; 'Visit Improves Ties with USA: President', *Dawn* (Islamabad), 17 Feb. 2002.

42 'Pakistan: War-Time Economy', *Oxford Analytica Brief*, 7 Nov. 2001, p. 2.

43 The Pakistan Finance Minister Shaukat Aziz claimed that Pakistan had secured new loans worth US$3.1 billion by April 2002. *Dawn*, 23 April 2002.

44 *Pakistan Economic Survey*, http://www.finance.gov.pk/survey/over.htm (accessed on 13 Aug. 2002).

45 Interviews with a Pakistani official, Jan. 2002.

46 Samina Yasmeen, 'Kashmir', *Economic and Political Weekly*, 16–22 Feb. 2002.

47 Seth Mydans, 'Pakistan's Hard Line on Terror Shows Signs of Softening', *New York Times*, 28 April 2002.

17 In the middle ground
India

Raju G. C. Thomas

THE DIZZY DECADE: 1991–92 TO 2001–02

It has been a decade of uncertainty for India following the end of the Cold War. India's swift and unconditional decision to support the US war on international terrorism in the aftermath of the terrorist attack on the World Trade Center reflected a new direction in the cycle of sudden revolutionary shifts in its foreign and defense policies.

The absence of a clear foreign policy direction began with the collapse of the USSR in 1991. During the Cold War, the Soviet Union had served as the anchor of India's foreign and defense policies, the high point being reached with the forging of a quasi-military alliance in August 1971, euphemistically called the Treaty of Peace and Friendship. Amidst the uncertainty surrounding the collapse of the Soviet Union in 1991, the treaty was renewed for another twenty years with the Russian Federation, although the purpose and utility of the treaty had become clouded. Shortly thereafter, with the new Russia suffering serious economic problems with little to offer, the Indian government sought closer military ties with the USA but achieved little success except for joint naval exercises and technological assistance for the development of its light combat aircraft and a few other weapons systems.

Following the US-led NATO bombing of Yugoslavia in 1999, India's coalition government led by the Hindu nationalist Bharatiya Janata Party (BJP) condemned the USA and sought closer strategic ties with Russia and China. The WTC bombing by al-Qaeda and the subsequent dramatic American political and military reactions that concentrated on South Asia generated an equally revolutionary response in India. Immediately after 9/11, the BJP-led coalition government offered the USA its intelligence data on radical Islamic terrorism, and military bases in India to conduct operations against al-Qaeda and the Taliban regime in Afghanistan. India claimed that for years it was also the victim of Islamic extremist terrorism in Kashmir supported by these radical Islamic forces.

At the outset of America's war on terrorism, President George W. Bush echoed the proclamation of Secretary of State John Foster Dulles at the beginning of the Cold War: 'Either you are with us or against us.' Like Dulles, Bush declared that there could be no policy options in between for other states. However, it has been

India's traditional foreign policy practice to declare itself on middle ground, expressed especially in its earlier Cold War doctrine of non-alignment between East and West. Under the continuing mantle of a diluted non-alignment policy, Indian responses now seemed to fluctuate on the extremes between the 'West and the Rest.'[1] However, these changes in India's foreign and security policies since the end of the Cold War were always modified and moderated by its economic dependency on the West, especially on the USA which is India's largest trading partner and investor, although India ranks well below China in economic importance to the USA, and, indeed, even below Singapore.

The two most dramatic swings in India's strategic perspective took place first following NATO's assault on Yugoslavia from 24 March to 8 June 1999; and then following the terrorist attack of 9/11. The radical nature of the transformation in India's world outlook following 9/11 is best illustrated by examining the stark differences in Indian foreign policy before and after.

BEFORE 9/11: AGAINST THE USA

The Indian decision to go nuclear in 1998 needs to be considered in the context of the new Western dominant world order. The unrestrained use of force against the remnant Yugoslavia in 1999 by an American-led Western alliance, provided an additional post-hoc justification for an Indian nuclear deterrent, especially when it had seemed counterproductive earlier against threats from China and Pakistan. NATO's bombing of Serbia over its Kosovo Muslim majority province, a situation not unlike Kashmir, provoked a flood of condemnations by Indian politicians, diplomats and the media.

India's permanent representative to the UN declared to the Security Council on 24 March 1999 that the attacks on the former Yugoslavia were 'in clear violation of Article 53 of the UN Charter. No country, group of countries or regional arrangement, no matter how powerful, can arrogate to itself the right of taking arbitrary and unilateral military action against others.' He added that the attacks were not authorized by the Council and were thus 'illegal.'[2]

Indian Prime Minister Atal Bihari Vajpayee declared 'NATO is blindly bombing Yugoslavia. There is a dance of destruction going on there.'[3] In December 1999, Indian Defense Minister George Fernandes observed that the aggression against Yugoslavia was 'the greatest injustice of the 20th century' and added that India was against a 'unipolar world' and 'favored a world without a world policeman, and in which the UN would act in accordance with its charter.'[4]

K. Subrahmanyam, the subsequent chairman of India's newly created National Security Advisory Board in August 1999, renewed India's case for a strong nuclear force posture: 'It is not accidental that the only countries voicing strong protests against the bombing in Yugoslavia happen to be Russia, China and India, all nuclear weapon powers.'[5]

NATO's use of force against Yugoslavia without sanction from the UN Security Council brought about several counter moves among Russia, China, India and

Indonesia. In July 2001, Russia and China signed a 'treaty of friendship and cooperation,' the first such treaty since the era of Stalin and Mao. It bound the two former communist giants for the next twenty years 'committing them to oppose jointly much of the framework for international security that the United States is seeking to erect after the Cold War.'[6] The first part 'obligated both to refrain from assisting opposition movements of ethnic minorities.'[7]

On 14 June 1999, a week after the hostilities ended in the Balkans, India and China established a 'Security Dialogue' which was stated by their respective foreign ministers to be a response to NATO's actions.[8] China also distanced itself from Pakistani actions in Kargil moving towards a more neutral stance. In January 2001, Indian Prime Minister Vajpayee and Chinese leader Li Peng agreed to complete clarification of the Line of Actual Control 'as soon as possible.'[9] Vajpayee stated that 'As two great civilizations and neighbors, India and China are engaged in the process of resolving, and putting behind us, past differences and forging a new and dynamic relationship for the 21st century for the benefit of our two countries and the world.' These statements reflect a return to prime ministers Jawaharlal Nehru and Chou Enlai's joint declarations of peaceful coexistence embodied in the 1954 Sino–Indian Treaty.

In the spring of 1999, there was some Indian interest in the call by then Russian premier, Evgenii Primakov, to forge a counter-alliance against NATO among Russia, China and India. Russian–Indian cooperation took more concrete shape during President Vladimir Putin's visit to India in October 2000, when a limited strategic partnership was established between India and Russia. Prime Minister Vajpayee stated that the two countries shared common concerns and interests, and that 'the history of the last five decades demonstrates that close Indo–Russian understanding is essential to peace and stability in Asia and the world. This is what makes India and Russia strategic partners. Our friendship is not based on short-term calculations, but transcends the twists and turns of history and politics.'[10] Putin claimed that a multipolar world was a safer world and the Indo–Russian strategic partnership would contribute to that desirable global condition.

The threat of Western dominance and the right of humanitarian intervention also drew Indonesia and India closer together. During an exchange of visits by Prime Minister Vajpayee and President Abdurrahman Wahid in January 2001, both the Indonesian president and Defense Minister Mr. Mahfud proposed a quadrilateral alliance of Russia, China, India and Indonesia.[11] Subsequently, Indian Foreign Minister Jaswant Singh claimed that India did not believe in alliances. However, five Indo–Indonesian agreements were then signed in Jakarta, including the formation of a joint commission for defense cooperation. Indonesia's desire for such an alliance was understandable. It had just suffered the loss of East Timor through Western diplomatic humanitarian intervention. Referring to what appeared to be a new appreciation of each other's bilateral concerns, Vajpayee declared that 'as multi-ethnic, multi-religious and diverse societies, both our countries support each other's unity and territorial integrity.'[12]

If nothing else, there existed a propensity at the end of the twentieth century to forge a diluted quadrilateral quasi-alliance relationship among India, Russia, China and Indonesia as a balance to NATO. However, such efforts to generate some semblance of countervailing power to the United States and NATO was limited even before 9/11 because of the economic dependence of all four countries on the West.

AFTER 9/11: WITH THE USA

Political and strategic conditions changed in the aftermath of 9/11. The United States and India – and indeed much of the rest of the world including Russia and China – found common cause in the war against this virulent form of trans-national terrorism. The Russia–China–India quasi-alliance momentum stalled suddenly, if it had not halted altogether. India was among the first countries to rush to the American side to offer military bases and logistical support to fight al-Qaeda in Afghanistan, having been the subject of al-Qaeda-sponsored terrorist operations in Kashmir as well. The United States, however, sought such facilities in Pakistan instead – it is adjacent to Afghanistan – while attempting to soothe India's fears of a return to the old Pakistani–American military alliance of the Cold War. The American policy has been to encourage rapprochement between India and Pakistan over Kashmir in order to facilitate its larger campaign against transnational terrorism.

During the visit of the Indian Prime Minister to Moscow in November 2001, Putin and Vajpayee proclaimed a common cause against transnational Islamic terrorism in Chechnia and Kashmir, as well as a common cause with the United States in combating global terrorism.[13] Nearly all states have jumped on the American anti-terrorism bandwagon with various degrees of conviction and sup-port. Within India itself, much of the vocal support for the US military campaign in Afghanistan came from primarily Hindu leaders and political analysts, espe-cially from members of the Hindu nationalist BJP. No public reports are evident of the reactions and sentiments among the nearly 150 million Muslim minority of India to al-Qaeda's attack on the World Trade Center and the subsequent Ameri-can bombing of Afghanistan. Whereas in the USA there has been some criticism that the American Muslim population, and the Muslim world in general, have not condemned enough al-Qaeda's attack on the WTC, there has been no similar criticisms in India of its large Muslim minority of failure to denounce publicly the attack on America. Unlike the involvement of a handful of naturalized or converted American, British and French Muslims, no Indian Muslims outside Kashmir have been involved in the al-Qaeda and Taliban movements.

Within two months of 9/11, Indian news reports indicated that the USA had proposed 'a major military alliance' with India which would provide India with a central role as counterweight to China on the one hand, and the Islamic states of West Asia on the other. India would provide the USA with land and naval training bases for its forces. The Indian Navy would be expected to safeguard American shipping interests in the Bay of Bengal and the Arabian Sea and 'in the event of these ships being attacked, the Indian navy was expected to engage the enemy.'[14] According to the Indian reports, India's Cabinet Committee on Security had rejected this proposal. However, by May 2002, a series of Indo–US military exchanges had begun exceeding some of the more feeble exchanges earlier.[15]

As on other previous occasions both before and after the Cold War, India's pursuit of an alliance relationship with the USA was curtailed severely by the continuing Indo–Pakistani confrontation over Kashmir, and by the prospect of nuclear war between the two hostile states. In the years following the series of nuclear tests conducted by India and Pakistan in May 1998, US officials and the American media called South Asia the most dangerous place on earth.[16] This view of impending nuclear war on the subcontinent unless something was done by the United States was voiced by President Clinton prior to his visit to South Asia in March 2000. Likewise, following 9/11, Deputy Secretary of State Richard Armitage told reporters on 11 October 2001 that Kashmir 'is the most dangerous place in the world,' and that 'the main purpose of [Secretary of State] Powell's trip would be to ensure that tensions between the two countries do not escalate.'[17] Indeed, during the American bombing of Afghanistan to root out Osama bin Laden and his al-Qaeda terrorist base, tensions escalated over Kashmir between these two newly armed nuclear weapon states.

The attack by the terrorist group *Lashkar-e-Toyba* on the Indian parliament in New Delhi on 13 December 2001 (thwarted by Indian security forces, costing the lives of seven security personnel and that of the four terrorists) was declared the equivalent of the attack by al-Qaeda on the World Trade Center, especially given the critical symbols to freedom and democracy that these targets represented. If the USA could conduct a war in distant Afghanistan to root out al-Qaeda, then why should not India have the right to conduct a war against the sanctuaries of the *Lashkar-e-Toyba*, the *Jaish-e-Mohammed* and other terrorist groups operating out of Pakistan?

Pakistan claimed that this was a freedom struggle and accused India of state terrorism in Kashmir. According to Pakistan, it was not enough for the USA to wage war against the Taliban and al-Qaeda in Afghanistan. If Southern Asia was to be stabilized, then Kashmir too must be settled. General Musharraf of Pakistan considered this one payoff for his country's cooperation with the USA in its war in Afghanistan. Meanwhile, there continued to be no basis for a settlement on Kashmir. Pakistan will not give up its goal to make Indian-held Kashmir part of Pakistan. India insists on the territorial status quo in Kashmir. The Indo–Pakistani rhetoric escalated as international attention focused on Afghanistan, Pakistan and India.

Premonitions of an impending Indo–Pakistani nuclear war in the midst of the 2001–2 war in Afghanistan was overblown, although precautionary measures to avoid such an eventuality may be necessary. There is no reason to believe that Indian and Pakistani leaders are less rational and responsible with their nuclear weapons than American, Russian and Chinese leaders. Some danger may lie on the Pakistani side where radical Islamic extremists, especially those in the military establishment who sympathize with al-Qaeda, could gain control of the nuclear weapons and delivery systems. A private Pakistani group that may have sought to develop such nuclear bombs for al-Qaeda operations worldwide including against India, was the Ummah Tameer-e-Nau (UTN). Founded by a Pakistani nuclear scientist, the UTN claimed to be a relief organization helping deprived civilians in Afghanistan. UTN was put on Washington's list of suspected terrorist groups.[18]

Nuclear weapons in the hands of the more extreme Kashmiri separatist groups may compel India to capitulate in future confrontations over Kashmir. Moreover, several Pakistani leaders have threatened the use of nuclear weapons if India were to launch a conventional attack on Pakistan. However, the periodic warnings by the West that India and Pakistan are on the brink of nuclear war may compound its dangers and become a self-fulfilling prophecy. Indeed, the frequency and intensity of such American forebodings had begun to look like wishful thinking. Too much professional credibility was put on line if these doomsday predictions were not to occur. However, while the Indian government and its supporters disagreed with such dire predictions, Pakistan and its allied Kashmiri separatists supported this thesis of imminent nuclear war. Raising its specter by Kashmiri separatists was intended to bring about US intervention while the world's attention remained focused on South Asia.

POST 9/11: NEITHER WITH NOR AGAINST THE USA

At the Asia conference in Almaty, Kazakhstan in early June, the leaders of both India and Pakistan declared that nuclear war was unthinkable. The Indian Defense Ministry stated 'India does not believe in the use of nuclear weapons. Neither does it visualize that it will be used by any other country.' Speaking on Russia's state-run RTR television, Pakistani President Musharraf said: 'Let me assure the whole world that our nuclear assets are in extremely safe hands and there is no vulnerability of these at all.' Was there really any doubt that Vajpayee and Musharraf would never escalate the Indo–Pakistani crisis into a nuclear war? Such doomsday forecasts by the US government and the drastic step of pulling all Americans out of the region, compounded its dangers. No such panic prevailed in India and Pakistan at any time.

Images of 9/11 and sympathy for the USA have now faded. The Indian rush into America's military arms has now slowed down although joint military exercises that preceded 9/11 have continued and advanced, moving from only joint naval exercises to joint air force ones as well. India's new Foreign Secretary, Kanwar Sibal, observed in early July 2002, that India's patience with Washington's South Asia policy was wearing thin. He criticized the grossly exaggerated claims of an imminent Indo–Pakistan nuclear war and the withdrawal of all American citizens when no such fears existed in South Asia. He asked: 'Did anyone see hospitals being readied, sirens being tested, even basic civil defense measures being operationalised?'[19] An indication of dissent may be seen in the response of India's Foreign Secretary, Kanwal Sibal, who observed 'One billion people did not feel threatened by an imminent nuclear war, but America said it did. There was no sign of India itself taking the threat seriously, but America decided to pull out its citizens. What else did they do? When Pakistan was test firing its missiles at the height of the tension, Washington did little more than express disappointment. If they were really that anxious, wouldn't they have done more?' He chastised the USA for its failure to condemn Pakistan's testing of missiles, and then rewarding Pakistan with $8 billion in aid without any appreciable change in Pakistani-sponsored cross-border terrorism in Indian Kashmir. The Indian Foreign Secretary then stated that India is not interested in having the USA act as mediator between India and Pakistan.[20]

Yet another American effort was made at the end of July 2002 with the visit of Secretary of State Colin Powell to both Pakistan and India to facilitate a resolution on Kashmir and revive Indo–American cooperation against common threats. The visit did not, as expected, make a major breakthrough in the Indo–Pakistan impasse. Former Indian foreign secretary J. N. Dixit observed that 'the Americans are going to repeat the mantra of restraint, and say that unless you talk to the Pakistanis, this can't be resolved,' and 'we will say you put more pressure on the Pakistanis.'[21]

Thus, the anticipated great Indo–American strategic cooperation against terrorism following 9/11 has not yet blossomed. The Pakistan factor continues to stymie the relationship as it did throughout the Cold War. The core of the Indo–American relationship has returned now to economic ties, more specifically, India's economic dependency on the USA. A July 2002 assessment by the Indian embassy in Washington observed that while India–US bilateral trade continued to grow, it still remained a small fraction of the global trade of the United States, with only about 10 percent of India's non-oil imports coming from the USA while almost one-fourth of India's exports go to it. American trade with India was less than 1 percent of its global trade and Indian goods have been 0.9 percent of total US imports for several years. The USA remains India's primary trading partner while India ranks twenty-second among countries exporting to it.[22] Therein lies the basis of 'post-post 9-11' India policy for the time being – at least, until the next unpredictable revolutionary change.

NOTES

1 The phrase was coined by Kishore Mahbubani in his 'The West and the Rest', *National Interest*, Summer 1991, pp. 3–13.
2 Quoted by former Indian Foreign Secretary, A. P. Venkateswaran, 'The Arrogance of Power', *Hindustan Times*, 1 April 2001.
3 Quoted by Anthony Faiolam, 'Air Campaign Ignites Anti-U.S. Sentiment', *Washington Post Foreign Service*, 18 May 1999.
4 'Indian Minister Praises Yugoslav Resistance to NATO', *Agence-France Presse*, 31 Dec. 1999.
5 *Times of India*, 3 May 1999.
6 See Patrick E. Tyler, 'Russia and China Sign "Friendship" Pact', *New York Times*, 17 July 2001.
7 This quotation and assessment is from Bruce A. Elleman and Sarah C. M. Paine,

'Security Pact with Russia Bolsters China's Power', *International Herald Tribune*, 6 Aug. 2001.

8 See Seema Guha, 'China, India to Set Up Security Dialogue', *Times of India*, 15 June 1999.

9 See 'India, China Decide to Stop Fencing Over Boundary', *Times of India*, 16 Jan. 2001.

10 Quoted from Press Trust of India report, *India Network News Digest*, Vol. 12, Issue 170, 4 Oct. 2000.

11 Amit Baruah, 'Wahid Supports Vajpayee Position on Kashmir', *India Network News Digest*, Vol. 13, Issue 8, 12 Jan. 2001.

12 From Amit Baruah, *India Network News Digest*, Vol. 13, Issue 8, 12 Jan. 2001.

13 Karen DeYoung and Dana Milbank, 'Bush, Putin Agree to Slash Nuclear Arms', *Washington Post*, 13 Nov. 2001; Peter Baker, 'A Familiar Bush Strategy on Disarmament', *Washington Post*, 13 Nov. 2001; 'Look Deep Into Putin's Eyes and Seal the Deal', *Los Angeles Times*, 14 Nov. 2001; Michael Gordon, 'U.S. Arsenal: Treaties vs. Non-Treaties', *New York Times*, 14 Nov. 2001.

14 *Hindustan Times*, 10 Nov. 2001. This newspaper was quoting India's leading newsweekly, *India Today*.

15 See Chidanand Rajghatta, 'India, US Tie Up Defense Under Shadow of N-War', *Times of India*, 23 May 2002.

16 An American editorial entitled, 'Danger Within Pakistan', stated that 'the world cannot afford to allow the region's two nuclear-armed nations to increase their tensions.' See *New York Times*, 26 Jan. 2000.

17 See 'Kashmir Most Dangerous Place: US', *Times of India*, 12 Oct. 2001. External Affairs and Defense Minister, Jaswant Singh, stated: 'I disagree with the assessment. We have disagreed with earlier also to this type of thesis being put up by the West. Rather than Kashmir, it was Afghanistan which is a flashpoint.' See 'India Rejects US Assessment of Kashmir as "Most Dangerous" ', *Hindustan Times*, 12 Oct. 2001.

18 John F. Burns, 'Uneasy Ally in Terror War Suddenly Feels More U.S. Pressure', *New York Times*, 21 Dec. 2001.

19 'New Foreign Secretary Says Travel Advisory Was a Political Act', *Financial Express* (Bombay), 9 July 2002; and 'Foreign Secretary Nails America for Double-Speak on Pakistan', *Hindustan Times*, 9 July 2002.

20 'Foreign Secretary Nails America for Double-Speak on Pakistan', *Hindustan Times*, 9 July 2002; and 'U.S. Can't Act as Mediator: Sibal', *The Hindu*, 9 July 2002.

21 *India Network News Digest*, Vol. 14, Issue 129, 26 July 2002. See also K. Subrahmanyam, 'Enduring Failures: US Dancing to Pakistan's Tune', *Times of India*, 26 July 2002.

22 See 'India and US: A Note on Trade and Commercial Issues: Comprehensive Note of the Commerce Wing of the Indian Embassy', 10 July 2002. From www.US-India Friendship.net

18 A rising power with global aspirations

China

Rex Li

In a rising power with global aspirations, Chinese leaders have shown enormous interest in changes in the international situation since 9/11. Their reactions to the USA's campaign against terrorism is significant in the shaping of US–China relations and of Asia–Pacific security. Here I consider China's official and public reactions to the terrorist attacks, examine elite perceptions of the nature and implications of 9/11 and analyze China's relations with the USA, Russia, Japan and other Asian countries.

CHINA'S OFFICIAL AND PUBLIC REACTIONS

China's official response was swift but cautious. President Jiang Zemin was among the first world leaders to send condolences to President George W. Bush. Chinese leaders decided immediately after September 11 to condemn the terrorist attacks and express sympathy with the victims but would not take sides in America's conflict with terrorists.[1]

Chinese leaders were concerned about terrorism, especially in the far-western province of Xinjiang where Muslim separatists were believed to be supported by Afghan-based groups, like those of Osama bin Laden, but were reluctant to offer unreserved support for America's anti-terrorist campaign. Chinese officials urged the USA to discuss anti-terrorist proposals at the United Nations Security Council. They insisted that any actions should be based on international law and the UN Charter.[2]

China demanded 'concrete evidence' from Bush before military strikes against suspected terrorist groups were launched. Any military actions, Chinese officials asserted, 'should have a clear orientation that should not hurt innocent people.'[3] While China had serious reservations over US operations in Afghanistan, it responded positively to Washington's call for international cooperation in fighting terrorism. Jiang was keen to maintain an image of China as a peaceful and constructive member of the international community.

Chinese leaders may have disagreements over the speed and direction of China's economic reform and opening up to the outside world, but their overriding consideration is to protect or advance China's national interest. No evidence indicates a division within the central leadership on this issue. As the General Secretary of the Chinese Communist Party and the Chairman of its Central Military Commission, Jiang appears to have full control over the key decisions on China's foreign and security policy. He has managed to silence the hardline generals who are alarmed by augmenting US influence in Asia. Indeed, the top Chinese leaders have spoken unanimously since September 11.

Reliable information on public opinion is scarce in China. Western media reports suggest that Chinese citizens had mixed feelings about the terrorist attacks, but were horrified by the scale of damage and the huge loss of life. Fourteen Chinese-owned companies were in the World Trade Center. However, they tended to blame the tragedy on the USA's 'hegemonic policy.' As a student at Beijing University said: 'Terrorism is wrong but I personally think this was a lesson for the United States. From now on, the US won't be so arrogant and reckless.' Another commented: 'Now they know how it feels to be bombed' – referring to NATO's accidental bombing of the Chinese embassy in Belgrade in 1999. Some even went further to say: 'Heroes, brave men who liberated the world . . . America under attack – it deserved it!'[4]

This sort of anti-American sentiment was widely expressed on Chinese websites and chat-rooms which reflected popular ambivalence towards the USA. The Chinese admired America's wealth and power but resented its dominant role in world affairs, especially its alleged attempts to frustrate China's aspirations to become a great power.

CHINESE ANALYSES AND INTERPRETATIONS

To understand the complexity of China's perceptions of 9/11, one has to go beyond the standard official reports or the sentimental views on Chinese websites. Over the past year, Chinese security experts and international relations specialists have had lively discussions on various aspects of the terrorist attacks and their implications. Published in specialist journals, this literature is written primarily for domestic consumption and is not normally reported in the state media.[5] It provides in-depth analyses of a whole range of significant issues which mirrors mainstream Chinese thinking on the world after 9/11. Most authors of these Chinese-language publications are prominent scholars and influential analysts whose views are likely to attract the attention of Chinese leaders and senior government officials.[6]

Chinese analysts invariably regard the 9/11 attacks as terrorist acts. They believe that they are of an extreme and evil nature which will have negative effects on both the USA and the world. While Chinese security specialists disapprove of many aspects of US foreign policy, they maintain that nothing can justify such barbaric acts.[7] They argue that international terrorism is rooted in an unjust international political and economic order which is largely dominated by a hegemonic power, namely, the USA. The wealth gap between the North and South, according to Chinese analyses, has widened in recent years. The situation is exacerbated by the process of globalization which has led to further economic marginalization of the South, creating a political climate conducive to the growth of global terrorism.[8]

Yang Yunzhong has argued that 9/11 should be seen as an extreme form of struggle between hegemonism and anti-hegemonism rather than a clash of civilizations between Islam and the West.[9] Tang Zhichao contends that the anti-American sentiments in the Arab world are the result of a failure of US policy in the Middle East and continued American military presence in the region.[10] Other Chinese analysts argue that 9/11 makes it more urgent to promote 'democratisation of international relations.'[11] Given the plethora of challenges in a globalizing world, some Chinese scholars such as Pang Zhongying believe it is essential to establish a new global order based on equality, justice and mutual respect.[12] Any international campaign against terrorism, he and others including Yang Jin maintain, should be led by the UN and conducted in accordance with international law. More important, the national sovereignty of independent states should not be violated in the name of fighting terrorism.[13]

Shi Yinhong has noted that most countries have readjusted their foreign policy and security strategy since 9/11.[14] The areas of cooperation among the major powers have expanded substantially which, according to Lu Zhongwei, is a positive development in international relations.[15] But Yang Yunzhong predicts that great power rivalry in Central Asia will increase which could result in instability in the region.[16]

Consensus exists among Chinese security analysts that America is the major source of global instability. The tensions between the USA and other countries, they assert, lie in Washington's ambitions to build a unipolar global system in an increasingly multipolar world.[17] They believe that America's desire to dominate the world has not been deterred by 9/11. On the contrary, according to Yang Yunzhong, the tragic events have provided the USA with an opportunity to expand its spheres of influence which has increased through the development of its anti-terrorist coalition.[18]

Chinese scholars have discerned some adjustments in US foreign policy since the terrorist attacks.[19] For a short period of time, Chu Shulong observes, the Bush administration appeared to be willing to abandon its unilateralism. But he points out that the flexibility in American policy is a reflection of pragmatic considerations rather than a fundamental change in US global strategy.[20] Guo Xiangang notes that the USA needs the support and collaboration of as many countries as possible to combat terrorism.[21] Despite its seemingly less unilateralist stance, America's basic strategic thinking is thought to be based upon the pursuit of hegemonism.[22] Chinese analysts generally claim that 'realism' has dominated US foreign policy thinking since 9/11.[23]

The terrorist attacks have inflicted an enormous financial damage to the USA and a devastating psychological shock to the American people, Shi Yinhong concurs, but they have enabled Bush to mobilize elite and popular support for his policies.[24] Military specialists such as Ge Lide are especially concerned about America's proposed plan to develop National Missile Defense (NMD) and

Theater Missile Defense (TMD) systems which could undermine Beijing's nuclear deterrent. They are disappointed by Bush's decision to withdraw from the Anti-Ballistic Missile (ABM) Treaty with Russia and to continue with the NMD project. The strategic aim of the USA, Ge concludes, is to achieve absolute security and global dominance.[25] Similarly, the real purpose of America's war in Afghanistan is less about capturing bin Laden than about shaping the future of the country. The war according to Shi Lan, Li Wenjing and others has also given the Americans a golden opportunity to move into the oil-rich region of Central Asia.[26]

Another concern of Chinese analysts is President Bush's reference to Iran, Iraq and North Korea as an 'axis of evil.' They are convinced that Bush is seeking to demonize these countries in order to increase his popularity, justify a huge rise in military spending and stimulate the American economy through increased arms production.[27] More worrying for China's security analysts is the shift in America's strategic emphasis towards the Asia-Pacific.[28] Zhou Jianming and others believe that the USA tries to maintain its military presence in, and fortify its security ties with, other Asia-Pacific countries with a view to containing China which is perceived as America's main rival and potential enemy.[29]

There is clearly a shared apprehension among Chinese specialists about rising US global influence. They seem to have different opinions, however, on the effects of 9/11 on international politics. Some analysts are more optimistic about the prospects for great power cooperation. Others believe that the USA would be more assertive in safeguarding its self-interest with or without the consent of other states.

IMPLICATIONS FOR CHINA'S REGIONAL RELATIONSHIPS

China, America and Japan

During the Clinton era the relationship between the USA and China was characterized as one of 'strategic partnership.' The Bush campaign instead saw China as a 'strategic competitor.'[30] Immediately after taking office, Bush took steps to strengthen America's security relations with friends across the Asia-Pacific, which Chinese leaders saw as encircling China. The mid-air collision of an EP-3E spy plane and a Chinese fighter jet over the South China Sea and the unauthorized emergency landing of the American plane on China's Hainan island in April 2001, led to a major diplomatic crisis between the two states.

After 9/11 some Western observers expressed the hope that US–China relations could be improved because Chinese support would be needed in America's battle against terrorism. Indeed, China's willingness to cooperate with the USA in fighting international terrorism has been welcomed by Bush. In Shanghai in October 2001 Bush referred to the USA and China as 'two great nations.' In December, the US government granted China permanent status as a normal trading partner which, according to the White House, marked 'the final stage in normalizing US–China trade relations.'[31]

While the 'war against terrorism' may have provided a new opportunity for Sino–American cooperation, it does not appear to provide a lasting basis.[32] This is because leaders in both countries have different views on the origins of terrorism, the approaches to fighting it and the expected outcomes of anti-terrorist cooperation. In fact, the expansion of America's anti-terrorist networks has led to a deeper concern in China about America's future role in the global system. On a variety of strategic, political and economic issues, the perceptions of Chinese and American policy-makers differ profoundly.[33]

From the dominant US perspective, China is a non-status quo power which, despite its impressive record of economic achievements over the past two decades, is still governed by a group of self-appointed communist leaders. Many US politicians and analysts fear that a non-democratic China with great power aspirations and growing military capabilities will be less likely to deal with unresolved disputes peacefully with neighbors. This would pose a significant challenge to the USA and allies in the Asia-Pacific.

A CIA report of 2002 estimated that China's ballistic missiles will increase several-fold by 2015 and that they would be deployed primarily against the USA.[34] Concerns of China's military modernization and its potential threat to Asia-Pacific security and US interests were expressed in a Pentagon report published in July 2002.[35] While China is no longer depicted as a 'strategic competitor,' the Bush administration's perceptions of China remain largely unchanged.

Taiwan is probably the most sensitive and potentially explosive issue in US–China relations. Bush has approved the sale of a massive arms package to Taipei and stated publicly that the USA would do 'whatever it took to help Taiwan defend herself.'[36] Despite the need to secure China's support for the 'war against terrorism,' Washington has not abandoned its commitments to Taiwan. If anything, it has developed closer defense ties with the Taiwanese military and allowed senior Taiwanese leaders and officials to visit the USA.[37] A leaked Pentagon report has allegedly suggested that nuclear weapons could be used against China in the event of a conflict across the Taiwan Strait.[38]

All this is resented by the Chinese who suspect that the Bush administration, like its predecessors, is exploiting the Taiwan issue to constrain Chinese actions. America's real intention, they believe, is to prevent the emergence of a strong and united China. Chinese leaders see their country as a rising power which will eventually become an economic superpower and a global strategic player. Their long-term goal is to challenge US domination and to replace it by multipolarity.

China and Japan are historical rivals and regional powers in East Asia. Despite a high level of trade, Chinese leaders are deeply suspicious of Tokyo's global and regional ambitions.[39] Of particular concern to the Chinese is the strengthening of the US–Japan security alliance since the mid-1990s. They suspect that the USA is seeking to build a stronger alliance with Tokyo in order to 'contain' China.

Japan's response to 9/11 has made the Chinese more wary of its security strategy. After initial hesitation Japanese Prime Minister Junichiro Koizumi decided to offer the USA all the necessary support in its 'war against terrorism.' This was appreciated by Bush who called Japan 'the bedrock for peace and prosperity in the Pacific' during his February 2002 visit to Tokyo.

The Chinese are convinced that the Koizumi government has exploited the fear of terrorism to push legislation through the Diet which would allow the Self-Defense Forces to be deployed beyond Japanese waters and air space. Tokyo's active diplomacy in the Arab world, Central and South Asia before and during the Afghan war, coupled with generous Japanese financial support for the postwar reconstruction of Afghanistan, have aroused apprehensions in Beijing. Chinese analysts believe that Japan's 'anti-terrorism diplomacy' is designed to expand the areas of its security cooperation with America and to raise its international status more generally.[40]

The worst fear of China's leaders is that Washington would involve Japan in the development and the deployment of a TMD system in Asia. This could enhance Japan's military capability and weaken China's strategic position in the region. China has a longstanding dispute with Japan over the sovereignty of the Diaoyu/Senkaku islands. Chinese leaders are also worried that Japan may support American military actions in a future conflict over Taiwan. Given the importance of Japanese investments and Sino–Japanese trade, however, China will seek to maintain a stable relationship with Japan.

China's relations with Russia and Central Asia

Sino–Russian relations have improved significantly since the collapse of the Soviet Union and their economic and security cooperation has expanded substantially. Of special significance is China's purchase of a variety of weapons from Russia, including Su–27 and Su–30 warplanes. In July 2001 the two countries signed a high-profile Treaty of Friendship which was clearly directed at the USA. Indeed, the leaders of the two nations have on numerous occasions used the term 'strategic partnership' to describe their relations.

This is why Chinese elites and analysts are deeply disturbed by Russia's active support for the war in Afghanistan.[41] While Chinese leaders seem to understand the political and economic motives behind President Putin's decision to collaborate with Bush,[42] they fear that an improved relationship between Russia and America would jeopardize the Sino–Russian 'strategic partnership.'[43]

Undoubtedly, the nuclear arms treaty signed in 2002 by Putin and Bush (see Chapter 19 on Russia for details) is viewed by the Chinese with misgivings. Defense Minister Sergei Ivanov made a special visit to Beijing to reassure Chinese leaders that Russia's improved relations with the USA and closer links with NATO would not be detrimental to Sino–Russian relations.[44] But it is doubtful that this alleviated uneasiness over Russia moving closer to the West. What worries the Chinese is that some Russian military officials are apprehensive of Beijing's defense modernization and growing military strength, regarding China as a potential threat to Russia's future security.[45] Nevertheless, China will strive to sustain its 'strategic partnership' with Russia in order to balance the USA.

Soon after the disintegration of the Soviet Union in 1991, China established diplomatic relations with the five newly independent Central Asian countries. During the past decade much progress has been made in China's economic, political and security cooperation with these countries. The most significant development was probably the establishment of a regional grouping in April 1996 called Shanghai Five which was transformed in 2001 into a regional security bloc, the Shanghai Cooperation Organization (SCO).[46] This organization was initiated by Chinese and Russian leaders who felt uncomfortable with growing US global influence. Chinese analysts believe that the USA has been trying to exert its influence in Central Asia through the development of political links, economic assistance and military penetration ever since the early 1990s. The decisions of some Central Asian countries to open their air space and military bases to America have therefore caused tremendous anxiety in China.

Central Asia is important to China in many respects. First, over 30 percent of China's oil supply is imported from the region. Beijing has actively cooperated with Central Asian countries on oil exploration and construction of oil pipelines. The presence of US forces is thus seen as a serious threat to China's energy security. Second, Western entry into Central Asia could affect China's economic interests.[47] Third, Central Asia's growing political links with the West could push it away from China. Should the USA gain a foothold in Central Asia, Chinese military analysts warn, it would pose an immense challenge to China's national security.

The concern that US involvement in Central Asian affairs could undermine the influence of the SCO may have been eased slightly by the agreement of Russia and four Central Asian states to adopt a charter making explict the aim to 'fight terrorism, prevent conflicts and promote security in Central Asia' and to create a permanent secretariat in Beijing.[48]

China and South and Southeast Asia

Traditionally, Pakistan has had a close military and strategic relationship with China and Beijing has been transferring military technology to Islamabad for some time. Unsurprisingly, the Chinese feel uneasy about the warming of Pakistan's relations with the USA.[49] President Musharraf has repeatedly assured Chinese leaders that US–Pakistani cooperation on fighting terrorism would not harm the friendship between China and Pakistan. But the Chinese suspect that a pro-American regime in Islamabad could help the USA extend its influence to Central Asia.[50]

India, another nuclear power in South Asia, is viewed by Beijing as a rival. Both China and India have great power aspirations and are suspicious of each other's ambitions. The Chinese believe that India seeks to become a dominant power in South Asia and the Indian Ocean, while the Indians regard China's growing nuclear capabilities as a threat to the security of India. They also have unresolved border disputes and Chinese leaders are resentful of the fact that India has hosted the Dalai Lama's Tibetan exile government.

The close relationship between America and India is often interpreted as an anti-Chinese coalition.[51] Chinese leaders were therefore pleased to see India playing a less prominent role in the war in Afghanistan. Concerned about conflict over Kashmir, Beijing has called for dialogue between President Musharraf and Prime Minister Vajpayee.

In Southeast Asia, China has strong trade and economic relations with most countries but it also has unresolved territorial disputes, such as those concerning the South China Sea. America's security role in Southeast Asia has been enhanced by various types of military cooperation with Indonesia, the Philippines and Singapore.[52] Indeed, the USA and Southeast Asian countries recently signed an anti-terrorism agreement which was referred to by Secretary of State Colin Powell as 'a political declaration that brings ASEAN and the United States together in a more intimate relationship.'[53] The USA is, the Chinese assert, using the 'war against terrorism' as a pretext to perpetuate its military presence in Southeast Asia with the aim of guarding against a rising China.[54]

Leaders in Southeast Asian states may wish to utilize US connections to strengthen their position vis-à-vis China but they would not like to see a Sino–American military confrontation. They tend to see China's rise as inevitable and hope to benefit from the huge China market. Meanwhile, China has much to gain from its economic interactions with Southeast Asian nations. Hence, the nature of their relations has not been changed by 9/11.

CONCLUSION

If there is a 'realist' tendency in US foreign policy since 9/11, China's perceptions and interpretations of international relations are equally 'realist' in orientation. China's leaders are certain that the Bush administration is exploiting the current situation to consolidate a unipolar position in the global system. They have serious doubts about the motives behind America's anti-terrorist campaign. Their nightmare scenario is a geostrategic situation where China is encircled by the USA through a series of security networks in Central, South, Southeast and Northeast Asia.

Despite this premonition, there are good reasons for Chinese leaders to work with the US administration. 9/11 has shifted the attention of US elites and media away from debate about the 'China threat.' Instead, Beijing's cooperation for anti-terrorism is sought by the Bush administration. To the Jiang leadership, joining the US campaign against global terrorism would help China elevate its status as a responsible power. More important, the success of Chinese economic modernization depends heavily on US investment and a stable international environment. As Chinese leaders are preoccupied with domestic challenges, such as leadership succession and the implications of WTO membership, it is not in their interest to have a difficult relationship with the USA.

Moreover, the Chinese government has been able to use the threat of terrorism to justify its suppression of Uighur separatists who are allegedly involved in organizing various terrorist activities. The US government's recent reference to the East Turkestan Islamic Movement (ETIM) as a terrorist organization has lent additional support for China's claims that the ETIM is linked to al-Qaeda and that it is aiming to establish an independent state of East Turkestan in Xinjiang. America's position on the ETIM has also enabled Beijing to renew its military cooperation with other SCO member states such as Kyrgyzstan which are believed to be threatened by the organization.

Thus, Chinese leaders are willing to collaborate with America on its 'war against terror,' hoping to develop a mutually beneficial relationship with Washington. This is reflected by Jiang's exceptionally mild reactions to America's withdrawal from the ABM Treaty and its plan to take military actions against Iraq. Nevertheless, China's leaders and elites remain skeptical of US global ambitions and strategic intentions.

NOTES

 1 Willy Wo-Lap Lam, 'China Sends Condolences to U.S.', 12 Sept. 2001, http://asia.cnn.com/2001/WORLD/asiapcf/east/09/11/china.us.reax/index.html
 2 'China Asks US to Look Beyond NATO', 13 Sept. 2001, http://news.bbc.co.uk/hi/english/world/americas/newsid_1541000/1541656.stm
 3 'China Demands US Attack Evidence', 18 Sept. 2001, http://news.bbc.co.uk/hi/english/world/asia-pacific/newsid_1550000/1550495.stm
 4 Jaime FlorCruz, 'China's Dilemma in the Fight Against Terrorism', 19 Sept. 2001, http://asia.cnn.com/2001/WORLD/asiapcf/east/09/19/ret.china.dilemma/
 5 Given space constraints only a small number of Chinese-language sources are cited in this chapter.
 6 For a discussion of the advisory role of Chinese policy analysts and security specialists in China's foreign policy-making process, see Rex Li, 'Unipolar Aspirations in a Multipolar Reality: China's Perceptions of US Ambitions and Capabilities in the Post-Cold War World', *Pacifica Review*, Vol. 11, No. 2, June 1999, pp. 116–18.
 7 See, for example, Shi Yinhong, 'Reflections on Three Major Issues After "September 11" ', *Xiandai guoji guanxi* (Contemporary International Relations) [Beijing], No.1, Jan. 2002, p. 45.
 8 See, for example, Niu Hanzhang, 'Terrorism and Anti-terrorism: Theoretical Considerations on a Different Type of War in the 21st Century', *Zhijie jingji yu zhengzhi luntan* (Forum on World Economy and Politics) [Nanjing], No. 6, 2001, pp. 41–4; Yang Jin, 'An Analysis of the Events of September 11 and the Approaches to International Anti-terrorism', *Jiaoxue yu yanjiu* (Teaching and Research) [Beijing], No. 11, 2001, pp. 55–7.
 9 Yang Yunzhong, 'The Profound Impact of the Events of September 11 on the International Strategic Situation', *Dangdai yatai* (Contemporary Asia-Pacific Studies) [Beijing], No. 3, March 2002, p. 5.
10 Tang Zhichao, 'Why America Is Hated by the Arabs', *Huanqiu shibao* (Global Times) [Beijing], 10 Jan. 2002, p. 6.
11 Ni Shixiong and Wang Yiwei, 'On Democratisation of International Relations', *Guoji wenti yanjiu* (Journal of International Studies) [Beijing], No. 3, May 2002, pp. 22–6.
12 Pang Zhongying, 'Peace for a New Century? – Reflections on the World Order', *Guoji jingji pinglun* (International Economic Review) [Beijing], No. 6, 2001, pp. 29–31.
13 Yang Jin, 'An Analysis', *Jiaoxue yu yanjiu*, p. 57; Wang Tingdong, 'The Events of September 11 and the Strategies Against Global Terrorism', *Shijie jingji yu zhengzhi*

(World Economics and Politics) [Beijing], No. 4, 2002, p. 53; Qian Wenrong, 'Anti-terrorism and the International Order', *Guoji wenti yanjiu*, No. 3, May 2002, pp. 27–32.

14 Shi Yinhong, 'On America's War Against Terrorism', *Guoji jingji pinglun*, No. 6, 2001, pp. 25–9.

15 Lu Zhongwei, 'Grasping the Overall Trend of the World Scene', *Xiandai guoji guanxi*, No. 1, Jan. 2002, pp. 2–3.

16 Yang Yunzhong, 'The Profound Impact', *Dangdai yatai*, pp. 10–11.

17 For a detailed examination of China's security perceptions of the United States, see Rex Li, 'Unipolar Aspirations in a Multipolar Reality', pp. 115–49.

18 Yang Yunzhong, 'The Profound Impact', *Dangdai yatai*, p. 5.

19 Guo Xiangang, 'The Changes in the Bush Administration's Foreign Policy over the Past Year and Their Implications', *Guoji wenti yanjiu*, No. 2, March 2002, pp. 34–5.

20 Chu Shulong, 'The Events of September 11 and the Bush Administration's Foreign Policy', *Heping yu fazhan* (Peace and Development) [Beijing], No. 4, 2001, pp. 5–8.

21 Guo Xiangang, 'The Changes in', *Guoji wenti yanjiu*, pp. 34–5.

22 Chu Shulong, 'The Events of', *Heping yu fazhan*, p. 8.

23 Feng Shaolei, 'The Re-emergence of Realism', *Wenhuibao* (The Literary Daily) [Shang-hai], 9 Jan. 2002, p. 4; Zhou Jianming, 'America Has Abandoned Its "Engagement Strategy" ', *Huanqiu shibao*, 14 March 2002, p. 7.

24 Shi Yinhong, 'The Events of September 11 and US External Posture', *Meiguo yanjiu* (American Studies) [Beijing], No. 4, Dec. 2001, pp. 21–8.

25 Ge Lide, 'America's Withdrawal from the "ABM Treaty" and the Prospects for the Development of the Strategic Anti-Missile System', *Shijie jingji yu zhengzhi*, No. 4, 2002, pp. 37–42.

26 Shi Lan and Li Wenjing, 'The Re-construction of Afghanistan: A New Contest', *Dangdai yatai*, No. 4, April 2002, p. 25; Zhang Wenmu, 'The War in Afghanistan and the Asymmetric World Structure', *Zhanlue yu guanli* (Strategy and Management) [Beijing], No. 2, 2002, pp. 42–3.

27 Wang Hongwei, 'Reflections on the "Axis of Evil" ', *Dangdai yatai*, No. 4, April 2002, pp. 22–4.

28 Yang Yunzhong, 'The Profound Impact', *Dangdai yatai*, pp. 5–7.

29 Zhou Jianming, 'America', *Huanqiu shibao*, p. 7; Chu Shulong, 'The Events', *Heping yu fazhan*, pp. 5–8; Yang Yunzhong, 'The Profound Impact', *Dangdai yatai*, p. 7.

30 This view of China was well articulated by Condoleezza Rice, 'Promoting the National Interest', *Foreign Affairs*, Vol. 79, No. 1, Jan./Feb. 2000, pp. 55–7.

31 BBC News, 'US Normalises Trade with China', 28 Dec. 2001, http://www.news.bbc.co.uk/hi/english/business/newsid_1731000/1731451.stm

32 I have offered a preliminary analysis of US–China relations in the first year of the Bush administration in a paper ' "Strategic Partnership" or "Strategic Competition"? US–China Relations in the Post-Clinton Era' presented at the Asian Studies Center, St. Antony's College, University of Oxford, 19 Feb. 2002.

33 Rex Li, 'US–China Relations: Accidents Can Happen', *World Today*, Vol. 56, No. 5, May 2000, pp. 17–20.

34 The National Intelligence Council, 'Foreign Missile Developments and the Ballistic Missile Threat Through 2015', Jan. 2002. The report is available on http://www.cia.gov/nic/pubs/other_products/Unclassifiedballisticmissilefinal.htm

35 BBC News, 'US Warns of Danger to Taiwan', 13 July 2002, http://news.bbc.co.uk/1/hi/world/asia-pacific/2125617.stm

36 David E. Sanger, 'U.S. Would Defend Taiwan, Bush Says', *New York Times*, 26 April 2001, p. A1.

37 For an analysis of the role of America in recent China–Taiwan relations, see Rex Li, 'War or Peace? Potential Conflict Across the Taiwan Strait', *World Defence Systems*, Royal United Services Institute for Defence Studies, Aug. 2002, pp. 157–60.

38 BBC News, 'US "Has Nuclear Hit List" ', 9 March 2002, http://news.bbc.co.uk/1/hi/world/americas/1864173.stm. Excerpts of the Pentagon's 'Nuclear Posture Review' can be found on http://www.globalsecurity.org/wmd/library/policy/dod/npr.htm

39 Rex Li, 'Partners or Rivals? Chinese Perceptions of Japan's Security Strategy in the Asia-Pacific Region', *Journal of Strategic Studies*, Vol. 22, No. 4, Dec. 1999, pp. 1–25.

40 Xu Zhixian, Ma Junwei and Liu Junhong, 'Japan: Retrospect and Prospects', *Xiandai guoji guanxi*, No. 1, Jan. 2002, pp. 33–4; Jin Xide, 'Japan's Security Strategy at the Crossroads', *Riben xuekan* (Journal of Japanese Studies) [Beijing], No. 2, March 2002, p. 6.

41 Zhu Feng, 'New Trends in US–Russian Relations', *Xiandai guoji guanxi*, No. 11, Nov. 2001, pp. 24–5.

42 Ibid., pp. 30–1.

43 Yang Yunzhong, 'The Profound Impact', *Dangdai yatai*, p. 13.

44 BBC News, 'Russia Reassures China Over NATO', 31 May 2002, http://news.bbc.co.uk/hi/english/world/asia-pacific/newsid_2016000/2016917.stm

45 Sun Jian, 'On Indian–Russian Relations', *Shijie jingji yu zhengzhi luntan*, No. 3, 2001, pp. 32–3.

46 Deng Hao, 'China's Relations with Central Asian Countries: Retrospects and Prospects', *Guoji wenti yanjiu*, No. 3, May 2002, pp. 8–9.

47 Ibid., p. 12; Dai Chaowu and Li Chunling, 'America's Policy Towards Central Asia After September 11 and Its Impact', *Shijie jingji yu zhengzhi luntan*, No. 1, 2002, p. 64.

48 Nikolai Gorshkov, 'Asian Security Bloc Boosted', 7 June 2002, http://news.bbc.co.uk/hi/english/world/asia-pacific/newsid_2031000/2031906.stm

49 Yuan Di, 'The Strategy of International Anti-terrorism: America, Pakistan and India', *Nanya yanjiu jikan* (South Asian Studies Quarterly) [Chengdu], No. 4, 2001, pp. 32–6.

50 Ma Jiali, 'An Analysis of the Changes in the Triangular Relationships Among America, India and Pakistan', *Xiandai guoji guanxi*, No. 11, Nov. 2001, p. 35.

51 Ma Jiali, 'The Changes in America's South Asia Policy After September 11', *Nanya yanjiu* (South Asian Studies) [Beijing], No. 2, 2001, p. 3.

52 US Department of State International Information Programs, 'Transcript: Admiral Blair Discusses Military Cooperation in Southeast Asia', 29 Jan. 2002, http://www.usinfo.state.gov/regional/ea/easec/blair9.htm

53 BBC News, 'ASEAN Makes Anti-terror Pact with US', 1 Aug. 2002, http://news.bbc.co.uk/1/hi/world/asia-pacific/2165552.stm

54 Cao Yunhua, 'The New Changes in the Geopolitical Structure of South East Asia', *Dongnanya zongheng* (South East Asia Review) [Nanning], No. 12, 2001, pp. 14–16; Xia Liping, 'America's "Return to South East Asia" and Its Impact on Asia-Pacific Security', *Xiandai guoji guanxi*, No. 8, Aug. 2002, pp. 18–22.

19 Former superpower

The Russian Federation

Mary Buckley

The terrorist attacks of September 11 provided President Vladimir Putin with an opportunity to raise the Russian Federation's status in world politics through joining the coalition against terrorism and by playing a diplomatic and military role in Afghanistan. Putin also wanted to improve Russian–US relations after their deterioration over NATO intervention in Kosovo. Eager for respect for Russia, Putin pressed for agreement on missile reductions, for a greater say in NATO's security policy in Europe and for a joint statement with President Bush on the Middle East. Putin wanted Russia to be seen as a great power, making a difference in world politics.

In Russia, however, Putin's critics insisted that he was making too many concessions to the USA. Bush may finally have agreed to sign a treaty on missile reductions after initially stating that a verbal agreement would do, but he refused to destroy his decommissioned weapons. NATO expansion eastwards was continuing and although the NATO–Russia Permanent Joint Council (PJC) was replaced in May 2002 by a new NATO–Russia Council (NRC), Russia had a voice but no vote or veto. Moreover, Western troops were in Kyrgyzstan, Uzbekistan and Tajikistan in Central Asia, US bases were being established in Kyrgyzstan and Uzbekistan and US military instructors were in Georgia providing training in counter-terrorism. By contrast, Russia had decided to pull out of bases in Cuba and Vietnam. In sum, Russia was suffering geopolitical losses in a world that appeared to many to be unipolar. Communists and nationalists voiced their discontent, pointing out that even the 1974 Jackson–Vanik amendment had not been removed, despite Bush's indications that he would work towards this. Instead, it became snarled up in the Congress due to a trade dispute over the import of US chicken legs.

This chapter traces the reactions of president, top ministers, political parties and public opinion in Russia to 9/11, war in Afghanistan, changing geo-politics and to the looming threat of war against Iraq.

BACKGROUND

Russian/US relations had soured considerably as a consequence of NATO's bombing in Serbia and Kosovo. Ninety–eight percent of Russians were against

NATO's actions and Russian politicians were unanimous in their condemnations, even if their emphases varied. Kosovo heralded the worst period of relations with the USA since the final disintegration of the USSR in 1991.[1]

Russia's status in the USA had also been downgraded due to the election in November 2000 of George W. Bush as US President. Bush duly abolished the post of Under-secretary of State on Russia and that of Special Ambassador-at-large on Russia and Newly Independent States.[2]

Putin's negative image in the US media at this time was of an impenetrable ex-KGB agent prone to authoritarian tendencies and ready to clip freedom of speech on television.[3] In Washington, Russia was viewed as an erstwhile superpower, significantly weakened by its loss of empire in 1989. Its hallmarks were identity crisis, enduring economic problems, crime, corruption and poverty, topped with human rights' abuses in Chechnia. Still enjoying a large Communist Party and several political parties with nationalist leanings, the Parliament was not pre-dominantly made up of liberal reformers. The elections to the Duma in 1993, 1995 and 1999 had not resulted in political compositions which endeared Russia to the IMF, foreign investors or the White House.[4]

Putin attempted to rebut his negative image and to suggest the great potential of Russia. His book *First Person* portrayed Putin as a hard-working and serious democrat, a good family man and dog lover, who saw no reason why cooperation between Russia and NATO should not develop further so long as Russia was 'treated as an equal partner'.[5] Bush, however, was reluctant to pay Russia the attention that his predecessor Bill Clinton had. Bush's National Security Advisor Condoleezza Rice is a highly informed and intelligent Russian scholar from Stanford University, but one who recommended toughness in dealings with the former superpower, not over-solicitude.

Through participating in the US coalition against terrorism, Putin could cooperate with other world states whose 'club' he wanted to join. Communists and nationalists at home, however, as well as some members of the foreign and defense establishment, were quick to suggest that Putin was selling out to the Americans, going soft on NATO expansion, still enduring hypocritical Western criticisms of Russian policy in Chechnia, not contesting US bases in Central Asia and giving in to the storage of decommissioned US nuclear weapons which could therefore be reactivated in the future. Putin also reluctantly accepted the US pull-out from the 1972 ABM Treaty and its declared intent to build a National Missile Defense System. Russia and China had been vociferous critics of reneging on the ABM Treaty, with Putin and President Jiang Zemin in July 2000 issuing a joint statement to the effect that it would lead to 'distortions of the balance of power,' but now Putin had muted his opposition.[6] Nationalists wondered if there was anything left for Putin to concede.

IMMEDIATE REACTIONS TO 9/11 BY PUTIN AND HIS MINISTERS

Putin condemned the events of September 11, announced Russia's support for the US anti-terrorist drive and declared that the Commonwealth of Independent States (CIS) must unite to fight terrorism.[7] In line with Putin's emphasis on cooperation with the USA, even Defense Minister Sergei Ivanov softened his earlier hostility due to events in Kosovo. After the planes flew into the Twin Towers, Ivanov telephoned Rice and US Secretary of Defense Donald Rumsfeld to give his condolences.[8] On television on 24 September, Putin then offered Russian cooperation, intelligence and airspace for humanitarian aid in the operation against the Taliban and al-Qaeda. He also volunteered to coordinate with Central Asian states ready to give their airspace.[9] 9/11 and the subsequent bombing of Afghanistan gave Putin a platform to indicate a commitment to broader changes in Russian–US relations. He toned down his opposition to NATO enlargement and announced a reduction of Russian troops in the Balkans. He also increased support for the Northern Alliance in Afghanistan.

On official visits Putin expressed his desire for Russia to be seen as a great European power and advocated a common security space in Europe.[10] In October, in a speech in fluent German to the Bundestag, Putin announced the importance of incorporating Russia into European economic, political and defense structures.[11] Again in October, he went to Brussels for an EU–Russian summit and for discussions at NATO headquarters. Here Putin indicated that Russia might reassess opposition to NATO expansion given the need for a global anti-terrorism coalition. Although he made clear that NATO had no need to expand since Russia was not a threat, he stressed that if NATO adapted to take due account of Russia's interests, then relations could improve.[12] The consistent message for Western leaders was that Russia was a self-sufficient state, capable of defending itself. Putin repeatedly conveyed that Russia was not asking to join NATO but rather sought common ground with it.

Putin agreed to monthly Russia–EU meetings on foreign and defense policy and supported a NATO proposal for a new body to oversee 'a widening and deepening' of relations.[13] Putin took advantage of every visit to Western Europe to stress how important the issue of global terrorism was to Russia, how he was ready to provide serious help in combating it, and how Russia should be consulted on matters of European security. He was not slow to point out that Russia had experience of terrorism in Chechnia and Daghestan, as well as bomb blasts in Moscow in 1999, so knew its destructive power too. He told reporters that bombings of Moscow apartments carried 'the same signature' as plane attacks in the USA.[14] Putin wanted Western leaders to get the message that terrorists in Chechnia had links with international terrorists. In return for his cooperation, he wanted better understanding in the West of what was happening in Chechnia.

Putin emphasized the importance of tackling terrorism whether in Chechnia or in Afghanistan with military might. When, for instance, British Prime Minister Tony Blair met Putin for the eighth time in Moscow in October 2001, Putin told him that, 'I have no doubt at all that military action can be effective. The foremost condition is the making of an effective alliance of countries to combat this problem and to keep it going for a long time.'[15] Putin made his backing clear and engaged in a flurry of diplomatic visits in Europe, the USA and China. His November summit on Bush's Texan ranch was given extensive publicity worldwide. As part of their strategic rapprochement, they agreed to make huge reductions in nuclear arsenals. US stockpiles would be cut from around 6,500 to between 1,700 and 2,200 and Russian ones from 6,000 to about 1,500. Bush emphasized that no treaty was needed, a cause of subsequent concern to Russian leaders. Constant diplomatic chiseling from Russia eventually prompted Bush to concede a treaty. This was one benefit which Putin managed to extract from Bush to which the US leader would not otherwise have agreed. Bush also indicated that he would work towards the repeal of the Jackson–Vanik amendment which imposed trade sanctions on the former USSR.[16] At the time of writing, this has yet to come to fruition.

Putin kept up his message on terrorism, reiterating to Bush in late October at the Shanghai summit that the fight required 'united efforts' and went so far as to say that agreement could be reached on problems thrown up by US plans for a missile defense system, which hitherto Russia had vociferously opposed.[17] Then in an interview in Greece in December, Putin declared improved relations with the USA to be a 'strategic policy.' He even dismissed concerns about closer US ties with Central Asian states and about US presence in the region.[18] Putin was calm about the USA's withdrawal from the ABM Treaty, but critical. He said it did not surprise him, but it was a 'mistake.' Prime Minister Mikhail Kasyanov reiterated this, with the words 'Russia will regret, but not worry about such a move.'[19] Putin's main concern about the USA withdrawing from the treaty were its strategic consequences. As he put it: 'the world cannot afford a legal vacuum in strategic stability.'[20] Above all, Putin wanted a new legal framework to define strategic relations. Whether in Brussels, Bonn, Athens, Bush's ranch in Texas, or Shangai, Putin seemed with each foreign visit to be more accommodating to the West. In December 2001, Foreign Minister Ivanov summed up 2001 as 'the year of Russia's return to the international arena as a key player.' Russia had improved relations with the USA, cemented links with China, India and Japan and made diplomacy visible in South America and Africa.[21]

Putin simultaneously played an active part in the conflict in Afghanistan by stepping up his support for the Northern Alliance. He met with some of its leadership in October in Tajikistan to discuss Russian military assistance and the future Afghan government.[22] Russia had long been a supplier of the Northern Alliance and now this came out into the open. This deal was estimated to be worth $40–$70 million.[23] Russian troops also became active inside Afghanistan, although this was publicly denied. In September 2001, Russian troops, tanks and military equipment were moved to the Tajik/Afghan border. The Russian 201st Motorized Rifle Division threw pontoon bridges across the Pyandzh river and with the help of Russian airpower fought to defend the bridgeheads against the Taliban. By October, Russian special forces were on the ground inside

Afghanistan with the task of pinpointing targets for bombs to destroy Osama bin Laden's mountain strongholds.[24]

Cooperation with the USA was not at the expense of Russia's relations with China. Putin was in regular contact with Jiang Zemin and informed him of the details of his US visit. The two reiterated their shared views on the ABM Treaty and of the need for the UN to play an active role in Afghanistan.[25] They, or their ministers, met regularly at meetings of the Shanghai Cooperation Organization (SCO) or 'Shanghai Six' (Russia, China, Kazakhstan, Uzbekistan, Kyrgyzstan and Tajikistan) and issued agreed statements on regional developments. At a meeting of SCO foreign ministers in January 2002, Ivanov announced support for Afghanistan becoming a neutral state and for the UN Security Council coordinating the struggle against international terrorism.[26] Prior to an SCO summit in June 2002 in Petersburg, Putin had talks with Jiang about his May summit with Bush and about recent summits on NATO and the EU.[27] The SCO became a fully-fledged international organization with a legal charter on 7 June. It created a joint anti-terrorism structure, to be based in Kyrgyzstan. Putin commented that 'we bear a special responsibility for security and stability in Central Asia.'[28]

On the subject of Afghanistan's future, Putin had met the Northern Alliance leadership opposition in Tajikistan in October.[29] By December, Russia prided itself on being the only state with a fully-fledged program of humanitarian aid in operation, with centers along the northern border of Afghanistan from which to transport goods.[30] Then after a visit to Kabul in February 2002, in which Foreign Minister Igor Ivanov met Hamid Karzai, head of Afghanistan's provisional administration, Ivanov announced that Russia would play an active role in developing Afghanistan and re-building the economy.[31] In February 2002, Defense Minister Sergei Ivanov excluded Russian involvement in developing the Afghan army, however, with the words 'They have been at war for 20 years – how can we teach them to fight?'[32]

Throughout these early reactions to 9/11, Foreign Minister Ivanov played a predictable diplomatic role, in line with Putin's priorities. On NATO expansion, according to US Secretary of State Colin Powell, Ivanov told him that Russia now has better relations with Poland, Hungary and the Czech Republic as members of NATO than when they were in the Warsaw Pact.[33] Ivanov, however, subsequently criticized the '19 plus one formula,' of 19 states plus Russia, arguing for equality and joint approaches.[34] He favored an 'upgrading' of Russia's relations with NATO and responded positively to Tony Blair's proposal for closer NATO–Russia cooperation and to Italian Prime Minister Silvio Berlusconi's subsequent backing.[35] Russia's responses to 9/11 and to war in Afghanistan set the backdrop to NATO's attempts to make Russian leaders feel more involved in NATO's decision-making process.

In December 2001, foreign ministers from nineteen NATO member states and from Russia met in Brussels to create a NATO–Russia Permanent Joint Council, an independent decision-making body, not a consultative one.[36] US Secretary of State Colin Powell visited Moscow in December and emphasized how Russia would participate in NATO's governing bodies, even though it was not a member.[37] Russian discontent about NATO, however, festered. In February 2002, NATO effectively acknowledged this by offering to form a new NATO–Russia Council (NRC), replacing the PJC.[38] At first Ivanov grumbled that he was unsure how this differed from the PJC since Russia still lacked a veto.[39] Finally, the NRC was depicted as twenty, or *dvadtsatka*, rather than 19+1 and was discussed by foreign ministers in Reykjavik in mid-May and formalized on 28 May near Rome.[40] Prior to that, in March, the Russian government had set up a working group to coordinate anti-terror work with NATO.[41]

Both Russia's role in NATO and the US withdrawal from the ABM Treaty were issues, however, which preoccupied the Russian defense minister. In December 2001, Ivanov had indicated that he supported a 'continuation of Russia's dialogue with the USA on the status of the ABM Treaty.'[42] Later in December, Ivanov attended a meeting of the PJC and also met Rumsfeld to consider the significance of US–Russian relations in light of US withdrawal from the ABM Treaty.[43] Ivanov told Russian commanders of the Strategic Missile Forces that forces would be both reduced and modernized.[44] On the controversial topic of the US presence in Central Asia, Ivanov actually told the press in February 2002 that this was 'positive' for Russia since it stopped 'the Taliban threat' spilling over Russia's borders. What mattered was that the US presence was only temporary and that 'they will leave once the operation is finished.'[45] In Rome, Ivanov also said that although chemical and biological weapons could be used in future terrorist attacks, Russian leaders were also worried about 'information terrorism' in which computer pirates could attack electronic databases and telecommunications channels, thereby paralyzing stock exchanges, financial institutions and national television channels.[46]

As one of the harshest critics of NATO's bombing of Kosovo, Ivanov was predictably quick to respond to Bush's remarks about North Korea, Iraq and Iran constituting an 'axis of evil.' Speaking in Rome in February 2002 at a conference of NATO defense ministers, Ivanov stressed that Russia was united with the anti-terrorism coalition, but that Moscow had different goals in the second stage of action. He reiterated his dislike of Bush's conception of an 'axis of evil' and informed listeners that 'Russia is supplying conventional weapons to Iran and will continue to do so because it is a normal commercial deal.'[47] In keeping with its good relations with so-called 'rogue states,' in December 2001 the Duma had also ratified a friendship treaty with Iran which provided for expanding military-technical and economic cooperation, including the supply of nuclear reactors.[48] The Duma did not, however, approve a proposal by the reformers in the *Yabloko* (Apple) fraction to write to the US Congress to express the Russian parliament's disapproval at US withdrawal from the ABM Treaty.[49] Vladimir Zhirinovskii actually argued that the US action could be beneficial to Russia since it 'unties our hands.'[50]

Notwithstanding concern about Bush's remarks on 'rogue states,' Putin proved to be a loyal coalition member. He reiterated Russia's resolve to combat terrorism after an explosion disrupted a Victory Day parade in Kaspiisk, Daghestan, in

May 2002, leaving 42 dead and more than 130 wounded. Putin condemned the 'scum' behind it and called for unity against international terrorism.[51] The Chechen leadership denied their rumoured involvement while authorities in Daghestan appealed to Putin to reinstate the death penalty for the culprits. In June, a controversial bill on extremism passed its first reading in the Duma, preceded by protests from human rights' activists.[52] Islamic leaders in Russia, however, urged Putin to accelerate his battle against international terrorism and to cleanse Russia of Wahhabism – whose adherents, they claimed, constituted a bunch of 'pseudo-Islamic provocateurs.'[53]

Putin's pledge to fight terrorism was reiterated with some pain after special troops on the 26 October 2002 stormed a Moscow theater that fifty armed Chechens had occupied on the 23rd and had taken around 800 people hostage, demanding a withdrawal of Russian troops from Chechnia.[54] Putin quickly asserted that the siege had been planned in 'foreign terrorist centers,' which Movsar Baraev, leader of the siege, denied.[55] Putin insisted that Russia would make no 'understandings' with terrorists and pledged preparedness to use the army to combat world terrorism.[56] Putin dubbed 23 October 'Russia's September 11' and portrayed himself as a world leader alongside Bush in tackling global terror.[57] He ordered a revision of Russia's national security policy and Sergei Ivanov called for greater flexibility for the armed forces in dealing with terrorism.[58]

REACTIONS ACROSS POLITICAL PARTIES

Support for Putin's reactions to 9/11 came from liberals and centrists, but was harshly criticized by the Communist Party of the Russian Federation (KPRF) and endured switching lines from nationalist Zhirinovskii.

Grigorii Yavlinskii, a liberal reformer and leader of *Yabloko*, agreed that 'Russia must unite with the anti-terrorist actions of the USA. She herself suffers from terrorism.'[59] Yavlinskii concluded that there would be no minuses for Russia, although he foresaw 'a flood' of refugees and insisted that 'the participation of Russian soldiers is out of the question. America will come out of the war having lost little. We will be left with an even greater duty, with a discontented people, with a sapped economy.'[60] *Yabloko*'s Democratic Manifesto of December 2001 included a section on 'Security and the Struggle with Terrorism.' It held that politics alone could not triumph over this 'evil,' but military action had to be under civil leadership and strict parliamentary and societal control.[61] *Soiuz Pravykh Sil* (SPS, Union of Right Forces), slightly to the right of *Yabloko*, held a similar position. Viktor Pokhmelkin, deputy leader of the fraction in the Duma, argued that 'Russia must participate in the action of retribution.' But the coalition 'can have no leaders' but should be based on 'the principle of equal cooperation of all countries.'[62]

Boris Nemtsov, one of SPS's leaders, held that the weaker the Taliban became, the stronger Russia would be, because it was the only regime in the world that supported the production of heroin, bringing death to young Russians.[63] Irina Khakamada, also a co-leader, pointed out that in the past Russia had supported the Northern Alliance and now continued to do so openly. She favored giving the Alliance arms, but also spoke out against sending in Russian troops. Khakamada stressed that agreement with the USA was needed to avoid a 'repeat of the Gorbachev era, under which as future allies, we never participated in making decisions.'[64] She pressed for Russia to be an equal, even if this meant joining NATO. Centrists echoed these concerns.

Aleksandr Gurov, a leader of *Edinstvo* (Unity) argued that Russia had more than once asked the world community to fight terrorism, but hitherto they had ignored it.[65] Speaking for the combined centrist movement *Otechestvo–Vsia Rossiia* (Fatherland–All Russia), Konstantin Kocachev agreed that a stand had to be taken stressing that a neutral regime in Afghanistan would best suit Russia's interests and also that there should be no double standards. Implicit was the point that terrorism in Chechnia was as unacceptable as the terrorist attacks of 9/11.[66] Sergei Kovalev of Fatherland–All Russia was more cautious. In his view, bombing Afghanistan was 'the crudest strategic error.'[67] In December 2001, the three centrist groups of *Edinstvo*, *Otechestvo* and *Vsia Rossiia* merged into a new centrist political party.[68] In February they each formally dissolved and formed *Edinaia Rossiia*, or Unified Russia.[69] This large centrist bloc in the Duma more or less automatically supports Putin's policies.

Those on the 'left' of Russian politics were more critical. Arguing against Russia's involvement in Afghanistan, Nikolai Kharitonov of the Agro-Industrial deputies group, indicated that the USA might withdraw quickly, leaving Russia as a 'new victim,' tied up in conflict. It was more important to annihilate bases which trained Chechen terrorists.[70] One of the loudest voices against Russia's involvement in Afghanistan was that of communist Ziuganov who lambasted Putin for his 'pro-American' foreign policy. In November, Ziuganov published his open letter to Putin before the President's flight to meet with Bush. He argued that a turnaround had occurred in Russian foreign policy, beginning in the spring of 2000, when Putin had pushed ratification of START II through the Duma, although it was not approved in the US Congress. Subsequent steps amounted to a return to a shameful pro-Western Kozyrev-style foreign policy. Andrei Kozyrev had been Russia's foreign minister from 1990 to 1996, much criticized by nationalists and communists. The expansion of NATO caused 'alarm' amongst Russians, but Putin's recent speeches in Vienna and in Helsinki could be taken as accepting the admission of Latvia, Lithuania, Estonia, Austria, Finland and Sweden.[71]

Ziuganov charged that Russia had denied support to the Balkans, given tacit agreement to the abduction of Milosevic, striven to remove Russian troops from Georgia and Prednestr, 'ignoring the interests of Russians, made victims of discrimination in the post-Soviet space.'[72] Putin had also decided to close bases in Vietnam and Cuba, yet agreed to temporary US bases in Uzbekistan and Tajikistan. Zuiganov warned that 'soon no geopolitical homefront will remain for Russia.'[73] In the background was the continued destruction of the Russian army. It was senseless, held Ziuganov, sharply to cut back on weapons whilst the USA was creating a new anti-missile defense system. In sum, Putin's foreign policy represented the 'third stage of treason of national interests' after Gorbachev and Yeltsin.[74] How, Ziuganov asked, would the USA feel if Russian forces billeted themselves in Mexico?[75] In February 2002, Ziuganov's message became 'liberal fascism is more terrible than nazism.'[76]

Nationalist opinion stressed above all the importance of Russian interests. Initially, Vladimir Zhirinovskii insisted that Russia should remain neutral.[77] Next he held that 'most important – is to try to keep Central Asia under Russia's influence.'[78] He maintained that it was not in Russia's interests to get mixed up with armed conflict begun by the USA and NATO. Zhirinovskii contended that if globalization meant that all the world had to work for America, then this was 'bad' and did not 'suit' Russia.[79]

In Washington in December, however, Zhirinovskii had another message to deliver. He told the National Press Club that the ABM Treaty and START accords were 'obsolete' and needed to be renegotiated. He also declared that NATO's founding documents should be rewritten to include Russia. He advocated that the USA, NATO and Russia should share responsibility for the world's trouble spots since they were the key military powers. He held that Russia's ties with Iraq, Iran and North Korea were advantageous to the USA in its fight against terrorism. He also revealed that he regretted his previous anti-American sentiments.[80] Then, remarkably, in a speech to his party congress in December 2001, Zhirinovskii suggested that delegates change the anti-Americanism and anti-Western provisions in the party program and instead join the coalition with 'Europe, North America and NATO.' He failed to persuade his supporters to make this volte-face official after ten years of the opposite line.[81]

Political parties, then, exhibited a wide range of views about Putin's leadership, how best to combat world terrorism and the significance of changing geo-politics. Divisions were also evident in public opinion, but more on some issues than others.

PUBLIC OPINION

Public opinion showed great sympathy for the Americans after 9/11, but revealed concern about the US presence in Central Asia, reluctance to take on the so-called 'axis of evil' and fluctuating attitudes on friendship with the USA.

In a nationwide survey of 24–29 September 2001, 80 percent of citizens considered that the attacks on the Twin Towers concerned all of humanity, 15 percent thought they were an internal affair of the USA and 5 percent did not know. Fifty-three percent believed that repeat attacks were possible in other countries, 27 percent disagreed and 20 percent did not know.[82]

Another nationwide survey of September 2001 asked respondents what they thought Russia's position should be in a conflict between NATO and opponents in the Muslim world (namely Afghanistan, Iran and Iraq). The majority – 54 percent – wanted Russia to remain neutral and maintain good relations with both. Only

9 percent favored military operations alongside NATO. Twenty percent backed moral support for NATO, with a break in relations with the others. A small 5 percent advocated backing for Muslim states. Most Russians did not want to see their country drawn into broader confrontations, and certainly not with longstanding friends.[83]

There was also anxiety about the strengthening of the US presence in Central Asia. A nationwide survey of January 2002 found 26 percent of respondents 'definitely worried,' 37 percent 'somewhat worried' (making 63 percent overall 'worried'), 19 percent 'not too worried', and 5 percent 'not worried at all' (making 24 percent overall 'not worried'), and 13 percent with no clear view.[84] Thus more were concerned than indifferent, whatever Putin said.

Attitudes towards the USA showed fluctuation in the first half of 2002. In March, across forty–four regions, one poll indicated that only 17 percent of Russians saw the USA as 'friendly,' with 71 percent holding the opposite view.[85] Another poll of late March revealed 37 percent described the USA as an 'ally' and 38 percent perceived it as an 'opponent.'[86] These two polls, however, came after the Russian defeat in figure skating at the Winter Olympic Games, which went down badly in Russia. In late April, another nationwide poll showed 4 percent of Russians feeling 'very good' about the USA and 55 percent 'basically good.' In contrast, 26 percent felt 'bad', 7 percent 'very bad' and 8 percent were undecided.[87]

Attitudes about Russia participating in any action to topple Saddam Hussein remained hostile. In a poll of March 2002, 42 percent of respondents wanted Russia to remain in the anti-terrorism coalition, but to stay on the sidelines in any operation against Iraq. Four percent advocated military backing for Iraq, 16 percent favored opposing the USA and giving diplomatic help to Iraq, 14 percent were ready to 'support but not participate' in US action and only 1 percent backed any Russian involvement with the USA.[88] Russian support then for bombing in Afghanistan far outweighed advocacy of challenging Hussein.

After Bush's visit to Moscow in May, two nationwide polls were conducted which asked what respondents thought brought Russia and the USA together and what pushed them apart. Fifty-one percent of those approached thought that the joint struggle against international terrorism brought them together. Twenty eight percent believed that mutually beneficial trade was behind it. Personal contacts for study, work and leisure was a reason given by 18 percent, as were peacekeeping and attempts to stop conflicts around the world. Sixteen percent named scientific and technological change and 15 percent cited fights against diseases and pollution. Various other replies attracting less than 10 percent of mentions totaled 30 percent. A pessimistic 10 percent declared that nothing brought them together and 8 percent did not know.[89]

In reflecting upon what pushed Russia and the USA apart, most respondents in May 2002 blamed what they perceived as different negative aspects of the behavior of US leaders and of US culture.[90] Thirty-eight percent blamed the high-handed attitude of Americans to other states and peoples, 36 percent noted the striving by the US authorities to widen their power and control of the world,

32 percent pointed to the refusal by US authorities to consider others' interests, 26 percent condemned the US style of wielding a 'big stick' (i.e. troops and bombs) and 25 percent stressed the large gap between the two countries' levels of economic development and military power. A lower 11 percent indicated the low-grade quality of US popular culture, another 11 percent pointed out that despite its wealth the USA was not interested in helping poor countries and 10 percent put the blame on the legacy of the Cold War and Russia's isolation from the world. Twenty-one percent gave 'other' reasons. Three percent declared that nothing pushed the two countries apart and 9 percent did not know. In both surveys, respondents could cite more than one reason.

Noticeable is that most respondents did not name Russian behavior or attitudes as a reason for creating a gulf between the two states. Only 10 percent mentioned Russia's isolation from the rest of the world, coupled with the legacy of the Cold War. Implicitly, then, Russia always favored good relations, only thwarted by US attempts to rule the world and not consider others. The reponse to the age-old Russian question of '*kto vinovat*'?, or who is to blame, was overwhelmingly, 'not Russia'.

As Bush's enthusiasm for war against Iraq grew, Russians remained skeptical. In a poll of September 2002, only 2 percent of respondents backed participation alongside the USA and 19 percent favored 'support but not participate.' Forty-one percent wanted to remain on the sidelines and 18 percent wanted to help Iraq. But only 2 percent advocated military help for Iraq and an indecisive 18 percent were unsure.[91] There was also 28 percent uncertainty about the justification for US military action against Iraq if Sadddam Hussein did not accede to the demands of the UN concerning weapons of mass destruction. Eight percent of respondents 'definitely' supported US action in this event, 20 percent 'probably,' 14 percent 'definitely not' and 31 percent 'probably not.'[92] Evidently, Russians were becoming more unsure.

MEDIA DEBATE

In Moscow in April 2002, round-table talks took place to discuss the anti-terrorism coalition after six months. The view that there was no partnership between the USA and Russia was bluntly put by General Leonid Ivashov, deputy director of the Academy of geopolitical problems.[93] This was echoed by Aleksandr Shabanov, deputy chair of the Duma's Foreign Affairs Committee, who held that since the USA was dominant in the world, equal relations were not possible.[94] Aleksei Arbatov, now deputy chair of the Duma Defense Committee and a member of the *Yabloko* faction, argued against having bad relations with the USA but cautioned against an 'America-centric' policy. He propounded that Russia should have good relations with a mix of countries, including Japan, India, South Korea and the EU, states whose leaders would also criticize the USA when necessary.[95] Viacheslav Nikonov of the Politika Foundation regretted that Russia lacked a cohesive strategy for relations with the West since its leaders were unsure of what they wanted.[96]

Articles critical of Putin's foreign policy had been increasingly visible in the Russian press since January.[97] The general complaint was that Russian leaders had made more concessions to the USA than they had reaped. Leonid Radzikhovskii in *Vremia MN*, like Shabanov after him, added that Russia could not be an equal partner of the USA since their GDPs were so different. But the USA, so it seemed to Radzikhovskii, was not keen to make Russia a 'lesser partner' either. The real disagreement was that 'Russia needs Western investments, and the West does not give them.'[98] Some, such as Mikhail Margelov, Chair of the Federation Council's Foreign Relations Committee, suggested that Russia may withdraw from the START II Treaty in response to the US withdrawal from the ABM Treaty.[99] And indeed, in May 2002, it was announced in Moscow that there were preparations to do just that[100] and in June it was formally declared.[101]

The press response in May 2002 to Bush's visit to Russia and to the treaty on arms reductions was generally favorable, but with varying degrees of enthusiasm. Most excited coverage in *Moskovskii Komsomolets* praised the 'new phase' in US–Russian relations, arguing that Putin's 'sharp turn-around' after September 11 was vindicated. It highlighted the 'fantastic luxury' of the meeting in the Kremlin and noted that the lessening of world tensions begun by US President Richard Nixon and Soviet General Secretary Leonid Brezhnev was complete. The question now was not whether the USA and Russia would maintain nuclear parity, but would Russia buy Boeing rather than the European airbus?[102] *Izvestiia* emphasized how Bush was overwhelmed by the cultural trappings of his visits to Petersburg and Moscow, forever turning his head in amazement, and gave coverage to the question and answer session between Bush and students of Petersburg University. One asked him if the USA would make it easier for Russia to join the WTO. Putin interjected 'good question,' and Bush answered 'Yes, I have already told Congress, we need to chuck out the Jackson–Vanik amendment. I vote in favor.'[103]

Krasnaia zvezda lacked the euphoria of *Moskovskii Komsomolets*. None the less, in its factual coverage of events it quoted Bush on the 'historic day' and Russian experts on 'the tranformation of relations.' It did not leave out, however, Putin's remark that 'not all ideas and initiatives' found a form to be agreed on paper. Given criticisms within the defense establishment, one would not have expected jubilation, although overall reporting was perhaps more positive than might have been anticipated.[104] *Nezavisimaia gazeta* was not ecstatic either. Igor Korotchenko wrote a long piece on US–Russian differences over Iran and on US criticisms of Russian–Iranian cooperation, asking whether the interests of the Russian industrial-military complex would prevail.[105] More sarcastically, Aleksandr Nagornyi in *Zavtra* in an article entitled 'The theater of two actors' lambasted the show of the two 'friends,' who shared the same platforms of Gorbachev and Yeltsin and who propped up oligarchic capitalism, typified by Anatolii Chubais. Nagornyi poured scorn on Putin's alleged agreement in private with Bush for the latter's proposed operation against Iraq.[106]

CONCLUSION

In the eyes of his harshest critics, Putin was acquiescing in the global geopolitical weakening of Russia in return for a formal document on arms reductions which merely acknowledged what was happening anyway. For Putin, however, being a participant in the coalition against terrorism meant taking Russia back on the world stage, being seen to be active on issues that mattered and with it gaining some status, influence and respect. The influence, of course, given the USA's overpowering military and economic might, was modest, but it meant that on some matters Russia would be consulted. There was little that US leaders could be persuaded to do that they would not have done anyway, but there was now some scope for making US decision-makers think more about Russian responses than they had before. Bush, for example, had not seen the need for a formal agreement on arms reductions, but due to heavy pressure from Russia, however, conceded a formal document. It seemed somewhat ironic, then, when on 13 May Bush announced, amid huge fanfare, an historic arms agreement between the USA and Russia that would put the Cold War behind them once and for all, that it was a document that initially Bush had not even wanted and in Russia to many it meant one more sell-out that achieved very little for Russia.[107] It was signed in Moscow on 25 May in grand surroundings, amid more back-slapping and with declarations on strategic and energy cooperation and joint statements on economic relations and on the Middle East.[108] Russia and other states in the world also insisted that the USA not dash to war against Iraq before weapons inspectors had done their job and before evidence was found that Iraq was guilty. Putin initially opposed a fresh UN resolution which included a clause permitting war, but finally supported Resolution 1441, although not the subsequent war.

What has Russia gained from its cooperation with the coalition against terrorism? According to Putin's critics, particularly those in the Russian defense establishment, very little. Even if there was greater appreciation in the West of the situation in Chechnia, criticisms of human rights' abuses by Russian troops were still made by the UN, USA and EU.[109] Although Russia has dismantled its Lourdes electronic intelligence center in Cuba, removing all personnel and equipment, NATO enlargement would not halt and Bush would not curtail his plans for a National Missile Defense system.[110] Although Bush and Putin agreed to reduce weapons stockpiles, the USA declared it would not destroy its weapons, merely put them in storage, prompting Russia finally to say that it might do the same.[111] Defense Minister Ivanov told Rumsfeld in Brussels that START II had now lost its significance and that negotiations should work towards START III.

Any hope of acceleration of membership of the WTO was partly dashed by the EU's setting of several conditions which would complicate Russia's membership. Leaders of EU states want Russia to veto any legislation which is not consistent with WTO norms. They are also keen for Russia to stop charging for the use of its airspace. Revenues from Western airlines help to subsidize Aeroflot.[112] Although Bush expressed his backing in Petersburg for overturning the Jackson–Vanik amendment and for working towards Russian entry into the WTO, and notwithstanding the fact that on 22 May the US Senate had passed a non-binding resolution for normal trade relations with Russia, the amendment was not lifted due to a dispute with Russia over US poultry imports. Nationalist critics in Russia now saw the Jackson–Vanik amendment embroiled in political football about chicken legs.[113] It is likely, none the less, to be just a matter of time before Russia is allowed into the WTO. China is reported to back Russian membership, believing that it will boost bilateral trade.[114] In late May, WTO Director-General Mike Moore predicted that Russia would be able to join before September 2003 due to recent progress towards entry, with agricultural issues remaining the barrier.[115] In a nationwide poll in Russia, 54 percent of citizens believed that it was in Russia's interest to join, 18 percent thought it to be against its interests and 28 percent did not know.[116] In June, the US government finally recognized Russia as a fully-fledged market economy, and Bush relayed the news to Putin by telephone. This was one benefit that Bush could deliver and it is likely to increase Russian exports to the USA. It has already boosted the Western demand for shares in Russian companies.[117]

Putin has arguably obtained for Russia as good a deal as he was likely to get from Bush. Russia not only succeeded in securing a treaty on arms reductions and in capitalizing upon Bush's visit to Russia to set the majestic scene for its signing, thereby once more showing off the splendour of the Kremlin and Petersburg to the world's media, but also triggered more efforts in NATO to make Russia feel better consulted through the new NRC. A NATO liaison office was also opened in Moscow in late May.[118] Putin made plain that he wanted Russia to be a member of the WTO and he received Bush's verbal support for this, likely to be fulfilled at some point in the near future. Putin was also quick to play a part in attempting to broker peace between India and Pakistan over Kashmir, a role accepted by members of the G7, a club Putin was anxious to become a regular G8. Given Russia's weak position post-empire and post-USSR, Putin had ended its isolation and marginalization and also boosted its visibility in world diplomacy. He may have wanted more than he obtained, but that was not politically feasible.[119] Although his critics would not concur, he arguably did reasonably well in a very short period of time in reinstating Russia as a serious global actor. In November 2002, agreement was also reached with the EU over the Russian enclave of Kaliningrad, which just three months earlier had appeared a thorny problem. At the meeting, however, Putin showed irritation at questions about Russian military tactics in Chechnia, about which Chris Patten, EU external relations commissioner, said there was no 'meeting of minds.'[120]

Putin is not without his domestic critics, some severe. Most recently, Boris Kagarlitsky has mocked Putin's imitation of US rhetoric about fighting global terrorism as adopting 'an ideological skeleton key' which justifies stepped-up war in Chechnia and also suggests that Russia is not acting alone.[121] Since, however, according to opinion polls, Putin's popularity remains high, it appears that better relations with the USA and NATO have not hurt him. In fact, in May 2002, he climbed back up from 72 to 75 percent popularity and maintained this rating throughout the autumn and into 2003.[122] Putin, moreover, is committed to establishing good relations with many states, from the USA and EU to China, India, Iran and elsewhere. This 'multi-vector' foreign policy holds appeal to centrists, reforming liberals and some patriots. So long as Russia has a wide ideological span, then criticisms from left groups are inevitable, even if they are often merely rhetorical. If Putin can take enough politicians, members of the foreign policy, defense and security establishments with him, and voters too, then his current course is likely to persist, barring international events of which he seriously disapproves.

NOTES

Special thanks are due to Professor Drumond Bone, former Principal of Royal Holloway, for granting sabbatical leave and to John Grimmer.

1   See Mary Buckley, 'Russian Perceptions', in Mary Buckley and Sally Cummings (eds.) *Kosovo: Perceptions of War and its Aftermath* (London: Continuum, 2002), pp. 156–75. Note here the error which wrongly names Russian Defense Minister as Igor Sergeev when it should be Sergei Ivanov.
2   Jury Sigov, 'Friends and Foes', *World Today*, Vol. 57, No. 4, April 2001, pp. 8–9.
3   See, for instance, *New York Times*, 11 May 2001.
4   See Stephen White, Richard Rose and Ian McAllister, *How Russia Votes* (Chatham, NJ: Chatham House Publishers, 1997) and
    http://www.RFE/RL.org/elections/russia99results/index.html, p. 1.
5   Vladimir Putin, *First Person* (London: Hutchinson, 2000), p. 177.
6   Radio Free Europe, Radio Liberty (RFE/RL), *Newsline*, Vol. 4, No. 129, Part I, 7 July 2000, p. 2.
7   Vlad Sobell, 'Russia Turns West', *World Today*, Vol. 57, No. 11, Nov. 2001, pp. 18–19.
8   *Krasnaia zvezda*, 13 Sept. 2001, p. 1.
9   Sobell, 'Russia turns West'.
10 http://www.RFE/RL.org/newsline/2001/10/031001.html
11 http://www.guardian.co.uk/waronterror/story/0,1361,653073,00.html
12 http://www.RFE/RL.org/nca/features/2001/11/221122084257.asp
13 http://www.guardian.co.uk/waronterror/story/0,1361,53073,00html
14 Ibid.
15 http://www.guardian.co.uk/russia/article/0,2763,563766,00.html
16 *The Independent*, 14 Nov. 2001, p. 8.
17 http://www.guardian.co.uk/russia/article/0,2763,578472,00.html
18 RFE/RL, *Newsline*, Vol. 5, No. 230, Part I, 6 Dec. 2001, p. 1.
19 Ibid., Vol. 5, No. 235, Part I, 13 Dec. 2001, p. 1.
20 Ibid., Vol. 5, No. 236, Part I, 14 Dec. 2001, p. 1.
21 Ibid., Vol. 6, No. 1, Part I, 3 Jan. 2002, p. 2.
22 http://www.guardian.co.uk/russia/article/0,2763,578468,00.html
23 Ibid., /0,2763,579009,00.html
24 For reports, see:
    http://www.guardian.co.uk/international/story/0%2C555510%2C00.html
    http://www.hindustantimes.com/Nonfram/041001/dlame65.asp
    http://www.csmonitor.com/2001/1015/p13s1-wosc.html
    http://www.rediff.com/us/2001/sep/29ny8.htm
25 RFE/RL, *Newsline*, Vol. 5, No. 220, Part I, 20 Nov. 2001, p. 2.
26 Ibid., Vol. 6, No. 3, Part I, 7 Jan. 2002, p. 2.

27 Ibid., Vol. 6, No. 106, Part I, 7 June 2002, p. 2.
28 Ibid.
29 http:www.guardian.co.uk/russia/article/0,2763,578468,00.html
30 RFE/RL, *Newsline*, Vol. 5, No. 229, Part I, 5 Dec. 2001, p. 2.
31 Ibid., Vol. 6, No. 23, Part I, 5 Feb. 2002, p. 2.
32 Ibid., Vol. 6, No. 29, Part I, 13 Feb. 2002, p. 1.
33 http//www.RFE/RL.org/nca/features/2001/10/26102001093516.asp
34 http://www.RFE/RL.org/nca/features/2001/11/21112001092005.asp
35 http://www.RFE/RL.org/nca/features/2001/11/21112001013001.asp
    RFE/RL, *Newsline*, Vol. 5, No. 220, Part I, 20 Nov. 2001, p. 1. In talks in Paris in
    January 2002 with President Chirac, Putin also stressed how he wanted to improve
    economic and political relations with the EU. In February, Putin said he supported the
    idea of inviting heads of EU states to St. Petersburg for the city's celebration of its
    300-year anniversary. See RFE/RL, *Newsline*, Vol. 6, No. 25, Part I, 7 Feb. 2002, p. 3.
36 Ibid., Vol. 5, No. 231, Part I, 7 Dec. 2001, p. 1.
37 Ibid., Vol. 5, No. 232, Part I, 10 Dec. 2001, p. 2.
38 Ibid., Vol. 6, No. 50, Part I, 15 March 2002, p. 2.
39 Ibid., Vol. 6, No. 47, Part I, 12 March 2002, p. 2.
40 *The Independent*, 29 May 2002, p. 10.
41 RFE/RL, *Newsline*, Vol. 6, No. 59, Part I, 28 March 2001, p. 2.
42 Ibid., Vol. 5, No. 229, Part I, 5 Dec. 2001, p. 1.
43 Ibid., Vol. 5, No. 238, Part I, 18 Dec. 2001, p. 1.
44 Ibid.
45 Ibid., Vol. 6, No. 29, Part I, 13 Feb. 2002, p. 1.
46 Ibid., Vol. 6, No. 23, Part I, 5 Feb. 2002, p. 1.
47 Ibid., Vol. 6, No. 23, Part I, 5 Feb. 2002, p. 1.
48 Ibid., Vol. 5, No. 240, Part I, 20 Dec. 2001, p. 1.
49 Ibid., Vol. 5, No. 237, Part I, 17 Dec. 2001, p. 1.
50 Ibid., p. 2.
51 RFE/RL, *Newsline*, Vol. 6, No. 86, Part I, 9 May 2002, p. 1; ibid., No. 87, Part I,
    10 May 2002, p. 1; ibid., No. 88, Part I, 13 May 2002, p. 2.
52 Ibid., Vol. 6, No. 107, Part I, 10 June 2002, p. 2; ibid., Vol. 6. No. 104, Part I, 5 June
    2002, p. 4.
53 Ibid., Vol. 6, No. 100, Part I, 30 May 2002, p. 2.
54 *Izvestiia*, 24 and 25 Oct. 2002, p. 1.
55 Ibid, 25 Oct.
56 *Izvestiia*, 31 Oct. 2002; RFE/RL, *Newsline*, Vol. 6, No. 204, Part 1, 29 Oct. 2002,
    p. 1.
57 *Itogi*, 5 Nov. 2002.
58 *Izvestiia*, 28 Oct. 2002; ibid., 4 Nov. 2002.
59 *Rossiiskaia Federatsiia Segodnia*, No. 21, 2001, p. 20.
60 Ibid.
61 http://www.yabloko.ru/Union/Program/manifest–2001-proj.html, p. 6.
62 *Rossiiskaia Federatsiia Segodnia*, No. 21, 2001, p. 21.
63 Radio interview, *Ekho Moskvy*, 8 Oct. 2001 at:
    http://www.nemtsov.ru/media/interview.phtml?date=2001–10–08
64 http://www.sps.ru/sps/16637
65 *Rossiiskaia Federatsiia Segodnia*, No. 21, 2001, p. 5.
66 Ibid., No. 21, 2001, p. 6.
67 http://www.RFE/RL.org/newsline/2001/10/031001.html
68 http://www.ntvru.com/russia/01Dec2001/ed_ot.html
69 *Nezavisimaia gazeta*, 11 Feb. 2002, p. 4.
70 *Rossiiskaia Federatsiia Segodnia*, No. 21, 2001, p. 6.
71 http://zavtra.ru/cgi//veil//data/zavtra/o1/415/11.html, p. 1.

72 Ibid.
73 Ibid.
74 'V Vashingtone voskhishcheny, v Moskve negoduiut',
    http://www.kprf.ru/komment.htm; RFE/RL, *Newsline*, Vol. 6, No. 26, Part I, 8 Feb.
    2002, p. 1.
75 http://www.kprf.ru/komment.htm.11.21.01, p. 1.
76 http://www.kprf.ru/news/press.asp
77 http://www.RFE/RL.org/newsline/2001/10/031001.asp
78 *Rossiiskaia Federatsiia Segodnia*, No. 21, 2001, p. 5.
79 Ibid.
80 RFE/RL, *Newsline*, Vol. 5, No. 229, Part I, 5 Dec. 2001, pp. 1–2.
81 Ibid., Vol. 5, No. 236, Part I, 14 Dec. 2001, p. 2.
82 http://www.russiavotes.org/terror.htm, p. 1.
83 Nationwide VCIOM survey, 24–29 Sept. 2001, N=1,600, at:
    http://www.russiavotes.org/terror.htm
84 Ibid., 25–28 Jan. 2002, N=1,600.
85 RFE/RL, *Newsline*, Vol. 6, No. 46, Part I, 11 March 2002, p. 2.
86 Nationwide VCIOM surveys, 22–25 March 2002, N=1,600 at:
    http://www.russiavotes.org/Mood_intnl_cur.htm, p. 3.
87 Ibid., 19–22 April 2002, N=1,603, p. 2.
88 Ibid., 22–25 March 2002, N=1,600, p. 1.
89 http://www.russiavotes.org/Mood_intnl_cur.htm
90 Ibid., nationwide VCIOM surveys, 24–27 May 2002, N=1,600.
91 Ibid., 20–23 Sept. 2002, N=1,600.
92 Ibid.
93 http://www.RFE/RL.org/nca/features/2002/04/04042002081008.asp, p. 1.
94 Ibid.
95 Ibid., pp. 2–3. See, too, http://www.strana.ru/stories/01/10/08/1714/68634.html
96 http://www.RFE/RL.org/nca/features/2002/04/04042002081008.asp, p. 2.
97 See, for instance, *Izvestiia*, 18 Oct. 2001, pp. 1 and 4; *Vremia Novostei*, 19 Oct. 2001,
    p. 3.
98 RFE/RL, *Newsline*, Vol. 6, No. 19, Part I, 30 Jan. 2002, p. 3.
99 Ibid., Vol. 5, No. 237, Part I, 17 Dec. 2001, p. 1.
100 Ibid., Vol. 6, No. 97, Part I, 24 May 2002, p. 2.
101 The Russian Foreign Ministry declared that the USA had not yet ratified START II
     and this had been one of the conditions of Russian acceptance. See ibid.,Vol. 6, No.
     111., Part I, 14 June 2002, p. 2.
102 *Moskovskii Komsomolets*, 26 May 2002.
103 *Izvestiia*, 26 May 2002.
104 *Krasnaia zvezda*, 25 May 2002.
105 *Nezavisimaia gazeta*, 24 May 2002, p. 1.
106 *Zavtra*, 29 May 2002.
107 BBC News, 13 May 2002, 22.00 hours.
108 *Izvestiia*, 26 May 2002, p. 1; http://www.vip.lenta.ru/26.05.2002
109 See, for instance, RFE/RL, *Newsline*, Vol. 6, No. 74, Part I, 19 April 2002, p. 2.
110 Ibid., Vol. 6, No. 17, Part I, 28 Jan. 2002, p. 3.
111 Ibid., Vol. 6, No. 50, Part I, 15 March 2002, p. 2.
112 Ibid., Vol. 6, No. 17, Part I, 28 Jan. 2002, p. 3.
113 Ibid., Vol. 6, No. 96, Part I, 23 May 2002, p. 1.
114 Ibid., Vol. 6, No. 105, Part I, 6 June 2002, p. 2.
115 Ibid., Vol. 6, No. 99, Part I, 29 May 2002, p. 2.
116 Nationwide VCIOM surveys, 19–22 April 2002, N=1,603 at:
     http://www.russiavotes.org/Mood_intnl_cur.htm, p. 1.
117 Ibid., Vol. 6, No. 106, Part I, 7 June 2002, p. 1.

118 RFE/RL, *Newsline*, Vol. 6, No. 98, Part I, 28 May 2002, p. 2.
119 For discussion of Kaliningrad, refer to ibid.,Vol. 6, No. 90, Part I, 15 May 2002, p. 3;
     ibid., Vol. 6, No. 93, Part I, 20 May 2002, p. 3;
     http://www.RFE/RL.org/nca/features/2002/04/24042002085513.asp
120 *The Guardian*, 12 Nov. 2002, p. 16.
121 http://www.RFE/RL.org/nca/features/2002/11/05112002161104asp
122 See http://www.russiavotes.org/Putinperf.htm

20 Negotiating the US presence

The Central Asian states

Sally N. Cummings

George W. Bush's 20 September statement that 'Every nation in every region now has a decision to make. Either you are with us or you are with the terrorists' had perhaps no greater immediate significance than for Central Asia. The unfolding US campaign against terrorism has catapulted the region to newly enhanced strategic importance. To different degrees all five Central Asian states – Kazakhstan, Kyrgyzstan, Tajikistan, Turkmenistan and Uzbekistan – have supported the fight against terrorism. The implications are profound and comprehensive as the region now suffers greater insecurity and increased vulnerability.

The five leaderships' practical offers of support have differed. While all proposed assistance in intelligence and air transport, three states – Kyrgyzstan, Tajikistan and Uzbekistan – have actually housed US troops and are viewed as the front-line states in the war in Afghanistan. The USA established a major operations base at Khanabad airbase outside Tashkent in Uzbekistan, from where it regionally ran the air war in northern Afghanistan. In southern Tajikistan, French aircraft are using the Kuliab airbase. Eleven coalition countries have set up a 1,500-man base at Manas airport in Bishkek, Kyrgyzstan, even though Kyrgyzstan does not have a border with Afghanistan. US officials have surveyed the airbase in Chimkent, in southern Kazakhstan, and US Air Force aircraft as of early July 2002 is permitted to land and refuel at Astana airport.[1] Even officially neutral Turkmenistan, which along with Uzbekistan and Tajikistan borders Afghanistan, has offered its territory as a primary humanitarian transit point. Notes Ahmed Rashid: 'This marks the first arrival of Western armies since Alexander the Great conquered the region in 334 BC.'[2]

For Central Asia, the impact of Afghanistan's failed state began well before 9/11. Two decades of conflict in Afghanistan had already had a major impact on the region which had borne a heavy number of casualties. In more recent years, the Islamic Movement of Uzbekistan (IMU), which is supported by the Taliban, has carried out incursions into Uzbekistan and Kyrgyzstan from bases in Afghanistan. The IMU was held responsible by the Uzbek government for the Tashkent 1999 bomb explosions, and its militants have since 1999 used southern Kyrgyzstan's Batken Region as a chief theater of operations both within the region and elsewhere. Refugees from the Afghan civil war have been a major problem for Tajikistan. Uzbekistani President Islam Karimov was quick to refer to his Organization for Security and Cooperation in Europe (OSCE) Istanbul speech in which he 'drew international attention to the problem of rapidly developing terrorism. I spoke about unprecedented consequences it might have for humanity, warning people to wake up and that time has come for us to realize the horrific face of terrorism.'[3]

Although no stranger to fighting terrorism, the Central Asian leaders' decision to join the US-led international coalition was a qualitatively new risk. The UN initially estimated that 1.5 million Afghans might flee to neighboring countries, many of whom would be co-ethnics of the five Central Asian peoples. And although the differentiation between Muslims and Islamic terrorists was clear to the majority of Central Asians, these were nevertheless five Muslim states (albeit with secular constitutions) with some extremist Islamist pockets, especially the Ferghana Valley and bordering areas. Moreover, ethnic Tajiks and Uzbeks particularly were key fighters in the Northern Alliance against the Taliban and the Taliban quickly warned both Uzbekistan and Tajikistan of likely reprisals if either of these states joined the USA in the fight against terrorism, warning that deep historical ties between the two states will remain long after the USA had left the region.[4] Nor could rising anti-US sentiment then be ruled out, particularly by the more militant parts of the population that Uzbekistan, Tajikistan and Kyrgyzstan saw themselves as housing, but also by populations more generally unwilling to countenance co-ethnic Afghanistani casualties and the possibility of being dragged into a war that over time they would see as not their own. The International Crisis Group observed: 'These nations were in a precarious state even before the current crisis . . . [their] governments have been inclined to repress even moderate and non-violent religious groups for fear that they will become significant sources of opposition.'[5]

The decision by all five presidents to join the anti-terrorist coalition is thus all the more considerable, and was made with Russia's approval. The Tajikistani government, in particular, made the need for this approval explicit, stating that consultation with Moscow was required.[6] Statements by the governments of Kazakhstan and Kyrgyzstan implied that Russia had agreed. The case of Turkmenistan and Uzbekistan is less clear-cut. Turkmenistan's position of positive neutrality made consultation with Russia less relevant, and Islam Karimov has since Uzbek independence made it a point to distance his country's foreign policy from Russia, the only organization to join the alliance of Georgia, Ukraine, Uzbekistan, Azerbaijan and Moldova (GUUAM).[7] Karimov thus couched his decision to join the fight as a historical and independent right, one to 'guard the honour of our people and nation'[8] and even if Russia 'does not like the fact that Uzbekistan is carrying out its own independent policy with regard to this issue. But, let me say once again, when the Soviet army invaded Afghanistan in 1979, starting a big war, no one asked for our approval.'[9] But even in these latter two cases, Russia's agreement is likely to have facilitated and accelerated their decision.

Despite presidential endorsement, dissenting voices arose in all five states. Said Ibrahim Usmonov, chairman of the Tajik parliament's International Affairs

Committee: 'If the United States launches an attack against Afghanistan, which will cause casualties among the civilian population, and damage to economic objects and cultural relics, it will become itself like the terrorists.'[10] The head of the banned Erk Democratic Party of Uzbekistan, Muhammad Solih, warned of 'spill-over outside any local operation' and the 'danger of it spreading across all Central Asian states.'[11] A EurasiaNet summary wrote just after the attacks that while '(M)any local officials and citizens sympathize with the United States, expatriates can find abundant breaches of this sympathy,' and noted by way of example how at Bishkek University in the Kyrgyz capital, vandals broke windows and left behind anti-American graffiti.[12] These statements' trepidation and some-times hostility reveal these populations' sense of vulnerability at being on the front line of war.

POPULAR OPINION

In the absence of reliable opinion polls, it is, however, hard to tell what the masses really felt about joining the coalition. We are assisted, however, by a few local surveys and a recent US State Department Research Office Poll taken in Kazakhstan, Kyrgyzstan and Uzbekistan.[13] The poll indicates how in the majority popular sympathies were with the USA, but there was no uniform reaction on how best to proceed, with Russia as the country that all three continue to entrust most to deal with problems in Central Asia. Majorities in all three opposed a permanent US military presence, while all three opposed reductions in Russian influence. Opinion in both Uzbekistan and Kyrgyzstan felt the campaign justified, with as many as 71 percent in Uzbekistan (compared to 50 percent in Kyrgyzstan), demonstrating how '[O]nly in eager ally Uzbekistan do a majority voice strong support.'[14] The most consistently opposed to US action (be it the campaign or troops) was in Kazakhstan. Whilst Uzbekistan and Kyrgyzstan both supported the campaign, 55 percent in Kazakhstan opposed the campaign (distinct from 39 percent who approved).

Even if it can be argued that popular opinion has little immediate impact in five states whose foreign policies are overwhelmingly the preserve of the presidencies, the five presidents had to tread carefully. For the three front-line states in particu-lar, two constituencies for public statements emerged, one international, the other domestic, which for Tajikistan and Kyrgyzstan included Russia. Promises to the international community were often followed by denials to the domestic and Russian, matched later by confirmations and presentations as faits accomplis. Uzbekistan's leadership legitimized the use of military bases to its population by vouching that they would be used solely for humanitarian and search-and-rescue purposes, promising to release documentation to this effect. There was little if any discussion with groups about the stationing of troops and the population learned only belatedly, and often via foreign news sources, of the decision. Both Uzbek and Tajik governments initially denied that any US planes landed on their terri-tory. Later Uzbek presidential spokesman Rustam Jumayev reiterated that the 'number of the American personnel serving the aerodrome does not exceed three figures.'[15]

The political control of local media thus plays a critical role in the reactions and in our assessment. The tightest control of the media is in Uzbekistan[16] and Turkmenistan, followed by Tajikistan, with Kazakhstan and Kyrgyzstan still a relatively more critical media (albeit considerably less so than in the mid-1990s). In Tajikistan, reported one source, authorities jammed the TV signal on the night of the attacks, forcing citizens to watch a national history show instead of news from the USA. In Kazakhstan the political elite is fragmented, with some elite groups owning their media outlets, giving them greater opportunity to influence and be influenced by popular opinion. Thus, we should expect the media in the most part to reflect elite rather than popular positions and for popular positions to be somewhat influenced by the media. On this basis the greatest congruence between elite and mass opinion may be in Kazakhstan; the least congruence probably in Uzbekistan, simply because the official pro-Americanism of the regime was relatively stronger.

UZBEKISTAN

This strength of official Uzbek support was laid out early by the Uzbek leadership. Already on 5 October Karimov stated:

> 1. Our country gives air space to the US Air Force. 2. Information exchange is to be organized between the security bodies of the two countries. 3. US transport aircraft and helicopters are to be permitted to land at a military aerodrome on the territory of Uzbekistan. . . . We are not giving that aerodrome fully to them. Our military aircraft will also remain there. 4. The USA's aircraft and helicopters will only be used for humanitarian purposes and to carry out search-and-rescue operations. We also express our principled approach on two important issues: 1. It is not admissible for military ground operations to be carried out against Afghanistan from the territory of Uzbekistan. 2. It is not allowed to carry out bombing assault operations from the territory of our country.[17]

By 13 October Uzbekistan and the USA had signed a legal foundation for bilateral relations and the fight against international terrorism.[18] These served to legalize the Uzbek role within the campaign and to counter what Karimov saw as international, mainly Russian, distortion of Uzbekistani initial reactions. Karimov blamed Russia for stirring up issues because of what he termed Russian envy of Uzbekistan pursuing its independent policy. As noted, leadership endorsement does not tell the whole story; some reports portrayed how many Uzbeks were either hesitant or against joining the USA. A July 2002 survey, mainly among the younger population, indicated that approval for Uzbekistan's support for anti-terrorism operations in Afghanistan had fallen to 60 percent from around

90 percent in October 2001.[19] Anti-American sentiments in the Islamized Ferghana Valley are likely to grow, both by virtue of the changes in Tashkent's foreign policy and due to the repressive measures taken by the authorities against dissidents, which continued.

Bush's language bears close resemblance to that used by Karimov in his own earlier and continuous fight against the IMU. Karimov denounced September 11 as 'the barbaric act of terror' and terrorism as 'that horrible evil.'[20] His press secretary Rustam Jumayev called this a joint struggle against the 'plague of the twenty-first century.'[21] Not only such language united the two countries: already in the 1990s a US–Uzbek strategic partnership had been developing. The US government saw in Uzbekistan the strongest state demographically and militarily; the largest of the Central Asian states with 25 million inhabitants and the only one perceived to have a functioning army. The USA had been developing military links with Uzbekistan, in 2000 pledging it several million dollars' worth of military equipment; it had also become familiar with Uzbekistan's military and airbase after military exercises with Uzbek, Kazakh and Kyrgyz troops as part of the Centrazbat exercises held under NATO's Partnership for Peace Program (PfP). US special forces have trained Uzbek troops in counter-terrorism methods and mountain warfare. Karimov reportedly was the only one of the five Central Asian presidents to receive a phone call in September from President Bush.

This growing partnership is embraced by Karimov. Uzbekistan's official stance was borne of self-interest. Uzbekistan could hope to weaken the banned armed IMU led by Juma Namangoniy, play a role in deciding Afghanistan's postwar destiny, shake off Western criticism of measures against religious organizations in Uzbekistan, attract investment both for defense and the economy overall and generally strengthen its own position in Central Asia, becoming a rival to Russia in the region. Economically, different figures are touted for how much Uzbekistan has received from the USA in return for its support. In security terms, it is now openly the USA's and EU's leading partner in Central Asia. Tashkent has attracted Western foreign dignatories eager to express their gratitude, including key State Department and EU officials, the OSCE chairman-in-office, Romanian Foreign Minister Mircea Geoana and the UN undersecretary-general for humanitarian affairs, Kenzo Oshima. The US ambassador in Uzbekistan, John Herbst, was quoted as saying Americans 'would never forget the moral support given for the actions in Afghanistan to combat international terrorism.'[22] Uzbekistan is increasingly opting for bilateral relations with the USA, reportedly deciding in June 2002 to leave GUUAM[23] and lukewarm in its support of the Shanghai Cooperation Organization, a body formed in 1997 to reduce US presence in the region.[24] Uzbekistan in June 2002 was, however, the only Central Asian state to participate in the PfP 'Best-Effort–2002' large-scale, multinational military exercises in Georgia.[25]

KAZAKHSTAN

Uzbekistan's prominence in the US fight against terrorism undercuts its regional rival Kazakhstan, whose international image as the region's economic engine and 'epicentre of peace' (the title of President Nazarbaev's 2001 book) is less prized after 9/11. The European Bank for Reconstruction and Development as recently as 2001 regarded Kazakhstan as leading economic reforms in the post-Soviet space. In 2001 Kazakhstan had recorded an unprecedented budget surplus, and with the post-Soviet region's highest per capita foreign direct investment level which it had managed to maintain since 1997, was looking forward to a sustained period of growth. September 11 security concerns have overriden economic ones, however. And while Kazakhstan's geographic distance from the area of combat kept it fairly insulated from the terrorist threat felt by its southern Central Asian neighbors, it now placed practical limits on its engagement, with the risk that forced detachment might smack of indifference.

The result has been a leadership and population both willing to empathize and help, but also reluctant to be drawn into any military operations and critical of the US choice of a military response. The Kazakh newspaper *Megapolis* carried twenty-six articles, including interviews with Kazakh MPs and opposition party members, questioning the legality of the US reprisal attacks on Afghanistan. Seydakhmet Kuttykadam, the leader of the Orleu (Progress) opposition movement, described the operation as a 'mistake,' one that the Pashtun Afghans would not forget. The leader of the opposition Communist Party of Kazakhstan, Serikbolsyn Abdildin, said what America was doing in Afghanistan was a kind of terror, aggression by a strong state against a weak one. Madel Ismailov, a member of the opposition Workers' Movement of Almaty, said that the Taliban was the product of the USA. The leader of the recently formed moderate Patriots of Kazakhstan Party, Gani Kasymov, and the leader of the pro-presidential Civic Party, Azat Peruashev, also voiced opposition to the US strikes against Afghanistan, saying that the USA had decided unilaterally. They were also critical of Uzbekistan's stance in the fight against terrorism.[26] Other Kazakhstani newspapers carried a series of articles that portend the fundamental destabilization of the region as a result of US intervention, including articles arguing that the Caspian Sea states would become a 'Balkans plus oil.'[27]

This reluctance partly explains why Kazakhstan, despite being the furthest from Afghanistan and the richest of the Central Asian states, was the first to close its borders and tighten visa regimes.[28] These measures have provoked complaints from human rights groups and neighboring states. Kazakh authorities refused to allow in 131 Tajik passengers on the Dushanbe to Moscow train, citing concerns over terrorism.[29] Over 150 Kyrgyz citizens who were working in Kazakhstan were reportedly expelled to their home country without being given any opportunity to finish their business.[30] An exception is being made with their co-ethnics from Afghanistan, who are being resettled in the Republic's northern regions as part of the post-independence government policy to redress the ethnic imbalance in favor of ethnic Kazakhs by inviting home its diaspora. Like Uzbekistan, Kazakhstan's regime is being accused of using the war on terrorism to tighten domestic security.

The Kazakhstani leadership has also been seen to exercise repressive measures more generally after September 11. This is partly because of domestic realignments, as some elite groups have perhaps felt emboldened in the post-September 11 world, more confident that the President would be distracted by foreign policy concerns. With the USA and Russia set to play a more active role in the region, both elite and oppositional groups saw the possibility of external support. Oppositional ex-Prime Minister Akezhan Kazhegeldin was reassured by what he foresaw as growing Western interest in the oppositional cause, and the Kazakhstani opposition has stepped up its attempts to unite, including with movements in other Central Asian states.

In foreign policy terms, since 1991 Nazarbaev has prided himself on his country's foreign policy of 'multipolarity,' which aims to have friendly relations simultaneously with Russia, Central Asia, the USA and the wider world.[31] Statements by Nazarbaev after September 11 suggest that Kazakhstan's role as broker between the US and Russia, and its policy of good relations with the wider world as part of its multivector foreign policy, require review, in an 'effort to strengthen predictability and stability in Kazakhstan's relations' in favor of stronger relations 'with its neighbors.'[32] Unlike Uzbekistan's unilateral approach, Kazakhstan favors multilateral fora, in particular, the Eurasian Economic Community, the Shanghai Cooperation Organization (SCO), and the Central Asian Cooperation Organization. Kazakhstan's more recent emphasis on the SCO is possibly part of a stronger position accorded to China in Kazakhstan's foreign policy calculations and the enduring importance of Russia. China has reportedly assured Kazakhstan of its readiness to help with entry to the World Trade Organization.[33] Either directly or indirectly, after 9/11 Kazakhstan was undergoing significant domestic and foreign policy realignments.

KYRGYZSTAN

President Akaev called the presence of anti-terrorist coalition military forces in his country as an 'additional shield in the fight against international terrorism,'[34] but this has not prevented the unfolding of tragic events at home in 2002, when several people died in anti-government riots. Kyrgyzstan's reaction to September 11 can only be termed generous, and in some locals' views, probably overly so, with too much granted too soon relative to its socio-economic fragility. Kyrgyzstan was the only Central Asian state without a border on Afghanistan to have welcomed US troops, with the US base at Manas International Airport now the largest of the region. Only Kyrgyzstan agreed to open its borders to refugees; accounting for over 90 percent of the 11,000 officially registered refugees in Kyrgyzstan, Tajiks have been granted official travel documents and free medical care – an exception in Central Asia.[35] Akaev's decision came, moreover, in the face of considerable misgivings. One poll cited more than 60 percent of Bishkek's adult population as against the US presence. Their reasons were: the possible decline in relations with Russia, terrorist reprisals on their territory and the involvement of Kyrgyzstan in military action.[36] They also feared that the already restless south would increase its militancy, even though Akaev reassured that the region's other militant regional Islamic organization Hezb-e Tahrir 'is active mainly in Osh and Dzhalal-Abad Regions[37] and in Kara Su.[38] However, leaflets, including in Russian, have lately been disseminated even in Batken Region[39] and in Tokmak.[40] In other words, they are trying to involve the country's all Muslim people in the process.'[41] The deaths of protesters in March 2002 were predominantly the product of previous instability and the regime's growing authoritarianism (the rioters were protesting about the incarceration of an opposition member), but September 11 has contributed generally to a heightened sense of vulnerability and flux.

Akaev's decision to override these concerns was dictated by geopolitical and economic needs. In his May 2002 state of the nation address, Akaev spoke of his country's support for the anti-terrorist coalition, which he compared with the anti-Nazi coalition in the Second World War, and the resulting increased import-ance of relations with the USA, but said that this did not mean that Russia was any less a key ally for Kyrgyzstan. He also gave relations with China special mention, and called for the border agreement with China to be ratified.[42] His reference to the increased role of the USA and China is perhaps borne out of frustration from Russia's dwindling role in the Republic. To many members of the Kyrgyz leadership, Russia had lost its geopolitical and economic interests in their country. Despite Akaev's recent renewed pro-Russian policies, such as granting Russian the status of official language in 2001, visits to Moscow and frequent public reassurances that the US forces would be temporary, Russia was perceived as less able and willing to provide the sort of economic aid the country's poor economic situation requires. After Akaev's spring 2002 reported announcement that he intends not to stand for re-election, they also perceive that Russia may envisage that a successor to Akaev is likely to be less pro-Russian. Economically, the IMF, USA and other Western states have considerably increased their aid packages, the IMF alone agreeing to a new $105 million assistance package that would be disbursed over a three-year period.[43] Like all of Central Asia, Kyrgyzstan hoped to gain from assistance in its own counter-terrorism campaigns, counter-narcotics efforts, border security and help with refugee overflows.[44] Nevertheless, both leadership and people see a continuing role for Russia; indeed, the US polls cited earlier indicate that the Kyrgyz 'trust their own government less than they do most of their neighbors and the powerful outsiders – and much less than their neighbors trust their own governments to act responsibly'.[45]

TAJIKISTAN

Kyrgyzstan's and Tajikistan's decisions were made in very fragile domestic politi-cal contexts. Like the Uzbeks, Tajiks became a prime target for Taliban reprisals. One article termed the US strikes 'someone else's war knocking on our door.'[46] Many feared the country ill-equipped to deal with any flood of refugees. Many are worried that fighting in neighboring Afghanistan could upset the delicate political balance in their own country, still recovering from a civil war of 1992–7. Tajik participation in a US-led alliance is complicated by the fact that the main domestic political opposition comes from the Islamic Renaissance Party, which dominated the anti-government United Tajik Opposition during the civil war. Russia has effectively propped up current president Imomali Rahmonov's regime.

Tajikistan's government, therefore, more than its neighbors, had to consider Russia's reaction to any agreement to join the anti-terrorist coalition. As noted, only the Tajik leadership explicitly stated that it would consult Russia before committing itself any further. While Rahmonov resolutely denounced the 'barbaric actions' and expressed 'his readiness to take joint measures,'[47] Tajik Prime Minister Oqil Oqilov announced on 14 September that 'everything should be carefully thought out and a coordinated view should be reached,' and that Russia would 'definitely' be consulted.[48] Russia's 201st Motorized Rifle Division has guarded the Tajik–Afghan border and in 2002 the locus of the Rifle Division was converted to a militarized base. Both to its domestic and Russian audiences, the leadership initially denied any media claims that it had already agreed to the USA stationing forces on its territory. Russia publicly endorsed Tajikistan's position as a front-line state: 'Tajikistan is the forward post for the fight against international terrorism in Central Asia,' Russian Security Council Secretary Vladimir Rushaylo said, explaining Russia's concern for the Republic's defense capacity. The presidents of the Central Asian republics took these words from Russia's envoy as evidence that Russia will not leave the republics of Central Asia alone to face the Taliban.[49] Unlike Kyrgyzstan, Tajikistan can count on its border with Afghanistan to keep Russia involved.

If Tajiks are unhappy to countenance the withdrawal of Russia from the region, they nevertheless see both economic and political benefits from a rapprochement with the West. In his annual address to parliament on 22 April 2002, Rahmonov said that while 'Russia was a reliable partner of Tajikistan, . . . economic cooperation between the two countries was unsatisfactory'[50] and leader of the Democratic Party Asliddin Sohibnazarov echoed his President by arguing that the USA 'is a rich country and it can materially help Tajikistan, which finds itself in a deep crisis. This Russia cannot.'[51] Nevertheless, Tajiks want Russia to stay. Like Kyrgyzstan, the country fears reprisals. It also welcomes a counterweight to Uzbek regional domination. And some note that by helping the USA in carrying out military operations in Afghanistan, Tajikistan can strengthen its international image as a country actually fighting terrorism,[52] not least, as Rahmonov declared, because his country 'was the only state that did not change its stable policy towards the Taliban regime' given that it supported the Northern Alliance.[53] Overall, Tajiks view the USA as economically beneficial but unable to supplant Russia's regional security role.

TURKMENISTAN

Turkmenistan's international image was strengthened in the immediate aftermath of September 11. One Russian commentator observed, 'Turkmenistan rubs its hands: the one who is rubbing his hands with glee is Saparmyrat Nyyazov.'[54] The international community before September 11 quietly tolerated rather than ostracized Niyazov's despotic regime, partly because the Republic did not disrupt the system, having decided in effect to withdraw from it by its policy of positive neutrality, accepted by the UN in 1995. Neutrality, and thus Turkmenistan's open relations with the Taliban after 1995, might have meant Turkmenistan being accused of either treachery or detachment, both inadmissable in Bush's war. Instead, the policy has been an advantage both to the regime's image and economic proposals. It has offered airspace and humanitarian corridors[55] without compromising its positive neutrality. Even its post–1995 courting of the Taliban is now judged by some in the international community as an advantage because of the intelligence it might offer. 'As a neutral state, we do not interfere in internal affairs of other countries,' Niyazov said, also emphasizing the importance of the UN 'but we cannot be indifferent to what is happening to our neighbors and we hope that the international community will make all efforts to bring soonest possible peace into Afghanistan.'[56] UK Ambassador to Turkmenistan Fraser Wilson stated that neutrality 'does not mean isolation from other countries, but on the contrary, cooperation with other countries without falling under their political influence.'[57] US Secretary of State Colin L. Powell began more frankly: 'For decades Turkmenistan was a victim of an undemocratic system. The damage it caused to the Turkmen people is immense and it will take a lot of time to repair it', but concluded 'Turkmenistan is a source of stability in Central Asia and its role in the region will grow even more.'[58]

Like the three front-line states, Turkmenistan saw possible benefits to cooperation. In comparison to Tajikistan, which relies on Russian border guards to patrol the Afghan frontier, Turkmenistan's 840-kilometer Afghan border is much more penetrable. With 1 million ethnic Turkmen living in Afghanistan, military action could send tens of thousands streaming across the border, with Turkmenistan's military unable to manage the flow. One commentator has noted how refugees from Afghanistan combined with increasing dissatisfaction with Niyazov's authoritarian regime could ultimately damage Turkmenistan's fragile stability.[59] Economically, Niyazov suggested pushing ahead the plans for a trans-Afghan gas pipeline, proposed by Turkmenistan in 2000, as a means of giving an economic boost to Afghanistan and assisting its people. According to the original proposal, the pipeline would cross Afghanistan and deliver Turkmen gas to Pakistan. By the end of May 2002 Niyazov had already signed a Memorandum of Understanding for the pre-feasibility study of the proposed Turkmenistan–Afghanistan–Pakistan Oil and Gas Pipeline Project.[60]

Like President Nazarbaev, Niyazov has reshuffled his domestic elite post-September 11. Abroad, the Turkmen opposition, like Kazakhstan's, increased its efforts, but it is premature to assess whether this increased international profile has increased the hand of the opposition. The country still has not shown pretensions to regional leadership. Niyazov was the only leader not to show at an informal summit between Central Asia and Russia. Instead he continued to pursue bilateral relations, with Iran, Russia and the USA. Overall, the country has now a higher international profile while contributing decidely less than the three frontline states; in his May 2002 state of the nation address, Kyrgyz President Akaev pointedly omitted Niyazov from his thanks for the support offered by Central Asian presidents.

CONCLUSIONS

The implications for Central Asia as a result of involvement in the US-led anti-terrorist coalition are multiple. Reactions have been formed in the context of these states' domestic conditions, their relations with each other and with the outside world. Domestically, 9/11 appears to have sparked contradictory political developments in the five states. On the one hand, the events have catalyzed political elite realignments, notably in Kazakhstan and Turkmenistan where the sacking of major political actors occurred, and increased repression – the war on terrorism seen by some as vindicating government policies that impose strict limits on the freedom of speech and movement. On 6 December, a day before Powell was due to arrive in Tashkent, Uzbekistan's parliament endorsed a proposal to make Karimov president for life. On the other hand, the activities and profiles of opposition movements have grown. This dual development is partly a product of the USA's own twin policy: while offering assistance to incumbent regimes and downplaying human rights abuses, the USA has also met and interacted with opposition leaders.

Relations between the five states have on the whole deteriorated since September 11. Many of the Central Asian populations are uncomfortable about the position accorded Uzbekistan by the USA and fear that Uzbekistan's aggressive policies will intensify. The 96 percent delimitation of the 1,200 kilometer Kazakh–Uzbek border on 16 November has been overshadowed by the respective governments' tightening of border controls and the punishment of illegal immigration. Kazakhstani media contain criticism of Uzbekistan's human rights records. The Kyrgyz government has accused its Kazakh counterpart of stalling on several agreements, notably on cross-border trade.[61] Uzbeks have again stopped the supply of natural gas to Kyrgyzstan because the Kyrgyz still owe them backpayments, and Kyrgyzstan has accused Kazakhstan of an illegal gas trade.[62]

Cooperation between the five states continues to be most effective when outside powers are involved, of which the SCO is one example, but the five also fear that the likely increased competition between regional powers may ultimately prove destabilizing. They continue to see their security alignments in flux, constantly renewing relationships with outside powers without committing to any one power in particular. According to the US State Department poll of Kazakhstan, Kyrgyzstan and Uzbekistan, all three continue to place more long-term trust in

Russia than in the USA, China, their neighbors or even the UN, probably because Russia continues to hold 'the image of stability and restraint,' while the USA remains unfamiliar. [63]

NOTES

1 Interfax-Kazakhstan, 10 July 2002.
2 'Central Asian Elites, Suddenly, Shift into Revolt', http://www.eurasianet.org/ (hereafter EurasiaNet), 5 Feb. 2002.
3 Uzbek Television, 26 Sept. 2001 cited by Summary of World Broadcasts via Newsbase World Monitoring at: http://www.newsbaseworldmonitoring.com/ (hereafter SWB via Newsbase).
4 Afghan Taliban radio from Balkh Province, SWB via Newsbase, 13 Oct. 2001.
5 International Crisis Group, 'Central Asian Perspectives on 11 September and the Afghan Crisis', posted by EurasiaNet, 4 Oct. 2001.
6 'On the Front Lines', *Transitions Online*, posted by EurasiaNet, 23 Dec. 2001.
7 In 1997 Georgia, Ukraine, Azerbaijan and Moldova united around the project of building a Europe–Caucasus–Asia transport corridor involving sea, river, railway and automobile routes for passenger and freight traffic. Uzbekistan joined them in 1998.
8 Uzbek Television, SWB via Newsbase, 9 Oct. 2001.
9 Uzbek radio, SWB via Newsbase, 26 Sept. 2001.
10 Daler Nurkhanov, 'US Moves Against Afghanistan Cause Concern in Neighboring Tajikistan', EurasiaNet, 20 Sept. 2001.
11 Iranian radio from Mashhad, SWB via Newsbase, 27 Sept. 2001.
12 A EurasiaNet Roundup, 'Potential Retaliation Fosters Concern Among Expats in Central Asia', EurasiaNet, 14 Sept. 2002.
13 'Russia Tops U.S. in Central Asia', Office of Research, Opinion Analysis, Department of State, Washington, 31 May 2002, prepared by Steven A. Grant. The interviews, conducted in January and February 2002, were all supervised by the Expert Center for Social and Market Research, a Tashkent-based polling firm. The author would like to thank Steven A. Grant for his assistance.
14 'Russia Tops U.S. in Central Asia', p. 6.
15 Russian news agency RIA, SWB via Newsbase, 15 Oct. 2001.
16 To control coverage of the coalition's war on terrorism, the leadership on 8 October 2001 introduced its own new TV station called 'Akhborot Plus', explicitly devoted mainly to Uzbekistan's stance on the current developments in and around Afghanistan. Uzbek Television, SWB via Newsbase, 8 Oct. 2001.
17 Khalq Sozi, SWB via Newsbase, 6 Oct. 2001.
18 Russian news agency ITAR-TASS, SWB via Newsbase, 13 Oct. 2001.
19 Zamira Eshanova, 'Uzbekistan: Survey Shows Waning Support for War on Terror', 26 July 2002, http://www.eurasianet.org/departments/insight/articles/pp072602.shtml The poll was conducted by the the Ijtimoiy Fikr public-opinion center.
20 Russian news agency Interfax, SWB via Newsbase, 12 Sept. 2001.
21 Russian news agency RIA, SWB via Newsbase, 15 Oct. 2001.
22 Russian news agency ITAR-TASS, SWB via Newsbase, 27 Oct. 2001.
23 Russian news agency ITAR-TASS, SWB via Newsbase, 14 June 2002.
24 The Shanghai Cooperation Organization's members are Russia, China, Kazakhstan, Kyrgyzstan and Tajikistan. Uzbekistan joined later.
25 The others were: Austria, Azerbaijan, Canada, Ukraine, Greece, Lithuania, Romania, Britain, Bulgaria, USA, Turkey, Moldova, Hungary, Armenia and Georgia.
26 *Megapolis* (Almaty), 18 Oct. 2001.

27 *Respublika* (Almaty), 10 May 2002.
28 Alima Bisenova, 'Kazakhstan Backs U.S., Takes Cautious Approach on Refugees', 24 Sept. 2001. See also, Kazakhstan Today news agency website, SWB via Newsbase, 24 Sept. 2001.
29 'Kyrgyzstan: A Safe Haven for Tajiks', EurasiaNet, 4 Oct. 2001.
30 Kyrgyz TV, SWB via Newsbase, 26 Sept. 2001.
31 Kazakh Khabar TV, SWB via Newsbase, 29 April 2002.
32 Kazakh Khabar TV, SWB via Newsbase, 29 April 2002.
33 Kazakhstan Today news agency, SWB via Newsbase, 14 June 2002.
34 Kyrgyz news agency Kabar, SWB via Newsbase, 4 April 2002.
35 'Kyrgyzstan: A Safe Haven'.
36 Kyrgyz public educational TV, SWB via Newsbase, 10 April 2002.
37 In southern Kyrgyzstan, mainly populated by Uzbeks.
38 A district in Osh Region, southern Kyrgyzstan.
39 In southern Kyrgyzstan, which was attacked by armed militants in 1999 and 2000.
40 A town in northern Kyrgyzstan near the Kazakh border populated mainly by Kyrgyz, ethnic Dungans (Chinese Muslims), Russians and Kazakhs.
41 *Vecherniy Bishkek* (Bishkek), 20 Sept. 2001.
42 Kyrgyz radio, SWB via Newsbase, 7 May 2002.
43 Chris Schuepp, 'Kyrgyzstan Opens Airspace to US Warplanes', EurasiaNet, 25 Sept. 2001.
44 Robert McMahon, 'Afghanistan: Neighbors Stand to Benefit from Joining Antiterrorist Coalition', EurasiaNet Partner Post from RFE/RL, 27 Sept. 2001.
45 'Russia Tops U.S. in Central Asia', p. 4.
46 Tajik newspaper *Asia-Plus*, SWB via Newsbase, 20 Sept. 2001.
47 Russian news agency ITAR-TASS, SWB via Newsbase, 12 Sept. 2001.
48 Russian news agency Interfax, SWB via Newsbase, 14 Sept. 2001.
49 *Kommersant*, 22 Sept. 2001.
50 Tajik television, SWB via Newsbase, 22 April 2002.
51 *Obshchaia Gazeta*, 15 Dec. 2001.
52 Tajik newspaper *Asia-Plus*, SWB via Newsbase, 20 Sept. 2001.
53 Tajik television, SWB via Newsbase, 22 April 2002.
54 *Obshchaia Gazeta*, 15 Dec. 2001.
55 Consignments are being delivered through two main corridors – via the capital Ashgabat and via the eastern town of Turkmenabat (formerly Chardzhou).
56 Turkmenistan.RU Internet newspaper website, SWB via Newsbase, 1 Nov. 2001.
57 Turkmen television, SWB via Newsbase, 7 Dec. 2001.
58 Neytralnyy Turkmenistan (Ashkhabad), SWB via Newsbase, 27 Oct. 2001.
59 Rustem Safronov, 'Turkmenistan: A Question Mark in Central Asia's Security Framework', EurasiaNet, 21 Sept. 2001.
60 Turkmen television, SWB via Newsbase, 30 May 2002.
61 Kazakh Commercial TV, SWB via Newsbase, 30 April 2002.
62 Kazakh Commercial TV, SWB via Newsbase, 1 April 2002.
63 'Russia Tops U.S. in Central Asia', p. 9.

21 International organizations

The UN, NATO and the EU

Joanne Wright

In the immediate aftermath of 9/11, many analysts commented on the unprecedented unity of the international community and that once again the world was on the verge of a 'new world order.'[1] However, there was much less certainty or indeed optimism about this compared to the post-Gulf War 'new world order.' The international response to Saddam Hussein's invasion of Kuwait was supposed to usher in a new world order based on international institutions, multilateralism and respect for international law. After 9/11 and the US response, it is said to be based on US unilateralism, hegemony and a very secondary (and from the USA's point of view a purely instrumental) use of international institutions. The USA's seemingly unilateral campaign against Iraq can also be seen to confirm this view.

The role of the United Nations (UN), NATO and the European Union (EU) in the response to the attacks of 9/11, does raise a number of interesting theoretical as well as practical questions about international organizations and their roles in responding to security problems. The UN, although prominent in much rhetoric, did not push itself nor was it pushed hard by others to play a significant role in the military response. NATO (and ANZUS) invoked for the first time its collective defense Article 5, but played virtually no role. The EU did its usual self-important posturing, but did not move to mobilize its recently declared operative rapid reaction force. It may also be possible to argue that this international institutional 'decline' is part of a trend that runs through Somalia, Srebrenica and Kosovo. However, before coming to any conclusions about the role of international institutions or the 'world order,' it is important to establish exactly how these international organizations reacted to 9/11.

This chapter examines in most detail the reactions of the United Nations. It focuses on Security Council Resolutions 1368 and 1373, both passed by the end of September. It also examines the general debate which took place in the General Assembly between 1 and 4 October, in which 90 percent of all UN member states took part. Although many of the UN's functions may appear to have been usurped by the USA and to a lesser extent the EU, it remains essential to both the USA and the international community in the fight against terrorism. The chapter then moves on to look more briefly at the reaction of NATO. The conclusion here too is that over the longer term NATO will continue to play a key role in counter-terrorism. Finally, the chapter considers the reaction of the EU which, while lacking in some respects, was also the most comprehensive response of all international organizations. It will also play a key role in the longer term.

The current world order is one in which the power of the USA has undoubtedly been enhanced. But just as President Bush and others have constantly warned that the battle against terrorism will be long and multifaceted, so too will the ramifications of 9/11. Indeed the longer the counter-terrorism campaign goes on, the more important international institutions will become and in all probability the more dependent the USA will become on them. It is thus too early and too simple to label the international system as unipolar.

THE UNITED NATIONS: THE SECURITY COUNCIL

On 12 September, the Security Council unanimously passed Resolution 1368 and even the manner in which it was adopted was in recognition of the previous day's events. The French President of the Council invited the members to adopt the Resolution not by the traditional method of showing hands, but 'by standing, in a show of unity in the face of the scourge of terrorism.'[2] The debate preceding the adoption of the Resolution, in which the representatives of all fifteen members spoke, contained several themes that were emphasized by all speakers. In addition to expressing condolences and sympathy for the American people, speakers stressed that the attacks the previous day represented an attack on the entire civilized world, on democracy and on the values of humanity.

The Resolution itself declared the events of 9/11 to be a 'threat to international peace and security.' It also expressed the Security Council's 'readiness to take all necessary steps to respond to the terrorist attacks of 11 September 2001' as well as recognizing the inherent right of individual or collective self-defense in accordance with the Charter.[3] Resolution 1373 passed two weeks later restated these points.[4] There has been some debate about whether these Resolutions were sufficient to justify the American military response a few weeks later and the international legal issues are to some extent clouded by the fact that the perpetrators of 9/11 were not a state.[5]

Nonetheless the facts remain that the Security Council did not provide and was not asked to provide authorization for military strikes against Afghanistan and al-Qaeda forces inside it. There is no doubt that many countries, especially Muslim ones, would have preferred a specific Resolution authorizing the use of force in the same way that Resolution 678 authorized the use of force against Iraq in 1990. But this was not necessary in terms of international law and was certainly not the preferred option of US leaders. In addition to ideological hostility towards the UN on the part of the Bush administration, lingering frustration in the USA from the failure of the Security Council to pass rapid resolutions in relation to Kosovo in 1999, and the US military's unease with the thought of working to the constraints of coalition fighting always made a US approach for Security Council authorization highly unlikely. The USA justified its actions in terms of the self-defense provisions of the UN Charter which Resolutions 1368 and 1373 explicitly recognized in their preambles. The USA, and the United Kingdom, also followed UN Charter provisions for notifying the Security Council of actions taken in self-defense.

Although several countries were to voice their concerns about the value of military action against terrorism and the scale of America's actions, there was no dispute of the USA's right to take action on the basis of self-defense against future possible attacks from al-Qaeda.[6] This degree of consensus is rare and in times past, the Soviet Union/Russia and/or China would at the least have been most vocal in their criticisms. But they both recognized the USA's response as being one of self-defense. So, although the Security Council did not specifically author-ize the use of force in Afghanistan, the international community, and especially the Security Council, was solidly behind the USA's right to take military action in Afghanistan.

In addition to the US military's reluctance to be straitjacketed within multi-lateral political and operational control, the Bush administration did not need the help of others to achieve its objectives in attacking al-Qaeda and the Taliban. However, in order to win the 'war' against terrorism the USA does and will need the support of many other nations and it is here where aspects of Resolution 1373 are both interesting and important.

Resolution 1373, drafted by the USA, was also adopted unanimously and quickly, and because it was adopted under the provisions of Chapter VII of the UN Charter it obliges states to take action and leaves them vulnerable to sanctions if they do not.[7] The provisions contained in Resolution 1373 can be grouped into five main areas aimed at curtailing terrorists' finance, their support, and their ability to travel, establishing their acts as serious crimes, and enhancing inter-national cooperation against terrorism. The Resolution also sets up a special Security Council Sub-Committee to monitor compliance with these obligations.

In terms of curtailing terrorists' finances, Resolution 1373 uses almost identical language to the United Nations Convention for the Suppression of Terrorist Finances which, at the time, had not been able to come into effect as too few states had ratified it. Basically, Resolution 1373 requires states to prevent and suppress the financing of terrorist acts, criminalize the financing of terrorist acts and freeze the assets of those involved in financing terrorist acts. Resolution 1373 further requires states to refrain from allowing their territory to be used in support of terrorist actions or to recruit members of terrorist organizations. It also singles out the supply of weapons as an area for attention by member states. In terms of preventing the movement of terrorists, member states are obliged to install effect-ive border controls and mechanisms for the issuance and verification of travel documents.

States are further obliged to bring to justice those participating in the 'financing, planning, preparation or perpetration of terrorist acts or in supporting terrorist acts,' and to ensure that these are established as serious offenses in domestic legislation. The Resolution emphasizes the importance of international cooperation in a variety of ways. It compels members to exchange information promptly to prevent terrorist attack and calls on states to intensify and accelerate the exchange of operational information 'especially regarding actions or movements of terrorist persons or networks; forged or falsified travel documents; traffic in arms, explosives or sensitive materials; use of communications technologies by terrorist groups; and the threat posed by the possession of weapons of mass destruction by terrorist groups.'[8] States are also called upon to enhance bilateral and multilateral cooperation as well as become parties as soon as possible to the various international conventions and protocols relating to terrorism.

This is certainly a very extensive and necessary framework for dealing with the international phenomenon of terrorism, and in UN terms it is unusual for this alone. But what is unique about this Resolution is the establishment of a Committee of the Security Council to monitor its implementation. States are called upon to 'report to the Committee, no later than 90 days from the date of adoption of this resolution and thereafter according to a timetable to be proposed by the Committee, on the steps they have taken to implement this resolution.'[9]

The Committee was subsequently established as the Counter Terrorism Committee (CTC). It is made up of all fifteen members of the Security Council and is chaired by the British representative, Sir Jeremy Greenstock. By 19 October, the CTC had established its first work program. This concentrated mainly on setting up the procedures and guidelines for states to meet their obligation to report to the CTC on matters pertaining to Resolution 1373. In particular states are asked to give an indication of:

- What relevant legislation (including regulations or other legislative machinery) is in place or is contemplated;
- What executive (i.e. administrative or non-legislative) action has been taken or is contemplated;
- What other action, if any, has so far been taken to implement the letter and spirit of Resolution 1373 (2001);
- What steps have been taken or are contemplated to enhance international cooperation in the areas covered by the Resolution 1373 (2001).[10]

States were asked to provide these reports by the end of December 2001. In January 2002, Sir Jeremy Greenstock was able to confirm that of a total membership of 189, 117 had submitted their reports, and that the CTC is currently analyzing them with a view to identifying and promulgating best practice and researching ways of assisting states.[11]

Providing states and international organizations with information is the other key component of the CTC's first work program. The CTC has invited all states and regional and international organizations to provide it with any information that might facilitate the implementation of Resolution 1373. It has established a website and several member states and international organizations have already deposited relevant information under the headings of legislative drafting, financial law and practice, customs law and practice, immigration law and practice, extradition law and practice and illegal arms trafficking.[12] The CTC has also been meeting regularly since its inception.

Such measures and such a framework for cooperation in countering terrorism are obviously necessary. Helping states put in place appropriate legislation and improve their policing and law enforcement systems as well as disseminating good practice seems both sensible and practical. Monitoring the level of compliance of states is also important and what is interesting to note here is that it increases quite dramatically the range of areas of 'domestic' policy that are now of legitimate international concern and will be subject to a degree of international scrutiny. This will need to be managed very carefully and sensitively if it is not to become seen as an instrument of big power, particularly Western, intervention.

These measures are also not without controversy. Having an appropriate legislative framework at both national and international levels implies some sort of agreement on defining what terrorism is and is not, and a lack of international agreement on this has been a serious handicap in the past. There is also little doubt that during the Cold War fewer states had interests in seeing international terrorism tackled in too vigorous a way as it formed part of their foreign policy.[13] Taking advantage of the consensus and indeed momentum to counter terrorism that was created by 9/11, will depend on the cooperation of the UN's major representative institution, the General Assembly, and its major representative figure, the Secretary General.

THE UNITED NATIONS: THE GENERAL ASSEMBLY AND THE SECRETARY GENERAL

The General Assembly was also very quick to condemn the terrorist attacks on the USA and to call for actions to be taken against those responsible and those who harbor them.[14] In addition, the General Assembly moved to postpone planned meetings in order not to add to the burden of the emergency services in New York. By the end of September, the General Assembly had agreed to a special week-long plenary session on the subject of international terrorism. This debate also showed a very high degree of international consensus but, at the same time, has raised questions about the value of the UN and its ability to play an active and distinctive role in a US-dominated international system. Such views, however, are based on a misunderstanding of the scale of the problem that international terrorism poses and, perhaps, an underestimation of the political abilities of the Secretary General.

The week-long plenary debate in the General Assembly took place during the first week of October. As a rule, states were supportive of the USA and its right to take action against al-Qaeda and the Taliban, although the representatives of some states were clearly uncomfortable with aspects of US behavior. Perhaps not surprisingly, Cuba and Iraq were the most openly hostile.[15] Cuba criticized US actions, accused the UN of inconsistency, and blamed the Security Council for having caved into hegemonic pressure from the USA:

The Security Council has been pushed to give legal support to hegemonic and arbitrary decisions made by the ruling Power, which violate the Charter and International Law and that trespass on the sovereignty of all States. . . . The Council uses the unbelievable method of turning into mandatory for all States some of [the] rules contained in conventions against terrorism, which only the States themselves are entitled to sign or not.[16]

Iraq also accused the USA of terrorist acts against itself, the Palestinians and against peoples in Africa, Latin America and Asia.[17] Although in much softer language, the representatives of other countries such as Iran raised concerns about the dominant power position of the USA. Further concerns about inconsistencies in international behavior in relation to international terrorism and Palestine in particular were raised by the representatives of Malaysia, Pakistan, Palestine and Saudi Arabia.

Two common themes stand in the debate. First, a reiteration of the view that 9/11 was an attack against humanity and that it must not provoke any sort of polarization between Arabs and non-Arabs or Muslims and non-Muslims. Speeches by the representatives of Indonesia, Spain and Germany are illustrative. And second, that all states must work to strengthen the international legal frame-work against international terrorism by ratifying and implementing the various UN conventions and protocols. Speeches by the General Secretary and the repre-sentatives of the European Union, Russia, Czech Republic, France, Japan, Indo-nesia, Turkey, China, Australia, Sweden, Canada and the UK emphasized this theme.

The UN currently has twelve conventions or protocols that deal with aspects of international terrorism. Four of these deal with aircraft and aviation and the vast majority of UN members are party to them.[18] One convention and one protocol deal with the safety of maritime navigation and fixed platforms and most states with maritime interests are party to these.[19] Two further conventions on diplo-matic protection and the taking of hostages are also widely supported.[20] There is a Convention on the Physical Protection of Nuclear Material (Vienna, 1980) which has 75 parties and 45 signatories, and a Convention on the Marking of Plastic Explosives for the Purpose of Detection (Montreal, 1991) which has 77 parties. The remaining two conventions are both the newest and the ones that members of the United Nations particularly called upon each other to sign and ratify after 9/11. Even six months later, the International Convention for the Suppression of Terrorist Bombings (1997) had only 59 parties and 58 signatories, which represents only 62 percent of the membership. The International Convention for the Suppression of the Financing of Terrorism has fared better but only after, and no doubt as a result of, the September bombings; indeed it only became operational in April 2002. By May 2002 this convention had 31 parties and 132 signatories.

Member states also called upon each other to implement in full the comprehensive Security Council Resolution 1373 discussed above. While it might be expected that the USA's close European and Asian allies would be very supportive, it should also be noted that both China and Russia who often play to anti-American sentiment in the General Assembly were very forthright in their views of Resolution 1373. The Chinese ambassador called for the Resolution to be 'faithfully implemented,'[21] and the Russian ambassador in welcoming specially the compliance aspects of Resolution 1373 called it 'a serious step towards an effective response to terrorist threat.'[22]

Altogether this is an impressive international framework,[23] but it is also an incomplete one, due to the obvious and perennial problem of defining terrorism. However, even before 9/11, work was underway to try and draft a new global convention on terrorism. In 1996 the UN's legal committee, known as the Sixth Committee, established an ad hoc group to look at the issue of terrorism and international measures to counter it. Although this ad hoc group ultimately produced the Convention dealing with terrorist financing, it has so far been unable to reach consensus on a more general convention. At the end of 1999, for example, a draft was introduced on 'measures to eliminate international terrorism,' but consensus was not achieved. Syria, Lebanon and Benin abstained on the basis that the text did not draw a distinction between the legitimate struggles of peoples for self-determination and terrorism.[24] This is the same sort of problem that dogged attempts at international cooperation throughout the 1970s and 1980s.[25] It was also a problem referred to in the debate after 9/11.

This inability to achieve international consensus is no doubt one aspect of a lack of faith in the UN's ability to play a major role in the events that followed the bombings. Several commentators noted that the UN had been sidelined in the crisis or that it was 'conspicuous by its absence.'[26] The UN's lack of presence in the crisis was also highlighted by the fact that the peacekeeping operation subsequently established in Afghanistan was authorized but not commanded by the UN Security Council. The Security Council did, however, authorize the UN special envoy dealing with Afghanistan, Lakhdar Brahimi, to move ahead with a conference to establish some sort of interim government for Afghanistan pending the creation of a more substantial constitutional convention.[27] Since the end of the Cold War the UN has had some success in reorganizing failed and fragile states, but little success in dealing with its primary concern of threats to international peace and security. The fact that the UN was not trusted to do the fighting or deal with security problems, does raise questions about its ability to deliver on its fundamental objectives. Dominique Moisi, while still referring to the UN as essential, suggests that it has become 'more like the Red Cross than the enforcer of peace – its original mission.'[28]

The UN's lack of a prominent public role in the security issues surrounding the attacks on the USA may also be due to a conscious decision on the part of its leaders and especially Kofi Annan. It was always clear that the USA was going to respond on its own without recourse to the UN. Annan was certainly aware of this and even before the end of September he was positioning the UN to play more of a long-term strategy based mostly on the conventions and protocols already mentioned. This longer-term role for the UN is also widely supported by the member states. In supporting the UN and Kofi Annan, the German foreign minister reiterated that the campaign against terrorism would be long term and would have to tackle the problem 'on all levels – financial, political, intelligence, police immigration and, of course, also militarily.'[29] There was also general support for the UN's role in organizing the Bonn Conference at the end of November and early December 2001 to establish an interim government and in providing post-Taliban administrative assistance.

The UN, imperfect as it is, remains the best option for a multifaceted and global campaign against terrorism. Even if a general convention against international terrorism, complete with a universally agreed definition, is not forthcoming the remaining conventions and protocols still serve useful purposes. They set the norms and standards which are the basis of international consensus. Further, the General Assembly encourages global dialogue and helps create vested interests in countering international terrorism.

A second reason why the UN has not perhaps played such a prominent role in Afghanistan is that it too learnt much from the Balkans disaster. Of all the international organizations involved, the UN emerged as the most discredited and there seems little doubt that UN officials feared that the USA would move to shift responsibility for post-Taliban Afghanistan to them.[30] But again this is not to say that the UN has no useful role to play. One particular function that the UN is taking on, especially through the Terrorism Sub-Committee, is the dissemination of information and best practice. In this it will be aided by both NATO and the EU.

NATO

The way the USA reacted to 9/11 does raise a number of important issues for NATO and its future. That the USA did not use NATO in any substantial way has led some to question its purpose.[31] The military campaign waged by the USA provided another illustration of the 'capabilities gap' between the USA and its allies, but in the overall campaign against international terrorism the use of military force remains a limited option. The application of force is only one function of the military. NATO will continue to play an important part in the campaign against international terrorism based largely on its engagement with the countries of East/Central Europe, Russia and Ukraine.

NATO's reactions to 9/11 were hugely symbolic even if its actual military contribution was very limited. On 12 September, NATO invoked for the first time its collective defense provision, subject to confirmation that 9/11 had been directed from abroad. This confirmation came after briefings from various US officials in late September and early October. By 4 October, the allies had agreed to eight measures which included intelligence sharing, enhanced security for US facilities, and overflight clearances and port access.[32] By 9 October, Operation Eagle Assist had been launched which was essentially to free US resources to go to Afghanistan. By its conclusion on 16 May 2002, '830 crew members from 13 NATO nations have patrolled US skies in the NATO AWACS for nearly

4300 hours in over 360 operational sorties.'[33] The French also took over some US military responsibilities in the Balkans to free resources to be used elsewhere. However, as mentioned above, American decision-takers did not choose to act through NATO in any substantial way.

NATO has been strengthening its role as a political organization ever since the end of the Cold War. The Partnership for Peace (PfP) initiative and the establishment of the Euro–Atlantic Partnership Council (EAPC) have clear political objectives of inclusive dialogue with the non-NATO countries of Eastern Europe, Russia and the Ukraine. NATO has been quick to use this PfP/EAPC framework to coordinate and improve international cooperation against terrorism and preparedness of emergencies. It has organized conferences and seminars to discuss new ideas and disseminate good practice. It has also sought to coordinate its work with other international organizations such as the UN, EU, Organization for Security and Cooperation in Europe (OSCE) and the Commonwealth of Independent States (CIS). Such roles are vital in improving intelligence and trust among countries which are all to varying degrees subject to international terrorism. They may also help control the spread of weapons and other dangerous materials that could be exploited by terrorists.[34]

The prominence that counter-terrorism now has is likely to strengthen this broadening and more politically oriented role for NATO. Indeed, counter-terrorism is a core part of a new agreement between NATO and Russia.[35] And while this may serve to give NATO a degree of focus that it has lacked since the end of the Cold War, it will also represent a shift away from NATO's fundamental orientation as a collective defense organization focused on Europe. Moisi has observed that NATO may become more like the OSCE which will make expansion much easier, especially the inclusion of the Baltic states.[36]

Even in a broader and more politically oriented form, NATO will still lack most of the economic, political and diplomatic resources that are also needed in an effective international response to terrorism. The EU, in theory, does have these resources and it has tried to combine them in a comprehensive response to 9/11.

THE EUROPEAN UNION

European Union members and officials were just as quick as their counterparts in NATO and the UN to condemn the attacks and offer solidarity to the American government and people. Also like NATO, there is some debate over the longer-term consequences of 9/11 for the EU. The leader of the EU Commission, Romano Prodi, believes that 9/11 will result in more integration within the EU, but others point to the 'big three' diplomacy of Britain, France and Germany to suggest that the EU as a separate entity remains a very limited actor.[37] Adding to these limitations is the weaknesses that the Europeans have both individually and collectively in providing a rapid military response to crises even close to home never mind those requiring 'strategic lift' capabilities. Providing an analysis of this debate is beyond the scope of this chapter, but it is clear that the response of the

EU and its member countries to international terrorism is crucial, not least because of the direct and indirect European links to international terrorism. However, the EU is also well placed to assist in countering terrorism outside its own borders, and even if it does not have a full range of effective military instruments, it does have a number of other political and economic weapons at its disposal. All this is recognized in the EU's Action Plan which was launched on 21 September.

The Action Plan proposed measures in each of six main categories. The first of these is police and judicial cooperation which includes a common definition of terrorism, common arrest warrant, joint member state investigation teams and enhanced police and intelligence cooperation. The second focuses on diplomatic activity including solidarity with the USA, consolidation of the European Defense and Security Policy and determined efforts to relaunch the Middle East peace process. The third included measures to send and distribute humanitarian aid to Afghanistan and the fourth contained measures to improve and standardize airport security across the EU. The fifth targets terrorist finance and advocates measures additional to the UN Convention for the Suppression of Terrorist Financing (which member states are also urged to ratify). The final category relates to emergency preparedness and aims to pool medical and scientific expertise in relation to weapons of mass destruction as well as improve the coordination of public health emergency planning.[38] Many of these actions have begun to be implemented by the EU and there is little doubt that the battle against international terrorism is very dependent on their successful implementation.

It is now clear that the EU will opt for a 'big-bang' enlargement to include eight to ten new members in time for the 2004 European parliamentary elections and then full membership in 2005. Such an enlargement obviously presents both difficulties and opportunities in the campaign against terrorism. The applicant countries did, through the mechanisms of Common Foreign and Security Policy (CFSP), fully associate themselves with the EU's response and its statements in the UN.[39] The full accession of eight to ten more countries to the EU's counter-terrorism regime as described above will enhance its effectiveness and bring benefits beyond the EU. But at the same time, these accession countries are going to struggle to ensure that their border controls and policing and financial accounting standards are adequate which has the potential to create weaknesses that could be exploited by terrorists. The process of EU enlargement has not been greatly affected by 9/11, but a successful EU enlargement will enhance the international campaign against terrorism.

CONCLUSION

There is no doubt that 9/11 is a date that will be used as a historical reference point. But as Timothy Garton Ash points out, it remains unclear whether it will be a 'John F. Kennedy type' (significant but not inducing major structural change) or a 'Berlin wall type' (major structural change).[40] If it is going to turn out to be a system changing event, then much depends on the US response: to what extent it involves the international community or acts alone. By the end of October 2001, the US Secretary of State Colin Powell was declaring that 'we're so multi-lateral, it keeps me up 24 hours a day checking on everybody.'[41] It is also true to say that the US version of multilateralism was and remains more like a series of bilateral negotiations and agreements than a systematic use of multilateral fora such as the UN or even NATO. Several commentators have discussed how 9/11 has left the USA in a dominant position in the international system, although it is important to note that 9/11 only confirmed a trend.

It is also tempting to see 9/11 as part of a trend of increasingly religious and increasingly deadly international terrorism.[42] The perpetrators were traced back to a loose organization shielded by a corrupt, despicable, internationally isolated and ultimately weak government that caved in quickly when military pressure was applied. While this may be broadly comparable to the US attack on Sudan in the early 1990s, it remains nonetheless a relatively rare configuration of circumstances. Thus it is very important not to conflate what happened in the USA and Afghanistan with the struggle against international terrorism.

In other senses though, the events of 9/11 were quite typical of international terrorism. The perpetrators utilized the territory, and the financial, education and telecommunications services of several countries. In targeting the terrorists' utilization of such facilities and services, even the USA is dependent on support from the international community and it is just such issues that both the UN and EU are tackling. It is important to control the supply of weapons and especially materials that could be used to create weapons of mass destruction, and these are also being targeted as specific areas of action by the UN and NATO. Again the USA cannot control weapons and materials by itself. But perhaps most importantly, while no one would deny the terrible devastation wreaked by 9/11, terrorism, including terrorism practiced by governments against their own people, remains a daily aspect of life. Any international coalition will only be effective if it is inclusive as well as comprehensive. Imperfect as they are, our major international institutions are the only vehicles for this. Events since 9/11, especially the Bali and Mombasa bombings, have reinforced this. Recent interactions between the American administration and the Security Council in relation to Iraq and weapons of mass destruction also demonstrate the continuing importance of international institutions and the fact that the world, like terrorism, is more complex than we would like it to be.

NOTES

1 The United States in the days immediately after the bombing did manage to secure the assistance of some new 'allies'. See 'Enlisting Iran', Leader, *The Guardian*, 25 Sept. 2001; D. Whitworth, 'Rogue Nation – Sudan Backs US Campaign', *The Times*, 29 Sept. 2001, p. 11; and G. Smyth 'Syrian Leader in Rome for Anti-terror Talks', *Financial Times*, 20 Feb. 2002. For a general 'new world order'-type article see P. Hain, 'Let's Use This Great Coalition', *The Independent*, 6 Oct. 2001.

2 United Nations Security Council, S/PV.4370, 12 Sept. 2001.
3 United Nations Security Council, S/RES/1368 (2001) 12 Sept. 2001.
4 United Nations Security Council, S/RES/1373 (2001) 28 Sept. 2001.
5 See for example, *Daily Telegraph*, 21 Sept. 2001, *The Guardian*, 22 Sept. 2001, *The Independent*, 25 Sept. 2001 and *Financial Times*, 8 Oct. 2001.
6 For a fuller discussion of this point and many of the other legal issues surrounding 11 Sept., see Christopher Greenwood, 'International Law and the "War against Terrorism" ', *International Affairs*, Vol. 78, No. 2, April 2002.
7 United Nations Security Council, S/RES/1373 (2001) 28 Sept. 2001. The wording states 'The Security Council – Acting under Chapter VII of the Charter of the United Nations'.
8 United Nations Security Council, S/RES/1373 (2001) 28 Sept. 2001, 3 (a).
9 United Nations Security Council, S/RES/1373 (2001) 28 Sept. 2001, 6.
10 United Nations, S/2001/986, 19 Oct. 2001.
11 http://www.un.org/News/briefings/docs/2002/terrorismpc.doc.htm
12 http://www.un.org/Docs/sc/committees/1373/INTRO.htm
13 See Michael Stohl and George Lopez (eds.) *Terrible Beyond Endurance? The Foreign Policy of State Terrorism* (New York: Greenwood, 1988); Barry Rubin (ed.) *Terrorism and US Foreign Policy* (Basingstoke: Macmillan, 1991); and Noam Chomsky *The Culture of Terrorism* (London: Pluto, 1988).
14 Kofi Annan, 'We Must Recognise Our Common Enemies', *The Independent*, 22 Sept. 2001.
15 Speeches and statements can be obtained from country specific text links at: http://www.un.org/list11001.html
16 http://www.un.org/terrorism/statements/cubaE.html
17 http://www.un.org/terrorism/statements/iraqE.html
18 The Convention on offenses and Certain Other Acts Committed on Board Aircraft (Tokyo, 1963) has 173 parties, the Convention for the Suppression of Unlawful Seizure of Aircraft (Hague, 1970) has 175 and the Convention for the Suppression of Unlawful Acts against the Safety of Civil Aviation (Montreal, 1971) has 176. There is also a Protocol (1988) supplementary to the Montreal Convention which has 117 parties.
19 The Convention for the Suppression of Unlawful Acts against the Safety of Maritime Navigation (Rome, 1988) has 55 contracting parties and the Protocol for the Suppression of Unlawful Acts against the Safety of Fixed Platforms has 60 parties.
20 The Convention on the Prevention and Punishment of Crimes against Internationally Protected Persons, including Diplomatic Agents (1973) has 119 parties and 25 signatories and the International Convention against the Taking of Hostages (1979) has 106 parties and 39 signatories.
21 http://www.un.org/terrorism/statements/chinaE.html
22 http://www.un.org/terrorism/statements/russiaE.html
23 There are some additional pieces of legislation that also have an impact on terrorism such as the UN Convention against Organized Crime.
24 See General Assembly Press Release GA/L/3140, 23 Nov. 1999.
25 The most often quoted example of the divisions in this era are Yasser Arafat's 1974 speech to the General Assembly when he said 'He who fights for a just cause, he who fights for the liberation of his country, he who fights against invasion and exploitation or single mindedly against colonialism, can never be defined a terrorist.' For a more detailed discussion of international cooperation during the 1970s and 1980s see Paul Wilkinson, 'Terrorism: International Dimensions', in William Gutteridge (ed.), *Contemporary Terrorism*, (New York: Facts on File, 1986), pp. 29–56.
26 See for example S. Rahman, 'Another New World Order? Multilateralism in the Aftermath of Sept. 11', *Harvard International Law Review*, Winter 2002, p. 44; and 'UN has a vital role to play', Leader, *The Independent*, 10 Nov. 2002, p. 3.
27 This conference subsequently took place in Bonn in late November and early

December 2001. In June 2002, an Afghan tribal assembly began preparing for a new constitution.

28 Dominique Moisi, 'Early Winners and Losers', *Financial Times*, 19 Nov. 2001, p. 15.

29 Joschka Fischer quoted in E. MacAskill, 'On the Brink of War', *The Guardian*, 22 Sept. 2001.

30 T. Judah and K. Bahoudin 'The Terrorism Crisis', *The Observer*, 21 Oct. 2001.

31 *Financial Times*, 19 Nov. 2001 and 14 Feb. 2002.

32 Full details at http://www.nato.int/docu/speech/2001/s11004b.htm

33 Lord Robinson, NATO Secretary General, 30 April 2002, http://www.nato.int/docu/update.2002/0429/e0430a.htm

34 This has also been cited by Kofi Annan and others as vital. See A. La Guardia, 'Annan Calls for Global Treaty on Terrorism', *Daily Telegraph*, 2 Oct. 2001, p. 6.

35 'Old friends and new', *The Economist*, 1–7 June 2002, pp. 25–7. The new NATO–Russia Council also provides Russia with an opportunity to play a role in the American development of missile defenses and NATO with the opportunity to play a role in the restructuring of Russia's armed forces.

36 Moisi, 'Early Winners and Losers'.

37 A. Grice and C. Stuart, 'War on Terrorism: EU Heavyweights', *The Independent*, 20 Oct. 2001.

38 For more details see http://europa.eu.int/comm/110901/index.htm

39 See http://www.un.org/terrorism/statements/euE.html

40 T. Garton Ash, 'Terror in America: A Moment That Will Define the 21st Century', *The Independent*, 13 Sept. 2001.

41 Quoted in Q. Peel, 'Keeping the Posse Together', *Financial Times*, 29 Oct. 2001.

42 Bruce Hoffman, *Inside Terrorism* (Columbia: Columbia University Press, 1999).

22 Perceptions of Afghan refugees

Joanne van Selm

The European Union's Council of Ministers for Justice and Home Affairs met on 20 September 2001, as part of its initial institutional reaction to 9/11 and its potential aftermath, including American intervention. The Council requested the European Commission to 'examine the scope for provisional application of the Council Directive on temporary protection in case special protection arrangements are required within the European Union.'[1] The Temporary Protection directive was then the only Commission proposal on asylum policy that had been accepted by the Council since the entry into force of the Amsterdam Treaty. Temporary Protection, as a means of dealing with the status and reception conditions for refugees fleeing a conflict or unrest, would be triggered if there were a significant influx into the EU. However, there was little chance of an influx, unless huge numbers of people found the ways and means to employ smugglers and leave the camps of Pakistan and Iran. While it was feared that 7 million Afghans risked starvation, the 13 million people still in the country stood little chance of leaving it, however afraid they were. As such, the statement that the EU was ready to receive Afghans was a symbolic foreign policy statement that, due to realities on the ground, could not clash with the internal policies of generally rejecting Afghan claims, or with domestic security fears attached to the arrival of new Afghan refugees who might include people who could be excluded from refugee protection on the grounds of involvement with terrorist organizations.[2]

Part of the reason why the EU leaders could safely make statements about receiving Afghanistan's refugees without actually contemplating the reality (as had been the case for Kosovo's refugees in 1999) was that the public imagination had not been fired to think about these refugees as people in need of more than tents, blankets and food parcels. Where public offerings of shelter (in their own homes), toys, clothes and bicycles, and outcries in the direction of governments, who were slow to pick up the public opinion trend and embrace the evacuation of refugees, became the mode in 1999 with regard to Kosovars, the Afghan refugees inspired no such sentiments.[3] A major reason for this was the lack of media access to Afghanistan, and thus to refugees or displaced persons in flight. Journalists were largely prevented from moving independently around the country, and concerns for their safety in doing so would be genuine amid bombardments and conflict. A further reason was the depiction of Afghans, over the last decade and more, as among the scroungers and bogus asylum seekers. Their land had been torn apart, left wasted by regime after regime since the 1970s, yet those who fled repression and the Taliban regime were rarely granted refugee (Convention) protection, and even less often granted true peace, safety and non-discrimination. The editor of UNHCR's magazine, *Refugees*, wondered if:

> Perhaps publics at large, focused for a moment on the crisis, will look behind the scare headlines and discover who refugees are – people just like you and me – and perhaps this time around the industrialized world will not walk away from Afghanistan in its greatest hour of need.[4]

This chapter addresses three issues: the images of the refugees, and the impact of these images on overall perceptions; the significance of longstanding perceptions; and the dilemma faced by authorities, which have international obligations to refugee protection and claims to security that they cannot ignore.

IMAGES

That the general public did not become attached to the refugees from Afghanistan can largely be put down to two phenomena in connection with the pictorial portrayal of the refugees and of Afghanistan: there was an absence of new images, and the presence of other images distracted, to an extent, from any focus on people. The citation above from UNHCR's *Refugees* did not become reality because new, strong images were not forthcoming meaning that the Afghan refugees from the end of 2001 did not become 'people just like us.'

No new pictures

Ironically, the most famous picture of a refugee in the world is a picture of a 12-year-old Afghan girl, taken in a refugee camp on the border between Afghanistan and Pakistan. It was taken in 1983, and became a global icon on its publication in 1985. It is a photograph taken by Steve McCurry, and it was the cover of *National Geographic*'s June 1985 issue. Everyone knows the image: haunting green eyes, as *National Geographic* describes them: 'piercing green eyes, shocked with hints of blue and fear, [which] gave away her story. Soviet helicopters destroyed her village and family, forcing her to make a two-week trek out of the perilous mountains of Afghanistan.'[5] Everyone wanted to know who the girl was. In January 2002 she was found: she had returned to Afghanistan. In April 2002, Sharbat Gula was again on the cover of *National Geographic* – and a new powerful image was found – but one which depended totally on the old image.[6] Sharbat Gula herself had never seen the photograph, and never been captured on film except on that one occasion, until the same photographer tracked her down.

The original photograph of Sharbat Gula is one of the most famous pictures in the world, arguably a picture that could never be matched. The new photographs of her aged by time and by the hardships of refugee camps and war, are not a let down. However, they do not have the same power – and given that she was already famous, if unknown, the world over, they hardly have the ability to make this representation of a refugee one with which the average persons finds empathy. In a sense, the fame of Sharbat's original portrait may be one of the reasons why no new images could emerge of refugees from Afghanistan, which could cause the hearts of Western publics to realize that these people feared the same people (the Taliban and al-Qaeda) that we fear. But they were in much closer proximity, so they ran away, seeking safety – a safety that it was nearly impossible for them to find.

In fact, unknown to many people, an image of an Afghan refugee won the World Press Photo 2001 prize in January 2002. That picture, taken by Danish photographer Erik Refner, shows the body of an infant boy being prepared for burial in a refugee camp in Pakistan. The picture was taken in June 2001, months before the US bombing began. While the picture may have technical qualities that impressed the judges, and cause an emotional reaction, it is not an image on which any campaign to increase acceptance of refugee arrivals from Afghanistan could be based.

Competing attention grabbers

Not only were there no new pictures of refugees, there were also at least two images with which it was hard to compete for attention in the flight from Afghanistan. In March 2001, the Taliban demolished two 1,500-year-old Buddha statues in Bamiyan. The threat to destroy the statues was met with international outcry. Some refugee advocacy groups highlighted the greater attention given to these objects of art and religious heritage compared with the limited positive attention for Afghanistan's refugees, displaced persons and suffering population, while using the renewed attention for Afghanistan to bring the refugees' plight to a wider audience.[7] At the end of 2001, the funds set up to restore the statues had donations far exceeding their target: the humanitarian funds to finance relief, assistance and reconstruction, were much bigger in terms of the amount sought, but had come nowhere near meeting their targets.

Also in the autumn of 2001, creatures in Kabul's zoo received enormous public attention. The focal point was Marjan, a one-eyed, 40-year-old lion, who had survived all the decades of fighting. On 26 January 2002, Marjan was found dead in his cage – only after an American vet had been flown in to tend to his needs. As the *Observer* noted: 'Cynics said the old cat generated far more attention than most of Afghanistan's needy human population. One British tabloid led a fund-raising campaign for him that netted £160,000.'[8]

Efforts to generate support for the displaced population of Afghanistan generally seemed to receive limited attention – perhaps again due to a lack of images. In a news conference on 11 October 2001, President George W. Bush announced the establishment of America's Fund for Afghan Children. It was presented as a fund to which American children would contribute in order to improve the lives of their Afghan counterparts. By March 2002, the Fund had received 390,614 letters containing donations of $4,289,455.11, and when other donations were added the total came to $4,648,516.63.[9] That is not insignificant, but does translate to less than a dollar per child in the USA – and to less than a dollar per child among the potential Afghan recipients. Administered by the Red Cross of America, the Fund called for letters to be sent to the White House – an announcement derided at a time when letters containing anthrax had been delivered in the Capitol area, causing the closure of Senate offices.

WHY IMAGES ARE NECESSARY FOR THE CREATION OF A 'PERCEPTION'

With funds for statues and animals grabbing the attention, the refugees stood little chance. A British television station provides the most telling proof of this suggestion: the Disasters Emergency Committee, an umbrella group of British aid agencies, hoped to announce an appeal at the end of September 2001. However, ITV, the main commercial station in the UK said that people would not respond, as disaster had not happened in Afghanistan yet, and people respond only after events, not in anticipation. What is more 'People need to see evidence of something happening' a source was cited as saying.[10] There simply were not enough powerful images: one director of the emergency committee pointed out that the problem was that people were dying quietly, and not photogenically in front of cameras.

Without images of the refugees, living or dying, people in developed states could not form a perception of the crisis faced by these Afghans. The pictures of the World Trade Center towers collapsing, and moving stories of survivors, family and friends from New York, the Washington area and elsewhere made for powerful television, as did images of armed service personnel, leaving behind families and heading to what was projected to be the USA's most dangerous war since Vietnam. The focus on the whereabouts of Osama bin Laden and Mullah Omar also made compelling and competing television and print stories. Together with the image-detractors described above, these factors meant that the general public was not becoming familiar with the refugees. Also most displaced people remained within Afghanistan's borders – inside which the international media were not easily permitted, as their security could not be guaranteed, and their presence could endanger the security of the complex military operation taking place. No individuals escaping Afghanistan *now* were being highlighted by the international media, and so the public perception of Afghan refugees was of a mass of *burkha* clad figures and dusty desert fighters to whom they found it difficult to relate.

EXISTING PERCEPTIONS

As all flights to and within the USA were grounded after 9/11, some of the people most traumatically affected by the inability to travel there were those who had been accepted, after strenuous scrutiny, for resettlement. They included Afghan families who had been waiting for years in Pakistan, India and other states, hoping for an opportunity to seek genuine safety and a better life. Only ten states in the world run active resettlement programs, and some six more states are starting them up. Resettlement involves the selection of refugees, in their country of origin or, more usually, in a country of first asylum, for relocation and a restriction-free future in a state which guarantees their residence and protection. Those resettled are refugees on arrival, not asylum seekers. The status of refugee has been granted after processing outside of the state of resettlement, either processing by its national authorities, or selection and recommendation by UNHCR. Having been selected as a refugee, but then being stranded in states of first asylum, some people were inevitably exposed to new dangers and renewed severe treatment by people who knew they had been ready to escape. The USA closed its resettlement program for much longer than the three days for which its airspace remained closed. Administrative delays due largely to the timing of events were one source of postponement and temporary closure. The program is renewed annually, in September. In 2001 it took until mid-November for the process of letters and signings between Congress, the White House and the State Department (which runs the program) to be finalized. Beyond that, the program saw fewer arrivals than planned during its first months of operation, largely due to security fears. Whereas some 20,000 might have been expected to arrive between September and December, only 2,000 did. While the security fears were originally thought to be centerd mainly on the applicants, in fact the security of Immigration and Naturalization Service staff who had to process the refugee applicants in their countries of first asylum was as much of an issue.

  Another state that has traditionally practiced resettlement on a large scale is Australia. Whereas the US program has operated at a level of 70,000–90,000 people per year for the last few years, the Australian program has involved some 12,000 places. In 2000–1 the number of places had not changed, but political decisions had been made to use a high proportion of those places not for offshore processing and resettlement, but for the onshore processing of spontaneously arriving asylum seekers. This was partly a response of the conservative Howard government to the increasing arrivals of people being smuggled by sea, often via Indonesia. In late August 2001 the *MV Tampa* incident had taken place: some 428 asylum seekers, for the most part Afghans, had been rescued at sea by the Norwegian vessel *The Tampa*. The captain, close to Australian waters at the time, requested permission to land his unexpected passengers on Christmas Island. This was refused. After furious debate between Australia, Norway and UNHCR, the tiny Pacific island of Nauru offered to allow the asylum seekers to land and be processed. Those who were acknowledged to be genuine refugees would be re-settled. Australian Minister for Immigration, Philip Ruddock, described the asylum seekers on board *The Tampa* as terrorists and hijackers: an unfortunate analogy in the eyes of many as the events of 9/11 unfolded. In fact, this perception of asylum seekers as terrorists and hijackers was sustained by Ruddock, Howard and their party, and is credited by many as fuelling their re-election success. In discussing the arrival of boats carrying asylum seekers in Australian waters and the links to terrorism, Peter Reith, Australia's Defense Minister, told one radio interviewer 'You've got to be able to control that (the right to refuse entry to boat people), otherwise it can be a pipeline for terrorists to come in and use your country as a staging post for terrorist activities.'[11] In contrast, New Zealand's Deputy Prime Minister replied to a parliamentary question: 'It is reprehensible to link the terrorist attacks in the US to refugees in New Zealand, let alone the Muslim community.'[12]

Refugees have suffered as victims of the aftermath of the terrorist attack through the reductions made to the US resettlement program. However, it was feared that the impact on asylum seekers and refugees generally could be greater. Refugee protection advocates in the USA and elsewhere held their breath in the days following September 11, fearing it would be discovered (as claimed originally) that some of the hijackers had claimed asylum either in the USA or Canada. Some of the 1993 World Trade Center bombers had used the asylum channel to remain in the USA: this had adversely affected US regulations on asylum seeking, particularly through the 1996 legal changes, which had instituted more detention of asylum seekers. In fact, none of the nineteen hijackers who orchestrated the attacks on September 11, or their suspected accomplices, appears to have applied for asylum in European countries, the USA or Canada. The more immediate legislative changes in the USA are therefore being made on the obtaining of a visa, and student entry – responding directly to the immigration categories used by the terrorists.

For years European governments had branded Afghan asylum seekers as among those who made invalid claims for refugee status. Of the 150,000 Afghanis who sought asylum in Europe in the 1990s, only 36,000 were recognized as refugees. Denials were based on an understanding that Afghans were not fleeing individual persecution as defined in the 1951 Convention. The hijacking analogy was, however, sustained during the trial of nine Afghans who had hijacked a plane and landed at London's Stansted airport in February 2000. Many of the hijackers and passengers sought asylum and it was believed that the plane had been specifically hijacked for that purpose. The nine were found guilty of hijacking in the UK in December 2001, but their conviction was overturned on appeal in May 2003. Fundamental in the latter judgment was the moment at which the hijackers sense of persecution ended. The basis of their claim was that persecution and the need for protection drove them to an illegal hijacking: they committed the crime, in other words, because they really needed asylum.

The existing perception of Afghan asylum seekers in most developed countries was thus negative. Without information to counter this view, or images to change the perception with the new crisis in that country, Afghanistan's refugees had little opportunity to make an impact on populations in the West, or to encourage those populations to inspire their governments to act on the refugees' behalf.

WHERE ARE THE REFUGEES?

Pakistan originally closed its border with Afghanistan in November 2000, as it already sheltered more than 2 million Afghan refugees. Although UNHCR and others had frequently requested that the borders be reopened, this had officially not been done. In the days immediately following 9/11, the US government specifically requested that Pakistan keep the borders closed as a security measure.[13] Not letting anyone out meant not letting bin Laden and al-Qaeda members out, as well as not letting refugees across. This stance may have made some sort of military and security sense, but it made little sense in human rights terms: refusing Afghans right to seek asylum in countries other than their own, and entailing *refoulement*. *Refoulement* is the act of returning a person who has applied for refugee status to the country in which he or she has reason to fear for safety, and the principle of *non-refoulement* is set out in Article 33 of the 1951 Refugee Convention. In any case, the terrorists had means, sophisticated, secret or otherwise, to cross the borders and regroup, without joining refugee convoys in trying to enter Pakistan in full view of the authorities.[14]

In the weeks prior to US military action in Afghanistan, UNHCR made plans to open camps to house up to 300,000 anticipated refugee arrivals in Pakistan. The UN agency became embroiled in difficult negotiations about the placement of camps, as the Pakistani authorities, not keen on new refugee arrivals, offered places with a range of dissatisfactory circumstances, including proximity to the Afghan border; the unsuitable nature of the ground composition; the absence of fresh water supplies and the location in largely anti-US areas of the country. The actual number of people crossing the border, even in the earliest weeks of bombardments by US forces, was much lower than expected. 'Only' 1,500–2,000 refugees were crossing the border into Pakistan daily according to NGO reports.[15] Many of these people were slipping across remote, unmanned border crossings, as the official border posts had publicly been re-declared closed by the Pakistani authorities.[16] While the Pakistani authorities were initially changing policies on border openings frequently,[17] the borders later remained officially closed, and refugees were resorting to the use of smugglers to reach relative safety in Pakistan. Many reports indicated US $50 was paid to smugglers – a significant amount of money to Afghans who had lost everything. Iran likewise limited inward border crossings and even deported some 2,000 people back of Afghanistan during the last months of 2001. While two or three thousand people crossed Pakistan's border checkpoints each day in the first week of the US bombing campaign over Afghanistan, some 50,000 people were reported to be gathering on the Afghan side in the eastern province of Paktia. But Pakistan held fast: General Pervez Musharraf, the military ruler of Pakistan, said 'We can only accept the bare minimum. We cannot open our borders to anyone who comes across.'[18] As Pakistan variously closed its borders and opened them intermittently to a few so-called vulnerable cases, and at the very least limited crossings by would-be refugees, the USA and its Western allies said little or nothing. There were no protests that refugees should not be kept backed up on the Afghan side of the border.

This contrasted sharply with the situation when Macedonia had closed its border crossing in early April 1999, leaving some 10,000 people stranded on the Kosovar and Serbian side of the frontier. Western governments rushed to protest, and to set up escape routes for the refugees and for Macedonia.[19] As images of Kosovar Albanians, trapped in no-man's-land, milling around railway tracks, and being sent walking back, away from safety along those tracks, were beamed around the world, governments leapt into action to use their diplomacy and the strategic offering of evacuation places to restore calm to Macedonia's political landscape. This was important also from the point of view of the NATO alliance. NATO had been present in Macedonia throughout the previous decade: at a time when its bases there were a focal point of preparation for peacekeeping missions in Kosovo, and when Macedonia's support for the alliance was most needed, the NATO states could not let support drift by not stepping in to protect the refugees who fled into Macedonia.

In the case of Pakistan there were intriguing differences and similarities in the situation. There were few pictures beamed around the world of Afghans waiting, still in Afghanistan, to cross the border: and those pictures that there were did not make the refugees 'look just like us,' in the way the Kosovar Albanians had.[20] Missing from the equation was an outpouring of public sympathy for the refugees in Afghanistan. Furthermore, those governments that had refugee resettlement programs had been closing them down or restricting them, so the atmosphere was not conducive to the provision of escape routes out of Pakistan and Iran, and via them out of Afghanistan.

By 6 November, 135,000 displaced persons had crossed the frontiers and registered with authorities, still not even half of UNHCR's contingency planning number. However, many tens of thousands more had been displaced within Afghanistan, leaving the local workers of international agencies scrambling to use supplies which were already present (and on occasion were being destroyed by US bombs). Furthermore, those people who were crossing the borders – while Pakistani guards' guns shot wildly into the air above them – were predominantly men fleeing conscription into the Taliban, it was suggested. Many of these were deported straight back to Afghanistan: and when it comes to public images, these men did not have the photogenic qualities required to instill sympathy.

The images were lacking, and thus domestic concerns to push for refugee protection assistance for Pakistan was absent. UNHCR was seemingly prepared and in place, if not fully operational, yet the refugees were not arriving. And whereas Macedonia had been urged to open its border during the Kosovo conflict and stop the human suffering, Pakistan was permitted to keep its border closed. There was diplomatic silence on the closure of the border and probably private relief for politicians that the border closure seemed firmly in place as far as their own publics were concerned, as popular fear of terrorists outweighed popular sympathy for refugees.

An unnamed UNHCR worker was cited in a Dutch newspaper as saying: 'Why are all these politicians visiting Pakistan now? It doesn't help anything. We are still the only ones who are screaming that the border between Afghanistan and

Pakistan must be opened, and opened now.'[21] President Musharraf claimed to fear the arrival of two million new refugees, and to prefer to see new camps set up within Afghanistan.[22] While leaders such as Dutch Prime Minister Wim Kok, visiting the region, could claim openly that the refugees would cross the border regardless of its closure if they really needed to, the reality was that few people were crossing because they feared the consequences. These included the actual reception on the border (with Pakistani guards shooting in the air and the orders to turn around), and the prospect of days, months or years in camps, which some had indeed left in order to return to Afghanistan during previous years of the decades' long wars in the country.

CONCLUSION: WHO RISKS WHAT WHEN THE IMAGES ARE ABSENT?

In 1999, NATO allies risked losing the support of Macedonia for their military intervention when that country felt overwhelmed by the sheer number of refugee arrivals. The Macedonian authorities and public saw NATO countries attempting to shirk responsibility for the refugees. For Pakistan, the loss of a strategic military ally was a risk the USA and UK, along with other Western allies, could not afford to take. If the situation had deteriorated so that Pakistan actually had to ask for help, the allies might have had to oblige. Yet the Pakistani government seemed to see asking for help as a potential embarrassment which might ultimately create instability domestically and internationally. The regime in Islamabad was caught in a dilemma: it could not, on the one hand, take care of a massive refugee flow, or bear the unrest a massive influx might set off which would be added to the disquiet surrounding its alliance with the USA against terror. On the other hand, it did not want to be blamed for a humanitarian disaster: and so the solution it found was to release the tension on the border only minimally, and only when it had to, by opening the border to let a few people through at moments of impending crisis, but never advertising the fact, which would only have had a magnet effect.[23] It was also not in the Pakistani government's interest vis-à-vis its own population to advertise how many people UNHCR could not count because they had disappeared into existing camps or to live with relatives elsewhere in the country. That would again risk social unrest, and add a new dimension of potential strain to the developing alliance with the USA.

The USA and other Western states clearly had strategic, security and political reasons for keeping the focus on the victims in the USA, and on the potential for further terrorist strikes, and away from the victims of decades of conflict in Afghanistan, and particularly from the new victims. Whether the absence of images was mere chance or not, it was to an extent fortuitous. With a governmental focus on assistance through the dropping by air of a few thousand food packages each night, which would help some people a little, there was also potentially a desire not to expose humanitarian holes in the overall policy with regard to Afghanistan and neighboring states.

Ultimately, one could perhaps say 'as usual,' those who risked the most from this lack of images were the refugees. Clearly, a rapid conflict, which might truly end the decades of war and bring reconstruction and development to the country, was the greatest goal for the refugees: but even if displaced for only a few days, people need assistance and protection in order to survive and to be productive in the long term. As they were turned away at the border, and forced into Internally Displaced Persons camps where they remained vulnerable to persecution by the Taliban, in Spin Baldak, for example, the refugees were denied the right to seek and enjoy asylum in other countries; they were victims of *refoulement* which the 1951 Convention specifically prohibits; and they were victimized repeatedly. Ultimately, the refugees risked their lives as a result of the lack of knowledge about their situation which 'just like us' images could have brought. As a result, the international community once again risked its entire refugee protection regime, established in the aftermath of the Second World War to insure that no individuals are lost in battles that disrupt and challenge the state system.

NOTES

1 *Conclusions adopted by the Council (Justice and Home Affairs)*, Brussels, 20 Sept. 2001, SN 3926/6/01 REV 6, para. 30.
2 Exclusion would be possible if the 1951 Convention's article 1F were to be appropriately applied, meaning that anyone who had committed a crime against humanity, or an act contrary to the principles of the United Nations, can be excluded from the provisions of the Convention which define a refugee and outline the basic rights attached to that status.
3 See Joanne van Selm, 'Perceptions of Kosovo's Refugees', in Mary Buckley and Sally N. Cummings (eds), *Kosovo: Perceptions of War and its Aftermath* (London and New York: Continuum, 2002) and Joanne van Selm (ed.), *Kosovo's Refugees in the European Union* (London and New York: Continuum, 2000).
4 Editorial 'The global fallout', *Refugees*, (Geneva: UNHCR), Vol. 4, No. 125, 2001, p. 2.
5 Steve McCurry, 'Unveiling the Face of War', http://www.nationalgeographic.com/ngm/100best/multi1_interview.html
6 'Found: After 17 Years an Afghan Refugee's Story', *National Geographic*, April 2002, which was that issue's cover and top story.
7 RFE/RL, 'UN: Humanitarian Crisis Coincides With Outrage Over Buddhist Statues', http://www.rferl.org/nca/features/2001/03/13032001113838.asp
8 Paul Harris, 'Marjan, the Lion of Kabul, Roars his Last', *The Observer*, 27 Jan. 2002, http://www.observer.co.uk/international/story/0,6903,640091,00.html
9 http://kidsfund.redcross.org/about.html
10 Felicity Lawrence and Matt Wells, 'Lack of Footage Stalls TV Disaster Appeal', *The Guardian*, 5 Oct. 2002
   http://www.guardian.co.uk/waronterror/story/0,1361,563729,00.html
11 Ray Wilkinson, 'After the terror: the fallout', *Refugees* (Geneva: UNHCR), Vol. 4, No. 125, 2001, p. 7.
12 Ibid.
13 Human Rights Watch, 'Closed Door Policy: Afghan Refugees in Pakistan and Iran', *Afghanistan, Iran and* Pakistan, Vol. 14, No. 2 (G) Feb. 2002, http://hrw.org/reports/2002/pakistan/index.htm, p. 23.

14 James Risen and David Johnston, 'Intercepted al-Qaeda E-Mail Is Said to Hint at Regrouping', *New York Times*, 6 March 2002.
15 'UN Agency in Dispute with Pakistan over Refugee Camps', *Financial Times*, 15 Oct. 2001.
16 Ibid.
17 Associated Press, 'Thousands of Refugees Pour Over Border into Pakistan', 19 Oct. 2001 http://news.independent.co.uk/world/asia_china/story.jsp?story=100376
18 Rory McCarthy, 'Borders Stay Shut to Fleeing Afghans', *The Guardian Unlimited*, 9 Oct. 2001 www.guardian.co.uk/waronterror/story/0,1361,565813,00.html
19 See Astri Suhrke, Michael Barutciski, Peta Sandison and Rick Garlock, 'The Kosovo Refugee Crisis: An Independent Evaluation of UNHCR's Emergency Preparedness and Response' by (EPAU/2000/001 February 2000 pre-publication edition) at http://www.unhcr.ch/cgi-bin/texis/vtx/home/opendoc.pdf?tbl=RESEARCH&id=3ba0bbeb4&page=research
20 Matthew J. Gibney, 'Kosovo and Beyond: Popular and Unpopular Refugees', *Forced Migration Review*, No. 5, Aug. 1999, pp. 28–30.
21 Frank Poorthuis, 'Wel even slikken, de mensen willen de grens over' ('Hard to swallow, the people want to cross the border'), *De Volkskrant*, 29 Oct. 2001 (author's translation).
22 Ibid.
23 Richard Lloyd Parry, 'Confusion on Frontier as Thousands Renain Standed in No Man's Land', *Independent*, 23 Oct. 2001, from http://www.independent.co.uk/world/asia_china/story.jsp?story=100956

23 The global economy

What has changed?[1]

Brigitte Granville

On September 11 2001, financial markets went into panic, stock prices plummeted all over the world while the prices of oil and gold soared. Fears were that the shock would have lasting effects on global trade and growth given the already precarious state of the US economy, and send the world economy into recession. However horrific, this shock did not in itself trigger a recession, thanks mainly to the US authorities' rapid economic policy response designed to bolster consumer confidence. This response comprised further interest rate cuts, with European monetary authorities quickly following suit, and further easing of fiscal policy in addition to the Bush administration's initial tax-cut package that predated the terrorist attacks.

In addition to the fact that the global economy has weathered the effect of the 9/11 attacks, on the policy level the attack may even have been beneficial. First, as already indicated, it stimulated even more aggressive easing of monetary and fiscal policy to boost demand. The US economy, crucial for global demand, followed the contraction of the third quarter with positive growth in the fourth quarter. Second, the terrorist attack has concentrated the minds of Western policy-makers on its economic origins, and in particular, the threat which global poverty poses to international security.

SCENARIOS OF GLOOM

Before 9/11, the economic downturn in the USA had centred on the sharp fall in manufacturing output, as inventories were run down amidst the unwinding of previous over-investment (especially in information technology and telecommunications). But the downturn had been cushioned by the resilience of consumer demand, despite the heavy indebtedness of US households and mounting job losses as enterprises retrenched. The fear after a terrorist act as horrific and unprecedented as the September 11 attacks was that this would strike a fatal blow to consumer confidence, transforming the existing US slowdown into sharply negative growth or a 'hard landing.'

This, in turn, would have triggered a global recession. The main transmission mechanism is the dependence of other economies on their export trade to the

USA and on global credit markets centred on the USA. The more a country depends on US exports for growth, the more the economy will head towards a recession in the event of any weakening of US demand. Similarly with finance, the more a country depends on external refinancing of maturing debt, the more adversely it will be affected by the capital outflow 'contagion' effect from distress in US credit markets.

With a slowdown in US demand, imports were bound to fall, affecting exporting countries mainly in Latin America and Asia depending on the level of their export dependency and the nature of exports. For these countries, weaker exports mean a deterioration in the current account, in turn leading to larger financing gaps, which will be difficult and expensive to fill in an environment of severely damaged confidence. The debt burden of the countries affected will increase as the cost of borrowing rises.

Even less open economic areas like the European Union were showing surprising signs of greater vulnerability to the US downturn – as reflected in the sharp manufacturing recession. As for Japan, there seemed no hope that the world's second largest economy could extricate itself from its home-made deflation trap and generate the demand necessary to offset economic weakness in the USA and so help avert global recession.

Oil producing countries in principle share other exporters' vulnerability to general demand weakness, mainly from – once again – the USA, as the world's largest energy consumer and oil importer. Military conflicts in Afghanistan and in Iraq created a potential threat to supply, which in turn supported the oil price. However, these concerns were short term.

WHAT CRISIS?

While some of these forebodings have become reality, notably the deep new recession in Japan and the financial and economic collapse in Argentina, these negative developments would most likely have happened anyway even without the September terrorist attack. But even where the impact of the attacks was most directly felt, fears of a resulting severe economic recession have proved overdone. First and foremost, the US economy, helped by a further round of aggressive monetary easing, withstood the initial blow to confidence. Although fears of recession persisted in 2002 as financial asset prices corrected sharply downwards, the economy did not experience a significant contraction.

After effectively stagnating in the first half of 2001, US growth already looked likely to move into negative territory in the third quarter as unemployment started to rise sharply. The immediate shock of the terrorist attack clearly aggravated this negative trend, and contributed to the GDP downturn for that quarter of −0.3 percent quarter over quarter and −0.4 percent year over year.[2] The effect on consumer confidence appears to have lingered in October 2001; but since then, consumer spending recovered, and meanwhile, the unwinding of industrial inventories has reached its natural limit, with a consequent positive turnaround in output trends. These processes were underpinned by the Federal Reserve making further interest rate cuts, while the Bush administration proposed an additional huge fiscal stimulus to the first round of tax cuts voted by Congress in the summer. Consensus expectations of a recession were thus contradicted, as GDP growth scraped back into positive territory in the fourth quarter (+2.7 percent quarter over quarter and 0.1 percent year over year).

Monetary authorities in Europe (the European Central Bank and Bank of England) followed the US lead in cutting their own interest rates. The turning point towards recovery was marked by the decision of the US Federal Reserve's Open Market Committee in February to leave interest rates unchanged – having reduced rates at each of its regular meetings over the previous thirteen months (the first cut occurred on 19 December 2000). This policy shift was partly designed to control long-term interest rates, which had started to rise as markets began to perceive the previous aggressive monetary easing as a prelude to higher inflation.

At the same time, the 'Fed' indicated that its policy bias remained in favor of further easing, as signs of weakness in the economy persist. In particular, some retrenchment by the highly leveraged households seems inevitable, and the consumer demand recovery at the end of 2001 was much exaggerated by car manufacturers' offer of interest free credit terms. Against this background, the positive output effect of inventory rebuilding in the manufacturing sector might be undermined by insufficient final demand. However that may be, at least the widely expected outcome of a full-blown recession caused by the September attack has not come to pass. Moreover, the factors favoring a 'double-dip recession' should be countered by the further effect of existing interest rate and tax cuts (2003 will see already enacted fiscal easing worth 1 percent of GDP materialize.

In the wider world economy, and in particular international trade, the picture mirrors that of the USA: short-term contraction giving way to a prospect of recovery coming sooner than previously expected. International trade during the second half of 2001 would have fallen anyway in the context of the recession in US and global manufacturing, but the September attacks must account for the extent of the contraction, even if its precise contribution is unquantifiable. The impact of 9/11 is most clearly traceable in specific sectors such as air transport and international tourism.

INTEGRATING THE POOR?

The terrorist attack on the USA has sharpened the focus of Western policy-making on the threat which global poverty poses to international security, and consequently on the need to ensure that the existing international economic order can be harnessed to effective strategies to reduce poverty.

The simplest income-based measure of poverty – about 300 million people (taking into account differences in cost of living) survive on less than $1 a day

– gives more than sufficient cause for alarm.[3] This is compounded by the grim web of causes and effects in which this reality of below-subsistence incomes is situated: political and economic instability, population displacement from civil conflict and regional wars, environmental degradation, the economic enslavement of women, and the spread of disease. It is of course clear that the perpetrators of the September attacks, like so many primary exponents of fanatical and murderous ideologies through history, were neither poor nor uneducated. But the extensive poverty and even more widespread hopelessness give these evil leaders fertile ground not only for recruiting their active foot soldiers, but also for building popular sympathy among the (in this case, Arab) masses.

As far as global poverty is concerned, 9/11 has thrown into stark relief the challenge for the world's richest and most powerful countries. This is to demonstrate that their system is part of the solution, rather than part of the problem. The mass street protests against globalization that became common in rich countries after 1999 appear based on the belief that international economic integration is part of the problem. The reverse is the case. In terms of integrating product (goods and services) and factor (labor and capital) markets across the world, the world's poor have been least integrated. This is because developed countries have restricted poor countries' access to the global marketplace by immigration controls (limiting labor mobility) and trade barriers to competitively priced goods.

Of these two problems, labor market fragmentation is perhaps the most important. The 1905 Immigration Act in the UK introduced national quotas on immigration virtually for the first time anywhere. The passport and its resulting inhibition of free labor mobility is a twentieth-century innovation.[4] Jeffrey Williamson shows how much of the very significant factor price convergence that occurred in the pre-First World War period, when the world economy was more integrated, was driven by emigration rather than international trade.[5] The present EU visa regime, for instance, is designed to prevent economic migration from developing countries. However, there are signs of a change of approach by rich European countries. This is due mainly to their own internal problems of skills shortages due to declining populations and social failures (especially in education); and the resulting greater openness to legal migration (notably in Germany) can be traced back to the late 1990s. However, there is still no early prospect of any such liberalization extending to the less-skilled workers of the poor countries that surround Western Europe.

The resulting dashed expectations contribute to the backlash in poor countries against the West and pro-Western governments and, at worst, can destabilize these countries and their economies, requiring yet more Western aid and intervention. Besides restriction on economic emigration from poor to rich countries, the other culprit is protectionist barriers to poor country exports. Restricted trade access for poor countries' primary resources and manufactures reflects the political and social pressures of rich country unemployment, and other internal structural weaknesses. The relative power of different interest groups within nations rather than some measure of overall national interest is the main determining factor in government policies toward international trade and development. Poor people in developing countries (earning $2 a day or less) work primarily in agriculture and labor-intensive manufactures. And yet the World Bank estimates in a report published in 2002 that the average poor person selling into globalized markets confronts barriers that are roughly twice as high as the typical worker in industrial countries.[6] The damage caused by discrimination against goods efficiently produced by poor countries such as food, textiles and clothing can be measured against faster integration which through lowering barriers to merchandise trade (elimination of import tariffs, export subsidies and domestic production subsidies) would increase growth and provide some $1.5 trillion of additional cumulative income to developing countries over the 2005–15 period.[7]

The IMF has highlighted the very limited progress to date with trade liberalization:

> Few industrial countries have allowed developing countries substantially unimpaired or unlimited access to their markets on a unilateral basis. Since the Uruguay round, progress in expanding market access has been largely confined to regional and bilateral trade arrangements, such as those negotiated between the European Union and various developing country groups, including its neighbors and former colonies. These relatively recent agreements, though welcome, have tended to benefit selected developing countries and not necessarily the poorest ones. The present system of trade preferences excludes a number of 'sensitive products' in precisely those sectors – primarily agriculture, textiles, and footwear – where many poor countries have the greatest potential to expand and diversify their exports.[8]

The most readily available route to this destination is the continued liberalization of the multilateral world trading system in the rules-based framework of the WTO. The November 2001 WTO ministerial meeting in Doha was always going to be a key test, after the fiasco of its predecessor in Seattle two years before. But its timing – just two months after the terrorist attack on the USA – gave the event a unique charge as the relevance of the international political economy to the most basic security threats had become clear. It was in this context that US Trade Representative Robert Zoellick framed his call at Doha for the launch of a new round of multilateral trade liberalization negotiations in terms of 'countering the revulsive destructionism of terrorism [*sic*].'[9] The successful conclusion of the Doha meeting, together with the June 2002 vote in the US Congress to give the Bush administration 'fast track' trade negotiating authority, may be reckoned among the most significant and positive ways in which the September terrorist attack has affected the outlook for the global economy. Since November 2001 when the Doha round was launched, progress in international trade negotiations has not been as rapid as expected but the negotiations continue.

Given that even in this improved environment, normalized trade access for poor countries remains a distant prospect, policy to combat global poverty will also remain focused in parallel on the only alternative to trade liberalization – namely, aid. Without entering here into the debate of the pros and cons of aid, if trade access is not improved and aid flows remain at their present low level,[10] there can be little positive to say about the West's policy towards very poor countries and about the prospects for a better, safer world as many of these countries are heavily indebted. But here too, there are some early signs that the terrorist crisis has concentrated minds. As regards the problem of poor country debt, the preexisting Heavily Indebted Poor Country initiative gains added relevance, and further government support may yet materialize for debt relief tied to the new anti-poverty conditionality. On aid more generally, the UK government's call for a new 'Marshall Plan' aimed at the poorest countries, by adding \$50 billion to existing annual aid flows in return for the developing countries' pursuing corruption-free policies for stability, opening up trade and encouraging private investment. The so-called 'International Finance Facility' was formally presented by the Chancellor of the Exchequer, Gordon Brown, at the Royal Institute of International Affairs on 22 January 2003.

The most striking concrete recent development on the aid front has flowed directly from the successful military campaign against the Taliban regime in Afghanistan. The \$4.5 billion of reconstruction aid for post-Taliban Afghanistan pledged at the Tokyo donor conference in January 2002 has a significance which goes wider than Afghanistan. It signifies an end to isolationism. During the last US presidential election campaign and right up to the September terrorist attack, the Bush team expressed a natural allergy to involvement in 'nation-building' in far-flung countries. After 9/11, such involvement has been revealed to be central to the most basic security needs. Leaving failed states like Afghanistan to rot in misery and isolation will result in their becoming breeding grounds for fanaticism and violence on a global scale.

This perception seems to be the basis for the use of US foreign aid in encouraging political reforms in the Arab world. It is too early to tell how systematic and effective US action in this area will prove. For instance, there has only been one case since 9/11 of US aid being withheld pending compliance with governance-related conditionality. This was Egypt, which is not representative of the failed state problem, although given that country's long-running status as a major recipient of US aid, this could denote the beginning of a greater willingness by the USA to apply more impartially by now standard governance principles in pursuit of broader development and poverty reduction goals.[11] More likely, however, political criteria will maintain their traditional supremacy; and in this context, that means US concerns about the socio-political context in the Arab world for the emergence of groups like al-Qaeda. The US demand for political reform of the Palestinian authority (set out in the May 2002 speech by President Bush on the Israel–Palestine conflict) is another good example for this trend. The most serious future challenge for the USA in the sphere of state building proper would come in the event that it achieves its objective of regime change in Iraq. At the very least, the USA would have to remain closely involved in that country having fought a war to make it into a protectorate.

CONCLUSION

Further military conflict, namely Iraq, has complicated this paradoxically benign picture. The challenge is to overcome the poisoned diplomatic atmosphere of the run-up to the Iraq war and ensure that a collaborative vision and generosity prevail in reconstructing Iraq and stabilizing the region, including Afghanistan. The USA should neither seek to act alone, such as resisting UN involvement for an interim administration in Iraq, nor be encouraged to do so by the festering resentment of its alienated partners in western Europe, Russia and China. At stake here is not only the future of Afghanistan, Iraq and neighboring countries, but also the survival of the secular global trend towards open economies and international trade on which the prosperity of the whole world – very much including the USA itself – strongly depends.

NOTES

1 The views expressed in this article are those of the author and not necessarily those of the RIIA. This article draws on materials contained in Brigitte Granville, 'Shaken', *World Today*, Vol. 57, No. 10, Oct. 2001, esp. p. 14.

2 The source is the US Department of Commerce, Bureau of Economic Analysis (NIPA), August 2002.

3 The figures used in public discussion are 1.2 billion people, a fifth of the world's population, survive on less than $1 a day and 2.8 billion on less than $2. These figures do not take into account differences in the cost of living. Sala-I-Martin from Columbia University estimates that 300 million people and about 1 billion live under $1 and $2 respectively. The differences in these two sets of figures are due to allowing for differences in countries' cost of living. Xavier Sala-I-Martin, 'The Disturbing "Rise" of Global Income Inequality', National Bureau of Economic Research Working Paper No. w8904, April 2002.

4 Lawrence Summers, 'Distinguished Lecture on Economics in Government, Reflections on Managing Global Integration', *Journal of Economic Perspectives*, Vol. 13, No. 2, Spring 1999, pp. 3–18.

5 Jeffrey Williamson, 'Globalization, Labor Markets and Policy Backlash in the Past', *Journal of Economic Perspectives*, Vol. 12, No. 4, Fall 1998, pp. 51–72.

6 The World Bank, *Global Economic Prospects and the Developing Countries, Making Trade Work for the Poor* (Washington, DC: The World Bank, 2002), p. xii: 'In general, tariffs in high-income countries on imports from developing countries, though low, are four times those collected from industrial countries (0.8 percent as opposed to 3.4 percent). Subsidies and other support to agriculture in the high income countries are particularly pernicious – and are now running roughly $1 billion a day – *or more than six times all development assistance.* Distortions in tariff codes – exceptionally high tariffs on developing country products (tariff peaks), embedded incentives against processing abroad (tariff escalation), and tariffs that are the higher once specified import ceilings are reached (tariff rate quotas) – and trade practices, such as frequent recourse to anti-dumping actions, are often more important impediments that keep the poor from taking advantage of trading opportunities.'

7 World Bank, *Global Economic Prospects*, p. xiii.

8 International Monetary Fund, *World Economic Outlook* (Washington, DC: International Monetary Fund, May 2000), p. 21.

9 'High Stakes at Doha', *The Economist*, 3 Nov. 2001, p. 14.
10 David Dollar and Lant Pritchett, *Assessing Aid, What Works, What Doesn't, and Why* (Washington, DC: World Bank Policy Research Paper, published for the World Bank by Oxford University Press, Nov. 1998).
11 See 'Slapping Egypt's Wrist', *The Economist*, 24 Aug. 2002, pp.13–14.

24 War without warriors

Christopher Coker

In a memorable lecture delivered in 1957 Raymond Aron noted how thinkers such as Auguste Comte and Herbert Spencer, both of whom were profoundly conscious of living in a period of transition, had been prepared to make prophecies about the future of warfare 'whose boldness and dogmatism astound us.' By the time Aron himself came to reflect on the subject the experience of two world wars and fear of another had made predictions about the future distinctly unfashionable. Instead the Cold War came to be marked by an acute concern with the present, a concern which shaped and, in some respects distorted, thinking about war and peace.[1]

The attack on the USA on September 11, 2001 almost demanded an intellectual as well as political response, but in engaging in it we do so at risk. The attack has been treated by many analysts as 'Year Zero,' the moment when everything changed. We should know enough from history to recognize that little changes overnight. We are all confronted by the modesty of history. In plying their trade historians and political scientists try to identify historic turning points and to date them precisely but history is more modest. Its essential dates remain secret for some time.

Whether the attack was a turning point only future historians can judge. In this chapter I am interested in quite another question: the extent to which those in the West no longer understand war as they once did. President Bush was quick to call the war on terrorism 'the first war of the twenty-first century' but if it was a war on the West's part, it was a war without warriors. The war in Afghanistan which followed a month later saw a largely instrumental form of war now pioneered by the United States. In terms of war, the gap between the USA and its enemies is now greater than it has been between any other societies in history.

LIKE FALLING CHERRY BLOSSOMS: THE SAMURAI SUICIDE BOMBERS

One of the most shocking elements of the World Trade Center attack was how a small group of fundamentalists, armed with their faith in Islam, were not only prepared to hazard their lives but seek out their own death. It was ironic that several politicians should have called the attack 'the Pearl Harbor of the twenty-first century' for the Americans had first come across suicide bombers in the war with Japan. Then the bombers were not crashing into buildings in New York but the decks of American warships in the great and bloody campaigns of Iwo Jima and Okinawa. But the Americans had first come across the phenomenon the previous summer. It was then that they had stumbled upon the *tokkotai*, the 'special forces' which flew suicide missions against American shipping. Better known as *kamikaze* pilots, the Japanese drew inspiration from the Kamikaze (or 'Divine Wind'), the typhoon that had destroyed the Mongol invasion fleet in the thirteenth century. Seven centuries later, faced with another invasion and given the desperate situation in which the high command found both itself and the country, it was inevitable it would engage in desperate measures.

The pilots who volunteered for kamikaze missions did so from a sense of duty. And like the Muslim pilots on 9/11, they had a lot of time to think about their decision for almost no one was sent off immediately after volunteering. In some cases the pilots waited weeks, even months before their assignment came, a fact which makes their commitment all the more remarkable. Before their mission they would don a white head scarf (*hachimaki*) with the rising sun emblazoned on the center. Sometimes, they also wore a ceremonial waist sash (*senninbari*), called a 'thousand stitch belt' because 1,000 women in Japan had sewn one stitch each in order to show the widespread national support for their actions. Often they composed death poems, traditional for samurai warriors prior to suicide. And many of those poems displayed a specifically Japanese characteristic: the poetic contemplation of nature at the moment of death. Thus in 1945 a 22-year-old pilot wrote:

> If only we might fall
> Like cherry blossoms in the Spring –
> So pure and radiant

So close are the Japanese to nature that they have a word for the season of cherry blossom viewing, *hanami*. Though this time it was the American sailors on their ships who viewed the fall and what they saw was for them a completely senseless loss of life which did some local damage but not enough to change materially the outcome of the war.

With their rigidly instrumental attitude to war the Americans thought the Japanese were mad. In June 1944 they commissioned a noted anthropologist, Ruth Benedict, to explain the kamikaze phenomenon. The central conclusion she reached in her study *The Chrysanthemum and the Sword* was that in war, as in peace, the Japanese had 'acted in character.' For unlike the West, Japan had a shame rather than a guilt culture, with all its humanistic implications for freedom and moral autonomy.[2] For guilt is experienced in the face of abstractions such as the moral law which is part, or becomes part, of the subject himself. The moral law is internalized. We feel guilty about our behavior to others. Our attention is turned to the victim. Shame, by contrast, is more narcissistic. It involves a strong sense of being at a disadvantage. This sense of powerlessness is doubled when it involves the outside world.

Benedict's analysis has not weathered well. Few anthropologists today would endorse her conclusions. But what of the Japanese, the subject of her study? What did they make of the American way of warfare? Largely, they too saw their American adversaries in an unflattering light. True, with their technological superiority – their B29 bombers, flame throwers and nuclear bombs the Americans were instrumentally formidable; but they seemed to lack the warrior's spirit. They did not fight to the death even though the motto of the Marines was 'Death before dishonour.'

And even as the war came to an end the Japanese were horrified rather than impressed with the ruthlessness the Americans showed, because it was largely manifest in 'disengaged' conflict: airpower. In March 1945 the USAF 'torched' Tokyo in a raid that claimed 120,000 lives. In *The World as Representation and Will* Schopenhauer speaks of music as 'pure will.' The Japanese were fascinated and horrified at the same time that the United States, a country which had wholly lost (or appeared to) the sense of war as representation had wholly preserved the idea of war as 'will.'

Whether or not we are living through a major turning point in our lives, the September 11 attack reintroduced the Americans to a different way of warfare. Once again they found themselves living in a different time zone from their enemies as they had in 1945. Both have a totally different understanding of war, and the role of the warrior. Both worlds are remote, psychologically and emotionally. The trouble is that they intersect from time to time through war or acts of terrorism.

EXPRESSIVE WAR

Contemporary history, it has been said, begins when those factors that are important in our own lives first began to take shape in our imagination. With the benefit of hindsight we can glimpse an intimation of the events of September 11 in a remarkable novel by Joseph Conrad which was published as long ago as 1906. Central to the story is a plot to blow up the Greenwich Observatory. Conrad was inspired to write the novel by a real event, an incident in Greenwich Park in 1894 in which a bomb exploded killing the anarchist sympathizer who was carrying it.

The novel was dedicated to H. G. Wells, 'the historian of the future.' And the dedication was nothing if not ironic. For although Conrad was a genuine admirer of Wells and his work he set out to challenge the heady optimism Wells had shown in his 'London' novels, *Love and Mr Lewisham* and *Mr Kipps*. Conrad's book is set in London but it is a metropolis which is not at peace with itself. For London, the center of the world in the early twentieth century, harbors an anarchist cell whose members are intent on the destruction of the bourgeois way of life. This was country he had explored before, notably in *Heart of Darkness* especially in the person of Mr Kurtz, who 'lies at the bottom of a precipice in which the sun never shines.' Conrad did not analyze the nihilism of the nineteenth century in the manner of Nietzsche but he knew the feel of it more consciously and keenly than his British contemporaries.

And he captured its spirit in the person of Mr Vladimir, the shadowy puppet-master who uses the anarchists for his own cynical ends. Cynical or not, he is a true nihilist in spirit. In conversation with the double agent Verloc, Vladimir waxes lyrical. What is needed, he muses, is a set of outrages that must be sufficiently startling to astonish the bourgeoisie. What act of terror would disconcert them the most? Not an attempt on a crowned head or a President – that would be mere sensationalism; not a bomb in a church otherwise that might be construed wrongly as a crime against organized religion; not blowing up a restaurant and the people eating in it for that might be dismissed as a social crime, the act of a hungry man. Not an attack on the National Gallery for no one in England would miss it. But what of an attack on reason? Pity it was impossible to blow up pure mathematics. The next best thing was zero longitude, on the one hand a very unreal concept, on the other something that was very real for the commerce and communications of a world centered on London. Such an outrage, Vladimir concludes, would be an act of 'gratuitous blasphemy' against the modern age.[3]

Blasphemy is the vernacular of the weak. It is expressive, not instrumental for it is not intended to change the world. To be blasphemous in a secular or irreligious age an act of terror must be aimed at the civic religion of the hour. In this case the act was designed to strike at the heart of the heady confidence of Edwardian England in progress. As a 'gratuitous' or 'meaningless' act it challenged its invincible faith in the future.

One reason for the consternation about anarchism at the time was its expressive not instrumental nature. Unlike acts of war, acts of terror did not seem to be aimed at any rational end or involve any concrete purpose: they appeared to be random. And the anarchists employed a new weapon not used by governments: not gunpowder but dynamite. This was a very expressive weapon too, a relatively new invention, a compound of nitroglycerine but much more powerful than its forerunner. Dynamite was from this time to become every anarchist's preferred weapon. The fear of being 'blown up' haunted popular culture.

When people use expressive violence for such ends much depends on the perspective of those involved, including perpetrators and victims, witnesses and bystanders. For expressive violence is intended to send a message. And that message is not intended to make people more frightened, or fearful but *anxious*. Freud tells us that all three are social constructs, that they vary from culture to culture, and even from era to era. In his 1920 study *Beyond the Pleasure Principle* he distinguished between the three according to the relationship between the subject and the danger. Thus fright refers to the state we fall into when suddenly confronted by a dangerous situation for which we are not prepared. Fear presupposes a definite object of which one is afraid and perhaps has been for some time. While anxiety refers to a state characterized by expecting and preparing for a danger that is pervasive but unknown and largely unknowable. Freud stressed the fact that common usage tended to employ each term interchangeably. It was an error he wanted to correct.[4]

Conrad's novel addresses the *anxiety* that all 'senseless' acts inspire in the complacent and sensible. Edwardian society was not frightened, or fearful of anarchism. It was anxious. Today the terrorist targets our anxiety in the risk societies we have become. For we too find violence meaningless and irrational. Terrorists play on our uncertainties and anxieties; our anxiety about the side effects of our own technological advances, and in the case of September 11 our anxieties about the underside of globalization. 'For the foreseeable future,' the US Defense Secretary had observed a few years earlier 'there are few who will have the power to match us militarily . . . but they will be dedicated to exploiting the weakness of our very strength.'[5] The more globalized the world, the more vulnerable the West apparently becomes. As we introduce more sophisticated technology new risks proliferate at an exponential rate. The information technologies of the 1980s facilitate international crime and assist terrorism. And it is now a commonplace idea that the risks we face are more catastrophic than those of the past because they are global.

The World Trade Center attack, therefore, threw into relief the *first* dialectical relationship of twenty-first century warfare: one between two worlds, the postmodern and the modern. The gap between them makes it possible for the former to use *expressive* violence against the other as never before because of the symbolic impact of violent acts in a globalized world. Symbolism is important: the meaning the use of violence has for the victim (anxiety, humiliation, both of which were involved on September 11) and the offender (status, prestige and reputation in his own group, in this case the Islamic world). These are precisely what symbolic action is all about. This does not mean, of course, that we are only dealing with 'symbolic' violence. Far from it: the anarchists and fundamentalists differ in this respect: one wanted to terrify, the other wants to kill – and to kill as many people as possible. What it does imply, however, is that the effective use of violence in a globalized age depends increasingly on its symbolic form.[6]

War in future will be increasingly expressive in nature. The sheer extent of America's military power demonstrated in its immediate response to the events of September 11 make this inevitable. It cannot be challenged in any other way. That is why we need an anthropologist's perspective for it is they who have found it useful to distinguish between instrumental (technical) and expressive (ritual, symbolic and communicative) aspects of human behavior. The former involve expediency and practical reason, the Aristotelian relation between means and goals. The latter involves meaning: what does violence 'say,' what does it express?

The problem is that we so want to understand violence primarily in utilitarian, rational terms, in terms of means and ends, that the question of what violence 'signifies,' 'says' or 'expresses' seems, at best, to be of secondary importance. And this despite the fact that there was a time when we too saw violence in expressive terms. Take the European duel and the honour code which was a historically developed cultural construction. What was at stake in these tests of strength was symbolic: identity, pride and meaning and the group membership implied in them. What was deployed and sacrificed for them was described by the German sociologist Simmel at the time Conrad was writing: 'To maintain honour is so much a duty that one derives from it the most terrible sacrifices – not only self-inflicted ones but also sacrifices imposed on others.'[7] But now, of course, we have gone out of the dueling business: and it is a mark of our civility that we have also turned our back on expressive forms of war. In instrumentalizing war as much as it has, the West has reached a point where it no longer understands the expressive element. Instead it tends to dismiss it as 'cowardly,' 'irrational' or 'barbaric.' To call violence by these names reflects a very Western bias for the technical, and tends to divorce cases of violence from their social context. However repugnant acts of terrorism may be, the one thing they are not is 'senseless.'

THE EXISTENTIAL WARRIOR

But what the warrior *is* is no less important too. Expressive violence is not only aimed at an enemy; it also affirms a way of life. We find this in all cultures though it is especially commended, for example, in *The Bhagavad Gita* where it is exemplified best by the great archer Arjuna who is instructed by Krishna to be unconcerned for consequences. A disinterested participation in battle is the path to follow if release is sought from *karma*. Violence is not only instrumental; it is the moral essence of the warrior, a secondary effect of martial art. For the true warrior war-making is not so much what you do but what you *are*.

In that sense, the true warrior is a *moral agent*. This sense of agency was clearly expressed in nineteenth-century Western literature too, though it usually took a secular form. One of the texts in which it is expressed most forcefully is Nietzsche's *Genealogy of Morals* in which we read: 'unconcerned, mocking, violent – thus wisdom wants *us*, she is a woman, and always loves only a warrior.' What sort of warrior is unconcerned? One for whom the means is an end, and which war is fought for its own sake. Who does the warrior mock? Clearly those still locked in the world of goals and purposes, those who fight for causes rather than for its own sake. For the true warrior violence is existential. There is, Nietzsche tells us in the first essay, 'no being behind doing . . . the "doer" is merely a fiction added to the deed.'[8]

Indeed back at the beginning of the twentieth century, the world Conrad understood so well, war was as much a means of realizing one's own humanity as it was a means of achieving the objectives of the state. 'You say that it is the good cause that hallows every war,' wrote Nietzsche, 'I tell you that it is the good war that hallows every cause.' 'Of course our cause sanctifies battle,' echoed that great twentieth-century warrior Ernst Junger (a man decorated with the Iron Cross in both world wars), 'but how much more does battle itself sanctify the cause?'[9]

Yet by the mid-twentieth century the existential dimension of war was dying in all advanced industrial countries, and for an example we need look no further than Japan, the land of the kamikazes. The author Mishima Yukio (who was often called 'the last samurai') achieved notoriety in 1970 by an ill-conceived coup attempt which ended with him taking his own life. From early youth he had been fascinated by the *Hagakure*, the textbook of Bushido (the Samurai ethos), which taught the importance of self-sacrifice. In a commentary on the work written a few years earlier Mishima made an impassioned plea for the return to the warrior values of the past. His concluding words form a *cri de coeur* for his own end, as well as that of the samurai tradition:

> We tend to suffer from the illusion that we are capable of dying for a belief or theory. What *Hagakure* is insisting is that even a merciless death, a futile death that knows neither flower nor fruit has dignity as the death of a human being. If we value so highly the dignity of life how can we not also value the dignity of death.[10]

For the samurai warrior death had meaning. So too did honour, courage and loyalty, all of which gave life meaning too. But by 1970 when Mishima staged his revolt, the warrior tradition was dead. His revolt and subsequent suicide (the samurai act of *seppuku*) were quickly forgotten. His call to arms found no resonance with the young to whom it had been directed.

The existential dimension of war, however, has survived in the non-Western world. The *second* dialectic of twenty-first century warfare is that between the instrumental and existential. To appreciate this better we must go back to the 1950s and the attempt to existentialize war itself, one associated largely though not exclusively with Franz Fanon, a psychologist from Martinique who played an active part in the Algerian revolution. Fanon was an intellectual as well as a psychologist but his writings had enormous appeal. His most famous patron, the French philosopher, Jean-Paul Sartre, claimed that 'in him the Third World finds itself and speaks to itself through his voice.'[11] Fanon later went on to produce an existential philosophy which praised the national liberation freedom fighter in quasi-Nietzschean terms as a warrior who finds in war an expression of his own humanity in the face of the inhumanity of life.

For Fanon took as his own starting point the belief that Africans were the victims of a situational neurosis, a socially constructed but very real situation of inferiority which they had internalized. As a psychologist who had looked after patients in Algeria and the West Indies, he traced the social origin of that neurosis to the attitude of white colonial society to their blackness. Violence was the only way of authentic self-affirmation. That is why one should not be surprised when they employed 'inhuman means'; it was the way that 'less-than-men' won their humanity in the eyes of their oppressors. The violence they employed was not the resurrection of savage instincts. Through violence a warrior 'comes to know himself in that he himself creates his self.' Fanon added that to kill a white man was not only to destroy an oppressor but also the man he oppresses at the same time. 'Make no mistake about it,' added Sartre, 'by this mad fury, by this bitterness and spleen, by their ever present desire to kill us . . . they have become men.'[12]

Although some writers now urge us to treat Fanon's writings as ironic, they were deeply felt. He saw violence as cathartic, an existential experience by which an individual liberated himself from his colonial status and recognized his humanity at the same time. His work scandalized many because it struck a blow against Western humanism. The European had become 'human' by denying humanity to others, or treating the colonized as little better than animals, or sub-human. The category 'human' was therefore empty of universal meaning because it was a European invention. A less apocalyptic view which is still widely held is that when humanists talk of the Rights of Man they mean 'universal' (i.e. Western) values which are themselves 'inhuman' because they deny both local culture and identity that alone made life humane.

Of course, the difference between Fanon's generation and that of bin Laden's today is pronounced. Fanon was born in the colonial world; he was shaped by a European sensibility. Whatever his critique of the West, his writings were part of the Western intellectual tradition and Western ideas, especially Marxism, were their chief point of reference. Today's Islamic fighters are not party to a Western philosophical discourse. They have no interest in strategies of authentication or existential realization and no interest in Marxist theories of emancipation. But, in one respect, their actions echo Fanon's ideas – the act of terror not only had an expressive meaning for the hijackers but an *existential* meaning as well. Even suicide can be life affirming.

Our own societies find this alienating for we no longer allow most of our soldiers (with one exception – special forces) to find war life affirming or to affirm their own humanity through violent acts. And we have shown little or no interest in the stylization of violence, the meaning and shift of meaning for the people who resort to it, as if the interest itself is somehow inappropriate. Our understanding of war, therefore, is somewhat ambiguous: on the one hand we pretend to know what it is; on the other we are finding it difficult to understand our enemies, so great is the psychological chasm between us.

THE BOURGEOIS VERSUS THE BARBARIAN

The response to the events of September 11 also revealed a *third* dialectic at play: or what Pierre Hassner has called the dialectic between 'the bourgeois and the barbarian.'[13] For whenever we see warriors in Africa or the Middle East we tend to see barbarians. Traveling around the world between 1993–7 Michael Ignatieff, seeking the identity of the 'post-modern warrior,' found them in the paramilitaries, guerrillas and warlords – in 'the barefoot boys with Kalashnikovs, the paramilitaries in wraparound sunglasses, the turbaned zealots of the Taliban who checked their prayer mats next to their guns.'[14] Barbara Ehrenreich too sees a new kind of war, more barbaric than the old, often fought by 'ill clad bands more resembling gangs than armies.'[15]

Sometimes, of course, we rely on the barbarians as we do in the war in Afghanistan (2001–2). For the Northern Alliance was no more than a bunch of warlords most of whom had supported themselves for years from the sale of heroin. Barbarous or not we have to cultivate them to do the fighting for us. The problem is not that they are in many cases 'savage' but that they always have been. The Afghan warriors the British fought, and professed to admire in their own way, were totally divorced from the Christian evangelical ethic which sustained the Victorians in their own idea of their civilizing mission. Not much has changed in the intervening years; but we have.

We now find all warriors and warlords criminal in their intent. As former US Senator Gary Hart wrote a few days after the World Trade Center attack, 'September 11 was the date on which the nature of warfare changed: the distinction between war and crime was eliminated.'[16] He was writing, of course, about a clear act of terrorism but some of our principle military analysts have been making the same claim for some time on a much wider canvas. The American journalist Robert Kaplan speaks of 're-primitivized man,' and regrets the re-emergence of warrior societies because he takes their re-emergence to be evidence of regression into a pre-modern condition.[17] Emerging patterns of violence, predicts Martin van Creveld 'will have more in common with the struggles of primitive tribes than with large-scale conventional war.'[18] Their way of fighting has no rules or moral conventions worth studying. Indeed they engage in operations that defy the classic Western understanding of logic or ethics. 'When we face warriors we face men who have acquired a taste for killing who do not behave rationally according to our definition of rationality, who are capable of atrocities that challenge the descriptive powers of language.'[19] So writes Ralph Peters, an influential American military analyst: 'America's enemies in future will be 'not soldiers . . . but warriors – erratic primitives with shifting allegiances, habituated to violence with no stake in civic order.' In the end, he writes, 'there is only rage.'[20]

What are they raging against? Like all 'barbarians' they are raging against the norms of civilized life. Let us return to Conrad's novel. What it tells us is that many people who resort to force wish to assert themselves against the centrifugal forces that appear to dispossess people of their history and warriors of their profession. Our own age, Jean-Francois Lyotard tells us, finds difficulty taking its own master narratives for granted. What is the postmodern age but one that shows 'incredulity towards grand narratives' and prefers the fragment or detail to the whole or the master text. We deconstruct texts; the fragment is the symbol of our condition and our authenticity. But, of course, we subscribe to a historical narrative: globalization, just as Edwardian England subscribed to the master text of modernity. Both are alienating for many. What makes globalization even more unsettling is that it threatens to change not the political configuration of the world so much as the very texture of history. For history is now made, or so the critics of globalization contend, not by the actors or agents of modernity – peoples or nation-states – so much as the global market.

And the market has a center, if only in our collective imagination. Today it is New York, the center of world trade. The building that bore that name which burned and then collapsed stood not just on an island along the edge of North America but in the homeland of the global imagination representing power and boundless possibility. But at the turn of the twentieth century, the time Conrad was writing, the future was to be glimpsed in London, the great metropolis with

Greenwich at its heart through which ran the line of longitude, the nerve end of the world's communications. Early twentieth- century writers like Wells and Conrad glimpsed a city that was the storm center of politics, that was fragile, pregnant with violence and social conflict. But in place of the confusion and chaos of the Victorian city, at least, the Edwardian city seemed to have a meaning; it seemed to have its own semiotic. The novelists embarked on a quest for London's urban legibility and they found it in the fact that it was the center of the world.

In *The Secret Agent* the attack on Greenwich is an attack on the heart of the world and its wholeness. And the novel ends with a chilling portrayal of the incorruptible fundamentalist, the anarchist professor walking the city's streets: 'He walked frail, insignificant, shabby, miserable – and terrible in the simplicity of his idea, calling madness and despair to the regeneration of the world.' Walking the streets with a lethal bomb in his pocket primed to blow up any challengers and himself into fragments he is 'a booby trapped Lyotard' (writes Frank Kermode) who would blow up, if he could, the master narrative of the world (progress) and London its chosen center.[21]

What is fragmentary today is the barbarian's wish to assert local history or make it on his own terms. In Don DeLillo's postmodern version of *The Secret Agent*, his much acclaimed novel *Mao 2*, the center of terrorist activity is no longer the West, the breeding ground of nineteenth- century nihilism, but the Third World, the focal point of Islamic fundamentalism. In the course of the book an American taken hostage in Beirut in the early 1980s asks his Islamic captor why he and his companions have turned to terrorism. 'Terror,' he replies, 'makes the new future possible. We live in history as never before.'[22]

We must expect more attempts to assert the local over the global. We fight, of course, for purely instrumental ends, for the 'interests of wider humanity' as Britain's Prime Minister told an audience in Chicago twenty-two days into the Kosovo War. They fight for themselves; for them the existential is the local, the assertion of their own values. As we face the 'barbarians' in the future we should be careful to respect them for their skills if not their intentions. Dismissing warriors (and yes even *some* terrorists) as criminals tends to be dangerous. For many have courage, the courage of their convictions however misplaced and alien to our own. We do not need to respect them but we do need to understand them. We do not condone their actions because we try to understand them either. We put ourselves in a better position to respond to them, to fight them in the future by taking their true measure. Making the enemy smaller than he is blinds us to the danger he presents and gives him the advantage that comes from being underestimated.

THE AMERICAN WAY OF WARFARE

For better or worse the United States has seized the future of war and for a time the future of humanity.

(George Friedman, *The Future of War*, 1994)

Writing in 1973, the historian Russell Weighley claimed that the American way of warfare was merely an offshoot of the 'European' and that American strategic thinking was 'a branch of European strategic thought.'[23] It is no longer. We now recognize, writes Edward Luttwak, that with its ritualized nuclear threats and mostly symbolic maneuvres the Cold War concealed the de-bellicization of the Europeans. Once a core activity of European societies, the Europeans themselves now watch from afar the wars of others.[24]

We can now see why Kant was right. War, he tells us, is natural, peace is not. It can only be made practical if so-called 'practical men' recognize that what is natural is not actually in their self-interest. What made Kant's ideas so much more realistic than many of the other peace manifestos of the past was his instinctual bias for dealing in institutions, not mentalities. He saw intuitively that without social change peace would be unobtainable. He called for a republican constitution, by which he meant a government of law, responsible to its citizens through representative institutions. Kant's ideal state is not aristocratic because in aristocratic societies the rulers lose nothing 'of their banquets, hunts, chateaux, court entertainments' even in wartime. Indeed war is 'a kind of pleasure policy' providing the most stunning entertainment of all. All this has changed dramatically. The aristocracy whose values, if not its members, dominated Europe up to the Second World War has vanished leaving only a memory of the warrior tradition behind. The meritocrats who run the European Union (its political class) may be less accountable than Kant would have liked but they derive neither profit nor status from war. Instead they find it increasingly distasteful.[25]

But if Europe is effectively out of the war business, America is not. And the Americans practice war in a particular way that is beyond both Europe's capabilities and even its technological understanding. If the American way of war can no longer be seen as a branch of European strategic thought, can it still be considered 'Western'?

As it happens, most features of the American way are still familiar, as we would expect of a country whose origins are Western. The Greek model still persists. War is still a system of thought which demands discipline, initiative and ingenuity on the part of soldiers at every level. It is still a science accessible to human reason. It still remains a democratic experience now that the Americans even fight humanitarian wars like Kosovo. But while the American style conforms to aspects of the Western model, it is vitally different in two key respects. Its emphasis on technology is ultimately not compatible with Western humanism; indeed it is leading us into a very different, post-human world. And its attempt to make war more humane for its own soldiers, and the viewers back home, is making it increasingly vulnerable to the kind of asymmetric strategies we saw demonstrated in the World Trade Center attack. This too is pushing it down the road to 'post-human warfare.'[26] It has embarked on a journey which only it can travel. The rest of us are spectators.

NOTES

1 Raymond Aron, *War and Industrial Society* (London: Oxford University Press, 1958), p. 3.
2 Ruth Benedict, *The Chrysanthemum and the Sword* (Cambridge, MA: Riverside Press, 1946). For the samurai poems see Marguerite Yourcenar, *That Mighty Sculptor, Time* (New York: Farrar, Straus & Giroux, 1992), pp. 73–5.
3 Joseph Conrad, *The Secret Agent* (Oxford: Oxford University Press, 1983), p. 34.
4 David Gentilcore, 'The Fear of Disease and the Disease of Fear', in William G. Naphy and Penny Roberts (eds.), *Fear in Early Modern Society* (Manchester: Manchester University Press, 1997), p. 190.
5 *The Washington Post*, 27 Aug. 1998.
6 Anton Blok, 'The Meaning of "Senseless" Violence', in Anton Blok (ed.), *Honour and Violence* (Cambridge: Polity Press, 2001), pp. 103–14.
7 Ibid., p. 113.
8 Arthur Danto, 'Some remarks on *The Genealogy of Morals*', in Robert C. Solomon and Kathleen M. Higgins (eds.), *Reading Nietzsche* (New York: Oxford University Press, 1988), pp. 13–14.
9 See my *War and the Twentieth Century* (London: Brasseys, 1994), p. 27.
10 Cited in Catharina Blomberg, *The Heart of the Warrior: Origins and Religious Background of the Samurai System in Feudal Japan* (Richmond: Curzon Press, 1995), p. 193.
11 Franz Fanon, *The Wretched of the Earth* (London: Penguin, 1967), p. xiii.
12 Ibid., p. 15.
13 Pierre Hassner 'The Bourgeois and the Barbarian', in Gwyn Prins and Hylke Tromp (eds.), *The Future of War* (The Hague: Kluwer Law International, 2000), p. 67.
14 Michael Ignatieff, *The Warrior's Honour: Ethnic War and the Modern Conscience* (New York: Henry Holt, 1997), pp. 3 and 5–6.
15 Barbara Ehrenreich, *Blood Rites: Origins and History of the Passions of War* (London: Vintage, 1997), p. 2.
16 *The Times*, 13 Sept. 2001.
17 Robert Kaplan, *The Ends of the Earth: A Journey at the Dawn of the Twenty-first Century* (London: Papermac, 1996), p. 30.
18 Martin Van Creveld, *The Transformation of War* (New York: Free Press, 1991), p. 34.
19 Ralph Peters, *Fighting for the Future: Will America Triumph?* (Mechanicsburg, PA: Stackpole Books, 1999).
20 Ibid., p. 52.
21 Frank Kermode, *History and Value* (New York: Oxford University Press, 1990), p. 134.
22 Don DeLillo, *Mao 2* (London: Vintage, 1992), p. 235.
23 Russell Weighley, *The American Way of Warfare: A History of US Military Strategy and Policy* (Bloomington: Indiana University Press, 1973), p. 408.
24 Edward Luttwak, 'Peace in our Time', *Times Literary Supplement*, 6 Oct. 2000, p. 9. See also Michael Howard, *The Invention of Peace: Reflections on War and International Order* (London: Profile, 2000), p. 104.
25 Ibid.
26 For discussion of post-human war see my *Waging War Without Warriors: The Changing Culture of Military Conflict* (Boulder, CO: Lynne Rienner, 2002).

25 Implications for the study of international relations[1]

Barry Buzan

Almost nobody disputes that the end of the Cold War had a profound impact on the pattern of international relations, and much of the last decade has been spent trying to determine the nature of the changes. Realists and particularly neorealists have focused on the shift from bipolarity to unipolarity and its consequences for international power politics. Globalists, whether of liberal or Marxian stripe, have focused on the rising importance of the economic and the transnational, and the consequent decline in salience of territoriality in general and the state in particular. Regionalists have promoted the view that since decolonization, regional patterns have become both more autonomous and more prominent, accelerated by the ending of the Cold War. Constructivists and others argue that we need to understand not just the changes in, and consequences of, the international distribution of power, but also the changes in, and consequences of, the normative structure of international society. Some think that normative continuity is dominant,[2] others that there have been significant changes.[3] Now there are claims that 9/11 has changed the world of international relations yet again. The undoubted drama and the ongoing aftershocks of the spectacularly ruthless terrorist attacks on the USA make such claims understandable. But are they true, or are they just a temporary hyperbole?

One way of addressing this question is to examine the prevailing set of theories used to think about international relations in general, and international security in particular. Do the events of 9/11 reinforce or question the pictures of the world, and the explanations of why things happened, offered by these theories? More broadly, how does the likely impact of September 11 compare to acknowledged major transformations of the international structure, such as the impact of the Second World War; the decolonization of the Third World between the mid-1940s and the late 1970s; and the ending of the Cold War?

This chapter sets out the prevailing theoretical approaches in a simplified form, explores the significance of 9/11, and argues that it is unlikely to have a transformative impact, though it will certainly cause some specific shifts of priority and focus.

FOUR THEORETICAL PERSPECTIVES ON THE
POST-COLD WAR INTERNATIONAL ORDER

The four principal theoretical perspectives on post-Cold War international security structure are neorealist, globalist, regionalist and constructivist.

The *neorealist perspective,* is widely understood. It is relatively clear and straightforward, and need not be elaborated. It is state-centric, and rests on an argument about power polarity: if not bipolarity, then necessarily either unipolarity or multipolarity (or some hybrid). This debate concerns the distribution of material power in the international system, which in neorealism determines the global political (and thereby also security) structure, and its interplay with balance of power logic.[4] Its interpretation of the post-Cold War structure of international security assumes that there has been a change of power structure at the global level (end of bipolarity), and it aims to identify the nature of that change in order to infer the security consequences. Neorealism does not question the primacy of the global level; its search for change is confined to a narrow range of options within that level: unipolarity or multipolarity. Neorealism is built around two levels, system and state, and is principally concerned to define and operationalize the system level. Neorealists either downplay or ignore all levels except the system one, or like Stephen M. Walt and Birthe Hansen, discuss the regional level empirically without considering its theoretical standing or implications except as an offshoot of the global level.[5]

The *globalist perspective* (by which I mean acceptance of the view usually labeled 'globalization') is widely discussed, but is neither simple nor clear. It can be understood as the antithesis of realism's (and neorealism's) statist, power-political understanding of international system structure. Globalization is mainly rooted in cultural, transnational and international political economy approaches. Perhaps its clearest guiding theme is the deterritorialization of world politics.[6] In its stronger versions (whether Marxian or liberal), deterritorialization sweeps all before it, taking the state, and the state system, off the center stage in the analysis of world politics.[7] Weaker versions retain the state and the state system, but put numerous non-state actors and systems through and alongside them:[8] 'territoriality and supraterritoriality coexist in complex interrelation'[9]; and 'Territorialization remains a check on globalization.'[10] In terms of structure, the globalist position is clearer as an attack on neorealism's state-centric approach, than as a statement of an explicit alternative. The global market, or capitalism, or various forms of world society probably best capture the underlying ideas of system structure in the globalist perspective, and the key point is rejection of the idea that an adequate sense of system structure can be captured by privileging states.

Globalization's hallmark is acknowledgment of the independent role of both transnational entities – corporations, non-governmental social and various political organizations – and intergovernmental organizations and regimes. Its focus is on how territorial sovereignty as the ordering principle for human activity has been redefined, and in some ways transcended, by networks of interaction involving varied actors and at many different levels, and feeding off the huge technological and social improvements in the capacity for transportation and communication of goods, information and ideas. The state is often a player in these networks, but it does not necessarily, or even usually, control them, and is increasingly enmeshed in and penetrated by them. Marxian and liberal versions of globalization differ more in their normative perspectives than in their basic understanding of what globalization means: here as elsewhere, they are mirror images of the same phenomenon. Both see the macro-structure of the international system as taking a center-periphery (or 'rich world–poor world'; 'developed–developing') form, with a core of societies (or elites) controlling most of the capital, technology, information, organizational and ideological resources in the system and shaping the terms on which the periphery participates. In the Marxian view, this structure is fundamentally exploitative, unequal, unstable and undesirable, whereas in the liberal one it is fundamentally progressive and developmental, and its tendencies towards instability, though serious, are not without institutional solutions.

As Victor D. Cha notes, little has been written about the links between globalization and security, not least because the security effects of globalization have been hard to distinguish from the more dramatic effects of the ending of the Cold War.[11] Cha, Ian Clark, Jean-Marie Guehenno and Jan Aart Scholte all argue that globalization is responsible for complicating the security agenda, while simultaneously reducing the elements of control that underpin the security strategy options of states.[12] Cha and Guehenno both think that globalization increases the incentives for states to pursue more cooperative security policies, especially at the regional level. This line of thinking has been much reinforced by the challenges posed by 9/11. Tarak Barkawi and Mark Laffey even want to sweep away state-centric security analysis and replace it with a center-periphery model.[13] From a security perspective, the academic debate about globalization matters less than whether and how either globalization in general, or specific aspects of it (e.g. financial flows, terrorism, trade liberalization, environment) become securitized by the actors in the international system. If globalization is seen and acted on as a threat by states and other actors in the system, then it plays alongside, and competes with, more traditional securitizations of neighbors, great powers or internal rivals.

The security perspective on globalization thus has two sides. The first highlights the dark side of the center-periphery structure. It is the successor to a long line of ideas extending at least as far as J. A. Hobson and V. I. Lenin, all emphasizing the unequal, exploitative and coercive aspects of relations between center and periphery: imperialism, colonialism, neocolonialism, *dependencia*, cultural imperialism, anti-hegemonism and suchlike. Risking oversimplification, one can see these ideas as stemming from the perspective of the periphery, and reflecting its resentments about its relative powerlessness, underdevelopment and vulnerability in relation to the center. In one sense, they reflect concerns that the practice of economic liberalism is a major key to understanding what generates the wider international security agenda.[14] At their most passionate, these ideas carry the accusation that the center-periphery structure generated and maintains the weak position of the periphery for the benefit of the core, citing cases such as Zaire, Angola and Iraq. This dark-side securitization of globalization is counterpointed by more upbeat liberal interpretations, more strongly rooted in the center, which acknowledge the inequalities and disparities, but see the process of globalization as the fastest and most efficient way to overcome them. Here, globalization should be a path to the erosion and eventual elimination of the traditional international security agenda (and in more radical liberal views also the state). The darlings of this perspective are South Korea, Taiwan and Singapore, all of which have transformed them-selves economically, and up to a point politically, within the embrace of globaliza-tion. Its key great power targets are China and Russia, where the hope is that economic liberalization (namely, penetration by globalization) will eventually gen-erate political liberalization and a lowering of threat perceptions. But even here there is a security dimension, mostly focused on the potential instabilities in the global trading and financial systems.[15]

The *regionalist perspective* rests on two assumptions: first, that the decline of superpower rivalry reduces the penetrative quality of global power interest in the rest of the world;[16] and second, that most of the great powers in the post-Cold War international system are now 'lite powers,' meaning that their domestic dynamics pull them away from military engagement and strategic competition in world trouble spots, leaving local states and societies to sort out their military-political relationships with less interference from great powers.[17] The regional level of security was also significant during the Cold War, and the security region-alist perspective generally holds that except when global powers are extremely dominant, as during the imperial era, regional security dynamics will normally be a significant part of the overall constellation of security in the international system.[18]

The regionalist perspective contains elements of both neorealism and global-ism, but prioritizes a lower level of analysis. Because the neorealist and the regionalist approaches are both rooted in territoriality and security, their relation-ship is potentially complementary (with the regionalists addressing the lower level marginalized by neorealists). Happily, it is relatively straightforward to include a regional level without causing too much disturbance to the theoretical archi-tecture.[19] Neorealism is in some respects strong on territoriality, and the potential harmony and synergy with the regionalist perspective is high, especially when states are the main actors. That said, room remains for conflict between neo-realism and regionalism when the security agenda moves to issue areas other than military-political, to actors other than the state, and to theories of security other than materialist.

Another potential conflict between neorealism and regionalism is in the latter's contention that the global level has lost salience relative to the regional one after the Cold War. Hardline neorealists might have trouble accepting the proposition that the system level is not always dominant. But in principle, the regionalist perspective should be able to incorporate neorealism's understanding of the global level into its own multi-level scheme (unit, region, inter-regional, global). Some linkage exists in the literature.[20] Multipolarity and unipolarity are more difficult to call, with lower competition at the global level, but also lower constraints on great power behavior. These structures could either allow more, or less, scope for the regional level than bipolarity. Anders Wivel goes further, presenting a whole theory of how variations in global polarity affect the regional level,[21] and Hansen postulates 'high regional activity' under unipolarity.[22]

The fit between regionalist and globalist perspectives is much less obvious and clean cut, not least because there is no uncontested conception of system structure at the heart of the globalist position (is it capitalism, or the global market, or world society?). Aside from the lack of specification concerning system structure, the problem lies in the globalist commitment to deterritorialization as the key to understanding both world politics and security. Because they are based on levels, both the neorealist and regionalist positions are incompatible with the extreme globalist idea that all levels are dissolving into one. But this opposition is often more apparent than real, and globalists have given little concern to security, and therefore address a different agenda. The moderate wing of globalists are keen to emphasize the interplay between territoriality and deterritorialization. It is, for example, already widely understood that many aspects of regionalization, especially the more cooperative ones of regional economic groupings, are responses to globalization.[23] Even if a deterritorializing trend is discernable, it still has much to do before levels cease to be a salient feature in the dynamics of international security. Although some of the new security agenda is deterritorialized, most notably in the economic and environmental sectors, territoriality remains a primary defining feature of many (in)security dynamics. In addition, while a core-periphery idea of system structure is attractive in some ways, it is too homogenized for regional security analysts. A regional approach gives both a much clearer empirical picture and a theoretically more coherent understanding of international security dynamics.

The *constructivist perspective* turns away from materialist approaches and focuses on the dynamics of human social interactions. Unlike the other three perspectives, constructivism offers no specific picture of what the world looks like. Instead, it pushes inquiry into the processes by which human beings construct inter-subjective understandings as the frameworks through which they relate to each other. Such understandings are in flux, but can also become sedimented so that they become durable structures in the social landscape. For example, sovereignty is not an essential condition that either exists or not, but a kind of social contract whose meaning is under continuous reassessment and renegotiation. Thus while sovereignty has proved durable for several centuries as a key social construct around which international relations has been organized, its substantive content has evolved. The rights, privileges, duties and expectations attached to sovereignty in the eighteenth century were different from those that attach to it in the twenty-first century, even while the basic territorial construction of the concept has remained intact. The constructivist approach does not focus on a particular level of analysis or a particular type of unit. In principle it applies to all of human social behavior.

These four perspectives, and the disputes amongst them, have largely shaped both the theoretical and the empirical debates about the post-Cold War international (dis)order. Does 9/11 call this general framework of understanding and debate into question?

THE CHALLENGE OF SEPTEMBER 11?

Since this exercise is being conducted shortly after 9/11 there has to be one big caveat: we do not yet know the full extent of what 'September 11' signifies. Is it to be largely a one-off spectacular with a tail of minor follow-ons, and fairly effective countermeasures? Or is it to be a more sustained and vigorous assault triggering diverse countermeasures of varying degrees of effectiveness? In the latter case, the particulars of 9/11 and war in Afghanistan have merely been the first installment of an 'event' that is not yet fully formed. Either way, one should not underestimate the capacity of humans to adapt to circumstances. Even a relatively sustained terrorist campaign of the 9/11 type would represent a very small addition to the statistical dangers to individuals that attend most forms of transportation, and are part of the daily risks of being alive. People generally accept that their routine activities carry a certain risk of death or damage, and this does not deter them from traveling, or from pursuing thrilling but dangerous sports. In countries where terrorism has been a constant background threat such as Britain, Spain or Sri Lanka, most people continue with their lives. There is therefore a reasonable possibility that 9/11 as it stands at the time of writing, or even '9/11 plus more of the same,' will quite quickly get drawn into the general background of the human condition. Only if the 'plus' was sustained on a very large scale or shifted to effective use of weapons of mass destruction, does a major change of assumptions about the nature of international relations become plausible.

The question is how well does the theoretical framework for understanding international relations stand up to the specific challenge of international terrorism manifested since 11 September, and the prominence that terrorism has since assumed on the international relations agenda? How does 9/11 impact on these theories? Even a cursory examination suggests that all four perspectives will have no difficulty claiming a slice of the action. Many well-established concerns on the IR agenda have been reaffirmed or reinforced by September 11.

Neorealism

Neorealists can focus on the USA as both the main target of, and principal respondant to, this wave of international terrorism. September 11 can be interpreted as a consequence of unipolarity (frustration in the periphery at American power, presence and influence, and the lack of a balancer to it), and the response as an example of the unipolar power structure in operation (bandwagoning in the form of a US-led coalition). Neorealists can look at the impact of 9/11 on realigning relationships amongst the great powers (reducing tensions between the USA on the one hand, and China and Russia on the other, by downgrading concerns about human rights, and upgrading the legitimacy of action to suppress 'terrorists'), and can also claim a strengthening of the state and territorial politics in the form of increased border and security measures and a general upgrading of the state's right to surveillance and inspection of activities of all kinds. For neorealists, 9/11 is interesting primarily for how it impacts on the way the USA conducts itself as the sole superpower. It will therefore increase interest in foreign policy analysis applied to the USA, and change the emphasis of the ongoing debate about American 'grand strategy.' Will the trend towards unilateralism and away from multilateralism that has become a key feature of US policy over the last several years be strengthened or mitigated? Is September 11 symbolic of the kind of reactions that a unipolar structure is likely to generate, and therefore a harbinger of future priorities for US security?

Three specific staples of the realist/security studies agenda seem likely to get reinforced by September 11. First is the concern that the proliferation of weapons of mass destruction (WMDs) is an under-attended problem in the international order, not only in the direct sense of transfers or leakage of military technology, but also in the much more complicated dual-use dilemma in which industrialization and world trade encourage the spread of technologies and expertise that can be used both for legitimate civilian purposes and to create weapons of mass destruction. The key focus here is on the nuclear, aerospace, chemical and biotechnology industries. This concern has previously focused on radical or rogue states, but now will expand to give attention to transnational terrorist organizations.

Second is the assessment that the revolution in military affairs (RMA) is both expanding a gap between the capability of the USA and all other actors in the system, and also opening up new possibilities for unprecedentedly precise use of force with low risk of casualties. Before 9/11 the RMA seemed to be having a distinctive effect on US foreign policy (encouraging unilateralism), while simultaneously generating a rather peculiar psychology between the very strong (seen as increasingly invulnerable in conventional military terms) and the very weak (seen as increasingly helpless and pushed towards either submission to the USA, or pursuit of alternative military means – terrorism or WMDs). These issues are likely to remain high on the agenda, particularly since the emerging US response to 9/11 is to increase its military capability in relation to the rest of the world. Any hope that the terrorist attacks would undermine America's enthusiasm for pursuing national missile defense has been blown away by a huge increase in its desire for defense against threats of all kinds.

This obsession with the pursuit of invulnerability feeds on the third and most recent realist idea, that the world is heading for a clash of civilizations in which lines of conflict will be shaped mainly by patterns of cultural differentiation, especially, but not only, that between the West and the Islamic world.[24] September 11 has undoubtedly reinforced parts of Samuel Huntington's interpretation, and increased the risk that it will become a self-fulfilling prophecy. To the extent that a 'clash of civilizations' mindset prevails in the USA, it will strengthen the position of realist thinking in American IR, and drive forward a policy of seeking security through military primacy and the ability to act alone.

Globalism

Globalists can claim a victory for deterritorialization by focusing on the transnational operations and methods of the al-Qaeda network, and the wider significance of religious identities that transcend the framework of states. Al-Qaeda's new and incredibly ruthless methods of mass suicide attacks and random biological assaults seem, *inter alia*, purpose-designed to dissolve the key territorialist assumption that the transmission of threats (especially threats of force) is closely linked to distance.[25] Globalists can also point to the economic effects of 9/11, emphasizing the extent to which the global economic order has transcended states, and how threats are now beyond the control capacity of individual states. For globalists, September 11 could become the iconic event that symbolizes the passage from a Westphalian international system, dominated by the military capabilities of states, to a post-Westphalian structure in which control of the means of force, along with many other capabilties, is in the hands not just of states but also of many other types of unit, most of them not territorially organized. Part of this picture is the emergent pattern of failed states, tearing holes in the global Westphalian political fabric and creating spaces for non-state actors on the dark side of world society.

In the globalist perspective, the international system has for some decades been divided into two worlds: a zone of peace and a zone of conflict.[26] Since the end of the Cold War the fault line between them has become a focus of instability and danger. September 11 will probably be read as reinforcing the core-periphery aspects of the two-worlds idea, though it should also strengthen the regionalist case for differentiating within the periphery.[27] But it may modify the understanding that in relation to the use of force, the zone of peace could largely set aside worries about being attacked, which would largely be confined to the zone of conflict. The threat of terrorism increases the threat of crossover violence in both directions (terrorism into the core, counter-terrorism into the periphery) though it does not modify the idea that interstate war will remain rare or even absent within the core, and normal in the periphery. To the extent that this perspective is based on the inequity of the liberal economic order, the periphery is threatened by two linked developments consequent on the collapse of bipolarity: first, the overwhelming military superiority of the West and the USA in particular, no longer balanced by a rival superpower; and second, the collapse of the political space generated for the Third World by superpower rivalry during the Cold War, and its replacement by a much more monolithic domination by the West. The center can now impose much more demanding legal, social, financial and political conditions on the periphery as the price of access to aid, trade, credit, recognition and membership in various clubs ranging from NATO and the EU, to the WTO, and can also wield increased pressure on states to conform to contested regimes (nonproliferation) or norms (democracy, human rights, anti-terrorism). Questions will be asked about whether this change of conditions contributes to international terrorism.

Within the periphery, the problem of failed states reinforces the globalist critique of realist theoretical and policy assumptions about how the international system is structured. This problem exists regardless of whether its causes are thought to be primarily in the operation of the capitalist international political economy, or in the inability of some societies and cultures to adapt themselves sufficiently to sustain self-government, provide for basic human needs, or approach prevailing 'standards of civilization.' There was a tendency after the ending of the Cold War to marginalize the problem of failed states (except, as in the Balkans, where they were located embarrassingly close to Western heartlands). It is likely that September 11 will have undermined that indifference, and replaced it with concern that failed states offer too many opportunities to the dark side of world society (mafias, extremists of all stripes, polluters and proliferators). If this new concern takes root, it will face the same difficulty that has confronted advocates of development since decolonization, which is that we still do not really know how to transfer 'development' to societies in which it has not arisen indigenously. It will be interesting to see whether new forms of mandate system come back into fashion, as they have in the Balkans.

September 11 also plays into globalist concerns about economic security, and the worry that the liberal international economic order (LIEO) is not intrinsically stable and may be subject to periodic crises. The traditional main areas of concern have been the regimes that regulate international trade and finance. Fears have focused on the possibility of protectionist reactions to the pain of competition undermining the liberal trading rules, and on the inherent unpredictability and volatility of any liberalized financial system as demonstrated by the 1997 crisis in East Asia. The economic consequences of 9/11 add new sources of stress to both these concerns. Will the institutionalization of greater security measures on travel and transport make the global economy stickier and less efficient, with potential big impacts on specific industries, and perhaps on expectations about levels of growth in the long run? This could be a rather fundamental issue given the political dependence of capitalist political economies on sustained growth if they are to avoid conflicts over unequal distribution. It might add a little to the existing debates about inequality, (under)development and aid, but is unlikely to change the basic political positions already consolidated around these questions (neoliberal versus economic nationalist and human rights).

A third worry about the instability of the LIEO has focused on the way in which transnational organized crime – particularly related to money laundering, and to the smuggling of drugs, migrants, women and weapons – has been facilitated by the LIEO, and has assumed a more global scale.[28] Terrorists and mafias have much in common in their organization and methods: network structures that penetrate state structures and patterns of regional and global security. Although their objectives usually differ, they may overlap at several points, particularly in matters concerning money and weapons. 9/11 will certainly enhance concern about this aspect of the LIEO. A fourth concern has been about the fragility of the LIEO's infrastructure. Already before 9/11 anxiety was noticeable about cyberwar and the vulnerability of the IT networks on which Western military and civil activity increasingly depend. Concerns about transportation infrastructure will now undoubtedly get higher priority than they did when the main threat to them was the price and/or availability of oil.

Regionalism

Regionalists can claim that 9/11 reaffirms the post-Cold War salience of regional security as a key part of the international order. Despite the transnational quality of its methods and organization, the al-Qaeda network is intimately tied into the dynamics of Middle Eastern regional security, and their interplay with the unipolar structure at the global level. Although there may be a kind of globalist element in al-Qaeda's securitization (a resistance of the worldwide faithful against the global cultural assault of capitalism), this does not seem to be the main motive. Much more prominent in their discourses are the placement of US forces in the 'holy lands' of Saudi Arabia, and US backing for Israel (as a 'crusader' invasion of Islamic territory and as the oppressor of the Palestinians). Thus, while al-Qaeda manifests itself as a deterritorialized, transnational player, neither its existence, its operation, nor its motives can be understood without close reference to both the regional structures of security and the interplay with the global level, that have been the main feature of the regionalist analysis. International terrorism of the type, and on the scale, unleashed since 9/11 does unquestionably strengthen the non-territorial aspect of security. But it is not separable from the main territorial dynamics, and it is nowhere close to replacing them as the prime structuring principle of international security. Its biggest impact may be to change not only the security dynamics within the Middle East and South Asia, but also the relationship of both to the USA, and the relationship of the USA to the other great powers. That would be no mean accomplishment, but it would amount to changes *within* the underlying territorial structure of international security, not a transformation *of* it. Regionalists will be able to play the powerful card that they offer the most promising path towards solving the al-Qaeda problem. Unless something is done about the Middle East, and the way that the USA plays into its regional security dynamics, the sources that feed al-Qaeda will remain bountiful.

Constructivism

Constructivists do not have a picture of the world to be challenged or reinforced by September 11. Their strength is in an ability to understand the discourses that underpin both organized terrorism and the responses to it, and the implications of these for the workings and structure of international society. If, as Robert Keohane thinks, 9/11 will raise interest in motives for violence (particularly religious ones),[29] then constructivists are well equipped to capture how such motives are to be understood. They will also point to the discursive moves now in competition to capture interpretations of 9/11, and show how these differ from material capabilities. Has 9/11 reinforced international society (by creating new areas of shared interests amongst states) or weakened it (by weakening the state structure itself, or by creating new divisions among states), or simply changed it (by bringing some norms to higher priority and pushing others into the background)? Those interested in a more disaggregated view of international society (where a variety of thicker, more solidarist regional international societies, such as the EU, are seen to be embedded in a thinner, more pluralist, global international society) may have their hand strengthened by the civilizational aspect of September 11. Pluralists who fear the rise of world society will have their hand strengthened by the way in which September 11 has highlighted the dark side of world society. Solidarists may find that their human rights agenda is knocked back by the demands of counter-terrorism against global uncivil society. Yet at the same time, the responses to 9/11 could advance solidarism by thickening the web of shared norms, rules and institutions among states.

CONCLUSIONS

September 11 does not require major changes to the debates about IR theory or to the agenda of IR. It is important to understand IR theory as pluralist in nature: not as a single dominant theory, but a number of contending perspectives and the tensions and debates among them.[30] Each of these perspectives captures an important aspect of the extremely complex world system, and the debates among them can be seen as ways of adjusting to the unfoldings of world history. It is unlikely (not impossible) that any event would bring one theory into clear dominance over all the others (and they are not mutually exclusive anyway). Pertinent questions are: does September 11 invalidate any of the existing theoretical perspectives on IR? Does it require new theoretical tools for understanding? Does it change the balance of claims amongst the contending approaches about their ability to capture the essentials of international relations? Does it change the nature of the tensions and questions that shape the debate amongst them?

The answer to all these questions is basically 'No.' September 11 adds the specific concerns of 'the war against terrorism,' but leaves much else intact with a few new twists and changes of emphasis. September 11 does not tip the balance in the debates about territoriality versus deterritorialization, or about the uses and limits of military power, or about the weight of material versus social factors in shaping international relations, or about state versus non-state actors, or about globalization versus unipolarity, or global level versus regional. It does not suggest the need for new theories, or even much in the way of new debates among existing theories. Neither does it much change the relative strength of the claims that the leading theories make to provide us with insight into international events. It affirms that all the theories have something important to tell us about what we should look at and how we should look at it, and in this sense it underlines Keohane's point that there needs to be less emphasis on rivalry amongst competing theoretical positions, and more attention paid to how to synthesize them.[31]

If these arguments risk sounding too complacent about the state of IR theory, note that Richard Little and I have argued elsewhere that IR has no reason to feel satisfied with its development as an intellectual enterprise. I stand by those arguments. But in the specific case of September 11 (so far) the sorts of challenges represented by this event fall fairly comfortably within the scope of existing debates, and do not suggest the need for radical departures or new developments. September 11 is not in the league of decolonization (which gave rise to development studies), or the Second World War (which established realism as orthodoxy) or the ending of the Cold War (which downgraded the priority of military security, stimulated constructivism, and raised the priority of historical understanding and questions of identity), or the oil crises of the 1970s (which spurred the revival of international political economy). Probably, it is not even in the league of Pearl Harbor, with which it has been (in some ways rightly) compared, because although it may have a significant impact on American psychology, it is unlikely to unleash a conflict on the scale, or with the consequences for the distribution of power and the nature of international society, of the Pacific War.

A better comparison might be the Cuba Missile Crisis, a relatively short, sharp event which caused a lasting change of perspective and a reconsideration of various policies among the leading powers. The Crisis turned attention to the domestic level, and stimulated inquiry into how foreign policy is made (which is not, strictly speaking, part of IR theory). In anticipating what kinds of changes and reconsiderations might follow on from September 11, the domestic level also seems likely to figure prominently. In general, there is the question about how the 'war against terrorism' will impact on the ongoing tension between the struggle to create and preserve civil liberties on the one hand, and the needs of states to create and maintain intelligence services, and to provide 'homeland security' on the other. In particular, attention will focus on domestic American politics, especially how the USA will see its future rights and responsibilities towards the rest of the international system. Because the USA is so centrally located in the international order, its leaders' attitudes are crucial. Before September 11, the country seemed to be shifting ground, away from the liberal international engagements of the Cold War decades, and towards a more self-centred, unilateralist stance, opposing and even attacking many of the institutional structures built up by US policy over the last half-century. Whether this drift represented just a temporary effect of a particularly conservative administration, or a deeper shift resonating with the less liberal sides of American exceptionalism, was a matter of debate. It remains so today, but with the pressures playing on it modifed by 9/11. So far, the impact of 9/11 does not clearly weigh in one direction or the other, and therefore does not seem likely to prove quickly decisive in this larger unfolding. In part, US unilateralism has been reinforced, but so also has awareness of the fact that the USA still needs other players onside if it is to be able to realize its own goals at reasonable cost. The imperatives driving the American RMA seem almost certain to be reinforced, but beyond that, prediction becomes impossible. In principle, 9/11 might open the way to major reconsiderations in the USA about both its dependence on oil and the nature and extent of its engagements in the Middle

East. In practice, resistance to such changes will probably be large, even though no great power competition is at stake in the Middle East, and US support both for Israel, and for unpopular pro-Western governments in the Arab world, is conspicuously counterproductive.

NOTES

1   I am grateful to Chris Browning, Tarja Cronberg, Rick Fawn, Stefano Guzzini, Lene Hansen, Ulla Holm, Pertti Joenniemi, Dietrich Jung, Viatcheslav Morozov, Noel Parker and Ole Wæver for comments on an earlier draft. Much of section 1 is drawn from work I have done jointly with Ole Wæver on *Regions and Powers: The Structure of International Security* (Cambridge: Cambridge University Press, 2003).

2   James Mayall, *World Politics: Progress and Its Limits* (Cambridge: Polity, 2000), p. 147.

3   Nicholas J. Wheeler, *Saving Strangers: Humanitarian Intervention in International Society* (Oxford: Oxford University Press, 2000).

4   Kenneth N. Waltz, *Theory of International Politics* (Reading, MA: Addison-Wesley, 1979).

5   Stephen M. Walt, *The Origins of Alliances* (Ithaca: Cornell University Press, 1987); Birthe Hansen, *Unipolarity and the Middle East* (Richmond: Curzon Press, 2000).

6   David Held, Anthony McGrew, David Goldblatt and Jonathan Perraton, *Global Transformation: Politics, Economics and Culture* (Cambridge: Polity Press, 1999), pp. 7–9; Ngaire Woods (ed.), *The Political Economy of Globalization* (Basingstoke: Macmillan, 2000), p. 6; and Jan Aart Scholte, *Globalization: A Critical Introduction* (Basingstoke: Macmillan, 2000), pp. 2–3.

7   Held *et al.*, *Global Transformation*, pp. 3–5.

8   Held *et al.*, *Global Transformation*, pp. 7–9; Scholte, *Globalization*; Woods, *The Political Economy*, pp. 1–19; and Ian Clark, *Globalization and International Relations Theory* (Oxford: Oxford University Press, 1999).

9   Scholte, *Globalization*, p. 8.

10 Clark, *Globalization*, p. 169.

11 Victor D. Cha, 'Abandonment, Entrapment, and Neoclassical Realism in Asia: The United States, Japan, and Korea', *International Studies Quarterly*, Vol. 44, No. 2, 2000, pp. 391 and 394.

12 Cha, 'Abandonment', p. 397; Clark, *Globalization*, ch. 6; Jean-Marie Guehenno, 'The Impact of Globalization on Strategy', *Survival*, Vol. 40, No. 4, 1998–9, pp. 5–19; Scholte, *Globalization*, pp. 207–33.

13 Tarak Barkawi and Mark Laffey, 'The Imperial Peace: Democracy, Force and Globalization', *European Journal of International Relations*, Vol. 5, No. 4, 1999, pp. 403–34.

14 Barry Buzan and Ole Wæver, *Liberalism and Security: The Contradictions of the Liberal Leviathan* (Copenhagen: COPRI Working Paper 23, 1998); Scholte, *Globalization*, ch. 9.

15 Barry Buzan, Ole Wæver and Jaap de Wilde, *Security: A New Framework for Analysis* (Boulder CO: Lynne Rienner, 1998), ch. 5.

16 Arthur A. Stein and Steven E. Lobell, 'The End of the Cold War and the Regionalization of International Security', in David A. Lake and Patrick M. Morgan (eds), *Regional Orders: Building Security in a New World* (University Park: Pennsylvania State University Press, 1997), pp. 119–20; David A. Lake, 'Regional Security Complexes: A Systems Approach', in Lake and Morgan *Regional Orders*, p. 61.

17 Barry Buzan and Gerald Segal, 'The Rise of the "Lite" Powers: A Strategy for Postmodern States', *World Policy Journal*, Vol. 13, No. 3, 1996, pp. 1–10.

18 Buzan, Wæver and de Wilde, *Security*; Buzan and Wæver, *Regions and Powers*.

19 Even as a fourth tier of system structure, see Ole Wæver, 'Europe: Stability and Responsibility', in *Internationales Umfeld, Sicherheitsinteressen und nationale Planung der*

Bundesrepublik. Teil C: Unterstützende Einzelanalysen. Band 5. II.A Europäische Sicherheitskultur. II.B Optionen für kollektive Verteidigung im Kontext sicherheitspolitischer Entwicklungen Dritter (Ebenhausen: Stiftung Wissenschaft und Politik, SWP – S 383/5, 1993), pp. 31–72; Ole Wæver, 'Resisting the Temptation of Post Foreign Policy Analysis', in Walter Carlsnaes and Steve Smith (eds), *European Foreign Policy Analysis. The EC and Changing Perspectives in Europe* (London: Sage, 1994); Ole Wæver, *Regional Realism: A Mildly Constructivist Interpretation of European Security with Implications for 'World Order'*, (Copenhagen: Danish Institute of International Affairs, Nov. 1997), paper presented to the 'New World Order: Contrasting Theories' Conference.

20 See, for example, Lake, 'Regional Security Complexes', pp. 61–2; and Randall L. Schweller, 'Realism and the Present Great Power System: Growth and Positional Conflict over Scarce Resources', in Ethan B. Kapstein and Michael Mastanduno (eds), *Unipolar Politics: Realism and State Strategies After the Cold War* (New York: Columbia University Press, 1999), pp. 41–2.

21 Anders Wivel, *The Integration Spiral: International Security and European Integration 1945– 1999* (Copenhagen: PhD Dissertation, Institute of Political Science, University of Copenhagen, 2000).

22 Hansen, *Unipolarity*, pp. 68, 81.

23 Buzan, Wæver and de Wilde *Security*, pp. 113–15; Peter J. Katzenstein, 'Regionalism in Comparative Perspective', *Cooperation and Conflict*, Vol. 31, No. 2, 1996, pp. 126–7; Andrew Hurrell, 'Regionalism in Theoretical Perspective', in Louise Fawcett and Andrew Hurrell (eds), *Regionalism in World Politics: Regional Organization and International Order* (Oxford: Oxford University Press, 1995), pp. 53–8.

24 Samuel P. Huntington, *The Clash of Civilizations and the Remaking of World Order* (New York: Simon & Schuster, 1996).

25 Robert O. Keohane, 'The Globalization of Informal Violence, Theories of World Politics, and the "Liberalism of Fear" ', (New York: SSRC, 2002), www.ssrc.org/sept11/essays/keohane.htm

26 Barry Buzan, 'New Patterns of Global Security in the Twenty-first Century', *International Affairs*, Vol. 67, No. 3, 1991, p. 432; James M. Goldgeier and Michael McFaul, 'A Tale of Two Worlds: Core and Periphery in the Post-Cold War Era', *International Organization*, Vol. 46, No. 2, 1992, pp. 467–91; Max Singer and Aaron Wildavsky, *The Real World Order: Zones of Peace/Zones of Turmoil* (Chatham: Chatham House Publishers, 1993); and implicitly in earlier versions, Karl W. Deutsch, Sidney A. Burrell, Robert A. Kann, Maurice Lee, Jr., Martin Lichterman, Raymond E. Lindgren, Francis L. Loewenheim and Richard W. van Wagenen (1957) *Political Community and the North Atlantic Area: International Organization in the Light of Historical Experience* (Princeton, NJ: Princeton University Press, 1957); Robert O. Keohane and Joseph S. Nye, Jr., *Power and Interdependence* (Boston: Little Brown, 1977).

27 Buzan and Wæver, *Regions and Powers*.

28 Robert Mandel, *Deadly Transfers and the Global Playground: Transnational Security Threats in a Disorderly World* (Westport, CT: Praeger Publishers, 1999); Phil Williams, 'Transnational Criminal Organisations and International Security', *Survival*, Vol. 36, No. 1, 1994, pp. 96–113.

29 Keohane, 'The Globalization', p. 1.

30 Ole Wæver, 'Four Meanings of International Society: A Trans-Atlantic Dialogue', in B. A. Roberson (ed.), *International Society and the Development of International Relations Theory* (London: Pinter, 1998), pp. 80–144.

31 Keohane, 'The Globalization', p. 7. See also Barry Buzan and Richard Little, *International Systems in World History* (Oxford: Oxford University Press, 2000); Barry Buzan and Richard Little, 'Why International Relations Has Failed as an Intellectual Project and What to Do about It', *Millennium*, Vol. 30, No.1, 2001, pp.19–39.

26 The war on terror

International implications

Mary Buckley and Rick Fawn

The recent terrorist attacks in New York, Washington, Kuwait, Yemen, Bali, Moscow, Mombasa, Riyadh and Casablanca, and wherever else they may occur, prompt a vast range of questions. Foremost on a domestic level are how liberal democratic societies cope with terrorist threats of unprecedented proportion while retaining their intrinsic values of political openness, tolerance, decency and celebration of diversity. Pressing at the international level is consideration of how foreign and security policies of consensus are formulated, especially when questions of the interpretation of religion become interwoven. Bringing both levels successfully together requires creating and sustaining tolerant societies and ensuring a high degree of international consensus. The fate of this tricky combination is under scrutiny in the complicated process of reconstructing Afghanistan. This chapter explores these issues briefly and argues that 9/11 and subsequent terrorist actions have provoked immense interpretative and policy challenges on the agenda of the early twenty-first century.

CIVIL WRONGS

In certain historical contexts, liberal, as well as illiberal, societies single out one ethnic or religious group for different treatment. Liberal democracies pride themselves on democratic constitutions (written or unwritten), on the rule of law, on freedom of speech, assembly and movement, and on fundamental rights in general, such as those of equality and habeas corpus (the right to a court hearing before long detention). In times of crisis, however, or periods of perceived necessity, these may become suspended, compromised or willingly flouted by policy-makers. Here the argument holds sway that the normally undesirable or unpleasant means justifies the noble end, usually deemed to be temporary.

Historical examples of crises allegedly justifying a curbing of human rights abound. Japanese Americans, for instance, were interned during the Second World War to protect the so-called 'national interest' after the Japanese bombing of the US base at Pearl Harbor. Through President Roosevelt's Executive Order 9066, 110,000 people of Japanese ancestry living in California, Washington, Oregon and Arizona were forcibly interned. More than two-thirds were citizens of the USA. A further 5,981 were born in camps.[1] In addition, 2,200 people of Japanese ancestry were forcibly removed from states in Latin America, 80 percent of whom were from Peru, and interned in the USA.[2] In Britain in the 1970s, at a time of vigorous attempts to tackle crime, Section 4 of the Vagrancy Act of 1824, the famous 'sus' offense, was used unevenly around England and Wales and hardly at all in Scotland. It allowed police to arrest an individual on suspicion of 'loitering with intent to commit an arrestable offence.'[3] Moreover, there was no trial by jury since the offense could only be tried in a magistrate's court. 'Sus' was disproportionately used against young black males in London, Merseyside and Manchester. One acquitted black Londoner was told by the magistrate that 'black youths who came into the West End to shop were asking for trouble.'[4] A moral panic about crime and the results of immigration fueled the situation.

A rather different example again is provided by the *Berufsverbot* (occupational ban) in Germany. This debarred so-called radicals, extremist right-wing or (more usually) left-wing persons from employment in public service, including in teaching.[5] This also affected minor public service posts not connected with security. The justification here was to prevent any return to an extremist past by barring those who questioned the constitutional order as laid out in the Basic Law. This caused much debate and controversy. Criticism was especially directed at the routine investigations conducted by the Federal and Länder Offices for the Defence of the Constitution *(Verfassungsschutz)*. The result was that many left wingers felt excluded from work for which they were qualified, and deemed their human rights curtailed. The argument was that the right to freedom of occupational choice was denied and therefore the principle 'freedom of occupation' was compromised. Fear of a return to something like Germany's Nazi past, however, was considered sufficient justification.

The means-end argument has also been used in non-liberal systems to justify acknowledged present unpleasantness as a sacrifice for a future utopia. The repressive Bolshevik one-party state with its secret police to combat counter-revolutionaries was dubbed a necessary means to a greater future good, as were purges within the Communist Party.[6] Liberal democracies, however, with different traditions are deemed 'above' the repressiveness of totalitarian systems. A history of liberal constitutionalism, as Fareed Zakaria has argued, renders democracy plausible. Lack of it may mean 'democratic tyranny' in states which are not historically 'ripe' and whose leaders attempt to democratize, as in Eastern Europe.[7] Each of these four examples has their own further complexities into which we cannot delve here.

It is worth noting, however, that President Gerald Ford declared the internment of Japanese Americans a 'national mistake' and in 1988 President Ronald Reagan signed legislation which amounted to a national apology, offering compensation to all surviving internees.[8] In 1993, following passage of the Civil Liberties Act, President Bill Clinton wrote a letter of apology to Japanese Americans, acknowledging a 'grave injustice.'[9] Then in 1998, Clinton formally apologized to Japanese Latin Americans for actions 'that unfairly denied you fundamental liberties.'[10] One interpretation of these apologies, if they are to mean anything, is that they should inform current approaches to citizens' rights at a time of national emergency. Arguably, one test of the strength of a democracy comes when rights are protected even when it would be more expedient to put them aside.[11]

The aftermath of September 11 has produced legislation in different states with the understandable and practical end of combating terrorism. This has been discussed above in chapters on the USA, UK, Germany and Russia (4, 5, 8 and 19, respectively). It is worth stressing, however, that the treatment of domestic suspects is different from those caught abroad. While governments may instinctively want to increase their powers of arrest and intrusion after terrorist attacks – as did Indonesia within a week of the October 2002 Bali bombing – Western governments have been limited in the extent of such measures against their own citizens. In the year following fresh British anti-terrorist measures, there was just one prosecution, and that was unsuccessful. While the US Patriot Act eased the legal restrictions on surveillance measures, such as wire-tapping, the Foreign Intelligence Surveillance Act Court dismissed some of the anti-terrorism measures that Attorney General John Ashcroft had introduced. When the American authorities arrested Yemenis in New York State on suspicion of terrorism, they did so after a long investigation and appealed to the Yemeni community for help.

Where defense of the civil rights of citizens in democracies seems undisputed – both in principle and largely in practice – the question of the treatment of non-nationals remains. One critical view is expressed by US lawyer Patricia Williams who argues that there is a new 'martial law' for the 20 million non-US citizens living in the USA because President George W. Bush is distinguishing between the constitutional rights enjoyed by citizens alone 'from human rights which do not have the same status.'[12] The detention center at Camp X-Ray in Guantanamo Bay is the most graphic example and has given rise in liberal circles to great unease. Here over 600 suspected al-Qaeda and Taliban fighters who had been captured in Afghanistan are held, often manacled, blindfolded and in small wire cells. As Singh notes in Chapter 4, in November 2001, Bush ordered that the prisoners would face secret trials by military tribunals. Williams has discussed the outcry against prisoners not being permitted to enjoy the usual legal safeguards against wrongful conviction and Bush eventually made some concessions. She has vigorously argued that issues of immigration, nationality, race, culture and categorization are bound up with the global expansion of anti-terrorism.[13] Illustrative of her thesis is the fact that all men from the Middle East entering the USA have been photographed and fingerprinted.

Amnesty International has alerted that the US Justice Department stopped releasing the figures of the number of detainees in the USA since 9/11 (initially it was around 1,200, mainly men from Muslim or Middle Eastern countries) and that the location of detainees is often unknown.[14] Television debates, such as those chaired by British journalist Jon Snow, ask why prisoners are in chains and are apparently deemed guilty rather than innocent until proven otherwise. One argument put in Snow's broadcast was that we now see a 'shadow justice system' in which there is a 'licensed political repression.' Whilst this is characteristic of totalitarian and authoritarian regimes, it is not supposed to be part of liberal democracy.

Certainly police need reliable information to conduct an effective 'war on terrorism' and also to pursue a careful one that does not flout democratic principles. As Rohan Gunaratna has contended in Chapter 3, better intelligence in Britain and police vigilance have resulted in the capture of more terrorists. Their imprisonment is essential if further innocent lives are to be spared brutal acts. However, it is worth stressing that the abuse of human rights, the suspension of habeas corpus and the harassment of certain groups of individuals *without due care* goes against the democratic tradition. Moreover, the risks inherent in means/ends approaches are those of threatened permanence and institutionalization. Liberal values are thereby compromised to such a degree that the state cannot accurately be deemed wholly 'liberal democratic.' If morality matters, then much deeper thought needs to be given to the dimensions of trade-off between perceived security needs and human rights.

Regardless of measures taken domestically or internationally towards a country's own nationals or foreigners, legal recourse for combating terrorism can be partially successful; as Paul Wilkinson has argued elsewhere, long imprisonment is the punishment that terrorists least like and the one which least serves their causes.[15] To be sure, incarcerated terrorists might prompt vicious acts by their collaborators to force their release. But this is a situation already faced by governments around the world, and particularly by the American, with the detentions at Camp X-Ray. Although the exact legal status of these detainees remains disputed, many are said to have supplied important anti-terrorism intelligence. Because of the unprecedented phenomenon of al-Qaeda's transnational operations and trans-ethnic composition, the 'war on terrorism' equally requires a high degree of international cooperation. This 'war' makes for strange political bedfellows and puts democracy at risk, but need not and should not entail its complete sacrifice.

STRANGE POLITICAL BEDFELLOWS: POLITICS, STRATEGY AND RELIGION

Despite expectations that the causes of and response to the 9/11 attack would be a religio-cultural chasm, the US-led coalition for the war in Afghanistan has been remarkably international. The US government has also stressed America's good relations with the Islamic world, including how it sought to come to the rescue of Muslims in Somalia, Bosnia and Kosovo. Bush has made statements, irrespective of course of how they may be received, that 'We treasure our friendship with Muslims and Arabs around the world.'[16]

Pakistani President Musharraf is hardly a paragon of democracy; indeed, having gained power through a coup, his political practices were critized before 9/11. But it is also possible he will feel more need to engage in democracy, and the success of Islamic parties in the October 2002 elections demonstrates the difficulties of democracy for him and his Western allies. Apart from debates about the universality of democracy, one cannot expect that more democracy in a country will necessarily flow from unprecedented cooperation with the USA. Indeed, new-found partners reject the notion. When the Bush adminstration signed an agree-ment with the former Soviet republic of Uzbekistan to provide it with security (separately from the stationing of American forces in Uzbekistan for the Afghan war), President Islam Karimov chastized Western governments for expecting rapid democratization.[17]

In pro-Western Jordan, post-September 11 anti-terrorism measures included restrictions on press freedom and jail sentences for slander of the monarchy. While called 'temporary,' such measures were also seen as creating the circum-stances in which potential supporters of al-Qaeda could flourish. As Human Rights Watch director Kenneth Roth warned, the American-led anti-terror fight 'is inspiring opportunistic attacks on civil liberties around the world.'[18] Anti-terrorism measures that limit liberties may in turn provide conditions for terrorism, as critics fight against them.

Apart from strong political consensus among major powers, much support for the war in Afghanistan was also generated in the Muslim world. Despite popular protests against the USA, Asian countries with large or majority Muslim popula-tions have not only rendered diplomatic backing to the war in Afghanistan but also assisted Western governments to foil plots against their physical interests in the region.

Changed international dynamics also mean that Islamic pariahs have been treated differently. Algeria, where over 100,000 deaths have resulted since 1992 at the hands of Islamic extremists, received a greater reception abroad accord-ing to diplomats. Said one, 'After September 11, they're on the good guys' side.'[19] US engagement in the Sudanese peace process, including Bush's signing the 'Sudan Peace Act' into law on 21 October 2002, marks a positive shift from its previous stigmatization as a rogue state. John Garang, leader of the People's Liberation Army that opposed the central government for nearly two decades, said 'if the international community can use the present environment [of domestic willingness for peace], and the post-September 11 situation, to achieve peace in this country, that would be good.'[20]

There is no question of course that religion can and has been used to ignite violence. Over 200 died in Kano, northern Nigeria, in mid-October 2001 in religious strife that stemmed from protests against the American bombing of Afghanistan. Separately, comments by Nigerian journalist Isioma Daniel in November 2002 that the prophet Muhammad might have married one of the contestants in that year's Miss World competition provoked violence that again resulted in the deaths of over 200 Nigerians in the northern city of Kaduna.[21] She was forced to flee the country when Imams called for her death. Despite seeming evidence that religion – especially Islam – is at the root of contemporary global conflict, many Western scholars of Islam have argued that distinctions must be made between the religion itself and the extremism of people like bin Laden.[22]

The future of Iraq is contentious, and most leaders, including the Bush administration, see that as qualitatively different from Afghanistan. Even with hesitation or out of diplomatic desperation, the Bush administration had still turned to the UN. When Bush called on the UN to do more on Iraq, it meant that Bush placed the UN at the heart of the Iraqi crisis although war would ultimately be waged without Security Council authorization. The irony of the Iraqi issue is that religion and culture appear not to be at the heart of the dispute. Iraq's Ba'athist regime has purported to run a fiercely secular state. The war in Afghanistan was, with caveats, acceptable to most of the world's governments. A second war against a regime, as deplorable as it may be, that, discovery by UN weapons inspectors or American evidence notwithstanding, had no proven supply of weapons of mass destruction or any link to al-Qaeda risked stretching the fight against terrorism to a perception of a war on Islam.[23] The relative silence that the Islamic Conference gave, for example, to the Israeli–Palestinian conflict during the Afghan war could be expected to evaporate. Religion could really then be perceived as the cause (or the cover) for wide-scale conflict. This is particularly of concern as the Israeli–Palestinian conflict would gain even further centrality to the Arab discourse with the West. There are parallels to the Middle East and Afghanistan: nation-building and terrorism appear interconnected. Through the aftermath of 9/11, reference to a Palestinian 'state' gained greater prominence in Western discourse.

Bush's initial use of 'crusade' was adopted by bin Laden who, in reiterating his jihad, called for Islamic resistance of the 'infidel forces' of 'Chief Crusader Bush under the banner of the cross.' Western values of human rights and democracy can easily be interpreted by others as excuses for imperialism, particularly a drive for the control over oil. A key means to substantiate the benevolence of Western intentions, especially towards the Islamic world, since 9/11 is the way in which Afghanistan is reconstructed.

Afghanistan and nation-building

The West's, or foremost the USA's, abandonment of Afghanistan after 1989 is the logical starting point for current Afghan history and its prospects for a better future. American and Pakistani intelligence services had succeeded in building up an effective military resistance to the Soviet presence. But when the last Soviet forces withdrew in February 1989 no plan or program was in place. To be sure, communist rule continued, but its lifeblood thinned with the collapse of the USSR two years later and the cessation of Soviet assistance. By early 1992, Pakistani-supported opposition groups seized power and created a nominal system of power-sharing. Burhanuddin Rabbani, in his turn as president, sought instead to retain power and attempted to eliminate his opponents with force. Afghanistan descending again into violence, Pakistani authorities switched their support to the Taliban that professed order and peace for the country.

With such dire recent history, assessments of Afghanistan's postwar settlement might benefit from the cliché of an improvement on nothing. The UN calls Kabul the most war-torn city in the world. For a people who have endured foreign interventions and war for much of their lifetimes, and who turned to the repression of the Taliban as a tonic against armed conflict, any future may be brighter.

And although foreign meddling is almost a cliché of Afghan history, foreign assistance must therefore now really deliver tangible sustenance and even prosperity, not only for the Afghans themselves but also if the 'war on terrorism' is to have any virtue. The international community signalled clearly that support for post-war Afghanistan meant the observance (or establishment) of human rights. In mid-November 2001, as Taliban control was reduced militarily to southern Afghanistan, the EU declared that reconstruction aid was specifically tied to the maintenance of human rights, while the UN, in promoting a conference for the formation of a provisional Afghan government, said that women should have an important role in it.

A multi-ethnic interim government, imperfect as it was, was created against considerable odds after the Bonn Agreement. The traditional Afghan Grand Assembly of the *Loya Jirga* was accordingly convened from 11–19 June 2002 and resulted in substantial backing for Karzai as leader, winning 1,295 of 1,638 votes. He in turn is credited with trying, despite the lack of experienced personnel, to build a multi-ethnic administration by making ethnically based senior appointments.[24] Such efforts have been further challenged by violence, including the February 2002 assassination of Aviation Minister Abdul Rahman, the assassination of Vice-President Haji Abdul Qadir four months later, and attempts on Karzai's life.

In these volatile circumstances it is all the more important that the international community, notably the West, fulfill its pledges to Afghanistan. The International Security Assistance Force (ISAF) – a 4,000-member force, drawn from eighteen countries and with a further nine volunteering personnel – is an important initiative, but the hesitation that other states had in joining it and the difficulty of finding a leader state augur poorly. Britain led ISAF for six months but was reported as 'keen' to pass the mandate on. Taking over ISAF command on 20 June 2002, Turkey was considered ideal as NATO's only Muslim (if secular) state and for having the Organization's second largest military. An American analyst was quoted on the Turks as 'being good allies who don't worry about whether to use force when it is required.'[25] Other candidates, notably Germany even after a direct appeal from Karzai, had backed down. ISAF gained a new lease when, in December 2002, the German government agreed to extend its commitment to ISAF for another year and to lead it jointly with the Netherlands.

ISAF's physical mandate has been restricted to Kabul, suggesting a limitation to international policing in Afghanistan. Karzai has pleaded, including directly to Kofi Annan, for ISAF's expansion beyond the capital. Even though the UN's deputy special envoy to Afghanistan, Spanish diplomat Francesc Vendrell, admitted that 'the international force needs to be deployed beyond Kabul and the Afghans want it – even the warlords say they want it,' this was not done.[26] For his part, Karzai has sought to bring all military force in the country under the control of the Ministry of Defence; those that refused would be deemed renegade forces and presumably subject to attack.[27] While the centrality of the

UN to the reconstruction is undisputed, with even Bush declaring on 11 October 2001 that the UN should assume responsibility for 'nation building' in Afghanistan, funding for postwar reconstruction remains essential, contentious and lacking.

Positive measures have, nevertheless, been made. According to one report: 'Thanks largely to the UN, 3 million Afghan children are back at school, 60,000 farmers have been given wheat seed, 24 million square miles of land has been cleared of mines, and Afghanistan is on the way to being free of polio.'[28] Karzai told foreign donors in mid-April 2002 that they must fulfill their aid promises and cease imposing what he saw as unrealistic requirements on the Afghan bureaucracy. But the European Commission, backed by the IMF, prepared a note warning the Afghan government that financial support was conditional on creating an accountable fiscal and monetary system, as if the country were simply facing corruption as an emerging market, not as a war-ravaged and impoverished society.

Reconstructing Afghanistan with extensive cooperation from its constituent groups could provide a testament to inter-faith, inter-political and inter-state cooperation, quite apart from helping to salve one of the worst wounds on the world torso, one that allowed infection to fester and expand. Creating the infrastructure for a healthier economy and society, run by Afghans and respecting indigenous faiths and cultures, would do much to undermine the ideological claims that bin Laden's followers can level against the West.

At his 10 p.m. news brief on 9/11 New York City Mayor Rudi Giuliani declared 'democracy is stronger than vicious, cowardly terrorism.' Democracy must prove itself so, by retaining and exercising its values in both domestic and international conduct in the pursuit of terrorists. For democracy, as much as it must bring wrongdoers to justice, risks denigrating itself if it reacts unethically. As American political forefather Benjamin Franklin cautioned two centuries before September 11, 2001: 'Those who would give up essential liberty to purchase a little temporary safety deserve neither liberty nor safety.'

NOTES

1 We are grateful to Professors Thomas Fujita-Rony and Craig Ihara of California State University at Fullerton for these data. Fujita-Rony, a specialist on this topic, recommends *http:www.javoice.com* as an informative website. He notes, however, that some sources incorrectly give 120,000 as the number of internees. For discussion of the internment of Ukrainian and Japanese Canadians, see: http://www. infoukes.com/history/internment/gulag/http://www.crr.ca/en/MediaCenter/FactsSheets/eMed CenFacShtFromRacismToRedress.1

2 http://www.cnn.com/WORLD/americas/9806/12/Japanese.reparations/

3 Martin Kettle and Lucy Hodges, *Uprising! The Police, the People and the Riots in Britain's Cities* (London and Sydney: Pan Books, 1982), p. 91.

4 Ibid.

5 http://www.eurofound.eu.int/emire/GERMANY/OCCUPATIONALBAN-DE.html

6 Barrington Moore, Jr., *Soviet Politics – The Dilemma of Power* (New York: Harper Torchbooks, 1965).

7 Fareed Zakaria, 'The Rise of Illiberal Democracy', *Foreign Affairs*, Vol. 76, No. 6, Nov./ Dec. 1997, pp. 22–43.

8 http://www.mtnbrook.k12.al.us/academy/6thgrade/camps/6jweb.htm

9 http://www.pbs.org/childofcamp/history/clinton.html

10 http://www.cnn.com/WORLD/americas/9806/12/Japanese.reparations

11 We thank James Putzel for this obervation.

12 Patricia Williams, 'This Dangerous Patriot's Game', *The Observer*, 2 Dec. 2001.

13 Ibid.

14 Ibid.

15 Paul Wilkinson, valedictory lecture, May 2002, University of St. Andrews. See the general discussion in Paul Wilkinson, *Terrorism versus Democracy* (London: Frank Cass, 2001), ch. 5.

16 Office of the Press Secretary, 10 Sept. 2002, http://www.whitehouse.gov/news/ releases/2002/09/20020910–7.html

17 The terms of the security agreement were kept secret, but American officials denied it constituted a 'security guarantee.' Roula Khalaf, 'Freedom Becomes a Casualty of the War against Terrorism', *Financial Times*, 16 Jan. 2002.

18 Reuters, 28 Jan. 2002.

19 Roula Khalaf, 'Algeria Reaps the Rewards of War against Terrorists', *Financial Times*, 15 Jan. 2002, p. 8.

20 Quentin Peel, 'Sudan's Rebels See Hope for Peace in the War on Terror', *Financial Times*, 15 Jan. 2002, p. 18.

21 Her article was originally published in the Nigerian paper *This Day*, 16 Nov. 2002.

22 See most recently, John L. Esposito, *Unholy War: Terror in the Name of Islam* (Oxford: Oxford University Press, 2002).

23 US and British officials and commentators have said that Iraq has both WMDs and connections to terrorism, but specific details have been few. See, for example, Richard Perle, Chairman of the Defence Policy Board: 'We know that he [Saddam] harbors terrorists, about which more evidence will emerge in due course.' 'Why the West Must Strike First', *National Post*, 14 Aug. 2002, p. A14.

24 Amin Saikal, 'Afghanistan after the Loya Jirga', *Survival*, Vol. 44, No. 3, Autumn 2002, p. 49.

25 Leyla Boulton and Richard Wolfe, 'US Search Yields Crucial Terror Data', *Financial Times*, 4 Jan. 2002.

26 Carola Hoyos, 'Troops in Kabul Urged to Expand Mandate', *Financial Times*, 24 Jan. 2002.

27 In a February 2002 diplomatic tour that included India and Iran, Karzai sought funds but also requested that neighbouring countries cease interference in Afghanistan and waging proxy wars in it. Karzai declared 'Every commander in every province has direct contact with foreigners. This is the reason he does not pay attention to the orders of the central government. If these contacts are cut, then the next day the commanders will pay their respects to the central government,' Charles Glover, 'Afghanistan Seeks to End Proxy Wars within Borders', *Financial Times*, 28 Feb. 2002, p. 14.

28 *Financial Times*, 5 June 2000, p. 8.

Selected bibliography

STUDY OF TERRORISM

Chomsky, Noam, *The Culture of Terrorism* (London: Pluto, 1988).

Clutterbuck, Richard, *Terrorism and Guerrilla Warfare* (London: Routledge, 1990).

Crenshaw, Martha (ed.), *Terrorism in Context* (University Park: Pennsylvania State University Press, 1995).

Hoffman, Bruce, *'Holy Terror': The Implications of Terrorism Motivated by a Religious Imperative* (Santa Monica, CA: RAND, 1993).

—— *Inside Terrorism* (London: Gollancz, and New York: Columbia University Press, 1998).

Juergensmeyer, Mark, *Terror in the Mind of God: The Global Rise of Religious Violence* (Berkeley: University of California Press, 2000).

Laqueur, Walter, *The Terrorism Reader* (London: Wildwood House, 1979).

Rapoport, David C. (ed.), *Inside Terrorist Organizations* (New York: Columbia University Press, 1988).

Rapoport, David C. and Alexander, Yohan (eds.), *The Morality of Terrorism: Religious and Secular Justifications* (New York: Pergamon Press, 1982).

Schmid, Alex P. and Jorgman, Albert J. et al, *Political Terrorism: An New Guide to Actors, Authors, Concepts, Data Bases, Theories and Literature* (Amsterdam: North Holland Publishing Co., 1988).

Stohl, Michael and Lopez, George (eds.), *Terrible Beyond Endurance? The Foreign Policy of State Terrorism* (New York: Greenwood, 1988).

Wilkinson, Paul, *Terrorism and the Liberal State* (London: Macmillan, 1977/1986).

—— *Terrorism vs. Democracy: The Liberal State Response* (London and Portland, OR: Frank Cass, 2000).

'NEW' TERRORISM AND 9/11 IN CONTEXT

BBC News Team, *The Day That Shook the World* (London: BBC Books, 2001).

Booth, Ken and Dunne, Tim (eds.), *Worlds in Collision: Terror and the Future of Global Order* (London: Palgrave, 2002).

Falkenrath, Richard A., Newman, Robert D. and Thayer, Bradley A., *America's Achilles' Heel: Nuclear, Biological, and Chemical Terrorism and Covert Attack* (Cambridge, MA: MIT Press, 1998).

Halliday, Fred, *Two Hours That Shook the World* (London: Saqi Books, 2001).

Heymann, Philip B., *Terrorism and America: A Commonsense Strategy for a Democratic Society* (Cambridge, MA: MIT Press, 1998).

Hoge, James F., Jr. and Rose, Gideon (eds.), *How Did This Happen? Terrorism and the New War* (New York: PublicAffairs, 2001).

Honderich, Ted, *After the Terror* (Edinburgh: Edinburgh University Press, 2002).

Laqueur, Walter, *The New Terrorism: Fanaticism and the Arms of Mass Destruction* (London: Phoenix Press, 2002).

Markham, Ian and Abu-Rabi', Ibrahim (eds.), *September 11: Historical, Theological and Social Perspectives* (London and New York: One World Publications, 2002).

Miller, Judith, Engelberg, Stephen and Broad, William J., *Germs: Biological Weapons and America's Secret War* (New York: Simon & Schuster, 2001).

Pazam Reuven, *Tangled Web: International Networking of the Islamist Struggle* (Washington, DC: Brookings Institution Press, 2002).

Satloff, Robert B. (ed.), *Campaign Against Terror: The Middle East Dimension* (Washington, DC: Brookings Institution Press, 2002).

Stern, Jessica, *The Ultimate Terrorists* (Cambridge, MA: Harvard University Press, 1999).

Talbott, Strobe and Chanda, Nayan (eds.), *The Age of Terror: America and the World After September 11* (New York: Basic Books, 2002).

AL-QAEDA AND OSAMA BIN LADEN

Alexander, Yohan and Swetnam, Michael C., *Usama bin Laden's al-Qaida: Profile of a Terrorist Network* (New York: Transnational Publishers, 2002).

Bodansky, Yossef, *Bin Laden: The Man Who Declared War on America* (New York: Random House, 2001).

Corbin, Jane, *The Base: In Search of al-Qaeda* (London and New York: Simon & Schuster, 2002).

Gunaratna, Rohan, *Inside al-Qae'da* (London: Hurst, and New York: Columbia University Press, 2002).

Reeve, Simon, *The New Jackals: Ramzi Yousef, Osama bin Laden and the Future of Terrorism* (Boston: Northeastern University Press, 1999).

AFGHANISTAN AND CENTRAL ASIA

Cooley, John, *Unholy Wars: Afghanistan, America and International Terrorism* (London and Sterling, VA: Pluto Press, 1999).

Griffin, Michael, *Reaping the Whirlwind: The Taliban Movement in Afghanistan* (London and Sterling, VA: Pluto Press, 2001).

Maley, William (ed.), *Fundamentalism Reborn? Afghanistan and the Taliban* (London: Hurst, 1998).

Rashid, Ahmed, *Taliban: The Story of the Afghan Warlords* (London: Pan, 2001).

——— *Jihad: The Rise of Militant Islam in Central Asia* (New Haven: Yale University Press, 2002).

Roy, Olivier, *Islam and Resistance in Afghanistan* (Cambridge and New York: Cambridge University Press, 1990).

Rubin, Barnett R., *The Fragmentation of Afghanistan: State Formation and Collapse in the International System* (New Haven: Yale University Press, 1995).

—— *The Search for Peace in Afghanistan: From Buffer State to Failed State* (New Haven: Yale University Press, 1996).

MODERN ISLAM AND INTERNATIONAL RELATIONS

Armstrong, Karen, *The Battle for God* (New York: Knopf, 2000).

Esposito, John L., *The Islamic Threat: Myth or Reality?* (Oxford: Oxford University Press, 1992; 2nd edn, 1995).

—— *Unholy War: Terror in the Name of Islam* (Oxford: Oxford University Press, 2002).

Halliday, Fred, *Islam and the Myth of Confrontation* (London: I.B. Tauris, 1996).

Hiro, Dilip, *Holy Wars: The Rise of Islamic Fundamentalism* (New York and London: Routledge, 1989).

Huntington, Samuel P., *The Clash of Civilizations and the Remaking of World Order* (New York: Simon & Schuster, 1996).

Kepel, Gilles, *Jihad* (London: I.B. Tauris, 2002).

Lawrence, Bruce B., *Shattering the Myth: Islam beyond Violence* (Princeton: Princeton University Press, 1998).

Lewis, Bernard, *The Political Language of Islam* (Chicago: University of Chicago Press, 1988).

Partner, Peter, *God of Battles: Holy Wars of Christianity and Islam* (Princeton: Princeton University Press, 1998).

Peters, Rudolph, *Jihad in Classical and Modern Islam* (Princeton: Princeton University Press, 1996).

Ruthven, Malise, *Islam in the World* (Oxford: Oxford University Press, 2000).

CONTEMPORARY US FOREIGN AND SECURITY POLICY

Gertz, Bill, *Breakdown: How America's Intelligence Failures Led to September 11* (New York: Regnery Publishing, 2002).

Kagan, Robert and Kristol, William (eds.), *Present Dangers: Crisis and Opportunity in American Foreign and Defense Policy* (New York: Encounter Books, 2000).

Lieber, Robert J., *Eagle Rules? Foreign Policy and American Primacy in the Twenty-First Century* (Upper Saddle River, NJ: Prentice Hall, 2001)

Mead, Walter Russell, *Special Providence: American Foreign Policy and How it Changed the World* New York: Alfred A. Knopf, 2001).

Nye, Joseph S., Jr., *The Paradox of American Power* (New York and Oxford: Oxford University Press, 2002).

Pillar, Paul R., *Terrorism and U.S. Foreign Policy* (Washington, DC: Brookings Institution Press, 2001).

Rubin, Barry (ed.), *Terrorism and US Foreign Policy* (Basingstoke: Macmillan, 1991).

Talbott, Strobe and Chanda, Nayan (eds.), *The Age of Terror: America and the World After September 11* (New York: Basic Books, 2001).

Woodward, Bob, *Bush at War: Inside the Bush White House* (New York: Simon & Schuster, 2002).

Index

Abdallah, Abu 44
Abdildin, Serikbolsyn 244
Abdullah, Crown Prince of Saudi Arabia 145, 146, 149, 150, 151
Abdullah, King of Jordan 17
ABM Treaty *see* Anti-Ballistic Missile Treaty
Abu Abdallah 44
Abu Doha 48
Abu Ghaith, Sulieman 44
Abu Hamza 47, 48
Abu Musa 44
Abu Qatada 47, 48
Abu Sayyaf ('Father of the Executioner') movement 37, 181, 182, 183–4, 185
Advice and Reformation Committee (ARC) 38, 46–7, 48
Afghanistan 3, 5, 15–23, 33, 167, 185; aid to 281, 316; 'barbarians' analogy 291–2; British citizens fighting for Taliban 47, 69, 70; Canada 79, 81–3, 84; Central Asia 239, 240–1, 242, 244, 247, 248; China 210, 213; coalition strength 313, 314; EU Action Plan 261; France 91, 96–7; geopolitics 2; Germany 103, 106–8; India position 202, 205; Indonesia position 177; interim government 33; international community support 254; Iran position 4, 125, 126, 127–8, 132; Iraq 130, 131; Israel support for war 160, 161; Italian attitudes 116–18, 119; lack of UN Resolution 253; limited UN role 6, 259; Mujahidin 37; Pakistan 5, 188, 191, 192, 193, 194, 195–7; peacekeeping operations 258; Philippines position 183; preparations for war against 12–15; al-Qaeda 38, 40, 41, 46; reconstruction 281, 310, 315–17; refugees 1, 7, 196, 265–75; Russia position 223–5, 228;

Soviet occupation 189–90; Syria position 136, 137–8; UK involvement 66, 67, 68–70, 72–3, 74, 75; US public opinion 55; US unilateralism 62, *see also* Taliban
Africa 5, 165–75; extreme left terrorists 30; fear of marginalization 1, 2, 4; al-Qaeda 40
al-Ahmar, Abdallah 139
aid 16, 169, 197–8, 281, 317
Akaev, Askar 245, 246, 249
Albright, Madeline 138
Algeria 25, 44, 95, 167, 171, 314; anti-colonial struggles 31, 32; Armed Islamic Group of Algeria 37, 39; Fanon 290; FLN 31, 168
Allbaugh, Joe 58
Alliot-Marie, Michèle 92
Amnesty International 312
anarchism 7, 287, 288, 293
Andang, Galib 182
Angola 299
Annan, Kofi 9, 128, 132, 172, 258, 316
anthrax attacks 16, 54, 58
anti-Americanism: Africa 170; Arab world 212; Central Asia 243; China 211; France 90, 92, 93, 98; Germany 102, 107; Iran 126; Russia 229
Anti-Ballistic Missile (ABM) Treaty, US abrogation 6, 56, 70, 213, 218, 222, 224, 226, 232
Arabs, Israeli 160–1
Arafat, Yasser 155–6, 157, 158, 159, 263*n*
Arbatov, Aleksei 231
ARC *see* Advice and Reformation Committee
Arendt, Hannah 28
Armed Islamic Group of Algeria 37, 39
Armitage, Richard 206
Aron, Raymond 28, 284